TELEWORKING: INTERNATIONAL PERSPECTIVES

Teleworking: International Perspectives is an up-to-date, groundbreaking and comprehensive assessment of teleworking. Inspired by a conference at Brunel University, which was sponsored by BT and the European Commission, the book features contributions from a range of international and interdisciplinary perspectives. As well as an original analysis of the theoretical context of the post-industrial and postmodern world, the book also contains detailed empirical studies examining teleworking in a number of different countries.

Contributors explore many of the main issues in teleworking, drawing on insights from business, economics, sociology and information systems. These include: conceptualising teleworking; the management of spatial, temporal and cultural boundaries; the possibility of the virtual organisation; integrating teleworking into an organisational perspective.

Teleworking: International Perspectives is a valuable introduction to teleworking and an important contribution to the debate on the future of work.

Paul J. Jackson is a lecturer in Management Studies at Brunel University, UK. **Jos M. van der Wielen** is a researcher and consultant for O&i Management Partners and former lecturer at Tilburg University, The Netherlands.

THE MANAGEMENT OF TECHNOLOGY AND INNOVATION

Series editors: David Preece, University of Portsmouth and John Bessant, University of Brighton/SPRU

The books in this series offer grounding in central elements of the management of technology and innovation. Each title explains, develops and critically explores issues and concepts in a particular aspect of the management of technology/ innovation combining a review of the current state of knowledge with the presentation and discussion of primary material not previously published.

Forthcoming titles:

THE MANAGEMENT OF TECHNOLOGY AND INNOVATION
Edited by David Preece and John Bessant

CREATIVE TECHNOLOGICAL CHANGE
Ian McLoughlin

TECHNOLOGY IN CONTEXT
Technology assessment for managers
Ernest Braun

TELEWORKING: INTERNATIONAL PERSPECTIVES

From telecommuting to the virtual organisation

Edited by Paul J. Jackson and Jos M. van der Wielen

London and New York

First published 1998
by Routledge
11 New Fetter Lane, London EC4P 4EE

Simultaneously published in the USA and Canada
by Routledge
29 West 35th Street, New York, NY 10001

© 1998 Selection and editorial matter by Paul J. Jackson and
Jos M. van der Wielen; individual chapters to their authors

Typeset in Baskerville by RefineCatch Limited, Bungay, Suffolk

British Library Cataloguing in Publication Data
A catalogue record for this book is available from the British Library

Library of Congress Cataloguing in Publication Data

Teleworking: international perspectives: from telecommuting to the
virtual organisation/edited by Paul J. Jackson & Jos M. van der Wielen.
p.   cm.
Includes bibliographical reference and index.
1. Telecommuting.   2. Virtual organisation and management.   I. Jackson,
Paul J.   II. Wielen, Jos van der.
HD2336.3.N48   1998
331.25—dc21
97–28677
CIP

ISBN   0–415–17354–X (hbk)
ISBN   0–415–17127–X (pbk)

CONTENTS

CONTENTS

CONTENTS

FIGURES

TABLES

CONTRIBUTORS

Georg Aichholzer is Senior Researcher at the Institute for Technology Assessment (ITA) of the Austrian Academy of Sciences and Lecturer at the Vienna University of Economics and Business Administration. His current fields of research are in the sociology of telework, evaluation of information technology projects and technology foresight. He has co-edited, among others, a book on technology policy.

Ann M. Brewer is an Associate Professor of Transport Management, Institute of Transport Studies, The University of Sydney. She is the author of four books as well as numerous research publications. Her current research investigates work organisation, distributed work practices and their impact on travel behaviour.

André Büssing, Ph.D., is Professor of Psychology and Chair of Psychology at the Technical University of München. He is currently directing projects on teleworking, new information and communication technologies in hospitals, occupational stress and burnout. He is on the editorial board of several journals, including *Work and Stress*. He has authored and edited eight books, including *Teleworking: Analysis, Evaluation and Design*, and has written numerous articles in journals.

Alistair Campbell is a Lecturer in the Department of Computing and Information Systems at the University of Paisley, Scotland. He has presented at UK national and international conferences and published papers in the areas of electronic commerce, virtual organisations and business transformation. Current research interests are in network and web forms of enterprise, and organisational learning.

Dima Dimitrova is in the final stages of her Ph.D. on telework at the University of Toronto. She is a Research Associate at the Centre for Urban and Community studies at the University and has worked for the Telepresence project and the Telecommuting project. She has co-authored several articles on telework, such as 'Computer Networks as Social Networks: Collaborative Work, Telework and Virtual Community' in the *Annual Review of Sociology*, 1996. Her current interests lie in the areas of new forms of work and the implications of information technologies for the workplace and organisations.

Patrizio Di Nicola is an Italian sociologist and co-ordinator of the European Telework Development Initiative. He is President of the Work and Technology Association, a virtual research centre based in Rome, where he is undertaking research into teleworking and virtual organisations. He is the author of books and articles on telework, the Internet and post-industrial society.

Steven Fireman is a doctoral student in the Department of Management and Organisation at the University of Washington. Following careers in information technology and the law, his research interests centre around the impacts of technology in the workplace, decision-making, motivation and negotiations. He is an author of 'An unfolding model of voluntary employee turnover', a lead article in the *Academy of Management Journal*.

Benjamin A. Goldman, Ph.D., is a consultant and author on various development and environmental issues. He has co-founded and directed several non-governmental organisations in the US, and is a former Lecturer at Tufts University. He has published numerous books and articles, and has been appointed to a variety of government advisory boards.

Lois M. Goldman, M.C.P., is a transportation planner who has worked for several governmental organisations in New York and Boston. Her 1996 masters thesis for Boston University is entitled 'A Planner's Guide to Telecommuting and Economic Development'.

Charles Grantham, Ph.D., is President of the Institute for the Study of Distributed Work in Walnut Creek, CA. He is also a founder of eWork Systems LLC, and has authored *The Digital Workplace* (Van Nostrand-Reinhold 1993). His current research projects include investigations into intellectual capital management, formation of electronic communities and distance learning.

Leslie Haddon is a Visiting Fellow at the Graduate Research Centre in Culture and Communication at the University of Sussex. He has worked on a range of projects examining the social shaping and consumption of various information and communication technologies and is co-author of *The Shape of Things to Consume: Bringing Information Technology into the Home*.

Martin Harris, Ph.D., lectures at the Department of Management Studies, Brunel University, England. He is joint editor of *Innovation, Organisational Change and Technology* (1997) (London: International Thompson Business Press). He has advised a number of public bodies on the social and economic aspects of information technology. Current interests include an investigation of internal markets at the BBC and a forthcoming book on the political and cultural consequences of the new ICTs.

David A. Hensher is Director of the Institute of Transport Studies, The

Australian Key Centre in Transport Management, The University of Sydney. He is an economist with skills in microeconomics, econometrics and business policy. He is on the editorial boards of all the major international transport journals, and has been a visiting lecturer at the most distinguished universities throughout the world. He is the author of five books and a significant list of research publications. He is regularly engaged as a consultant on the crucial transport issues and projects in Australia, and has also held senior advisory positions in Australian transport.

Maeve Houlihan is a doctoral student at the University of Lancaster's Department of Behaviour in Organisations. She has lectured and researched at University College Dublin and her current research focuses on organisational behaviour in the context of new information and communication technologies.

Paul J. Jackson lectures in Management Studies at Brunel University, England. He holds a doctorate in Management Studies from Cambridge University. He has been a European Research Fellow at the Work and Organization Research Centre, Tilburg University, The Netherlands. He has undertaken international speaking and consultancy assignments on new technology and flexible working, innovation and organisational learning. He is also a co-founder of the International Workshops on Telework series and the International Telework Foundation. He is currently researching and publishing in the area of innovation in virtual organisations and small businesses and the Internet.

Scott A. Johnson worked for AT&T for nine years in management positions, including in a virtual office environment. He is currently completing a doctorate in Organizational Behavior and Human Resources Management at Arizona State University, where he is also part of a faculty team responsible for teaching business students. His research interests focus on the management of service employees and he has most recently been published in the *Journal of Market-Focused Management* ('Psychological Contracts and Fairness: The Effect of Violations on Customer Service Behavior', with D. Blancero and C. Lakshman, 1996).

Martin Kompast is a teacher of physics and mathematics. Since 1993 he has been an Associate of the Institut für Gestaltungs- und Wirkungsforschung, Technische Universität Wien, participating in research on the use of computers in design (architecture, theatre, film) and on telework arrangements in the computer industry. He has been actively involved in a series of school reform projects and developed innovative approaches to teaching physics.

Ari Luukinen is one of the pioneers in the field of Telework in Finland. He has worked as a researcher and in project management since the late 1980s. Originally an economist, he has worked both in universities and business in close connection to government. Recently he has been active in research and development projects funded by the Finnish state and the EU. Among other things, he has been involved in theme groups on telework as well as the Finnish Labour Relations Association.

Paul McGrath is Lecturer in organisational behaviour at the Graduate School of Business, University College Dublin. His current research interests include management practices within knowledge-intensive firms and social issues within virtual organisational arrangements. He has published a number of articles and book chapters on the topics of organisational decline and change management.

Kiran Mirchandani is working on the Social Science and Humanities Research Council of Canada (SSHRC) Postdoctoral Fellowship at the Department of Management, St Mary's University, Canada. She holds a Ph.D. in sociology from McGill University, Canada, and has published articles on gender, work and organisations. She is currently conducting a project on the social and economic implications of work-at-home arrangements in Atlantic Canada.

Ruggero Parrotto works for Telecom Italia, where he is Industrial Relations Research Projects Manager. He is a member of AISRI (Italian Association of Industrial Relations Studies) and he is the author of books and articles on information society, human resources management and telework.

Juhani Pekkola is Senior Researcher, Licentiate of Social Science at the Ministry of Labour, Helsinki. Since 1983 he has worked for the Ministry of Social Affairs and Health and for the Ministry of Labour, related to research and development activities in the area of labour relations and telework. During 1996 he was Project Co-ordinator for The National Workplace Development Programme and since 1997 has been Project Secretary for The Team for the Information Society.

Constance Perin is a cultural anthropologist specialising in the study of organisations and work systems. She is the author of three books and several articles analysing American culture and professionals' work and careers. She has held Guggenheim, Fulbright, and Ford Foundation fellowships and visiting appointments at universities in the US and Europe. She is currently a Ph.D. visiting scholar in the Program in Science, Technology, and Society at the Massachusetts Institute of Technology.

Lars Qvortrup is Professor in the Department of Communication, Aalborg University. His research areas include: the theory of the artificial; IT and regional development; the aesthetics of multimedia and telework. He is the author of fifteen books in Danish and English, including *Mellem kedsomhed og dannelse* ('Between Boredom and "Bildung"') and approximately 100 papers in journals and books, including *The Social Construction of Humancentredness* (1996). He is a member of the editorial board of the journal *Cybernetics and Human Knowing*.

Janet W. Salaff is a Professor of Sociology and Principal Investigator of the Telecommuting Project, as well as serving on the Executive Committee of the Knowledge Media Design Institute (KMDI) of the Computer Sciences Department, University of Toronto. She has co-authored many books, such as *Working Daughter of Hong Kong: Filial Piety or Power in the Family?* She has written numerous articles on various aspects of telework which include telework and the family, specifically young children and the elderly, control and co-ordination in telework and the organisational implications of telework. She is currently interested in virtual organisations.

Koji Sato is Associate Professor in the Faculty of Economics, Kanagawa University at Yokohama and also a Senior Research Fellow at the Institute of Public Policy, George Mason University in Virginia. His research interests focus on regional industrial policy, communications policy and telework. He is a member of the International Flexwork Forum and has served on several telework related government committees in Japan. He is a co-author of several books, including most recently *Regionale Modernisierungspolitik* published by Leske and Budrich, Germany.

Wendy A. Spinks is Assistant Professor in International Studies at Josai International University. She is a founding member of the International Flexwork Forum and has served on several telework-related government committees in Japan. Her major research interest is corporate applications of telework and her most recent publication is a 30-part series on telework in the *Nihon Keizai Shimbun*, Japan's major economic daily.

Lennart Sturesson is Research Assistant at Tema Technology and Social Change, Linköping University, Sweden. His study of Swedish efforts to implement telework is part of research into discrepancies between information technology as presented in visions and as used in real life, carried out by the research group, Man, Information Technology, Society. He is editor of two books about the information society, the most recent with Magnus Karlsson, *The World's Largest Machine: Global Telecommunications and the Human Condition* (1995).

Reima Suomi is Professor of Information Systems Science at Turku School of Economics and Business Administration, Finland. His research interests focus on telecommunications management, including telework and telecommunication cost structures. He has published in journals such as *Information and Management*, *Human Systems Management* and *Information Services and Use*.

Ina Wagner is a Professor at Technische Universität Wien and Head of a Centre for CSCW research. She holds a Ph.D. in physics from the University of Vienna. She has edited and written numerous books and authored over 80 papers on a variety of technology-related issues, amongst them a feminist perspective in science and technology, ethical and political issues in systems design, computer support of hospital work, CSCW and networking. One of her main current interests focuses on the multi-disciplinary design of computer systems for architectural design and planning.

Jos M. van der Wielen is a researcher and consultant for O&i Management Partners in Utrecht, The Netherlands. He has a degree from the Free University of Amsterdam and has lectured in Organisational Psychology at the Department of Policy and Organisational Sciences at Tilburg University. He is currently completing his Ph.D. thesis at Tilburg University on the social and organisational implications of telework. He has been involved in telework research since 1990 and has written several articles and book chapters on telework and virtual organising. He is a co-founder of the International Workshop on Telework Series and the International Telework Foundation and is on the editorial board of *Telewerken*.

Marya Zamindar is a researcher and consultant to the Finnish Ministry of Labour. She has been responsible for managing country reporting projects to the OECD and the EU in the areas of enterprise flexibility and Finnish labour policy, and has published reports on telecommuting, enterprise flexibility and in-firm training. Her work also involves consulting in Russia, advising clients on how to create local labour agreements within St Petersburg organisations. Marya received her BA from Johns Hopkins University and her MA in Public Policy from Georgetown University, Washington.

FOREWORD

The idea of 'telework' has been with us for more than 20 years. Ever since its introduction it received great interest from many different sides. Managers and employees were the first to experiment with electronic distance work, but soon city planners, transportation experts, telecommunication firms, computer vendors, employment agencies and many others also showed a keen interest. Telework was heralded as the solution to many different problems. It was expected that rearranging work with respect to space and time, using new information and communication technology, would resolve traffic congestion, save energy, eliminate skill shortages, offer employment opportunities for the handicapped, reduce labour and overhead costs, increase work flexibility and reconcile the conflicting demands of work and family.

While convenient as a notion into which everyone could project his or her desires, telework also appeared to suffer from evasiveness and lack of substance when it came to research and practical work. Many attempts were made to define telework in a satisfactory way, but with little success. It appeared impossible to come up with an unequivocal definition that covered the essence of what telework was supposed to be and that differentiated it from other forms of work. As a consequence it has not been possible to make reliable assessments of the scale of use of telework, nor of its development and growth perspective. It so happened that estimates of the scale of use differed by a factor of 10 or more, and that some researchers called telework a marginal phenomenon, while others depicted it as a genuine revolution.

In recent years scholars have begun to realise that telework discussions often revealed a problematic focus, that the early fascination with technology and the way people could use it had diverted attention from the organisation as the place in which work is performed and had blurred the organisation's role in the economy. More and more scholars became aware that it was not only the on-line worker who was of interest, but also the change in organisational functions and forms enabled by new technology. At present one can witness a transition to another vocabulary. Some authors prefer to speak about dispersed organisations, distributed organisations, network organisations, virtual organisations, and so on, rather than about telework. The focus is shifting towards the alternative ways in which organisations can use information technology for realising their business purposes – production, marketing, sales and distribution of goods and services – repositioning and restructuring themselves with respect to time and place.

This book gives the first clear account of this transition. It marks a new stage in our thinking on distributed work. It shows how old notions are now being abandoned and replaced by concepts referring to the rearrangement of organisational processes. This opens a new perspective on organisation and work that gives scientists a chance to effectively describe and analyse the changes made with the help of information technology, many of which are radical and pervasive indeed. This perspective is not only useful for research and theory, it is also promising with respect to further innovations in organisation and work. Needless to say, I would wish this important book to have a large and attentive readership.

Professor Robert A. Roe
Scientific Director of WORC

PREFACE AND
ACKNOWLEDGEMENTS

By the mid-1990s the debate on teleworking seemed to be stuck in an orbit around certain issues and perspectives. Many of the articles and events dedicated to the subject tended to replay the discussions that had dominated the previous decade. Traditional issues such as reducing commuting, work flexibility and cutting overheads were central items on such agendas. Telework was promoted as very much a 'plug and play' solution for problems as wide-ranging as worker motivation and corporate competitiveness. This was often reinforced by discussion of several popular cases of teleworking, giving the impression that teleworking success stories could be easily emulated. This also came at a time when the wider practical and intellectual context was concerned with ideas such as corporate restructuring and 'reinvention' – more systemic responses to organisational problems and opportunities. This left a widening gulf between teleworking – which increasingly became seen as a tactical tool – and more fundamental responses that addressed long-term imperatives for corporate survival.

A two year project was therefore conceived. This was intended to start moving the debate on telework out of orbit and create a new sense of gravity around a revised set of issues and perspectives that embraced more contemporary imperatives – such as those concerned with the opportunities of Internet-based working and virtual organisation. This began with an international workshop and concluded with the production of this book. As workers in the field we were aware that a great many developments (both theoretical and practical) had taken place over the years, and that there was an appetite within the telework community for such a venture.

A workshop on 'New International Perspectives on Telework' was thus held at Brunel University, England, in the Summer of 1996. This brought together an international and interdisciplinary group of over 60 researchers and consultants from 14 European countries, as well as Australia, Canada, the US, Israel and Japan. These included transport theorists, sociologists, management scientists, economists, philosophers and anthropologists. The workshop therefore enabled participants to take a fresh, more holistic look at the teleworking agenda and helped to provide a kick-start for a new debate on the subject.

The original workshop was made possible by the support and hard work of a number of people. For her many hours of toil leading up to and during the workshop, we would like to thank Liz Ackroyd from the Centre for Research on Innovation, Culture and Technology at Brunel University. For their moral support and advice, thanks are also due to Adrian Woods from the Department of Management Studies, Brunel University, and Rob Roe from Work and Organization Research Centre (WORC), Tilburg University. We must also thank WORC for their financial support of the Workshop. For helping to organise and chair workshop sessions we must thank Ian McLoughlin and Martin Harris from the Department of Management Studies, Brunel University; Tharsi Taillieu from the Department of Work and Organisational Psychology, University of Leuven; and Sandra Schruijer, from the Department of Policy and Organizational Sciences, Tilburg University. For their financial help, thanks are also due to both British Telecom, especially Mike Maternaghan and Mike Tate, and the European Commission, DG XIII in the person of Maarten Botterman.

In producing the book we must give particular thanks to the series editors, especially David Preece; and from Routledge, Stuart Hay. For reading parts of the book draft we should thank Reinout de Vries, Lisa Harris and Ian McLoughlin. If you would like details on future international workshops and publications on telework by the editors please get in touch via e-mail. Paul J. Jackson can be contacted at pauljjackson@compuserve.com and Jos M. van der Wielen at vdwielen@nedernet.nl

1

INTRODUCTION

Actors, approaches and agendas: from telecommuting to the virtual organisation

Paul J. Jackson and Jos M. van der Wielen

Ideas, like commodities, have fashions. They come and go. One year something's in; the next it's out. But as tastes change and markets shift, we often find things coming around again – repackaged, refocused – sometimes reborn. Those who have followed the topic over the years may recognise the same pattern in discussions of telework. Trumpeted in the 1970s as an answer to energy consumption and commuting demands (for example, Nilles *et al.* 1976), the 1980s saw telework relaunched as a flexible working arrangement, by which job and family demands could be balanced, skill shortages addressed and economic peripheries integrated with core regions (Kinsman 1987; Huws *et al.* 1990). In the 1990s we find more attention being given to issues of workplace design, facility management and the need to manage work time and work space to encourage productivity and effectiveness (for example, Becker and Steele 1995).

In this sense, the ground sometimes appears to shift beneath teleworking discussions. Yet while the world may move on, many people still see telework as an answer waiting in the wings. The difficulty this presents is that the concepts and theories available to inform such discussions often reflect the priorities, mind-sets and values of earlier contexts. But as circumstances change – due, for instance, to the globalisation of markets and production, economic restructuring and the diffusion of new technologies such as the Internet – the need to question our old assumptions about teleworking becomes evermore important.

As interest in the idea is renewed, many different stakeholders become involved in discussing and promoting telework. These include, for instance, transport ministries, telecom companies, personnel managers and flexible workers. The consequence of this is that the meaning, role and value of telework became more ambiguous. To achieve a more thorough understanding of the complex nature of the phenomenon, therefore, we need to take a fresh look at the theories and concepts developed until now, rethink old assumptions and reconceptualise the issues at hand. To find new ways of looking at teleworking

1

opportunities, we must build bridges with adjacent debates – on restructuring, re-engineering, business networking, and so on – as well as with relevant disciplines, such as social geography, economics, IT-sciences and work psychology. In short, we need to develop new, integrative perspectives that provide more robust ways of analysing and theorising teleworking phenomena and so aid the task of understanding, implementing and managing it. A recognition of this – and the fact that there is a range of interests involved – is essential if the debate on teleworking is to move forward.

This book presents a concerted effort to develop new perspectives. We intend it to provide a timely contribution to the debate on telework. In so doing, it draws upon a range of international experiences and reflects the variety of disciplinary backgrounds of the contributors. The present chapter provides an introduction to this by looking at the main teleworking approaches, actors and agendas. It starts with a discussion of the three dominant approaches to the subject. Next, the complexity in telework caused by the array of actors involved in research and practice is examined. The chapter then discusses the key social and organisational issues involved in teleworking developments, before concluding with a look at the emerging agendas that need to be addressed.

Different approaches to telework

Teleworking phenomena have been approached in many ways: as an icon of technological innovation, as a 'new way of working' or as a modern lifestyle for young dual-career couples with children. In conceptual terms, several authors have attempted to characterise developments using terms like 'remote working', 'distance working' (Holti and Stern 1986a and b) or 'outwork' (Probert and Wajcman 1988). Others seek to categorise the various *forms of* telework, like 'homework', 'alternative officing' and 'mobile working' (see Gordon 1996). Alternatively, distinctions have been made between residential workers with a fixed central workplace, hybrid workers with central and decentral workplaces, and nomads with no fixed workplace (for example, Stanworth and Stanworth 1991). More analytical approaches, such as Brandt (1983) and Holti and Stern (1986b), have sought to categorise flexible work arrangements according to forms of spatial dispersal and means of co-ordination (from market to hierarchy).

In theoretical terms, efforts have taken place to integrate teleworking issues within different contexts of change. These range from the role of teleworking within organisations (Lenk 1989; Stanworth and Stanworth 1991; Jackson 1992) to the broader issues of economic and industrial restructuring (for example, Pfeffer and Baron 1988; Probert and Wajcman 1988; Van der Wielen 1991; McGrath and Houlihan, this volume). In developing new ideas and lines of analysis we must therefore start by identifying the conceptual, methodological and theoretical strengths and weaknesses found in existing approaches.

Back to the future: technology, symbolism and telework

The last two decades have seen the steady realisation of teleworking ideas in the world of work. In the 1970s, at the time when Nilles *et al.* (1976) introduced the notion of 'telecommuting' (the American synonym for telework), research was aimed at giving public policy-makers technology-supported solutions for several societal problems, such as urban crowding, energy shortages, transportation congestion, environmental pollution and the peripheralisation of economic regions. The main idea here was that geographical dispersion of the labour force from central business districts would significantly decrease the number of daily commuters, with IT used to bridge distances.

The idea was adopted by futurists such as Toffler (1980), who integrated the notion of telecommuting into broader speculations about the future of Western society. Telecommuting here was encompassed by Toffler's notion of the 'electronic cottage', and became an important icon in revolutionary (post-industrial) predictions about the birth of the Information Society. The electronic cottage exemplifies a disjuncture with previous ways of living and working. This involves a new world in which technology allows for a reintegration of work, family and community, and contrasts with the harsh divisions caused by life under industrialism. The approach sees IT as the fundamental factor explaining economic development, and the emerging information economy more generally.

Several problems are created by this line of thinking. One is that discussions of telework, as well as the technologies that support it, may pay more attention to symbolic issues than those of practical usefulness (see also Sturesson, this volume). This treats telework as a *vision of the future*, rather than considering its practical merits as a technology-supported work innovation. Another problem is that the role of technology in social and organisational change is under-theorised and treated in a deterministic way (Jackson 1992). It is presumed, for instance, that technologies will be appropriated and configured in ways that accord with teleworking, rather than supporting alternative arrangements in general.

It is now widely recognised that while fundamental changes in organisation and production are associated with technological advances, we cannot regard technological development as a unique, independent factor determining social and organisational change. We instead need to understand the adoption of IT as *a social and political process*, in which actors do not passively 'adapt to' new technologies but actively shape them to their own ends, transforming them as they conceive of new configurations (for example, McLoughlin and Harris 1997).

Telework as an objective phenomenon

As the amount of studies on the subject shows, there is enormous interest in ascertaining the extent, shape and potential of teleworking. However, in order to gain a picture of developments in the field, there is a need to define the phenomenon under study. Moreover, in extrapolating from this to identify the potential for, or growth in, telework, we need to establish a link between telework development and changes in areas of technology, the economy, industry, demographics and society.

Conceptual difficulties therefore compound the problems involved in theorising and predicting telework developments. As the literature shows, defining telework is easier said than done (see for instance, Huws *et al.* 1990; Korte and Wynne 1996; Quortrup, this volume). The presence of information technology in a particular work arrangement does not in itself define it as telework. Moreover, whilst it might support its development and help to accelerate the rate of adoption, the diffusion of new technologies does not correlate in a straightforward way with the growth in teleworking. This in part explains the difficulties involved in (and failures of) projecting a spread in teleworking based on the take-up of technology. The same goes, of course, for the relationship between teleworking and the growth of information processing work.

Despite this, understanding the viability of telework, the reasons behind its use and the potential for its growth, has been a matter of interest to many people. Initially, this mainly concerned governments, consultants and academics, although in more recent years it has been vendors of the technology who were keen to track and extrapolate trends. So far as this latter group is concerned, there is a clear interest in the market potential for products targeted at potential teleworkers and their organisations.

Forecasts and estimates of teleworking developments

Many studies have sought to calculate existing and future teleworking developments. Statistics fall into three general areas: measurements of actual *penetration* (for example, Huws *et al.* 1990; Korte and Wynne 1996); estimates of the *potential* for take-up (Nilles *et al.* 1976); and *predictions* of future growth (Holti and Stern 1986b). In setting about the task in each of these areas, a variety of definitions, approaches and methods have been used. Certain studies (such as Kraut 1987, 1989; Find/SVP 1995) place the *home* as a defining attribute, while others include a variety of workplace arrangements. Others place new technology or activities related to the spread of new technology as a central factor (Find/SVP 1995). So far as *calculations* are concerned, some figures are based on occupational employment data, others on home-based work statistics, whilst some utilise opinion surveys regarding awareness and interest in teleworking.

Nilles *et al.* (1976), for instance, estimated the number of US information workers in 1978 at 48.3 per cent or 38 million of the total US workforce (78.6 million in 1970) and 55 per cent by the year 2000. This was used to suggest a massive potential for telework. Simarly, Kraut (1987) sees a significant potential for teleworking growth through analysis of data on 'professional occupations' (such as para-legal personnel, computer systems analysts and computer programmers). These, he argues, are growing quickly in percentage terms and are likely to be accompanied by a rapid growth in teleworking.

4

More recently, Miller estimated the total number of homeworkers/teleworkers in the US at 5.5 million (4.5 per cent of the workforce) – including about 876,000 full-time telecommuters – based on the number of part-time teleworkers in the US (Miller 1990). A similar study conducted by Find/SVP a few years later indicated that 9.1 million workers in the US workforce could be considered tele-commuters, an increase of almost 100 per cent compared to 1990 (Find/SVP 1995).

In Europe, the potential for telework has also been considered vast. In an early study, Holti and Stern (1986b) reported that whilst the actual amount of tele-workers in Europe was still very small, it was expected to rise dramatically within 10 to 15 years. The European Commission, who are actively promoting and supporting telework developments, even expects as many as 10 million tele-workers in Europe by the year 2000 (see Qvortrup, this volume). An opinion survey, conducted with more methodological rigour, and based on a sample of more than 16,000 households in the Federal Republic of Germany, France, Italy and the UK, showed that 13 million workers (14 per cent of the labour force) showed serious interest in home work (Huws et al. 1990).

A recent study by Korte and Wynne (1996) on the penetration of telework in the five largest countries of Europe (Germany, France, Britain, Italy and Spain) concluded that the actual penetration of telework in European organisations is around 5 per cent (1.1 million workers). Extrapolated for the whole of Europe this would mean 1.25 million teleworkers. This study shows that the extent of telework practice varies considerably beween member states: nearly half of European teleworkers live in Britain (560,000), France has 215,000, Germany 149,000, with Southern Europe lagging far behind – Spain has 102,000 and Italy 97,000.

In many cases, though, the *rigour* of methods used to collect data is variable. As Kraut (1987) acknowledges, approaches based on occupation and employment data are often unreliable, and provide only a rough indication of the 'outer limits' of possible developments. Such difficulties are also reflected in figures based on homeworking statistics. The problem is that these accounts may fail to consider a number of important social, economic, legal and political forces that also influ-ence the spread of telework. In addition to this, many studies are often under taken by (or on behalf of) vendors and funding bodies who seek to promote teleworking or to legitimise the allocation funding. Where the actors involved here have considerable power and profile, they may therefore be in a position to skew the debate in terms favourable to themselves.

A central problem in quantitative studies of telework is the way in which the lack of conceptual clarity frustrates cross-study comparison (see Kraut 1987; Huws et al. 1990). Given that surveys are undertaken by a variety of organisa-tions, with different interests and concerned with different analytical variables, it is therefore no surprise that the operational definitions used do vary. For instance, telecommunications companies wishing to promote the use of the Internet among teleworkers may place more emphasis on *technology* as a defining feature than would gender studies researchers looking at the impact homeworking has on domestic role conflict. In other words, what we choose to call 'telework' and then go on to study also depends on *why* we conduct the study in the first instance. Since we cannot say incontrovertibly what is or what is not telework, it is perhaps better to look at the usefulness of such studies given the purposes for which they were intended.

The search to understand telework in the above manner involves a distinctly 'objectivist' approach to the subject. It is concerned with ascertaining the shape, variants and extent of teleworking (how many are doing it, where, in what jobs and so on). Accompanying this, we also find an attempt to illuminate the motives behind the schemes in question, as well as the forms of employment involved, and the means of control and management exercised (see also, Huws 1993). The objectivist stance then, presumes the *existence* of teleworking phenomena 'out there' in the world, and that they can be identified, placed in (often pre-defined) conceptual categories, counted and then analysed. In this case, the researcher stands 'outside looking in'.

However, the shortcomings of the objectivist stance are not simply that it entails the use of data that makes for difficult comparisons, but that it also tends to rely on concepts and categories that people in organisations may not recognise. Moreover, it may discuss issues in terms that the actors involved would not employ themselves. For example, the introduction of call-centres may not be viewed as a form of teleworking by the companies involved, even though such innovations correspond to many teleworking orthodoxies, such as the use of IT to provide remote services. For these reasons we also need to consider the viewpoint of telework which seeks to 'get inside' organisations and understand the way phenomena are treated.

Telework as a conceptual representation

In a world that has seen the rise of the World Wide Web and a whole array of multimedia technologies, discussions of telework that emphasise the role of IT in facilitating homeworking may often ignore many broader business pressures and opportunities. And yet this comes at a time when technological advance outstrips the expectations many would have had even at the start of this decade. Often, discussions of telework have been eclipsed by other 'big(ger) ideas' such as re-engineering, web-based working and virtual working.

Restructuring trends, such as downsizing, de-layering, or 'rightsizing' – despite their well-discussed shortcomings – have helped to ensure corporate survival, competitive repositioning, as well as lowering operating costs (Keen 1991). Developments in business process re-engineering (Hammer and Champy 1993; Davenport 1993) have produced a greater attention to process management and redesign, and an increase in customer focus. We can also observe the loosening of hierarchical structures towards independent and smaller units. The intention here is to achieve strategic flexibility by externalising or eliminating activities that are not seen as vital to core processes (Van der Wielen *et al.* 1993). This has sometimes been accompanied by the use of IT to create new (often dispersed) structures that involve the creation of inter-business networks and project teams (Jackson and Van der Wielen 1997).

What this illustrates is that while the *concept* of telework may lack currency in many quarters, the ideas with which it is associated (IT-facilitated flexibility, remote service provision, increased efficiency, lower overheads and operating costs) are often pursued through other programmes of change (see Jackson, this volume). Technology is indeed playing an instrumental role in support of many teleworking orthodoxies, although such developments are not articulated in tele-working terms. Hence, the same issues, pressures and opportunities that are cen-tral to teleworking debates are also conceptualised as part of other organisational developments and work initiatives.

A concentration on 'teleworkers', as people who work remotely from their central offices by using IT, may leave one blinkered to developments in areas of general business process and policy. In this instance, teleworking provides an *alternative perspective*, which illuminates possibilities for reorganisation based on IT-supported dispersed working. In this sense, rather than presuming the existence of *instances* of telework 'out there' in the world, teleworking ideas provide new ways of *representing* work phenomena. As such, this helps us to get *inside* situations and actively *frame* issues to identify new business solutions and opportunities.

In many ways, the use of telework-related ideas as a 'framing device' is what occurs in discussions of 'virtuality'. In contrast to telework, there is less concen-tration here on individual work tasks or jobs, particularly flexible work arrange-ments. Instead, such discussions focus on issues of IT-supported work dispersal. There have been several terms used to describe the work phenomena involved here: for instance, 'cyber business' (Barnatt 1995); 'virtual corporation' (Davidow and Malone 1992); and 'virtual organisation' (Birchall and Lyons 1995). In the more radical approaches, such as Barnatt's, organisational structures become synonymous with the cyberspace through which relations are articulated. In this sense, organisations are seen to operate in an 'information space', rather than a material world, situated in time and space. The 'representational landscape' on which this takes place is supported by the discourses, images and metaphors provided by new forms of IT, particularly the more evocative ones such as virtual reality and the World Wide Web (see Jackson 1997).

The ideas underpinning these approaches demand some elucidation. For example, virtual organisations sometimes imply an atomisation of actors, in which they are treated not simply as employees or human beings, but as *market actors* (cf. Birchall and Lyons 1995). This is more so where cyberspace is treated as a 'marketplace' (for example, see Gates 1995: 6) in which economic transactions take place and which provides 'perfect information' about products (including labour) (see Jackson 1996). Although internally consistent, such perspectives are also based on simplified images of people, work, market decisions, as well as time and space. Moreover, they are constructed through certain discourses that have their own ideological connotations (symbolic, in the information view; free-market economics, in the case of cyberworking). We need to challenge and supplement them with the insights offered from different theoretical vantage points, such as those that concentrate on the social constitution of organisations.

The ability to represent issues in teleworking and virtual organisation to serve a range of agendas is something that lies at the heart of the subject's complexity. It is to this matter that we now turn.

Understanding teleworking's complexity

1997 saw the relaunch of the *Star Wars* trilogy, and the famous scene where Luke Skywalker and Han Solo visit a bar on the planet Tatooine, surrounded by an array of weird and wonderful creatures from all different planets. On the face of it, these creatures have little in common. Yet they have found a common-meeting place because of a shared interest in drinking and having a good time. In a similar way, the idea of telework – and the conferences, publications and projects dedicated to it – forms a common-meeting place for some similarly different animals (metaphorically speaking). These include:

- information systems designers, hardware vendors, telecom companies
- policy-makers in transport planning, urban planning, rural regeneration and environmental protection
- personnel managers, equal opportunities managers, flexible work specialists
- business redesign experts, researchers and consultants on new organisational forms
- psychologists and sociologists of work
- anthropologists and social geographers
- economists
- line managers and business owners searching for new ways of working.

These parties have a shared interest in teleworking because of its implications for the way we work, live, travel and purchase and consume goods. It offers some radical sociotechnical disjunctures that cut across many areas of practical and academic concern. As such, it provides a meeting ground for people who would usually not meet. This, of course, is a potential strength of teleworking discussions, in that such people bring a range of views, analyses and prescriptions to the subject.

Yet the range of actors involved, and their differences in background and outlook (especially in academic disciplines), is also a source of complexity. Reasons for interest may lead to different approaches to the subject, and alternative conceptualisations of the phenomena involved. In addition, the context within which this takes place is also likely to influence which actors engage in debates and developments. For example, skill shortages, oil crises and road traffic pollution have all been a spur to certain actors getting involved at particular points in time. We need therefore to understand the relation between teleworking concepts and issues, practical developments, the networks of actors that take part and the contexts within which these occur.

This is also important for another reason. By examining the actors, motives and strategies employed in teleworking developments, we can appreciate in a more robust way the relation between changes in technology, work and organisations. This provides a useful antidote to the deterministic way in which technology is sometimes treated. To do this, we will turn to the ideas espoused by 'actor network theories'.

Actor network theory

Actor network theories have been developed to address the way that technologies form and stabilise into particular configurations (see, for example, Callon 1986, 1987; Latour 1988; Law 1991, 1997). The approach involves examining the 'heterogeneous associations' (human, technological, conceptual, material, etc.) which constitute such networks, and the means by which they are changed or consolidated. It sees the formation of these associations as a process of 'translation', in which the elements of the network (e.g. workers, technologies, buildings) take on a role defined for them by a *translator* (such as a manager, engineer or even a company (Callon 1986, 1987)). Translation is achieved through a strategy of *problemisation*, in which a scenario is constructed such that membership of the network best serves the solution to an actor's problems, or the means of seizing certain opportunities. If successful, this creates what Callon calls an 'obligatory point of passage' for the actors involved – that they can only solve their problems through membership of *this* network. Following this, the next stage of the translation process can begin. This involves a series of *displacements*, through which a range of entities is mobilised to ensure stabilisation of the network.

We can see an example of this in teleworking if we follow the strategies sometimes employed by telecom and IT companies. To push their products and services, such companies need to translate clients' needs and problems in terms that involve the sale of IT devices and telecom services. One way of achieving this might be to persuade clients that teleworking (using their technologies and services) is an 'obligatory point of passage' in meeting, for example, the desire of individuals for work flexibility, or for a company to collaborate better with allied businesses. The success and stability of these translations rely on a whole series of heterogeneous alignments. For example, home-based workers must be willing and able to turn their houses into workplaces. Managers must have attitudes towards supervision and control that are not based on physical surveillance. This alignment cannot, of course, be guaranteed, even where 'problemisation through telework' seems attractive. To appreciate the dynamics involved here, we need to understand two other processes that are crucial to the formation of actor networks: *simplification* and *juxtaposition*.

Besides their membership of any one network (such as a work organisation) –

which involves a particular role (as a worker, for example) – actors are also members of juxtaposed networks in which they perform other roles. For example, as well as working for an organisation, individuals are also members of family or social networks. In travelling to work, they take part in additional networks, which involve a heterogeneous association of vehicles, travel fares, energy consumption and environmental damage (noise, pollutants, etc.). However, in attempting to enrol them into these networks, the actors are looked upon in terms of those properties compatible with membership of the network. Callon (1986) and Law (1991) warn, though, that the actors in question may reject such simplifications, since their role in juxtaposed networks may more strongly influence them. This is especially the case where such networks conflict. For example, the role of parent (in the family network) is not always compatible with that of a worker. This is especially true where work involves spending considerable time at locations away from the home, especially where this requires long commutes and job-related stress.

Understanding the actors involved in teleworking networks

Using actor network theories in telework helps us to make sense of the complex web of relationships and agendas. Where we take teleworking to imply a reduction in commuting, those who are members of transport planning and environmental protection networks (typically, government ministries and agencies) have a clear interest. Where this is accompanied by a shift in demand for housing and public services, urban planning authorities also have a stake. Where they view telework as a means of bringing jobs to depressed or remote regions, further agencies are likely to become interested. These may include those charged with rural regeneration or the social inclusion of local communities. Where they see it as a means of promoting IT innovation more generally, ministries for trade and industry, as well as technology transfer and innovation centres, may also see a role to play.

As for work-related matters, problems and issues exist in which managers from a variety of functions have an interest. These range from personnel in real estate and facilities management, to those developing flexible work packages and remote services. Individual employees seeking to secure a better balance between on-site working and the home may also see incentives. We can also include here entrepreneurs wanting to establish SOHO (small office, home office) arrangements. Finally, as far as workers' interests are concerned, we must also recognise the influence that works councils and trade unions may seek to make.

In the consultancy and research communities, telework provides an opportunity to sell advice and undertake studies. It defines a market and focus at which projects, books and research proposals can be targeted. Finally, we can add those organisations mentioned above – telecom and IT companies – that may benefit from telework innovations through the provision of the technologies that support it.

Yet while telework provides the meeting ground for all the above actors, their motives in getting involved in developments clearly diverge. Additionally, though taking actions that promote teleworking may be of mutual benefit, each actor may prefer alternative alignments. One reason for this is that in the complex world outside that of (simplified) teleworking translations, membership of other networks may better serve actors' interests. For example, the desire to balance better job and family demands is translated in telework as a problem about *commuting* and *work location*. The workers involved may reject this, and choose instead to see the *real* problem as one of long hours or inflexible *work times*. As such, job-sharing, part-time working, flexitime or term-time working may all be seen as alternative solutions. Additionally, other associations created by office-based networks, such as social contact and the opportunities to impress one's superiors, may be another reason to reject the telework alignment.

The danger of network simplification is something of particular relevance to actors involved in the supply side of telework. For example, unless the role of telework is also in alignment with clients' business strategies and other responses to strategic challenges, it may be difficult to provide a persuasive translation of their opportunities and problems in terms that favour a teleworking response. Similarly, the promotion of telecentres and satellite offices also demands understanding clients' requirements in terms other than simple access to technology or low-cost accommodation. For instance, the need to build personal relationships with customers, and to project image and prestige by having offices sited in commercial centres, may militate against remote working.

This also highlights the need for a better appreciation of the symbolic aspects of space and the built environment. We must be cognisant of the fact that certain places – the home, the office, town centres, even entire cities and countries – evoke particular meanings and experiences. This has important implications for both office and work location (see also Kompast and Wagner, this volume).

There is also an issue here as far as IT, telecom and consultancy companies are concerned. By employing telework-related concepts and ideas as their problemisation strategies, these companies necessarily translate clients' problems and opportunities into terms that they can address through IT supported work configurations. There is a danger, though, that such strategies may downplay the social and organisational dynamics of different work configurations in favour of a 'technical fix'.

Perhaps more problematical is that the more radical the work concept, the greater demands for change and psychological adjustment it places on people. For example, managers used to having all functions beneath the same 'roof', with employees operating under the watchful gaze of their supervisors, may lack the sort of values, attitudes (particularly that of trust) and behaviour needed for more virtual forms of organisation to operate. As such, appropriating new technologies to create new business models and ways of working may require an alignment that involves a whole *turnaround in thinking* (cf. Handy 1995).

The same also goes for the *skills* needed to manage under these arrangements. For example, managers dealing with remote employees, (virtual) team members who may seldom meet and home-based individuals managing the psychological boundaries between work and non-work, all need to develop new abilities if they are to profit from the new ways of working (see Part 2 of this volume).

To address these issues we will turn now to the changing nature of modern organisations and the issues they highlight for successful change.

Rethinking social and organisational issues in telework

Where telework has been promoted based on the notion that it is technologically feasible and economically desirable to reduce office space, eliminate commuting and start working at home, results have often been poor. This is particularly so where such ideas illustrate some common, yet flawed, premises concerning the nature of work and organisation, as well as the social aspects of technological change (Van der Wielen *et al.* 1993; and Taillieu 1995; Jackson and Van der Wielen 1997). Such 'supply driven' approaches tend to highlight the shift in physical workplace (from company offices to working at home), giving little attention to the organisation of work. This creates the impression that work is an individual activity, rather than a collaborative effort. Many test cases, pilot studies and experiments therefore failed to recognise that the work place is not primarily a *physical* location but the locus of *collective endeavour* (Hirschheim 1985; Jackson 1992; Gillespie and Feng 1994).

Many advocates of teleworking have underestimated the social and organisational changes neccesary for successful innovation (see Forester 1988; Dürrenberger 1989; Gordon 1988; Olson 1988; Jackson 1992; Van der Wielen 1991). In several cases the advantages of telework did not outweigh the (unexpected) social and organisational problems linked with the relocation of workplaces (see Olson 1988; Dürrenberger 1989). Moreover, given that many approaches focus on the technological possibilities for dispersed working, they tend to downplay broader problems with which organisations are having to cope. Insufficient attention is often given to the rapidly changing business environments. Such approaches therefore failed to develop a meaningful vision of how telework could be introduced as a viable, strategic solution. However appealing, the substitution of transportation and geographical dispersion of workplaces cannot be isolated from the broader influences on production (Van der Wielen 1991; Van der Wielen *et al.* 1993). Despite this, only a few authors have questioned the underlying assumptions of initial approaches to telework, or sought to develop it within a more meaningful conceptual framework (for example, Holti and Stern 1986b; Huws *et al.* 1990). This is essential if we are to understand the transition from a modern society based on bureaucratic mass-production to a postmodern one based on flexible, client-oriented production. This would allow telework to be appreciated as part of a broader transformation of organisations, involving the dispersal of activities in space and time (cf. Harvey 1989; Van der Wielen *et al.* 1993).

Organisation, space and time

In the days in which mass-production was the dominant basis for organisation, industry depended largely upon a concentration of people, tools and resources in a common setting. Rigid bureaucratic structuring – the ability to routinise and repeat activities – proved to be the key success factor for production (Hassard 1989). This relied on co-ordinating the activities of employees by synchronising their movements in time and space (Pollard 1965). This also provided for worker discipline, since co-ordination and control could take place in face-to-face settings under the watchful eye of a supervisor (cf. Foucault 1979).

Such spatial and temporal structures are also reflected in the cultural values and norms of an organisation. Mass-production industry, for instance, relied on a culture of punctuality, precision, discipline, obedience and conscientiousness to support time-space concentration and maintain coherence of the collectivity (see Erneste 1989). As such, co-ordinates of space and time have served as surrogates of performance and discipline. Time-span and presence, for instance, are used as indicators of performance, with (in)visibility often reflecting status and hier-archical position (Giddens 1987). The spatial-temporal concentration of workers in conventional work practices is therefore not simply a product of technical decisions and requirements, but is a highly social and political phenomenon (cf. Thompson 1967; Foucault 1979; Marglin 1974).

New forms of spatial-temporal cooperation

Increasing environmental turbulence has confronted bureaucratic, hierarchical organisations with their inability to adapt to changing circumstances and their failure to reduce uncertainty. Global competition, shorter life cycles of products and services, and pressure to speed up product development and rate of innov-ation, have forced management to replace rigid hierarchical structures with more fluid and dynamic horizontal relationships (Taillieu 1989). In an environment of rapid change, requiring constant innovation, a more 'organic' or 'integrative' organisation is needed (Moss-Kanter 1991). The impact of this on corporate strategies and forms is to de-legitimise bureaucracy, weaken the power of hier-archy and loosen the employment relationship (ibid.). By redistributing activities organisations aim to reduce complexity, increase flexibility, improve efficiency, and create new strategic opportunities.

The redistribution of activities also causes existing boundaries between differ-ent internal organisational units to disappear. At the same time, the external boundaries of organisations become more and more blurred. As a result, new organisational forms emerge that are characterised by temporal and spatial dis-persion (Van der Wielen 1991; Van der Wielen *et al.* 1993; Gillespie and Feng

1994). These dispersed, or 'virtual' organisations are designed to overcome time-and-place constraints associated with rigid bureaucratic structures. They are also based on a different design philosophy with regard to how, where and when work should be done.

For instance, the integration of dispersed activities demands new forms of co-operation, co-ordination and control. Consequently, telework becomes not simply an experiment in cost-efficient production, but more importantly, an exercise in self-management by the workers themselves. It demands reduced input control, and output-oriented management and supervision. Where work takes place in the home, workers may need to develop the skills involved in managing the psychological and social boundaries between work and non-work. The design of new information systems must address the need for better knowledge management and organisational learning. Where workers seldom operate at a central site, issues of commitment, loyalty and organisational identity become important. In cases where IT allows for individuals to work together across space, better team-building skills are needed. This is especially so where *inter-organisational* (as well as spatial) boundaries dissolve. In this case, the need to establish *trust* between the parties is essential if such arrragements are to succeed.

To understand these emerging issues we need to develop a new agenda for teleworking. This demands new perspectives on the subject – new ways of looking at phenomena and new ways of addressing them.

The parts of the book: developing a new agenda for telework

In Part 1 of the book, Making Sense of Teleworking Concepts and Contexts, we take a look at practical and theoretical developments that have taken place in the area of teleworking. A bridge is built here between debates on telework and broader discussions of virtual working and virtual organisation. This part also seeks to locate teleworking developments as part of a more encompassing framework involving the changing spatial and temporal dynamics of work and organisation.

Part 2, Understanding and Managing Boundaries in Telework, examines the consequences of new ways of working for different work and non-work boundaries. It highlights the need to manage time, space and social relationships in new ways. It also provides an analysis of the symbolic nature of time and space and how they relate to the meaning and experience of work itself.

In Part 3, Integrative Frameworks for Teleworking, we examine how teleworking ideas can be integrated into planning and strategy development to address a range of problems and issues, both inside and outside organisations. This illustrates the different interests and agendas involved in teleworking, and the need for frameworks that help to combine issues from different points of view.

The final part of the book, Part 4, Actors, Networks and Experiences: International Cases of Telework, draws on examples from both Europe and North

America to illustrate the strategies and experiences of different actors involved in a variety of teleworking forms.

Part 4 is followed by a short conclusion, which draws together the books' chapters and discusses the consequences of these for future research and practice.

References

Barnatt, C. (1995) *Cyberbusiness*, Chichester: Wiley.

Becker, F. and Steele, F. (1995). *Workplace by Design: Mapping the High Performance Workscape*, San Fransisco: Jossey-Bass Publishers.

Birchall, D. and Lyons, D. (1995) *Creating Tomorrow's Organisation*, London: Pitman.

Brandes, W. and Buttler, F. (1985) 'Alte und neue heimarbeit: eine arbeitsökonomische interpretation', in *SAMF arbeitspapiere* 4: 75–91.

Brandt, S. (1983) 'Working-at-home: how to cope with spatial design possibilities caused by the new communication media', *Office Technology and People*, Elsevier Science Publishers, North-Holland.

Brocklehurst, M. (1989) 'Homeworking and the new technology: the reality and the rhetoric', *Personnel review*, 18: 2.

Callon, M. (1986) 'The Sociology of an Actor Network: The Case of the Electric Vehicle', in Callon, M., Law, J. and Rip, A. (eds), *Mapping the Dynamics of Science and Technology*, London: Macmillan.

—— (1987) 'Society in the Making: The Study of Technology as a Tool for Sociological Analysis', in Bijker, W.E., Hughes, T.P. and Pinch, T.F. (eds) *The Social Construction of Technological Systems*, Cambridge, MA: MIT Press.

Christensen, K. (1988) *The New Era of Home Based Work: Directions and Policies*, London: Westview Press.

Davenport, T.H. (1993) *Process Innovation: Reengineering Work Through Information Technology*, Boston: Harvard Business School Press.

Davidow, W.H. and Malone, M.S. (1992) *The Virtual Corporation*: New York, HarperCollins.

Dürrenberger, G. (1989) 'Vocational Territories', in Ernste, H. and Jaeger, C. (eds) *Information Society and Spatial Structure*, London: Belhaven.

Erneste, H. (1989) 'The Corporate Culture and its Linkages with the Corporate Enviroment', in Erneste, H. and Jaeger, C. (eds) *Information Society and Spatial Structure*, London: Belhaven.

Find/SVP (1995) 'The new home office consumers', *Interactive Consumers*, 2, 1. January.

Forester, T. (1988) 'The myth of the electronic cottage', *Futures*, June. 227–40.

Foucault, M. (1979) *Discipline and Punishment*, New York: Vintage.

Gates, B. (1995) *The Road Ahead*, London: Viking.

Giddens, A. (1987) *Social Theory and Modern Sociology*, Cambridge: Polity.

Gillespie, A. and Feng, L. (1994) 'Teleworking, work organization and the workplace', in Mansell, R. (ed.) *Management of Information and Communication Technologies: Emerging Patterns of Control*, London, ASLIB (Association for Information Management).

Gordon, G.E. (1988) 'The dilemma of telework: technology vs. tradition', in Korte, W.B., Robinson, S. and Steinle, W.J. (eds) *Telework: Present Situation and Future Development of a New Form of Work Organization*, Amsterdam, North-Holland.

—— (1996) *Telecommuting, Teleworking and Alternative Officing Homepage*, Gil Gordon Associates, http://www.gilgordon.com

Hammer, M. and Champy, J. (1993) *Reengineering the Corporation*, New York: Harper Business.

Handy, C. (1995) 'Trust and the Virtual Organization', *Harvard Business Review*, May–June: 40–50.

Harvey, D. (1989) *The Condition of Postmodernity*, Oxford: Blackwell.

Hassard, J. (1989) 'Time and Industrial Sociology', in Blyton, P., Hassard, J., Hill, S. and Starkey, K. (eds) *Time, Work and Organisation*, London: Routledge.

Hirschheim, R.A. (1985) *Office Automation: a Social and Organizational Perspective*, Chichester: Wiley.

Holti, R. (1994) 'Telematics, workplaces and homes: the evolving picture of teleworking', in Andriessen, J.H. and Roe, R.A. (eds) *Telematics and Work*, Chichester: Wiley.

Holti, R. and Stern, E. (1986a), *Distance Working Study: Conclusions and Recommendations for Action*, FAST internal paper, London: Tavistock Institute.

—— (1986b) *Distance Working*, Commission of the European Communities, Directorate General Telecommunications, Information Industries and Innovation, Luxembourg.

Huws, U. (1993) 'Teleworking in Britain', Employment Department, Research Series No. 18, London.

Huws, U., Korte, W.B. and Robinson, S. (1990) *Telework: Towards the Elusive Office*, Chichester: Wiley.

Jackson, P.J. (1992) 'Organisational change: the role of telework', paper presented at the conference 'The Challenge of Change: the Theory and Practice of Organizational Transformations', Cardiff: Cardiff Business School.

—— (1996) 'The Virtual Society and the End of Organization: Feeling Our Way in the Dark', Keynote address to the World Wide Web Federal Consortium's Web Masters Workshop, Washington, DC, August.

—— (1997) 'Information Systems as Metaphor: Innovation and the 3 Rs of Representation', in McLoughlin, I.P. and Harris, M. (eds) *Innovation, Organisational Change and Technology*, London: Routledge.

Jackson, P.J. and Van der Wielen, J.M.M. (eds) (1996), *New International Perspectives on Telework: From Telecommuting to the Virtual Organisation*, Proceedings Vol. I and II, WORC, Tilburg, The Netherlands.

Jackson, P.J. and Van der Wielen, J.M.M. (1997) *New International Perspectives on Telework: Report of the London '96 Workshop 'From Telecommuting to the Virtual Organisation'* 31 July–2 August 1996, Work and Organisation Research Centre, Tilburg, The Netherlands.

Keen, P.G.W. (1991) *Shaping the Future: Business Design through Information Technology*, Boston, MA: Harvard Business School Press.

Kinsman, F. (1987) *The Telecommuters*, Chichester: Wiley.

Korte, W.B. and Wynne, R. (1996) *Telework: Penetration Potential and Practice in Europe*, Amsterdam: IOS Press.

Kraut, R.E. (1987) 'Predicting the use of technology: the case of telework', in Kraut, E. (ed.), *Technology and the Transformation of White-collar Work*, Hillsdale: Lawrence Erlbaum.

—— (1988) 'Homework: what is it and who does it?', in Christensen, K. (ed.) *The New Era of Home Based Work. Directions and Policies*, London: Westview Press.

—— (1989) 'Telecommuting: the trade-offs of home work', in Siefert, M., Gerbner, G. and Fisher, J. (eds) *The Information Gap: How Computers and Other New Communication Technologies Affect the Social Distribution of Power*, New York: Oxford University Press.

Latour, B. (1988) 'The Prince for Machines as well as for Machinations', in Elliot, B. (ed.) *Technology as Social Process*, Edinburgh: Edinburgh University Press.

Law, J. (1991) 'Introduction: Monsters, Machines and Socio-Technical Relations', in Law, J. (ed.) *A Sociology of Monsters*, London: Routledge.

—— (1997) 'Tradition/Trahision: Notes on Actor Network Theory', Centre for Social Theory and Technology, Keele University.

Lenk, T. (1989) *Telearbeit: Möglichkeiten und Grenzen einer telekommunikativen Dezentralisierung von betrieblichen Arbeitsplätze*, (Telework: possibilities and constraints for decentralization of working places with telecommunication), Betriebswirtschaftliche Schriften, Heft 138, Duncker and Humblot, Berlin.

McLoughlin, I.P. and Harris, M. (eds) (1997) *Innovation, Organisational Change and Technology*, London: Routledge.

Marglin, S.A. (1974) 'What do bosses really do? The origins and functions of hierarchy in capitalist production', *Review of Radical Political Economics*, 6: 60–112.

Miller, T.E. (1990) *1989 Home Office Overview*, New York, NY: Link Resources.

Moss-Kanter, R. (1991) 'The Future of Bureaucracy and Hierarchy in Organizational Theory: A Report from the Field', in Bourdieu, P. and Coleman, J.S. (eds) *Social Theory for a Changing Society*, Boulder: Westview Press.

Nilles, J.M., Carlson, F.R., Gray, P. and Hanneman, G.J. (1976) *The Telecommunications-Transportation Trade-off*, Chichester, Wiley.

Olson, M.H. (1988) 'Organizational barriers to telework', in Korte, W.B., Robinson, S. and Steinle, W.J. (eds) *Telework: Present Situation and Future Development of a New Form of Work Organization*, Amsterdam: North-Holland.

Pfeffer, J. and Baron, J.N. (1988) 'Taking the workers back out: recent trends in the structuring of employment', *Research in Organisational Behavior*, 10: 257–303.

Pollard, S. (1965) *The Genesis of Modern Management*, London: Edward Arnold.

Probert, B. and Wajcman, J. (1988) 'Technological change and the future of work', *Journal of Industrial Relations*, September: 432–48.

Roe, R.A., Van den Berg, P.T., Zijlstra, F.R.H., Schalk, M.J.D., Taillieu, T.C.B. and Van der Wielen, J.M.M. (1993) 'New concepts for a new age: information service organizations and mental information work', *The European Work and Organizational psychologist*, 2, 4, special issue on New Information Technology, Lawrence Erlbaum Associates.

Stanworth, J. and Stanworth, C. (1991) *Telework: the Human Resource Implications*, London: Institute of Personnel Management.

Taillieu, T.C.B. (1989) 'Trends in Management and Organization', Department of Work and Organizational Psychology, Tilburg University, The Netherlands.

Thompson, E.P. (1967) 'Time, Work Discipline and Industrial Capitalism', *Past and Present*, 38: 56–97.

Toffler, A. (1980) *The Third Wave*, London: Collins

Van der Wielen, J.M.M. (1991) *Telewerk: omgevingsinvloeden en verspreiding van activiteiten*, (Telework: environmental influences and dispersion of activities), working paper, Tilburg University, Tilburg, The Netherlands.

Van der Wielen, J.M.M. and Taillieu, T.C.B. (1995) 'Recent conceptual developments in telework research', *Proceedings of the 13th Annual Conference of the Association of Management*, 13, 2, Vancouver, British Columbia, Canada.

Van der Wielen, J.M.M., Taillieu, T.C.B., Poolman, J.A. and Van Zuilichem, J. (1993) 'Telework: dispersed organizational activity and new forms of spatial-temporal coordination and control', *The European Work and Organizational Psychologist*, 3, 2, special issue on New Information Technology: 145–62.

Part 1

MAKING SENSE OF
TELEWORKING CONCEPTS
AND CONTEXTS

The chapters that form Part 1 have two main aims. First, given the conceptual ambiguity in telework discussions, and the links that are often made between telework and virtual work, they address some of the conceptual problems involved in accounts of these subjects. Second, because teleworking and virtual working issues are often poorly integrated within wider debates on economic, techno-logical and social change, the authors examine frameworks that provide a more robust theorising of these issues within broader contexts of development.

In Chapter 2, Lars Qvortrup traces the origins and developments in tele-working concepts, stressing the importance of a purpose-based definition. For Qvortrup, telework should be linked to an individual's work situation, macro-sociological changes and the individual's life form. He identifies three life forms – self-employed, wage earner and career-oriented person – which are characterised by the way work and leisure time are related, and involve different attitudes and values towards work and family life. These different life forms, according to Qvortrup, are essential for explaining innovations in new forms of work.

In Chapter 3 Constance Perin looks at the social and cultural implications of work schedules, flexibility and project work, and contrasts the different time space scheduling demands of industrial and modern production systems. The latter illustrate the greater scope for temporal and spatial flexibility in the way in which much modern work is carried out. This is particularly shown by developments in project work and temporary organisation. As part of this, Perin argues that old demarcations between industrial and household production systems, paid and unpaid work, are becoming outdated.

Paul McGrath and Maeve Houlihan in Chapter 4 consider the relevance for telework of the postmodern perspective on organisations. They identify the macro-level changes that characterise the new organisational structures and forms of economic activity that are viewed as postmodern. The chapter summarises the contrasting imperatives of modernism and postmodernism as described by Clegg (1990). In order to incorporate teleworking into such frameworks, the authors identify additional dimensions that need to be added. They conclude that telework impacts on organisational arrangements in three main ways: to increase centralisation and control; to decentralise and empower; and to facilitate micro-enterprise.

In Chapter 5 Martin Harris examines some of the conceptual and theoretical questions raised by debates on virtual organisation. He notes that the development of these forms has, in common with other related social and organisational transformations, generally been treated as part of a paradigm shift and rejection of Fordist/Taylorist modes of organising. Harris argues instead for a more sophisticated reading which recognises continuities as well as discontinuities in ways of working. To reframe the debate in a way that recognises the co-existence of 'virtual' and Fordist forms, Harris points to the work of Fukuyama (1995) and Clegg (1990). These are used to help identify the role of culture and divergent organisational rationalities in understanding the way organisational forms come about.

2

FROM TELEWORKING TO NETWORKING

Definitions and trends

Lars Qvortrup

Introduction

The current telework terminology is becoming more and more problematic because it focuses on the remote work location of individual workers instead of emphasising the important organisational dynamics made possible by advanced communications and the networking aspects of computer-mediated work. Consequently, current quantifications of teleworkers have failed. Counting teleworkers is like measuring a rubber band. The result depends on how far you stretch your definition.

Still, as a concept for individual persons' working conditions telework and related terms are relevant. But in order for us to benefit analytically from these concepts they must be context-oriented, i.e. related to the concerned persons' life form situation and to his or her organisational context. Particularly, it is crucially important that specific ways of organising telework are adapted to the specific life form of the potential teleworker. In my opinion this is a pre-condition for understanding the organisational dynamics related to telework, and thus for making telework socially acceptable.

What is telework? The history of a changing concept

The history of telework definitions

How do we define telework? This is not just an academic discussion. On the contrary, our understanding of telework has major impacts on the way in which we organise telework, on the identification of potential teleworkers and telework regions, on the specification of pros and cons of telework, and of course on the statistical registration of teleworkers. Only if we know what telework is, is it possible for us to establish the appropriate organisational frameworks, to identify which geographical regions can and cannot benefit from telework initiatives, and of course to actually count the number of teleworkers.

So, what *is* telework? Is it 'electronic homework' – which already sounds a bit old-fashioned? Is it 'telecommuting', using the well-known concept coined by Jack Nilles in 1973 (Nilles *et al.* 1976)? Or is it 'flexiwork', a term becoming more and more popular in Europe? As I will exemplify, all three names have been used as the defining term for telework.

During the 1970s and 1980s in Europe telework was looked at with quite some scepticism. At that time, telework was often termed 'electronic homework', con-notating unskilled, low-paid office work from the home, either based on a full-time contract or on a freelance relationship with the employer. Normally, the connotations of this definition of telework were negative. The typical teleworker was exemplified by the housewife with child-care responsibilities who, in isolation from the working office community, performed monotonous wordprocessing for a remote employer. Critical literature used 'electronic homework' as the termin-ology for 'telework' in order to emphasise what was thought to be a close connec-tion between today's telework and early industrial homework. For instance, Maciejewski related telework closely to traditional homeworking (Maciejewski 1987: 2f). According to critical analyses, the main group of potential teleworkers were female office workers. The foreseeable impact of telework was therefore social isolation, dis-organisation of workers and further centralisation of man-agement and control (for instance Bahl-Benker 1988; Dobbertheim 1985; Lux 1985; Moran and Tansey 1986; Vorjans 1987). In Denmark a similar approach has been articulated in Vedel (1984 and 1986).

Even if skilled work was added to this definition, it was still based on the assumption that telework was organised in relation to a central office with employees working at a distance from their basic place of work. In the United States in 1985 Margrethe H. Olson, Chairman of the National Research Coun-cil's Planning Panel on Office Workstations in the Homes, defined telework (or, rather, 'telecommuting', which was and still is the dominant American term) as simply 'people working at home with computers connected to offices many miles away' (National Research Council 1985:1; also Olson 1982 and 1988), and with only minor modifications in 1986 Cross and Raizman confirmed this definition: 'Telecommuting means performing job-related work at a site away from the office, then electronically transferring the results to the office or to another location' (Cross and Raizman 1986: 3f).

In the United States, the discussion of telework started much earlier than in Europe, not least thanks to the 'telework prophet' Jack Nilles who introduced the idea as early as 1973 (Olson in National Research Council 1985; and Nilles *et al.* 1976). The first systematic analysis of the pros and cons of telework at a societal level was published in 1976 by Nilles together with co-editors Carlson, Gray and Hanneman (Nilles *et al.* 1976). Here, the human and economic costs and benefits of the physical travel to and from work were compared with the costs and bene-fits of staying at home and using a telecommunications link to communicate with the employer. Generally speaking, in the US the discussion of telework has been closely related to the commuting problems from home to central offices or big cities with traffic problems. Consequently, the dominating term has been 'telecommuting' (this still seems to be the case, see Nilles 1994).

It is, however, not difficult to give examples of types of work which do not fit into the above definitions, yet still would be instinctively conceptualised as telework. This has been realised by many telework researchers – for instance, Huws (1988: 71), who emphasised that official definitions of the late 1980s might exclude a large proportion of people actually teleworking from home.

First, many teleworkers live as sole employees at their own, home-based business. They may be private consultants, working at home, sending reports of information to single customers or to subscribers of the said service. They may, for instance, be architects, working part time at home, telefaxing or e-mailing their designs and construction plans, part-time commuting in order to physically supervise the construction of a building, or they may be information providers, selling information to a mass market, for instance via Internet standards such as the World Wide Web.

Second, many teleworkers use telecommunications in order to avoid travelling to their customers or clients, or, similarly, end-users pick up their information commodity at a distance through the telecommunications network. Examples are video-communication-based interaction, or public, computer-based social service provision at a distance – perhaps even home shopping and home banking belong to this category.

Third, with the expansion of electronic network accessibility and the growing availability of portable computers, work may be performed 'everywhere' (at the office, at home, on travel), using computers and telecommunication, one example being the flexible consultant or the journalist, transmitting his or her reports via a modem from any corner of the world. In order to express this growing flexibility, and, presumably, to support positive connotations, the current dominating official term in Europe is: 'flexiwork'.

The distortion of a term

Still, both electronic homework, telecommuting, flexiwork, plus an abundance of other terms are used for telework. Just to mention a few: teleworkers, telecommuters, flexiworkers, distance workers, electronic homeworkers, teleguerrillas, home-based nomads, electronic moonlighters, satellite office workers, mobile teleworkers, full- and part-time homeworkers, telecottage workers, etc. However, obviously, they are not synonymous. Even worse, they are based on different – technical, geographical, organisational, legal and so on – criteria, which means that they cannot be combined into a coherent system of sub-categories.

Based on examples like the above a number of researchers have concluded that it does not seem appropriate to define telework along any single parameter or dimension (Korte 1988: 375; Steinle 1988: 9; Huws et al. 1990: 9). As an example, Huws *et al.* suggest that an adequate definition should include three variables: the location of work; the use of electronic equipment; and the existence of a communications link to the employer or contractor. In their book they present the following definition. Telework is

> work the location of which is independent of the location of the employer or contractor and can be changed according to the wishes of the individual teleworker and/or the organisation for which he or she is working. It is work which relies primarily or to a large extent on the use of electronic equipment, the results of which work are communicated remotely to the employer or contractor. The remote communications link need not be a direct telecommunications link but could include the use of mail or courier services.
>
> (Huws *et al.*1990: 10)

Huws *et al.* present a number of good arguments for proposing this definition. First, telework is not covered by 'telecommuting', i.e. by the substitution of telecommunications for commuting, partly because (according to Huws *et al.* 1990: 2) a number of surveys have shown that the desire to save on commuting for many teleworkers is *not* an important motive,[1] and partly because many sole employees have no choice to but work from their home (self-employed service and information providers). Second, telework certainly is not covered by 'electronic homework'. It can be organised in many other ways, as for instance in local satellite centres, neighbourhood centres, etc.

Still, a number of problems remain. If it is accepted – and there is good reason for doing so – that telework can be organised in many ways, an additional problem of definition emerges: what about remote branch offices in, say, banks, insurance companies, decentralised social service offices, or libraries? Should work executed at such branch offices be defined as telework? In addition, it is a problem that Huws *et al.*, under the concept of telework, include work the products of which are not exclusively distributed electronically, but also via mail services. Although their point is that there is little difference between distributing a text through an electronic mail service or on a diskette via the traditional mail service, in my opinion the inclusion of all kinds of distribution makes the definition of telework too broad. The problem which is not fully realised by Huws *et al.* is that 'telework' is not defined by work contents, but by the organisational and technical context of work. In other words, exactly the same work qualifies as 'telework' in one technical context, but not in another. Finally, one must ask what is exactly meant by 'contractor'. Are subscribers of electronic network information services 'contractors' of this service? As I have indicated in the above examples, such providers of electronic information services should, in my opinion, be covered by the definition of telework.

First sub-conclusion

It is obvious that it is extremely difficult to define telework. However, the difficulties are not necessarily rooted in the lack of skills among researchers. On the contrary, the problem may spring from the nature of telework itself. Consequently, I would support Stern and Holti (1986) in that one is tempted to conclude that 'the term has become as distorted and so lacking in conceptual meaning as to defy serious investigation' (Stern and Holti 1986: 7).

As a first conclusion, among the vast number of terms, three telework categories seem to have attracted attention: electronic homework, telecommuting and flexiwork. However, while on the one hand they obviously do not have the same meaning – and while none of the three terms covers the whole spectrum of meanings represented by telework – on the other hand they are difficult to compare, because they are based on different conceptual criteria. *Electronic homework* has clear political connotations, both critical (being sent back home to old-fashioned isolated cottage work) and positive (the idyllic electronic cottage (Toffler 1980) reminding us of Laura Ingalls Wilder's little house on the prairie); thus the term evokes clear premodern associations. *Telecommuting* focuses on the wage earner's commuting problems; normally it does not include independent, home-based micro-enterprises and its main rationale lies in society's reduction of transportation time and traffic pollution. Here, the dominating connotations include modernity's separation of workers and means of production, and its dream of creating a rationally planned society. Finally, *flexiwork* is of a more recent origin; it reflects current organisational changes, while also having obvious connotational advantages – for instance, in a European Commission Telework Programme context, the term arouses postmodern associations. However, none of these terms covers the full spectrum of telework. Also, they are not compatible. Thus, with their present definition, they cannot be used for a sub-classification of telework as the generic term.

Current definitions: towards a more dynamic approach

If we look at analyses of telework from the 1990s, implicitly or explicitly the conclusion has been made that there is no reason to believe that an unambiguous and restrictive definition can be established. However, definitions are still being proposed, the difference being that they are less ambitious, less exact and more inclusive and dynamic than earlier. In the *Handbook for Teleworkers* published by ExperTeam TeleCom and IDATE telework is defined as 'work carried out at a place other than that where the results of this work are needed using information and communications technology' (Becker *et al.* 1994: 12). In its lack of specification the handbook seems to have accepted as fact that 'telework' evades a strict definition.

The orientation towards flexibility and dynamism is represented by a number of recent publications. In *Teleworking Explained*, Gray, Hodson and Gordon define teleworking as 'a *flexible* way of working which covers a wide range of work activities, all of which entail working remotely from an employer, or from a traditional place of work, for a significant proportion of work time' (Gray *et al.* 1993: 2, my emphasis). Even more outspoken, Wierda, Overmars & Partners in their *Handbook Teleworking. Code of Practice* define teleworking as 'flexibilization of work in the aspects of time and place where the geographical separation is bridged by telecommunication and micro-electronics' (Wierda, Overmars & Partners 1994: 4). A similar trend can be found in the US. According to Tele-commute America's homepage telecommuting 'is an encompassing concept that has emerged as an umbrella term referring to the wide range of alternative officing arrangements. The term is often used to symbolise the substitution of computing and telecommunications technology for the traditional automobile or bus commute' (Telecommute America 1995; Christiansen *et al.* 1996: 15). Per-haps the most radical – in the sense of dynamically oriented – definition can be found in Britton's *Rethinking Work*. According to his definition, telework 'covers a range of new ways of working, using telecommunications as a tool, and for at least part of the time outside a traditional office environment' (Britton 1994: 23).

The crisis of the telework concept

One of the problems of the concept of telework is that its borders are very vague; if one tests the concept empirically, i.e. through specific examples, one repeatedly realises that it is almost impossible to specify what is and what is not telework. On the face of it, the concept seems unambiguous, 'telework' signifying the situation where a person works at one place and delivers the work products to another place through telecommunications. But what about the big group of *flexiworkers*? They work at home, at the office, while travelling – does this make them tele-workers, and exactly *when* do they make the 'quantum leap' from being 'ordinary' workers to becoming 'teleworkers'? What about academics or bureaucrats, i.e. people in modern public administrations, are *they* teleworkers? They work at home, at their office, they go to meetings and conferences, and normally they communicate continuously via telephone and modems with their departments, their colleagues, their clients and students. Most of them, however, would not consider themselves 'teleworkers', but 'just' ordinary academics and adminis-trators using telecommunication equipment more and more extensively. What about those millions of people working in the financial sector? Most of these work at branch offices with working relations partly to local customers, partly to their head office, to foreign exchange dealers, etc. So, in reality, do not local banks qualify as telework centres? Taxi drivers certainly are true flexiworkers, using telecommunications to interact with their employer, their central office and their customers. People working in supermarkets are on-line, connected to banks, stocks, suppliers, etc. from when they arrive in the morning until they leave, but we would never call a small local supermarket a satellite work centre.

Second sub-conclusion

While the current conceptually liberal approach to telework reflects the growing understanding of the fact that new information technologies have broader organisational impacts than just moving the place of work, it certainly does not solve the conceptual crisis of telework. As telework researchers we still lack a common conceptual language. Particularly, when doing telework research or when making telework statistics we often count those people who for some reason or another *experience* themselves as teleworkers, while others with very similar working conditions are not recorded (also Huws 1993: 1). Also, the practical definition of the concept is often influenced by the political context in which it is used, turning research into a kind of academic propaganda. Here, I can fully support the conclusion of Luc Soete *et al.* that as telework seems to be 'one of the major forms of new modes of work which will be established in the Information Society ... a much higher quality of debate on teleworking ... ' is certainly needed (Soete *et al.* 1996: 22f).

Telework statistics: the problem of counting the uncountable

The difficulties of counting teleworkers

While all the above-mentioned definitions of the 1990s certainly reflect current organisational flexibilisations, from an operational point of view they are not very useful. For instance, how would one make statistics with such broad definitions?

For reasons of definitions, it is difficult to perform quantitative telework surveys, and even more difficult to transform such surveys into concrete predictions. As an example, based on a telework survey covering fourteen European companies, Huws *et al.* in their above-mentioned book on telework in Europe concluded that '(g)eneralisations are ... fraught with danger' (Huws *et al.* 1990: 148). Consequently they warned that '(t)ranslating the results of such surveys into concrete predictions is notoriously difficult' (Ibid.: 201). Still, they concluded that 'telework is likely to grow steadily, albeit more slowly than early commentators predicted. Teleworkers who are home-based all the time are likely to be outnumbered by part-time and occasional teleworkers who are otherwise office based. A majority of the workforce will not be engaged in telework' (Ibid.: 207f).

Past and current optimism

Nevertheless, the short history of telework is filled with over-optimistic predictions. In 1971, AT&T predicted that by 1990 all Americans would be working from home (Korte 1988: 374), and ten years later another forecast modified the 1990 figure to 50 per cent of the entire American workforce (Steinle 1988: 7). In the early 1980s futurists forecast that 15 million people would be teleworking two or three days each week by 1990 (Cross and Raizman 1986), and at the same time the Institute of Future Studies at the University of South California assumed a number of 20 per cent in 1990 and 40 per cent in the year 2000 (Korte 1988: 374). Although the expectations have been modified from year to year, in 1987 it was still a common belief among employed people in Europe that it would be entirely feasible to decentralise about two-thirds of all jobs, implying that roughly 80 million jobs in Europe could be carried out from the home or from locations near the places where people live (Steinle 1988: 7).

Over the last few years, the European Commission has been much engaged in telework development. In the White Paper presented by Head of Commission, Jacques Delors, in late 1993, and discussed by Heads of State in December 1993, the development of telework, along with other uses of information infra-structures was given high priority.

At the same time, the European Commission decided on a new set of telework stimulation actions. Most started in January 1994. Over 30 co-operative actions should bring together more than 150 organisations, with a further 150 other sponsoring and associated bodies. Their principal objectives were:

- to encourage companies to experiment with and implement telework networks;
- to examine the practical problems associated with teleworking, particularly across the European Union's internal borders;
- to evaluate what new developments in technology were required;
- to analyse the impact on business organisation, industrial competitiveness, the environment and energy consumption; and
- to provide support and co-ordination for regional and national initiatives in this field.

The target of the European Commission's telework initiatives was to create tele-working centres in 20 places by the end of 1995 involving at least 20,000 workers. The aim was for 2 per cent of white-collar workers to be teleworkers by 1996; and to have created 10 million teleworking jobs by the year 2000.

Third sub-conclusion: the problem of measuring a rubber band

However, with the recent trend towards organisational flexibility and 'rightsizing', with the structural transformation of rural society and its need for economic diversification, with the changing organisational attitudes, leaving traditional organisational conservatism behind, with the growing social and infrastructural problems of urban regions, and with increasing political and social awareness of the need for organisational change and support of telework, the number of teleworkers *is* expected to expand.

According to the results of the TELDET survey (Korte *et al.* 1994, and personal communication) the actual total number of teleworkers in 1994 in France, Germany, Italy, Spain, and the UK was approximately 1.1 million, representing about 1 per cent of the total workforce. In terms of absolute figures the UK reached top figures with 560,000, followed by France with around 215,000 teleworkers. Italy and Spain, but also to some extent Germany, are at an early stage of telework diffusion. This *does* represent a growth trend, not least as regards the *awareness* of telework. When comparing the results from the surveys in 1994 with comparable surveys in 1985 it is 'apparent that interest in telework among the workforce ... has risen dramatically from 1985 to 1994 and in European countries by a factor of three to four' (Korte *et al.* 1994: 3).

The TELDET results can be compared with a telework survey conducted by Analytica in 1992. Here, a more restrictive definition of telework is used: a teleworker is defined as someone who:

1   has worked for the employer in question for at least ten days, or an equivalent number of hours, in the four weeks immediately prior to the survey;
2   has been based at home for at least 50 per cent of his or her time;
3   has a direct contact with the employer, which might or might not confer employee status;
4   uses both a telecommunicating device and a computing device in the course of carrying out his or her work;
5   would not be able to work remotely without the use of this technology

(Huws 1993: 3).

Huws concludes that calculations based on her survey suggest that in the UK less than one worker in 200 is a genuine teleworker. With 22 million wage earners in 1992 (Gray *et al.* 1993: 276) this equals less than 110,000 teleworkers.

Going in the opposite direction Gray *et al.* state that in 1992 there were 1,224,000 teleworkers in the UK (ibid.: 277) and 6,243,000 teleworkers in the USA. These figures represent the addition of the following categories: self-employed and small business sector; formal, wholly employed in major organisations; informal, wholly employed in major organisations; mobile teleworkers in cars; possible size of the tacit teleworking population of major organisations, less those included in the earlier categories (and thus duplicated). One of the big figures for this table is the latest 'possible size of the tacit teleworking population of major organisations' which is estimated at 528,000 (the UK) and 2,880,000 (the US). This figure is based on considerations of Franklin Becker of Cornell

Table 2.1 Surveys of teleworkers in the UK

TELDET (1994)	560,000
Analytica (1992)	110,000
Gray *et al.* (1992)	1,224,000

University concerning the number of desks occupied and unoccupied at an unspecified 'large office' in the US, and on some confidential guesses of an unnamed information technology manager at an anonymous 'major institution in North America' who thinks that 12.5 per cent are unofficially homeworking during a typical day. These – and only these – considerations lead to the following conclusion: 'We can guess-timate that between 12.5 % and 0 % are home working – say 6 %' (ibid.: 276).

If one compares these three surveys, the dilemma is obvious. On the one hand one may count what is measurable, knowing that this does not represent what is instinctively understood as teleworking. On the other hand one may count all teleworking, knowing that this is not measurable. Doing the latter should at least, however, avoid operating with exact figures.

Telework and life form

The importance of a purpose-based definition

As demonstrated above, the definition of telework has become more and more distorted. One possible conclusion is that the category should be given up. However, in my opinion this is not appropriate in all cases. Instead, the term should be used much more in relation to specific analytical purposes. For instance, when one talks about organisational changes, i.e. at a macro-sociological level, one should avoid the individual category 'telework'. But when focus is made at the impacts of such changes for individual persons (employees and self-employed persons), of course a term must be used which reflects their situation as individuals. Here, a well-defined generic concept for 'telework', 'teleworker' and 'teleworking', as well as sub-categorisations following a common standard, are needed. However, as I have argued, 'telework' does not signify the work contents, but the working situation within an organisational and technological context. Consequently, an appropriately defined telework concept should link the individual working situation partly to macro-sociological organisational changes, and partly to the individual person's general life situation.

Telework: electronic homework, telecommuting and flexiwork

In order to fulfil this purpose I will return to some of the categories presented in the beginning of this chapter. However, the idea is to give them a social interpretation in order partly to connect them to the general life situation of individuals in a modern society, partly to relate them to current organisational phenomena.

In this context, I will maintain *telework* as the generic term. Here, I agree with the definition given by Jack Nilles in 1988. Fifteen years after having launched the concept of electronically mediated distance working, Nilles proposed a broad definition of telework, simply stating that telework 'includes all work-related sub-stitutions of telecommunications and related information technologies for travel' (Nilles 1988: 301, and 1994: xix). Thus, the concept of telework is used for all kinds of electronically mediated work-related interactions across distance: inter-actions with the employer at the company headquarters, with colleagues in a central office, or at other workplaces, and – as either an employee in a large company or an independent home-based or shared-facility-based self-employed person – with contractors, subscribers and customers.

However, the generic term must be broken into sub-categories in order to specify the many different modes of telework which can be found today. Here, it is relevant to include all the above-mentioned three sub-concepts.

These three sub-categories can be defined as seen in Table 2.2:

Table 2.2 Sub-categories of telework

Category	Definition
Electronic homework	Work at home delivered through telecommunications to an external customer
Telecommuting	Work for an employer performed at distance, using computers and telecommunications
Flexiwork	Work performed 'everywhere' (at the office, at home, in travel) using computers and telecommunications

Telework and life form

Many definitions and categorisations of telework are not based on any explicit rationality, but often mix different (technical, organisational and social) criteria. However, the inherent idea of the above tripartite definition of telework is to build on a social rationality. Each of the three basic categories of telework is related to a basic life form in modern society. This implies that one type of telework is related to one social category, while others appeal more to other social roles and positions. However, we have seen again and again that telework has been identified with only one of the above sub-categories, thus narrowing the scope, and we have seen that one social group has unconsciously used their own implicit definition of telework, thus subsuming others under their specific favourite type of telework, and under their (but not necessarily others') most appropriate organisation of telework.

Basically, in our modern society there are three historically rooted life forms[2]: the self-employed's, the wage earner's and the career oriented person's life form. The *self-employed's life form* is of course most dominant among people who are associated with self-employment: farmers, artisans, shopkeepers, manufacturers. The *wage earner's life form* is, as indicated by the term, tied to being a wage earner. The *career oriented person's life form* refers to occupational groups aiming at a career, especially within larger enterprises and organisations (Storgaard and Jensen 1991: 124).

The basic idea of these 'life form' categories is that the form of work is closely related to the whole life form. Thus, all three categories can be defined by the way work and leisure time are related (see Figure 2.1). While wage earners place leisure time above work, career oriented persons prize work above leisure time. In comparison, self-employed people are very reluctant to draw a line between working hours and leisure time. They cherish other values, such as running their own farm or firm, and they do not experience any significant conflict between family life and working life (Storgaard and Jensen 1991: 125ff).

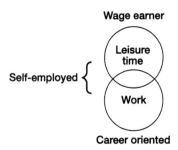

Figure 2.1 Life form categories

This also implies that different life form representatives have different attitudes to work. For career oriented people, work is a goal in itself (you live to work), while for wage earners work is rather a means to improve family life and leisure time (you work to live). While the former go to work in order to work, for the latter the social and interactional qualities of work are important: having a job is a key to social interaction at the workplace. Finally, the self-employed cannot really tell the difference between leisure and family time and work.

In addition, these life forms have different historical roots and interactional relations. The self-employed's life form is rooted in traditional (rural) society and is related to stable, positional interaction relations. The wage earner's life form is rooted in modern society with its urbanised personal interaction relations. Finally, the career oriented's life form is related to hyperpersonal interaction patterns and connotates postmodernity.

From this analysis it is much easier to characterise the three different forms of telework, and it is also much more understandable why one form of telework attracts one life form representative, but not necessarily other life forms (Figure 2.2 slightly modifies the illustration in Storgaard and Jensen 1991: 127).

Ways to organise telework

Having characterised the main forms of telework and their relations to life forms, social history and interaction types, I will now look at ways in which telework has

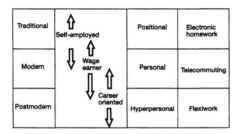

Figure 2.2 Life form interactional relations

been organised, one purpose being to demonstrate that different life form categories can be related to different ways of organising telework.

I think that the following five categories cover most of the spectrum:

1   *Electronic home-offices* In this form the worker undertakes paid employment either entirely at home or predominantly from a home base, with none or few visits to the site of an employer or client.

2   *Shared-facility centres* In this form a building, an office or a work centre is equipped with various new information technology facilities both for on-site work and for communicating at a distance. These facilities are shared by a number of users who may be employees of different companies, independent freelance professionals or small businesses unable to afford such facilities on their own, and the centres are placed in residential areas or in rural villages.

3   *Satellite work centres* These centres are placed in residential areas or in rural villages, but they are owned by a specific company which has relocated part of its operations at a distance from an original or main site. The operations in the branch office are normally relatively integrated ones, and the branch communicate with the head office by means of new information technology.

4   *Private Enterprise Centres* These centres are privately owned, and they provide information technology-based goods and services largely, if not entirely, at a distance. Those working at such enterprises are likely to be employees living locally, but the customers and clients of the enterprise are located at a distance. Typically, these centres are placed in rural regions, providing services for urban companies.

5   *Flexible work facilities (flexiwork)* Here, the distance workers may be located in more than one place: they are mobile, using portable equipment and telecommunication facilities, partly working at home and on trains and planes, partly at the central office or at shared-facility centres.

How should these different types of telework organisation be understood? In the current context I would prefer to analyse the different organisational forms in relation to the different life forms. It is my hypothesis that different life forms and types of human relations are related to different types of work organisation. The appropriate way to organise self-employed teleworkers is through electronic home-offices, often developing into small telework enterprises providing information-based services. For wage earning teleworkers, electronic home-offices should normally be avoided. Here, it is much more appropriate to establish satellitework centres or private enterprise centres, because they provide most of the qualities of a traditional place of work. Finally, career oriented teleworkers will normally favour flexi-facilities. Shared-facility centres like, for example, tele-centres, should be attractive for all categories; however, their weakness may be that they do not have any obvious specific life form profile (see Figure 2.3).

The trend towards networking

The dominating current trend in Europe seems to be that telework is performed by skilled information workers using computers and telecommunications for *flexible work*, i.e. working part time at home, part time in the office, and also bringing their portable computer on trains, aeroplanes, and to hotels, or visiting intelligent buildings. With the above life form categories this trend is easy to understand. It reflects the strong career oriented tendency of current urban life, making us less and less tied to positional or personal networks. With its celebration of electronic networking and its highly mobile work ideal, flexiwork is closely related to hyper-personal forms of personal interaction. Consequently, the current explosion of telework as flexiwork is an obvious example of convergence between a social and a technological development trend. The downsizing of computers, the increased independence of mainframes and the growth of networking opportunities go hand in hand with the growing dominance of the career oriented lifestyle.

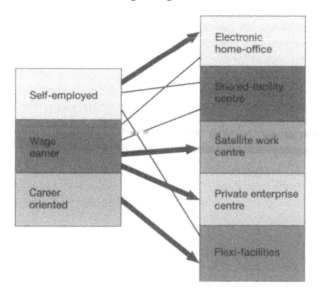

Figure 2.3 Life forms and work organisation

Thus, apart from contributing to a conceptual framework for telework research, my point in discussing the lack of statistical appropriateness of telework concepts is to emphasise the fact that the conceptual problems do not necessarily only reflect research problems, but that they are also the result of more fundamental structural changes in work relations and in organisational forms made possible by advanced communications. These changes should of course be part of telework research. Instead of focusing strictly on 'telework' as a static category one should rather consider 'the diffusion and impact of these applications of NIT (new information technology) communications in the spatial organization of work' (Stern and Holti 1986: 7). Earlier, when the organisational context was given *ex ante*, there was a tendency to focus on the *individual* worker's relation to the organisation. At that time, telework was synonymous with moving the place of work away from the organisational centre, everything else being equal. Today, with information workers working at different places and for changing – and even non-localisable – organisations, one should rather focus on the *structural* changes of modern organisations.

As early as 1983, Turoff and Hiltz went one step further, arguing that current office technologies make the concepts of centralisation and decentralisation outmoded, substituting a structure based on fluid networks by means of which teleworkers – or rather, they would say, knowledge workers – become members of *ad hoc* groupings formed around particular projects. These groupings – or 'online communities', as they were later coined by Hiltz – are not restricted by time or space, but are only based on the specific knowledge project which relate a number of project participants (Turoff and Hiltz 1983; Huws *et al.* 1990: 32)

The most well-known example of 'networking' in 'online communities' is provided by computerised conferencing systems used by groups of scientists working within the same research speciality. Typically such systems provide *message systems* which enable members to send private communications to individuals or groups on a topic of discussion, *conferences* which build up a permanent transcript on a topic of discussion, and *notebooks* where text processing features may be used to work on jointly authored reports (Hiltz 1984).

Based on such examples, Hiltz totally changes the definition of an office. 'Usually', she writes, 'one thinks of it as a place, with desks and telephones and typewriters. In thinking about the office of the future, one must instead think of it as a communications space, created by the merger of computers and telecommunications.' According to Hiltz these computer-mediated communication networks can best be thought of as a new kind of social system, in which the familiar social processes in the workplace and the organisation become subtly altered by electronically mediated interactive processes, creating new kinds of 'online communities' (Hiltz 1984: xv and 30).

In the context of telework, Huws *et al.* accepted the same kind of definition. Looking into the future, they believed 'that the traditional concept of the workplace as a fixed geographical space will be replaced by more abstract notions of the working context as a set of relationships, a network, an intellectual space' (Huws *et al.* 1990: 208). This 'network office' is coined *The elusive office.*

The consequences of broadening the scope can be found in many areas, a characteristic example being the discussion of computer interfaces. Still today, the computer interface is related to the desktop metaphor, the desktop being the appropriate horizon of an individual person's working situation. Currently, however, with very fundamental structural changes of organisations and with the emergence of 'network organisations', 'virtual offices', 'electronic libraries', 'intelligent buildings', etc., we should move our focus away from the adjectives of these compound concepts to their nouns: we are experiencing that we are not just putting new adjectives to otherwise unchanged nouns, but that we are changing the noun itself, i.e. the 'nature' of organisations, offices, libraries, buildings, etc. Consequently, the user interface should include and integrate buildings, office equipment, human relations and facilities; organisational structures and their design should reflect the need for continuous reproduction of organisational identity and of individuals' positions within organisations. Thus, the emerging user interface does not just include the desktop, but includes organisational culture, loyalties, working relations, continuous establishment and re-establishment of work teams, identification of individual organisational positions, and so on.

Also, the discussion of *telework* should learn from this trend. If we stick to the individual approach of telework, we may risk forgetting about all those important things below the surface, as Gil Gordon recently put it:

> Telework as we typically discuss it is only the tip of a growing iceberg. Above the surface is the visible issue of remote work locations and how to use them effectively, a subject about which we have learned a great deal and which is no longer . . . much of an issue. Below the surface are related issues of flexibility in the workplace in general, managerial (in)competence, rethinking of office space requirements and designs, transportation and land use planning, and . . . 'life after bureaucracy' – the prospects for organizational forms other than traditional hierarchical structures.
>
> (In Britton 1994: 26)

Notes

1 However, a contradictory conclusion can be found in the Empirica survey report from 1985. In a summary of the main findings it is emphasised that 'commuting costs (in terms of time spent) play a decisive role in determining attitudes towards electronic home-based work' (Empirica 1986: 21)

2 This specific analysis of life form was introduced by the Danish sociologist Thomas Højrup, (1983, 1984, and Højrup and Rahbek Christensen 1989); the idea to combine life form analysis and sociological analysis of information technology was introduced by Storgaard and Jensen (1991), and the following analysis is very much based on their categorisations. As regards the combination of life forms and telework categories I have been inspired by discussions with my MA student Janne Larsen.

References

Bahl-Benker, A. (1988) 'Humanisierung oder moderne Sklaverei? Wie Telearbeit Arbeit und Leben verändert', in M. Beck-Oberdorf, B. Bussfeld and B. Meiners (eds) *Wo liegt der Frauen Glück? Neue Wege Zwischen Beruf und Kindern*, Köln.

Bangemann, M. (1994) *Europe and the Global Information Society, Recommendations to the European Council* (the Bangemann Report), Brussels.

Becker, H. *et al.* (1994) *European Telecommunications Handbook for Teleworkers*, ExperTeam and IDATE.

Benhamou, Eric and McCracken, Ed (1994) *Smart Valley Telecommuting Guide* (Version 1 – Limited Distribution).

Britton, F.E.K. (1994) *Rethinking Work: An Exploratory Investigation of New Concepts of Work in a Knowledge Society*, EcoPlan International, RACE, Luxembourg.

Christiansen, Andreas Haaning, Jacobsen, Kåre Nordahl and Karlsdottir, Anna (1996) *Her og der. Et studie af højtkvalificeret fjernarbejde* (Here and there. A study of highly qualified distance work). Working Paper No. 126, Department of Geography and International Development Studies, Roskilde University.

Cross, T.B. and Raizman, M. (1986) *Telecommuting. The Future Technology of Work*, Dow Jones-Irwin, Homewood, Illinois.

Dobbertheim, M. (1985) Teleheimarbeit: Elektronische Heimarbeit – Gefahr oder Chance? Stuttgart.

Empirica (1986) 'Trends and Prospects of Electronic Home Working. Results of a Survey in Four Major European Countries', Commision of the European Communities, Luxembourg.

Gray, M., Hodson N. and Gordon, G. (1993) *Teleworking Explained*, BT and John Wiley and Sons, Chichester.

Hiltz, S.R. (1984) *Online Communities, A Case Study of the Office of the Future*, Ablex Publishing Corporation, Norwood, New Jersey.

Højrup, T. (1983) *Det glemte folk. Livsformer og centraldirigering* (The forgotten people. Life forms and central government), The Danish Building Research Institute, Hørsholm.

—— (1984) 'Begrebet livsform. En formspecificerende analysemåde anvendt på nutidige vesteuropæiske samfund' (The concept of life form. A mode of analysis applied to current Western European societies), *Fortid og Nutid* (Past and Present), 31: 194–218, Copenhagen.

Højrup, T. and Christensen, L.R. (1989) 'Introduktion til livsformsanalysens grundbegreber' ('Introduction to the basic concepts of life form analysis'), in Christensen, L. R. (ed.) *Livsformer*, Kulturbogen, Ringe.

Huws, U. (1988) 'Remote Possibilities: Some Difficulties in the Analysis and Quantification of Telework in the UK', in Korte, W. B., Robinson, S. and Steinle, W. J. (eds) *Telework: Present Situation and Future Development of a New Form of Work Organization*, North-Holland, Amsterdam.

—— (1993) *Teleworking in Britain*. A Report to the Employment Department, London.

Huws, U., Korte, W.B. and Robinson, S. (1990) *Telework: Towards the Elusive Office*, John Wiley and Sons, Chichester.

IDATE (1994) *Advanced Communications for Cohesion and Regional Development – the Case of Lorraine*, unpublished ACCORDE case study.

Korte, W.B. (1988) 'Telework. Potential and Reasons for its Utilization from the Organization's as well as the Individual's Perspective', in Rijn, F. v. and Williams, R. (eds) *Concerning Home Telematics*, North-Holland, Amsterdam.

Korte, W.B., Robinson, S. and Steinle, W.J. (eds) (1988) *Telework: Present Situation and Future Development of a New Form of Work Organization*, North-Holland, Amsterdam.

Korte, W.B., Kordey, N. and Robinson, S. (1994) *Telework Penetration, Potential and Practice in Europe*, TELDET Report No. 11.

Lux, B. (1985) *Bedingungen und Auswirkungen von Telearbeit oder Bleibt Informationstechnisch gestützte Heimarbeit eine Randerscheinung?*, Hamburg.

Maciejewski, P.G. (1987) *Telearbeit – Ein Neuer Berufsfeld der Zukunft*, Decker's Verlag, Heidelberg.

Moran, R. and Tansey, J. (1986) 'Distance Working: Women and Environments', FAST Occasional Papers No. 78, Brussels.

National Research Council (1985) *Office Workstations in the Home*, National Academy Press, Washington, DC.

Nilles, J.M. (1988) 'Traffic Reduction by Telecommuting: A Status Review and Selected Bibliography', in *Transportation Research*, 22A, 4: 301–17.

Nilles, J. M. (1994) *Making Telecommuting Happen. A Guide for Telemanagers and Telecommuters*, Van Nostrand Reinhold, New York.

Nilles, J.M., Carlson, F.R., Gray, P. and Hanneman, G.J. (1976) *The Telecommunications-Transportation Tradeoff*, Wiley, Chichester.

Olson, M.H. (1982) 'New Information Technology and Organizational Culture', *MIS Quarterly Special Issue*: 71–92.

—— (1988) 'Organizational Barriers to Telework', in Korte, W.B., Robinson, S. and Steinle, W.J. (eds) *Telework: Present Situation and Future Development of a New Form of Work Organization*, North-Holland, Amsterdam.

Page, A. *et al.* (1994) 'Guidelines for Establishing a Regional Telework/Telematics Forum', ECTF International Secretariat.

Qvortrup, L. (1992) 'Telework: Visions, Definitions, Realities, Barriers', in OECD (ed.) *Cities and New Technologies*, OECD, Paris.

—— (1993) 'Hi-Tech Network Organizations as Self-Referential Systems', in Bøgh, P. *et al.* (eds) *The Computer as Medium*, Cambridge University Press, Cambridge.

Soete, Luc *et al.* (1996) 'Building the European Information Society for Us All' First Reflections of the High Level Group of Experts, Brussels.

Steinle, W.J. (1988) 'Telework: Opening Remarks on an Open Debate', in Korte, W.B., Robinson, S. and Steinle, W.J. (eds) *Telework: Present Situation and Future Development of a New Form of Work Organization*, North-Holland, Amsterdam.

Stern, E. and Holti, R. (1986) *Distance Working Study*, FAST Occasional Papers No. 92, Brussels.

Storgaard, Kresten and Jensen, Ole Michael (1991) 'Information Technology and Ways of Life', in Cronberg, T., Duelund, P., Jensen, O.M. and Qvortrup, L. (eds) *Danish Experiments – Social Constructions of Technology*, New Social Science Monographs, Copenhagen.

Telecommute America's homepage: http://www.att.com/Telecommute_America

3Com Europe (1994) *Guide to Teleworking*, 3Com Europe Hertforshire.

Toffler, Alvin (1980) *The Third Wave*, William Morrow and Company, New York.

Turoff, M. and Hiltz, S.R. (1983) 'Working at Home or Living in the Office', *Information Processing*, September.

Vedel, Gitte (1984) *Aldrig længere væk end telefonen. Distancearbejde i Sverige* (Never further away than the telephone. Distance work in Sweden), Copenhagen Business School, Copenhagen.

—— (1986) *Ude af øje – ude af sind* (Out of sight – out of mind), Samfundslitteratur, Copenhagen.

Vorjans, B. (1987) *Tele-Heimarbeit: Möglichkeiten, Probleme, Perspektiven. Sozio-politische Auswirkungen neuer Informations- und Kommunikationstechnologien am Einzelbeispiel*, Peter Lang, Frankfurt.

Wierda, Overmars and Partners (1994) *Handbook Teleworking. Code of Practice.*

3

WORK, SPACE AND TIME ON THE THRESHOLD OF A NEW CENTURY

Constance Perin

Like bicycles, trains, planes and spacecraft, information technologies have come to unsettle the fundamental cosmologies through which we have understood ourselves in space and in time. We might say the same of the sometimes more welcome but perhaps more ambiguous disturbances that biotechnologies provoke. As genetic engineering and organ transplants ask us to recreate the meanings of health, life and death, we are forced to reconsider our understandings of what we have seen to be life's inevitabilities. By comparison, the ways in which computerised communications allow people to reposition themselves in space and time can appear trivial. These new modes may become commonplaces ultimately, but in the meantime the questions they raise about what we have taken for granted are as momentous for how we understand our present and future experiences of living and getting a living, of individual and collective life itself.

The evidence has been mounting for several years now that the very idea of working partly in an office and partly at home or in a place remote from a central office raises questions about the moral and social principles around which we organise our working and living relationships. Can we trust the conversations we have with those we cannot see? Can we make room in the sacred space of home (organised around the principle of love) for the profane space of work (motivated by a monetary principle)? Can managers believe sufficiently in workers' judgement, self-interest and good will to lower the whip of personalised control? Can the quality of work and employee productivity be measured substantively rather than only quantitatively? Can the work of making a living be reorganised to take as much account of the work of living? (Perin 1991, 1996).

Over the last decade and more, my research has been focusing on the cadre of salaried professionals and technical employees in the US and Western Europe for the reason that culturally they are likely to respond 'yes' to the above questions: they are said to enjoy greater managerial and collegial trust (Zussman 1985), they expect to work at home as an adjunct to working at the office, their higher level of self-management allows them greater schedule flexibility (to attend school plays and civic meetings), and the cadre as a whole has come to be populated by about as many women as men. Even within this cadre, however, employees' experiences of temporal and spatial flexibility are at odds with organisational authority and work systems. And at odds as well with the cadre's own understanding of what it takes to advance professionally and financially: they believe that being 'absent' from the office (especially when working from home) will be disadvantageous to their careers and their employers believe it to be impossible to supervise people out of their sight. The nineteenth-century 'panopticon' principle of control over industrial production – co-location, presence and visibility – remains active at this millennial moment.

A source of this persistence is a symbolic scheme where co-presence sustains owners' moral and actual authority and distance undermines it. This 'presence' discourse has yet to yield to 'performance' discourse, another moral and technical system that would evaluate outputs instead of counting inputs. It would recognise the value to individuals and organisations of the self-management implicit in temporal and spatial flexibility. Together, the semiotics of time and space and the panopticon principle override communicative, competence and household logics: the communicative logics of substituting presence with asynchronicity and virtual presence, the competence logics of time for thinking without interruption in a high 'noise' office and the household logics of self-scheduling to meet the routine and non-routine exigencies of domestic households (Perin 1991).

Social and moral imperatives that employees themselves introduce against spatial and temporal flexibility reinforce the symbolic system and the disciplinary principle. 'Going to the office' is driven almost as much by personal and social interests as by financial need. Besides enjoying pleasures in their work, professionals especially locate much of their identity in their office influence and relationships, and no matter how trying or challenging their colleagues, bosses and work are, being 'in the office' is an important social experience that can, often enough, enhance their work and their lives. It had better; an enjoyable workplace can be a necessary counterpoint to the built-in coerciveness of making a living, and for some few men and women the workplace is as much a respite from stressful domestic demands (Hochschild 1997) as home is respite from office stresses. Another source of employees' rootedness to workplace is that in this same decade industrial restructuring has clouded the career prospects of many; there may be even less willingness to be invisible to bosses and to colleagues who are also competitors for a steady job, interesting work and higher pay, even for only two days a week.

The overarching moral and social principle around which today's working and living relationships are organised is that the paid work of industrial production and the unpaid work of household production are 'separate spheres'. The untoward consequences of this principle in our time have belatedly been made more apparent, perhaps only because over the last few decades two-earner households among those in white-collar occupations are becoming as widespread as they have always been for those in blue-collar occupations. Given a century-and-a-half of industrialisation, why do the survival imperatives of work remain so much stronger than the temporal, spatial and moral imperatives of personal fulfilment, child-raising and community involvement? Of the responses that might be made to this question on various grounds – philosophical, political, moral, economic – mine will be largely cultural and social.

The project organisation

Over the last decade or so professional work of all kinds has come to be organised into 'projects' bringing together various specialties around a common problem, usually temporarily; each specialist remains permanently assigned to a function or department. For the non-routine (or less routinised) work activities that distinguish professional and many technical employees from others wearing white collars (Midler 1995) project management models have become a standard organising technology. Off-the-shelf models define specific steps for developing input and output requirements, defining work phases, specifying tasks, making cost estimates, allocating resources, scheduling reviews and deliveries, and tracking project activities in monthly, quarterly, and annual reports about progress and expenditure. Through project reporting systems, managers monitor strategic and research goals to see that financial and contractual obligations are being met. These systems also furnish managers with data for evaluating employees' performance – whether they meet their obligations and accountabilities project-by-project and meet organisational criteria for productivity, innovation, creativity and career progress, among others.

The project format appears to have become a ubiquituous 'batch production' technology for short runs, for repetitive operations, and for one-of-a-kind outcomes, at all scales of innovation and complexity. Project management models descend from the decades of the 'scientific management' scheme of Frederick Taylor, who in turn extended the observational principle of Jeremy and Samuel Bentham's Panopticon: an all-seeing, centralised surveillance and control system. Today, project management models attempt to approximate factory Taylorisation in non-manufacturing activities (construction, biotechnology, product design, software development). They are also used to rationalise approaches to so-called 'ill-structured problems' (first generation technologies, organisational change) (Shenhar 1991, 1992).

Industrial and household production systems: relating paid and unpaid work systems

How do these models relate to the temporal and spatial flexibility men and women need for integrating the work of living and making a living? The differences between industrial and household production systems are defined by conventionalised meanings understood not as being arbitrary but as natural. Coded in 'industrial' and 'household' are Western understandings of 'money' and 'love', 'public' and 'private', 'work' and 'home', 'work' and 'leisure', 'adults' and 'children', and all that symbolises them materially, socially and institutionally (Nippert-Eng 1996; Perin 1988). These semiotics produce persistent organisational, professional and personal issues that managers, employees and families are, consciously or not, addressing. My sketch of these differences suggests the domains in which data and theorising are needed:

> The Industrial Production System is a monetised social unit, whose work systems are believed to be rationally ordered and highly predictable. The Household Production System is a non-monetised unit for generational reproduction and caretaking, for personal development, for private life, and for maintaining and supporting health and well-being; its activities are believed to be affectively ordered and relatively unpredictable.

> Cognitively and emotionally, employees performing paid work focus their attentions preponderantly on remunerated obligations and tasks and their meanings for their organisational future. They interpret their experiences partly in terms of their role in their organisation's economic, social and cultural structures and partly in terms of their life goals, priorities and non-work situations. Away from their paid work (wherever located), when at home and during leisure, they focus on unremunerated obligations and relationships, interpreting their experiences partly in terms of familial and communal structures and partly in terms of occupational and career interests.

The incentives and rewards of participating in industrial production contrast so markedly with those of household production that managers do not trust employees to fulfill their paid duties at home. Another difference is between the random activities associated with 'home' and unsynchronised with industrial clock-time and the predictable activities of 'work'. For example, younger children's activities are seen as highly random and will therefore interfere with paid work, whereas school-age children's activities are increasingly predictable, thereby allowing for an office-like, regularised work-at-home schedule. Hence the widely accepted advice that employees with younger children at home should hire caretakers or not work at home. Parents' experiences may run counter to these beliefs, however: the sleep needs of younger children can leave large chunks of uninterrupted time, while the psychosocial needs of school-age children can require parental energy and attention.

Within project organisations, random events are as likely as routines, and the day itself is punctuated by coffee breaks, hallway conversations, last-minute meetings, unexpected tasks. One common experience of the office/home pattern is that managers soon learn that their industrial realm is more randomly organised than they assume, as seen in ubiquitous crisis management when they want employees right there. After tele-commuting programmes are established, managers observe that they plan work more efficiently and design more effective meetings. At home, employees may reverse the expected order by keeping random interruptions to a minimum (voice mail, child-care) and by incorporating household production into industrial production, e.g. taking planned breaks by walking the dog, starting supper.

Paradoxically, however, managerial distrust of industrial work in household space is active only when employees are at home during the regular industrial workday and workweek. Most professionals and technical workers are expected to complete tasks or respond to schedule pressures even if they have to work overtime at home in the evenings and at weekends. Upon learning that an employee needed computer equipment at home to keep up with a heavy schedule as a project manager, one manager arranged for it quickly. A few weeks later, when he asked how her work was progressing, she said, 'It's much better now that I can get so much more done during the day away from the telephone and other interruptions.' The manager was surprised, 'You mean that you're sitting home during the week? I only intended the equipment for you to use during evenings and weekends.' After this, she was free to work at home if she discussed it with him ahead of time. (In the 1980s IBM gave computer equipment to employees only on the condition that they use it for overtime work.) On the other hand, evening and weekend work may represent employees' own time-shifting, where they voluntarily work at these times in order to use scheduled office hours for family and personal concerns. In this case, 'overtime' is a self-managed flexibility strategy.

Beginning as temporal innovations, flexible schedules in industry have become spatial as well. They recognise, however faintly, that it is through their external, non-work and unpaid activities that employees sustain their individual capacities to contribute to their organisations' well-being. Company-time is not always life-time. But firms acknowledge this relationship mainly by recognising those non-work activities that debilitate their employees' at work capacities (e.g. health-care benefits, firm-supported programmes for alcohol- and drug-abuse prevention and treatment, child-care facilities that make it possible for some employees to work at all and to work at irregular hours). As studies have consistently shown, 'flexible' schedules and places of work are truly flexible only for those on the top organisational rungs.

The new sense of flexibility as being both temporal and spatial, the unprecedentedly high levels of dual-earner households in all socioeconomic groups, the longevity of parents, and the persistence of gender role stereotypes at work and at home suggest that the nature of the relationship between the paid work of industrial production and the unpaid work of household production is under great pressure to change. But studies of project management tend to concentrate on the internal structural questions posed by a 'matrix organisation'. They address practical tensions between functional departments (to which specialists owe their allegiances for professional and career development) and the parent organisation that controls resources (Midler 1995) and suggest that projects are 'temporary organisations' with special characteristics within the larger organisation (Goodman 1981; Lundin and Soderholm 1995; Packendorff 1995). The internal operations of projects within their organisational contexts are one aspect of the anthropology and sociology of work systems. Once juxtaposing project activities with schedule flexibility, distance working, and an office/home pattern, external contexts become equally significant. What is the relation between industrial paid work and households' unpaid work? Unacknowledged, project management models and practices control both.

A research prologue

A number of new questions arise when acknowledging the ubiquity of the project organisation of work, the technologically created opportunities for space-time flexibility, the competing time pressures on dual-earner households, the new highs in female employment, and such new social forms as networks, alliances and teams. Are project management models more than just practical tools for systematising professional and technical work? Do they obviate alternative approaches to organising work and non-work activities – that is, are they as much social, cognitive and cultural systems as they are technical systems? Do the models' premises, expectations and implementation conventions foreclose other ways of understanding individual and interdependent work processes? How do these models reinforce or moderate career and survival imperatives? Several issues deserve deeper consideration in order to begin to respond to such questions empirically and theoretically.

Across the 'boundaries': rights and obligations at work, at home and in the community

Project management models and the schedules and work-plans they result in constitute an implicit contract and set of promises. These elaborate on and specify obligations in the employment relationship, which is itself shaped by explicit and implicit expectations, demands and commitments. The 'psychological contract' between employees and employers acknowledges that although all expectations and commitments may not be spelled out, those that are taken for granted are equally operative. Looking at these mutual expectations as systems of 'rights and obligations' acknowledges their structural significance. Professionals' 'contracts' with families and communities are no less binding but likely to be only implied (until they decide to dissolve them). These non-organisational contracts are unlikely to be organisationally acknowledged.

How do professionals evaluate their work and non-work priorities, including career and other organisational considerations? That is, how do they relate their unpaid obligations to families and communities to their employment rights and obligations? How might they rewrite the provisions of their employment and non-employment 'contracts' (Kingdom 1996; Nippert-Eng 1996; Williams 1996)? Their rights in and obligations to firms, no less than families, are colloquially expressed as 'commitment and loyalty', but in the workplace these often translate into employers' expectations of office presence and work-related travel that can colonise household and personal time (Perin 1991). Commitment and loyalty are also signified by 'willingness to work long hours . . . [perceived] as an *indicator* of some valuable, yet hard to observe, characteristics of employees' (Landers *et al.* 1996: 1; emphasis in original). Again, temporal inputs rather than substantive outputs are the basis for evaluating employees and, again, this expectation relies on a presence model rather than a performance model of professional work (Perin 1991: 257–61). The presence model appears to underlie project management models and thereby perpetuates workplace and work schedule inflexibility.

In internal labour markets structured by formal rules, 'new problems such as work/family difficulties are solved through the introduction of new formal programs, i.e., work/family programs' (Osterman 1995: 683). Calling their non-work obligations 'difficulties' is a result of that original failure to recognise the life context of employees' obligations to household members, relatives and communities and the moral and personal satisfactions their rights in these relationships provide. These contribute to their well-being not only away from work but at work as well. The cultural postulate of the encapsulated 'ideal worker' is the source of this analytical and practical neglect – imagining employees as being single men or women with few if any competitors for time, attention, commitment and loyalty. Without this controlling myth, there would be no category of 'work/family difficulties'.

Gender matters: obligations at home define rights at work, and vice versa

The evidence continues to confirm that males' at-home obligations, if not also their rights, remain traditionally defined. No matter what age or at what educational level fathers, husbands and partners are, men take on far fewer obligations than women to use their time for caretaking and domestic tasks; women with children are likely to work half again as much at home as at their workplaces (Perkins and DeMeis 1996: 85–6). Even when men regard themselves as co-earners and co-providers and even when they believe that 'work and family roles should be shared equally . . . [they performed] an average of 40 per cent of the family tasks' (Perry-Jenkins and Crouter 1990: 154).

What is the relationship between the persistence of at-home patterns to the persistence of at-work norms and expectations? This persistence largely accounts for women's higher at-home workload, and, when (over)time at work is seen as a measure of 'loyalty' and career 'commitment', their inability to be 'ever available' counts against women's advancement opportunities (Seron and Ferris 1995). Where such employers reinforce a predominantly 'homemaker' perception of women, do they also advance a 'breadwinner' perception of men? If so, this is likely to influence men's understandings of their domestic obligations or make it difficult for them to act on alternative beliefs.

Are at-home gender roles influenced by at-work gender norms and expectations (Anderson and Tomaskovic-Devey 1995; Rowe and Snizek 1995)? How do men and women compare in their definition of and use of their workplace right to request time for their parental, spousal and communal obligations? Do their employers' policies and informal decisions define their workplace obligations differently? If so, how are their respective rights to career-enhancing tasks defined?

Cultural and social properties of projects in time and space

Project management models are a technique for reducing uncertainty and managing risk in organisational activities. They are understood as self-evident, straightforward techniques for planning, tracking, controlling and co-ordinating human, technological and financial resources and tasks. Their formal structures, represented visually in PERT configurations, in Gantt charts and 'waterfall' or tree structures, can also be seen, however, as cognitive templates that set expectations of linearity, transparency and predictability. The models also carry implicit promises of helping managers and project participants to anticipate and reduce financial and technical mis-steps, and in turn they elicit promises from them. Rhetorically, the format of 'milestones' and 'deliveries' is a quasi-contract (often levying penalties for missed milestones, for example). The simultaneous existence of other projects, likely to draw on the same resource pools, paradoxically increases organisational uncertainty and risk. These also increase professionals' levels of project 'density' (their number of assigned projects) and their task 'congestion' (the queue of task demands). Employees experience high density as 'fragmented' involvement, which, they report, can prevent them from learning new skills and can diffuse their attention, a low density of involvements can deepen their skills or isolate them, in that their opportunities to broaden their repertoires can be foreclosed. This technology intricately influences career systems.

In the variation of their levels of uncertainty and risk, projects are guided by rules-of-thumb that suggest how to categorise and manage them appropriately (Wheelwright and Clark 1992). When projects face few uncertainties and rely primarily on technical competence, managers can proceed 'by the book' to pay most attention to the formal steps and to technical content. But where uncertainty is higher because people are expected to be creative and innovative and projects are more vulnerable to failure, managers are instead faced first with process and organisational issues and second with control and content issues –

organisational processes such as developing teamwork, building consensus, sharing information and managing conflict (Buchanan 1991).

Those dynamics constitute the province of project managers, whose job is to corral resources and foster co-operation within and across organisational, occupational, technological and institutional units. They typically orchestrate activities, often without themselves being a topical specialist and often without commensurate authority. Hence there is a large literature providing advice for this cadre (e.g. Frame 1995), which only recently has begun to be complemented by a developing research literature concerned with 'stressing behavioral aspects [of project management] rather than techniques' and conceptualising projects as temporary organisations (Goodman 1981; Lundin and Soderholm 1995: 437; Packendorff 1995).

Project management models thereby embody a particular set of understandings about how to reduce the uncertainty of outcomes and the risk of financial loss and technical failure over time. These draw on a limited set of assumptions about work activities: arithmetic assumptions that work activities can be added, multiplied, divided and subtracted; geometric assumptions that they intersect and are tangential; logical assumptions that they form definitive categories, sets and subsets. Together with linearity, these characteristics of project management models can promote mechanistic expectations of exactitude rarely fulfilled in practice (Midler and Boudes 1996: 3). Despite their task of co-ordinating the work of specialists over social time and space, these models tend to assume away the social and cultural dynamics of project work and neglect its further temporal and spatial intersections with career and family concerns. Projects are not structured to consider these dimensions systematically; whether project activities take them into account in practice depends on the concerns, sensitivities and influence of project managers and participants.

Project social dynamics and organisational theory

'Projects' are structural elements of organisations that significantly affect organisational objectives, work schedules, task design, assignments and careers. The design of projects and their management are the concerns of at least four constituencies, each likely to have differing goals and time horizons: subject matter leaders, professional employees, firm executives and administrators. The relative influence of each occupational culture is revealed in actual project design and in project activities. Combining a structural and experiential focus on projects and their management provides primary evidence of the dialectic between structures and practices – that is, how formal organisational policies are informed and modified through practices and vice versa (Barley 1986). When do these result in work design and schedules where employees' participation is 'high' and 'low'? What implications do these differences have for temporal and spatial flexibility in project design and schedules? What fora are available for discussing and negotiating demands on financial, temporal, professional and material resources?

Project social organisation varies. The one constant is what some employees call the 'core group' to describe those doing the 'real work'. Then there are those who work solo, or as a duo, trio, or quintet. These vary for each project during its different phases. 'Core' also implies that there is often a 'periphery' of people contributing a small number of 'hours' and infrequently appearing at meetings. These shifting relationships organised by the nature of projects and tasks suggest that the unit of analysis in 'organisational' studies may more productively be seen as the project and the work systems it defines.

Time reckonings: project time, career time, household time

Criteria for employee performance, efficiency and productivity are highly dependent on calendar and clock time (Clark 1985), which neglects the multiplicity of time reckonings to be found in any organisation. Each has an implicit set of '"repertoires" of rules, structures and forms of action [that] meet the varying rhythms of demand, competition and regulation' (Whipp 1994: 103). While these can be assumed to vary by occupation and industrial sector, they have been little studied or conceptualised with reference to career and family time reckonings (Dubinskas 1988). A project staff, for example, may represent people in a variety of career and life cycle stages that influence the desirability of task assignments. Differences in career and household time reckonings are themselves sources of organisational conflict as well as of co-operation, as when employees adjust work arrangements to accommodate one another's temporal and spatial needs. When those in households without children observe the 'perks' afforded those with children there can be resentment and bitterness.

> The central "time problem" for organisational sociology is to penetrate behind the metaphor of clock time, because existing approaches to the "time dimension" rely totally on clock time. Essentially this view of time follows Newton's mistaken claim that time is separate from events [which is] the same time concept [of] seventeenth-century classical mechanics . . . [M]odern theories of time have, since the theorising of Bergson . . . and the development of quantum mechanics, claimed that time is *in* the events. According to the modern viewpoint time-reckoning systems are constructed by selecting various events in the form of sequences or trajectories, from arrays of events which can be apprehended relative to one another . . . Time is therefore relative, not absolute.
>
> (Clark 1985: 36, 40)

How professionals reckon the time their activities need (event time) is likely to differ depending on the context. According to a study of hospital staff, their intimate, local knowledge of their activities' temporality is rarely reflected, however, in time/cost accounting and timetabling (Zerubavel 1979). The tendency is to imagine a Tayloristic homogeneity rather than a plurality of time-reckoning rationales. When limited in their 'richness of time-ordering devices', organisations may become overly reliant on 'fixed routines' and unable to see both near-term and far-term implications together, as occurred in the failure of UK merchant banks in 1979–84 (Pettigrew and Whipp 1991: 174).

Projects, pace and productivity

In highly competitive markets, project designers may assume that accelerating the pace of work will also speed up innovative products. A study of 72 projects from 36 Asian, US and European firms in the 'high-velocity' computer industry finds that project designers modify conventional project management models by compressing steps and offering incentives for meeting tight schedules and by 'skimping on analysis and information, slashing conflict, or being centralised' (Eisenhardt and Tabrizi 1995: 86). These tactics do not, however, guarantee market success. Nor are they the only approaches to achieving speed-up. Pace can be accelerated in three ways, this study claims: through more tightly connected experts, more focused leadership and more frequent milestones; through 'real time interaction, flexibility, and improvisation'; through less linear, iterative 'experiential tactics', especially where uncertainty is greater, and, where it is less, through 'a rational engineering perspective'. By experiential tactics is meant 'improvisation, testing, milestones, and powerful leaders' who maintain employees' motivation (ibid.: 104, 107, 108). The dynamics of iteration and flexibility needed for innovative projects appear to depend on these social processes combined with activity-based understandings of temporal issues. The engineering perspective that dominates project management models tends instead to be linear and additive (Whipp 1994: 107).

Taking into account the value to business and scientific success of improvisation, leadership, iteration, learning and small-group relations would open the possibility of alternative scenarios for the design of work. Defining tasks and relationships differently may also make them more amenable to flexible scheduling. Redesigning project work may promote self-managing workgroups that can consider their members' priorities for career time and family time (Bailyn et al. 1996), a study that supports long-term observations (even by engineers!) that 'work-group autonomy . . . [is] the most rational form of organising work to cope with the spatial and temporal characteristics of work in modern enterprises' (Clark 1985: 46).

Projects across organisations: networking, time, and space

The viability of growth industries is partly due to the information and collegial networks that employees build and use. The survival of small biotech firms, for example, has been found to depend partly on the intensity of their external social relationships, recent studies in the USA and in France, Britain and Canada report; these agree that biotech firms' external collaborations contribute to innovation (Clarysee 1996; Liebeskind *et al.* 1995; Walsh *et al.* 1995; Zucker and Darby 1995). Professionals' 'social work' to develop and maintain networks and alliances is as much part of project design and management as their technical work.

Social networks are grounded in 'norms of trustworthy behavior in exchanges of information . . . reciprocity, respect for individuals' intellectual property rights, and honesty in research' (Liebeskind *et al.* 1995: 9), as observed within and across biotechnology firms. Those cultural properties of successful collaboration, exchange and access to valuable resources take time to develop and to be appreciated by each partner, but they provide the benefit of reducing the costs of knowledge acquisition and the costs of hierarchical organisation (ibid.: 23). Organisational support for '*both the internal and external exchanges* that are essential to the firm's survival and success . . . may be *the* critical capability for knowledge-based firms . . . However, self-coordination across organisational boundaries cannot take place without (at the very least) organisational permission or (at the very best) active organisational support' (ibid.: 24; emphasis in original). To exploit the benefits of collaborations, however, firms need to 'develop certain routines or build up certain resources' (Clarysee 1996: 40), which suggests the integration of these social processes into project designs, tasks and schedules especially for internal and external meetings.

The empirical and conceptual bases of theories of networks and alliances have heretofore overlooked the work design implications of those social and cultural processes. Nor have they extended organisational boundary-crossing issues to include the relationships between professional and household obligations (Nohria and Eccles 1993; Powell 1990). Likely to be structured by schedules, milestones and deliverables defined by clock and calendar time, project activities may overlook the business and scientific significance of work activities such as networking, reading, attending meetings; they may make conventional or outdated assumptions about the characteristics of careers and life stages; they may assume that independent work predominates over interdependent work; they may structure work believing that the time needed for resolving conflicts and for competing for resources, for example, is an interruption and a problem and not inherent in project-based organisations.

The end of a myth: the office is no place for 'real' work

Temporal and spatial flexibility is widely regarded as a 'privilege' or 'reward' and 'non-salary' benefit. These ideas of privilege, reward and extra benefit do not recognise that distance working already relies on unpaid household resources without acknowledging or compensating them. The centrifugal force of industrial work has long been felt in households across occupations of all kinds. For professional and technical employees today to accommodate the demands on them, they may begin the regular workday well before leaving home and after they return at night. They may be preparing presentations to give on trips, using their private telephones to co-ordinate with colleagues, managers and vendors, writing up reports of trip meetings and contacts, and so on. For themselves as well as their household members, these are more likely to be regarded as intrusions, inconveniences and interferences with domestic life than as 'benefits' and 'rewards'.

The split between industrial and household production systems is founded on outdated presumptions, in the experience of many who have exercised the option of working at home some days out of the working week. Only at home can they count on uninterrupted stretches of time for 'my real work' of writing plans, reports, suggestions, recommendations, specifications and for the contemplation, deep reading and 'incubation time' the quality of their work depends on. During a project's 'idea phase,' for example, a major task is reading and reflecting, without interruptions that divide attention and fragment time. Not only does home provide a refuge from meetings (often of questionable utility and quality), from the undisciplined demands of bosses, from a frantic, competitive atmosphere, from office politics and time-wasting, but so does any time away from the office and from telephones, e-mail and fax when on trains or planes, or in hotel rooms. The myth dies hard, however, when it comes to demands for employees to be 'ever available' – the at-home daily schedules of telecommuters may reproduce their in-office schedules. In one case, most of those working at home two days a week felt that they were more available electronically than before, perhaps because they are less mobile at home than in the office.

'That which is associated with the private sphere . . . is necessary for "public" activities' (Mirchandani 1996: 288). So concludes a study in which 50 female and male salaried professionals in public and private organisations described their ways of working between home and office. Their 'real work' is that on which they are 'measured', the very heart of the job they are paid to perform – and their own standards for its quality can be met best at home when interruptions and pace are under their control. Their unpaid household production – its emotional 'work' as well as its practical labours (food shopping, cooking, cleaning and laundering) – women and men alike regard as 'non-work'.

The subtleties of 'boundary' analysis in social life (Nippert-Eng 1996; Perin 1988; Zerubavel 1993) are lost in industrial discourse, at least in the United States, which perpetuates the myth of discontinuities between paid and unpaid activities. An 'open door' between work and home – not a territorial fence, wall or gate – perhaps better captures the experiences of the continuities and discontinuities of the threshold shared by paid and unpaid work. To arrive at systematic understanding of the surroundings in which we live and make a living requires a shift in focus from mythology to the realities and complementarities of production, paid and unpaid, industrial and social. Only then will we have grounds for reconsidering moral and social principles we have inherited not chosen.

Acknowledgement

This work has been supported partly by the Center for Coordination Science, Sloan School of Management, Massachusetts Institute of Technology, and partly by a grant from the Alfred P. Sloan Foundation to the Radcliffe Public Policy Institute, Radcliffe College, Cambridge, Massachusetts.

References

Anderson, C.D. and Tomaskovic-Devey, D. (1995) 'Patriarchal pressures: an exploration of organisational processes that exacerbate and erode gender earnings inequality'. *Work and Occupations*, 22, 3: 328–56.

Bailyn, L. (1993) *Breaking the Mold: Women, Men, and Time in the New Corporate World*. New York: The Free Press.

Bailyn, L., Rapoport, R., Kolb, D. and Fletcher, J., (1996) *Re-linking Work and Family: a Catalyst for Organizational Change*. MIT Sloan School of Management, April, Working Paper No. 3892-6.

Barley, S.R. (1986) 'Technology as an occasion for structuring: evidence from observations of CT scanners and the social order of radiology departments'. *Administrative Science Quarterly* 31: 78–108.

Buchanan, D.A. (1991) 'Beyond content and control: project vulnerability and the process agenda'. *International Journal of Project Management* 9, 4: 233–9.

Clark, P. (1985) 'A review of the theories of time and structure for organizational sociology'. *Research in the Sociology of Organizations* 4: 35–79.

Clarysee, B. (1996) *Innovative Productivity in the Biotech Industry: Integration and Collaboration as Dynamic Capabilities*. Seminar paper. Sloan School of Management Organization Studies Group, April.

Dubinskas, F.A. (ed.) (1988) *Making Time: Ethnographies of High Technology Organizations*. Philadelphia: Temple University Press.

Eisenhardt, K.M. and Tabrizi, B.N. (1995) 'Accelerating adaptive processes: product innovation in the global computer industry'. *Administrative Science Quarterly* 40, March: 84–110.

Frame, J. D. (1995) *Managing Projects in Organizations: How to Make the Best Use of Time, Techniques, and People*. San Francisco: Jossey-Bass.

Goodman, R.A. (1981) *Temporary Systems: Professional Development, Manpower Utilization, Task Effectiveness, and Innovation*. New York: Praeger

Hochschild, A. (1997), *The Time Bind: When Work Becomes Home and Home Becomes Work*. New York: Metropolitan Books.

Kingdom, E. (1996) 'Cohabitation contracts and the private regulation of time'. *Time and Society* 5, 1: 47–60.

Landers, R.M., Rebitzer, J.B. and Taylor, L.J. (1996) 'Ratrace redux: adverse selection in the determination of work hours in law firms'. *American Economic Review*, June: 329–48.

Leiter, M.P. and Durup, M.J. (1996) 'Work, home, and in-between: a longitudinal study of spillover'. *Journal of Applied Behavioral Science* 32, 1: 29–47.

Liebeskind, J.P., Oliver, A., Zucker, L.G. and Brewer, M.B. (1995) 'Social networks, learning, and flexibility: sourcing scientific knowledge in new biotechnology firms'. NBER Working Paper no. 5320, October. Cambridge, MA: National Bureau of Economic Research.

Lundin, R.A. and Soderholm, A. (1995) 'A theory of the temporary organisation'. *Scandinavian Journal of Management* 11, 4: 437–55.

Midler, C. (1995) ' "Projectification" ' of the firm: the Renault case'. *Scandinavian Journal of Management* 11, 4: 363–75.

Midler, C. and Boudes, T. (1996) 'Project management learning programs within firms: managerial fashion or organizational learning?' In G. Garel and C. Midler (eds) *Aspects of Society and Business Organized by Project*. IRNOP '96 Proceedings, 'Research Conference on Project Management and Temporary Organizations', June: 129–39. Paris.

Mirchandani, K. (1996) ' "Real work": professional telework and its challenge to the public–private dichotomy'. In P. Jackson and J. van der Wielen (eds) Proceedings of the Workshop *New International Perspectives on Telework: From Telecommuting to the Virtual Organisation*, London 31 July–2 August 1996, 2: 308–20. Tilburg, The Netherlands: Tilburg University Press.

Nippert-Eng, C. (1996) *Home and Work: Negotiating Boundaries Through Everyday life*. Chicago: University of Chicago Press.

Nohria, N. and Eccles, R.G. (eds) (1993) *Networks and Organizations*. Boston: Harvard Business School Press.

Osterman, P. (1995) 'Work/family programs and the employment relationship'. *Administrative Science Quarterly* 40: 681–700.

Packendorff, J. (1995) 'Inquiring into the temporary organization: new directions for project management research'. *Scandinavian Journal of Management* 11, 4: 319–33.

Perin, C. (1988) *Belonging in America: Reading Between the Lines*. Madison: University of Wisconsin Press.

—— (1991) 'The moral fabric of the office: panopticon discourse and schedule flexibility'. In P.S. Tolbert, and S.R. Barley *Research in the Sociology of Organizations 8, Organizations and Professions*: 243–70. Greenwich, CT.: JAI Press.

—— (1996) 'Project management models as social, cultural, and cognitive systems: relating paid and unpaid work schedules'. In P. Jackson and J. van der Wielen (eds) Proceedings of the Workshop *New International Perspectives on Telework: From Telecommuting to the Virtual Organisation*, London 31 July–2 August 1996: 292–304. Tilburg, The Netherlands: Tilburg University Press.

Perkins, H. W. and DeMeis, D.K. (1996) 'Gender and family effects on the "second-shift" domestic activity of college-educated young adults'. *Gender and Society* 10, 1: 78–93.

Perry-Jenkins, M. and Crouter, A.C. (1990) 'Men's provider-role attitudes: implications for household work and marital satisfaction'. *Journal of Family Issues* 11, 2: 136–56.

Pettigrew, A.M. and Whipp, R. (1991) *Managing Change for Competitive Success*. Oxford: Blackwell.

Powell, W.W. (1990) 'Neither market nor hierarchy: network forms of organisation'. *Research in Organizational Behavior*, 12: 295–336.

Rowe, R. and Snizek, W.E. (1995) 'Gender differences in work values: perpetuating the myth'. *Work and Occupations* 22, 2: 215–29.

Seron, C. and Ferris, K. (1995) 'Negotiating professionalism: the gendered social capital of flexible time'. *Work and Occupations* 22, 1: 22–47.

Shenhar, A. (1991) 'Project management style and technological uncertainty (Part 1): from low- to high-tech'. *Project Management Journal* XXII, 4: 11–14.

—— (1992) 'Project management style and the space shuttle program (Part 2): a retrospective look'. *Project Management Journal* XXIII, 1: 32–7.

Walsh, V., Niosi, J. and Mustar, P. (1995) 'Small-firm formation in biotechnology: a comparison of France, Britain and Canada'. *Technovation* 15, 5: 303–27.

Wheelwright, S.C. and Clark, K.B. (1992) 'Creating project plans to focus product development'. *Harvard Business Review*, March–April: 70–82.

Whipp, R. (1994) 'A time to be concerned: a position paper on time and management'. *Time and Society* 3, 1: 99–116.

Whipp, R. and Clark, P. (1986) *Innovation and the Auto Industry: Product, Process and Work Organization*. London: Frances Pinter.

Williams, J. (1996) 'Restructuring work and family entitlements around family values. *Harvard Journal of Law and Public Policy* 19, 3: 753–7.

Zerubavel, E. (1979) *Patterns of Time in Hospital Life*. Chicago: University of Chicago Press.

—— (1981) *Hidden Rhythms: Schedules and Calendars in Social Life*. Chicago: University of Chicago Press.

—— (1993) *The Fine Line: Making Distinctions in Everyday Life*. Chicago: University of Chicago Press.

Zucker, L.G. and Darby, M.R. (1995) 'Present at the revolution: transformation of technical identity for a large incumbent pharmaceutical firm after the biotechnological breakthrough'. NBER Working Paper Series no. 5243, August. Cambridge, MA: National Bureau of Economic Research.

Zussman, R. (1985) *Mechanics of the Middle Class: Work and Politics Among American Engineers*. Berkeley: University of California Press.

CONCEPTUALISING TELEWORK

Modern or postmodern?

Paul McGrath and Maeve Houlihan

Introduction

Co-ordinated research on the topic of telework has long been hampered by the marked absence of any coherent and agreed upon conceptual framework for the topic (Jackson 1992). This chapter will attempt to address this deficiency by developing a broadly based conceptual framework for telework within the context of organisation behaviour/organisational studies. The purpose of the framework is to help explain the seemingly contradictory trends and developments in this area and to aid the development of a unified and systematic research agenda. Telework will be examined within the reputed movement of organisations from modern to postmodern forms drawing primarily from and extending the work of Clegg (1990). It will be argued that telework, broadly defined, can be seen as both a modern and postmodern manifestation and often adopts a hybrid form. Two case studies will be used to illustrate the applicability of the framework.

Our point of departure was telework as a manifestation and intrinsic component of the postmodern organisational form (Clegg 1990). As will be explored below, postmodernism is presented here as a conceptual receptacle sufficiently broad to encompass a wide range of parallel contemporary societal and organisation specific developments such as flexible specialisation (Piore and Sabel 1984), post-industrialism (Bell 1973), network structures (Miles and Snow 1992), the information society (Webster 1995) and, indeed, the virtual organisation (Davidow and Malone 1992). Following the arguments of Harvey (1990) and Kumar (1995), postmodernism is not presented here as a massive and radical rupture with the past but as the crystallisation of a set of relatively profound changes (economic, political, social and cultural) at the end of the twentieth century that have clear continuity with the past. In this context postmodernism is seen as the latest, though radicalised, phase of modernism.

Before progressing it is worth briefly highlighting the key assumptions underpinning this work. First, the primary focus of this study is on the use of telework by existing medium and large business organisations. In this regard it confines its consideration to full-time employees engaged in teleworking activity. The issue of telework involving self-employed contractors will be addressed at the end of the chapter. Second, the unit of analysis is primarily the individual organisation as opposed to any network relationship within which the organisation may be involved. Third, the tentative framework presented is blatantly modernist in orientation. No apologies are made for this in that our concern is to talk about real organisations with real implications for real people (Parker 1992). Fourth, the framework presented below is hindered by the obvious conceptual limitations of any modernist dualistic framework. A partial solution to this problem will, however, be suggested at the end of the chapter. Fifth, the framework is largely speculative and has not been empirically tested. Finally, the ideas in this chapter are constrained by the authors' experiences of telework within Ireland. This final issue warrants further brief explanation in that Ireland may present a rather unique and possibly constraining context within which to examine trends within telework.

Ireland, at a national policy level, is projecting itself as a nation eager to become a true information society, the 'intelligent island of Europe'. This image is reinforced by a relatively young and highly educated workforce, the highest growth rates of any economy in Europe, a sophisticated telecommunications infrastructure and a strong and rapidly growing computer/telecommunications hardware and software sector within the country. New information and communication technologies are seen as enabling Ireland to overcome its lack of natural resources and locational disadvantage (being an island behind an island on the edge of Europe) and compete effectively in the new global information economy. Notwithstanding this vision, Ireland, with a few notable exceptions, appears to have a very traditional and conservative management ethos within industry, with poor investment in employee and management training and a questionable uptake in the usage and perceived strategic importance of information and communication technologies. A 1997 Government-sponsored report 'Information Society Ireland. Strategy for Action' highlighted the very low level of public awareness of the idea of an information society or of the technologies necessary for participation in such a society. Ireland is currently estimated to have approximately 15,000 teleworkers representing 1.1 per cent of the workforce, one of the lowest percentages in Europe (Bertin and Roberts 1996). Bearing this context in mind it should be noted that we were unable to find any company, private or public, beyond certain sales and consulting operations which have traditionally had a mobile workforce, that engaged in teleworking with full-time employees on a systematic level. A number of companies did, however, have informal arrangements whereby a small number of core employees would be occasionally facilitated to work from home or some other remote location.

What is telework?

The first step in the development of the framework was to establish some clarity over the meaning of the term 'telework'. Rather than going down the tortuous and disputed route of trying to establish a clear definition of telework we identified a number of its key defining features which would, in turn, be used to develop the conceptual framework. Drawing on the telework literature and in particular the work of Brandt (1983), Holti and Stern (1984), Allen and Wolkowitz (1987) and Jackson (1992) the following particular defining features of telework were identified:

Multiple manifestations: Telework comes in many different guises. Moorcroft and Bennett (1995) have identified a number of telework arrangements which are illustrated in Figure 4.1. Telework typically encompasses four of the categories in Figure 1 namely, (a) homeworkers (the stereotypical teleworker, employees or self-employed who work at home, on the road, at client sites and occasionally in the central office or a combination of all four); (b) neighbourhood work centres (typically telecottages or business exchanges providing local office space for employees and self-employed teleworkers); (c) nomadic staff (including sales executives and training specialists); and (d) satellite offices (typically off-shore, back office operations involving administrative or specialist services that have been hived away from main sites to take advantage of skill availability and lower overhead costs) .

Flexible location and employment status: Brandt (1983) in his discussion of new work design possibilities, identified location and affiliation of workers as key dimensions of telework. He predicted a gradual shift away from permanent, salaried employees located in a central office building towards a wide variety of combinations of workers' location and affiliation (Brandt 1983: 3). Atkinson (1984) presents a similar though more formalised and sophisticated analysis of variable employment contracts from an organisational/managerial perspective. As mentioned earlier our primary focus is on permanent employees engaged in telework arrangements.

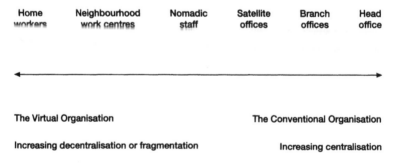

Figure 4.1 What is telework?
Source: Moorcroft and Bennett 1995. Used with permission.

Centrality of information and communications technologies: In general, telework is assumed to be work that is mediated or supported by advanced information and communication technologies, whether via telephone lines, faxes, computers, modems or video conferencing (Nilles *et al.* 1976; Huws *et al.* 1990). This, in turn, enables work to be carried out remote from its source at a place other than where the results of the work are needed.

Information-based work: Linked to the importance of information and communication technologies, we see telework as primarily concerned with service-type activities and, therefore, highly-information intensive. This view ties in with the literature on the information society (Webster 1995) where the gathering, processing, storage, retrieval and manipulation of information assume great economic importance. In addition, the search by organisations for sustainable competitive advantage is increasingly turning to the issue of the exercise of 'specialist knowledge and competencies, or the management of organizational competencies' (Blackler 1995: 1022). This type of knowledge is seen as essential in the successful functioning of new organisational forms based on networks, partnerships or contractual arrangements – the postmodern organisational form (Blackler 1995). It is this shift in the nature of business and organisational activities that has partially facilitated the adoption of more distributed work arrangements and forced organisations into more collaborative, network relationships with other organisations.

Bearing these features in mind the challenge set was the development of a framework that was sufficiently broad and flexible to cater for the rich and highly complex dynamic that is telework.

Developing a tentative framework

As was mentioned earlier, our initial point of departure in the development of our framework was telework as a manifestation and intrinsic component of the broad concept of postmodernism. Jackson (1992: 8) highlighted the frequent appearance of telework 'in the same vortex as discussions on Post-Fordism and flexibility', but has cautioned against a simplistic inclusion of telework within this complex and troubled model. While telework can be seen as a manifestation of the casualisation and externalisation policies of the flexible firm, this is obviously only a partial picture and does not do justice to the complex reality of teleworking. We wish to stay within the flexible firm debate by examining the contemporary postmodern perspective on organisations and considering its relevance, or otherwise, as a home for telework.

Postmodernism is a term that has been increasingly and heatedly debated in recent years. Kumar points out that there are 'far more books and articles telling us what is wrong with post-modern theory than there are statements in its favour or even, for that matter, telling us clearly what it is' (1995: 139). The debate concerning the utility or otherwise of postmodernism in organisation studies is in its infancy but remains equally heated and inconclusive. A number of recent contributions in the organisational studies field have tried to put some structure on the postmodern debate. One such approach is provided by Parker (1992) who develops two perspectives on post-modern writings. The first perspective is post-modernism (hyphenated) as an historical periodisation. Parker's argument is that society is entering a new epoch, beyond modernity. From an organisational per-spective the focus is on understanding these new times and designing appropriate organisational structures and adopting new management and information tech-nology practices to cope with the increasing disorganisation, messiness and attendant need for flexibility. As will be elaborated in the next section, this view of postmodernism is a realist ontology deeply rooted in conventional modernist discourse (Parker 1992). Parker's second perspective, postmodernism (unhyphen-ated) is an idealist epistemology and refutes the reality of any true 'meta-narrative'. The work of Cooper and Burrell (1988) and Burrell (1988) best typify this perspective. Parker's postmodern epistemologic stance embraces the work of Baudrillard, Lyotard and Derrida. It rejects the idea of rational progress, totalis-ing control and embraces the reality of instability, uncertainty and dissensus. Attempts to discover 'truth' are merely forms of discourse of which there are a multitude of equal significance. The main thrust of this approach is a rejection of the meta-narrative of modernity with its associated baggage of liberalism, enlightenment, progress through science and industrialisation and a general disillusionment with politics.

While this distinction in terms of periodisation and epistemology is artificial and limiting, it is useful in that it facilitates a more orderly analysis of much of this diverse and complex literature. The periodisation approach fits snugly with the requirements of late capitalism celebrating 'mass culture, consumerism and commercialism' (Kumar 1995: 193). On the other hand, the epistemological approach can be seen as a reaction against capitalist culture resisting pressures towards standardisation, ethnocentrism and homogenisation. The focus here will be on postmodernism as periodisation, but periodisation which contains strong continuity with the past. Postmodernism in this sense is 'postmodern capitalism' (Harvey 1990; Jameson 1992), a capitalism sufficiently distinctive at a cultural, political and economic level, a 'capitalism with a new face, one that shows many peculiar and unexpected features' (Kumar 1995: 195). However, as should become apparent this simple distinction increasingly breaks down in the face of analysis with the periodisation and epistemology perspectives becoming indistinguishable at times.

Postmodernism, as a movement, emerged primarily from the cultural sphere (predominantly art and architecture) but has been slowly embraced by an ever increasing circle of social life. A number of writers (Bell 1973; Piore and Sabel 1984; Lash and Urry 1987; Crook et al. 1992; Stehr 1994) highlight the impact of postmodernism on the economy. In their view postmodernism can be seen in the gradual emergence of a new structure and organisation of economic activity which can be summarised in terms of the following interrelated, macro-level changes:

Disaggregation and diminishing size of organisations: There will be a clear shift away from traditional bureaucratic/Fordist organisational arrangements towards greater structural diversity, collegial forms of work, self-employment and an ever expanding range of flexible work practices. Collaborative networks or interdependencies between economic sectors and organisations will become increasingly important.

Globalisation: Markets and competition adopt a global orientation. Deregulation and anti-protectionism increase in pace.

The emergence of the symbolic economy: Symbolic commodities such as capital movements, exchange rates, credit flows, statistics, fashion regimes, computer programmes assume a pivotal role in the world economy increasing uncertainty and the rate of obsolescence. The service economy will become increasingly influential and the distinction between goods and services will become increasingly ambivalent.

Shift to knowledge work: There will be an increasing emphasis in advanced economies on intellectual labour and on knowledge and learning in shaping work and the ability to work. While there is general acceptance that the conditions of work have changed there is no agreement as to whether the management of intellectual labour represents a new paradigm of management or simply a more technologically sophisticated 'intellectual assembly line'.

The eclipse of time, distance and place: As commodities and services increasingly embody information and knowledge, the constraining nature of time, place and distance diminish allowing for many more locational configurations than was previously the case. This 'irrelevance' of time and place is linked with technological advances which provide the means by which the size and volume of information flows can be exponentially increased.

The fragility of the future: The postmodern economy will increasingly be subject to a rise in indeterminacy. The fragility of markets and the need of organisations to become more flexible are further compounded by the nature of technological developments. Linear progress is no longer assumed to be inevitable.

Working within these broad economic trends the postmodern organisational form is invariably defined, described or contrasted with the modernist/ bureaucratic form. Both Harvey (1990) and Hassard (1994) suggest that postmodernism can be seen as both a progression from modernism and as a rupture with or negation of modernism. Harvey (1990) has produced a collage of terms to represent 'Fordist modernity' and 'flexible postmodernism' as two regimes of accumulation and regulation that 'hang together' as distinctive and relatively coherent types of social formation (Harvey 1990: 338). Harvey suggests that while an examination of the oppositions within each profile would suggest that postmodernism is a reversal of the dominant order found in Fordist modernity, another way of looking at the table is as a representation of the totality of political – economic and cultural – ideological relations within capitalism (ibid.: 339). As he explains:

> To view it in this way requires that we see the oppositions across as well as within the profiles as internal relations within a structured whole . . . It helps us dissolve the categories of both modernism and postmodernism into a complex of oppositions expressive of the cultural contradictions of capitalism. We then get to see the categorisations of both modernism and postmodernism as static reifications imposed upon the fluid inter-pretation of dynamic oppositions. Within this matrix of internal rela-tions, there is never one fixed configuration, but a swaying back and forth between centralisation and decentralisation, between authority and deconstruction, between hierarchy and anarchy, between permanence and flexibility, between the detail and social division of labour . . . The sharp categorical distinction between modernism and postmodernism disappears, to be replaced by an examination of the flux of internal relations within capitalism as a whole (Harvey 1990: 339–42).

Harvey's contribution provided the needed flexible context for our framework. However, we felt that his collage of terms was too conceptual and diverse for our purpose and so turned to the work of Stewart Clegg. Clegg's work, *Modern Organizations: Organization Studies in the Postmodern World* (1990) expresses similar sentiments to that of Harvey and represents one of the most sophisticated empirical analyses, to date, on postmodernism (periodisation) as it applies to work organisations. This work, as Clegg himself explains, is 'an analysis of distinctive, emergent and possible postmodern practices' (1990: 15) in an organisational setting and can be seen as an attempt to ground the notion of a postmodern organisation in empirical data (Parker 1992: 4). His approach, which is clearly objectivist in intention (Hassard 1994: 317), is to identify the structural characteristics of postmodern organisations based on a comparative study of Swedish, East Asian, Italian and particularly Japanese business enterprises. He sees these empirical examples of postmodern organisations as different from the dominant bureaucratic model of the past. These empirical tendencies raise questions as to the continual utility and validity of modernist organisation theory in providing a framework for understanding organisations. He sees organisation theory as a creation of modernity 'springing as it does from Weber's modernist vision of the modernist world' (Clegg 1990: 4). Weber's bureaucracy was seen as the epitome of rationality and technical efficiency and gave rise to the TINA (There Is No Alternative) tendency (Clegg 1990: 58) within organisation theory where the need for efficiency and industrial growth was seen as requiring large organisations with a high division of labour. From this perspective, Clegg sees postmodernism as a reversal of the modernist tendency of differentiation.

Clegg adopts a 'modes of rationality' approach focusing on elements of 'power' and 'institutions' perspectives – what agents actually do in accomplishing the work of organisations. His approach is also pluralist in orientation allowing for diverse modes of rationality (Clegg 1990: 17) in seeking understanding. He regards Weber's bureaucratic ideal form with its mechanistic structures of control built upon the principles of division of labour and legal-rational authority as the epitome of the 'modernist' organisation. Contemporary literature typically refers to this model as Fordism which embraced Taylor's empirical approach to work and added the linear semi-automatic assembly line and machine-paced and machine-dominated work design (Aglietta 1979: 118). The Fordist model, Clegg suggests, entered a stage of internal and external crisis in the 1970s and from the various organisational responses to this crisis the term 'postmodern organisation' emerged. Clegg identifies the components of a postmodern organisation (typically portrayed as a contemporary Japanese business organisation) by developing a contrast with an ideal form of modernist (bureaucratic/Fordist) organisation. The contrast is developed by examining how each type might typically handle what Clegg identifies as seven 'organisational imperatives' (from Blunt 1989), perennial problems faced by any administratively co-ordinated recurrent and routine activity, which occur between transacting agencies and which all effective forms of organisation must be capable of resolving. The contrast or comparison developed is not to suggest that all Western organisations conform to the modernist ideal but to assist in developing thinking about our organisations outside our strongly modernist assumptions. Clegg suggests that the postmodern organisational form, while remaining relatively ill-defined, is an empirical reality. He views it as a model which may become widely imitated and diffused but cautions against it being read as a blueprint:

> Postmodernism can be about possibilities denied by the project of modernity. Yet no necessity attaches to the future of organisational diversities. The view of this book [sic] has been that everything depends upon the indeterminate outcomes of struggles for meaning and power in and around organisations, struggles which take place under quite distinct national and institutional patterns ... It is certainly never a simple matter of organisational design as an intentional process – this is the rationalist illusion of the modernist age (Clegg 1990: 235).

Figure 4.2 summarises the contrasting imperatives of modernism and post-modernism. The dimensions contain a number of implicit factors. Focusing on the modernist organisation, we see a high concern with mass consumption; high diversification; technological determinism; large size; a high level of structural differentiation; tall hierarchy; job specialisation; de-skilling; rigid production systems; formalised power and authority structures; compartmentalised information flows; highly formalised and externalised co-ordination and control; a focus on individual accountability; the dominance of profit centres with short term focus on quarterly or annual return-on-investment and capital budgeting techniques; individualised effort-related bonus systems; and autocratic and untrusting

Figure 4.2 Organisational dimensions of modernity and postmodernity
Source: Clegg 1990. Used with permission.

leadership. The postmodern organisation, in contrast, is concerned with niche consumption; Keiretsu form; technological choice; small size; de-differentiation, tenure; self-managing teams; multi-skilling flexible production systems; informal and internal control combined with a high level of socialisation and indoctrination; empowerment through training and learning; long-term planning; rewards for the core workers linked to seniority and organisational performance; and trusting open transformational leadership.

Clegg (1990) put forward two main postmodern alternatives. First, postmodern enlightenment, largely following the Swedish experience, involves an increase in industrial democracy and an associated increase in the skill levels and quality of work-life of labour. The second alternative, postmodern seduction, largely based on the Japanese experience, raises a cautionary note in arguing that the post-modern form may be based on a highly segmented labour force 'where an enclave of privileged workers would be formed on highly exclusivist principles of social identity, such as gender, ethnicity and age, characteristics which were tightly coupled to the processes of skill formation' (Clegg 1990: 234). However, this casualisation of the workforce can also be readily embraced by the modernist form in its efforts to reduce costs, reduce size and to become more flexible in the face of increasing environmental uncertainty.

Clegg's work provides an interesting and challenging framework but unfortunately, from our perspective, has a shortfall in that it has an almost exclusive focus on large manufacturing organisations. Telework, while having a presence in the manufacturing sector, is primarily a manifestation of the ever increasing service sector and the attendant emergence of the information society (Galbraith 1967; Drucker 1978, 1993, Coulson-Thomas 1991, Handy 1989). Reflecting this reality we propose four minor additional dimensions to Clegg's framework to enable it to fully embrace the complexity of telework.

Dimension 8 – Technology: centralised vs. dispersed

The central issue here concerns the tendency for highly centralised and controlled mainframe or PC networks within modernist organisations as opposed to a focus on flexible end-user computing in the postmodernist frame. The key difference is the extent of individual autonomy and discretion in the use of hardware and software.

Dimension 9 – Activity: production / dataprocessing vs. information / knowledge

As was identified earlier, the espoused development of an Information Society implies a shift in focus from manufacturing and simple data processing to information and knowledge-based work. While there is considerable futuristic debate as to the nature of this new, emerging age and its implications for organisations, most commentators tend to give a high level of emphasis to the key roles of creativity, innovation and knowledge and to the fact that these are only attainable through people who must now become the key assets of any organisation. Contemporary analyses of the processes of knowledge creation and cognition have sought to identify core activities but have unlayered a complex web of processes. Weick (1995) uses the term 'sensemaking' to describe this multi-level, complex, often tacit process of seeing. Boland and Tenkasi (1995) emphasise that knowledge production involves communication between 'communities of knowing'. They characterise communication that strengthens 'within community' knowledge as a process of perspective-making and communication that improves the ability to take the knowledge of others into account as perspective-taking. They characterise the essential process by which these activities occur as one of information processing and narrativising of unusual events. Clearly much remains to be understood about these processes but the essential point to be stressed is that knowledge work is an activity involving complex processes rather than a simple concept of information processing.

Dimension 10 – Knowledge: embodied / embedded vs. embrained / encultured / encoded

While the postmodern form suggests a tendency away from data processing towards knowledge creation it can also be suggested that there is a shift in the nature of knowledge in use. Blackler (1995), drawing on the extensive literature on organisational learning, identifies five common images of knowledge: embrained, embodied, encultured, embedded and encoded. Embodied knowledge is partially explicit, action oriented and can be explained by reference to situations where successful problem-solving depends more on an intimate knowledge of the situation rather than abstract rules. Embedded knowledge is knowledge which resides in the systemic routines of organisations. Embrained knowledge is abstract knowledge dependent on conceptual skills and cognitive abilities. Encultured knowledge refers 'to the process of achieving shared understandings' (Blackler 1995: 1024) and is closely related to the process of socialisation and acculturation. Encoded knowledge is information conveyed by means of signs and symbols and typically occurs in books, manuals and codes of practice. Blackler suggests that recent commentaries on the emerging significance of knowledge work suggest a growing shift in interest and emphasis from embodied and embedded knowledge to knowledge which is embrained, encultured and encoded.

Dimension 11 – Time and Space: static vs. dynamic; fixity vs. mobility; centralisation vs. localisation

A recurring theme within postmodernism is the issue of time/space compression. Postmodernism exists in 'neutral time', 'eternal presentness' (Kumar 1995: 147), or, in Foucault's words, 'a moment, I believe, when our experience of the world is less that of a long life developing through time than that of a network that connects points and intersects with its own skein' (in Soja 1989: 10; quoted in Kumar 1995: 147). Advanced technology, linked to the increasing informational/ symbolic nature of workflows has facilitated time/space distanciation and compression (Harvey 1990; Giddens 1990) in turn allowing organisations to 'achieve a speed, flexibility and reach in their operations simply undreamt of by earlier generations' (Reed 1996: 580). Relating this issue to the telework literature, Jackson (1992) suggests that telework involves new forms of spatial relationships within organisations. In his view industrialisation was about separating work from home and the attendant focus on centralisation about bringing the worker to the work. New information and communication technologies may challenge, if not reverse this philosophy through their facilitation of connectedness from a distance. Time boundaries may also be transcended via technology and global location.

These four additional dimensions are integrated in Figure 4.3 below and should be considered as extensions to Figure 4.2.

When combined, Figures 4.2 and 4.3 represent a tentative framework within which to view the development of and evolving nature of telework.

The cases

Preliminary research was carried out on two Irish companies, both subsidiaries of foreign multinationals. To protect their confidentiality the companies will be referred to as 'Telebed' and 'Outsource Inc.'. Semi-structured interviews were conducted with staff from each company, predominantly senior managers. The following analysis will loosely follow the various dimensions detailed in Figures 4.2 and 4.3.

Telebed

Telebed is the reservation centre for European customers for a large multinational conglomerate encompassing a hotel chain, holiday resorts, travel agencies and, indirectly, an international airline. The company employs around 25 employees. Calls, primarily by telephone, are received into the centre from around 15 different European countries. The centre operates a flexible rota

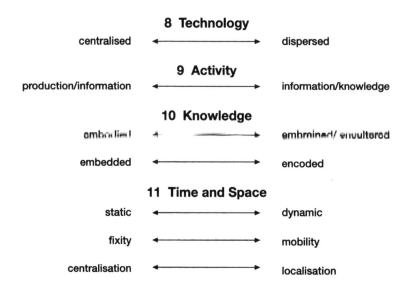

Figure 4.3 Additional organisational dimensions of modernity and postmodernity

system between the hours of 7 a.m. and 8 p.m. Irish time thereby catching the core hours of most European time zones. At present the centre processes around 700 calls per day.

Telebed is one of four call centres established by the company outside the USA. It was attracted to Ireland due to the suitability of the time zone, the availability of staff with language abilities, reasonable telephone tariff rates and an attractive government incentive package. Telebed has a highly specialised and focused strategy, largely determined by its parent company. Its central concern is the provision of a blanket, high quality holiday/business service based on an understanding of and maximum response to the varying cultural dynamics of European customers. Working arrangements are highly formalised and most work processes highly programmed due to the requirements of a centralised reservation database which prompts the employees to ask certain questions. Staff are, however, encouraged to interact at an informal, interpersonal level with their customers with a view to encouraging the development of a successful and enduring business relationship. Control is exercised through strong socialisation and ongoing training and through tight computer-based surveillance and random call monitoring. Operations staff are paid on an hourly basis and earn a commission on the revenue generated on each call which can account for up to 20 per cent of gross salary. Despite the Tayloristic appearance of working arrangements in Telebed, the employees appeared to be highly motivated, enjoying the pressurised nature of the work. In addition, employee turnover rates were substantially lower than equivalent USA operations. The technologies in use are highly centralised and have a substantial impact on behaviour. The activity is primarily one of information or data processing with the knowledge component consisting largely of embedded knowledge. In terms of time and space both, in reality, are centralised but the company does attempt to create the illusion of localisation primarily by insisting that all calls are answered in the language of the customer.

Outsource Inc.

Outsource Inc. is a relatively new strategic business unit within the Irish subsidiary of a large USA-based computer company engaged in manufacturing, software development and support services. It provides the European hardware and software support services for a number of global computer companies and currently employs around 250 employees, mostly on a permanent basis. Most of the employees have third-level technical educational qualifications and are located in a central office in Dublin, Ireland. The remainder of the employees, logistical support staff and engineers, are based in six different European countries. In a way, the mobile engineers represent the stereotypical conceptualisation of the teleworker/homeworker (see Figure 4.1). They are mostly permanent employees and typically operate from home in their base country. They have the ability to make twenty-four-hour mobile or PC-based contact with the Dublin office and are only required to make occasional visits each year to the Dublin office for training, performance review and general socialisation purposes.

While the strategic focus of Outsource Inc. is relatively specialised at present (technical support for personal computers and associated software) it has begun to become more diffused as its potential client base expands due to the merging of the IT and communications industries. Its core competencies are technical excellence and quality customer care. It operates between 6. a.m. and 6 p.m. Irish time with a view to covering the main working hours of most European time zones. The company currently operates in six European countries. Customers can access the company via telephone, e-mail, fax, the Internet and electronic data interchange and are dealt with in their own language. The Dublin office, where most of the employees are based, is relatively hierarchical. The work system, while relaxed, is formalised and focused on the individual. Staff are largely recruited with the relevant technical skills and tend to remain within their area of expertise. There is tight, constant computer-based performance monitoring and a strict system of monthly quality assessments. The reward system is primarily salary based with progression up the scale contingent on meeting individualised performance targets. The technology in Outsource Inc. is moderately centralised, consisting of a distributed PC local area network supported by an expert system to aid technical diagnosis of problems. Its core activity is knowledge based, given the problem orientation of the customer contact. The nature of the knowledge in use is, however, difficult to categorise. Customers typically contact Outsource Inc. with a technical problem and the employee is expected to find a technical solution to this problem in the shortest possible time. Referring to the knowledge dimension on Figure 4.3, there would appear to be strong elements of embodied and embedded knowledge as well as encoded and embrained knowledge within the company. An expert system is available to staff to aid common diagnoses but tends not to be used by the more experienced staff. In terms of time and space, as with Telebed, we find a relatively centralised operation providing a highly geographically mobile service with a high emphasis on the illusion of localised, in temporal and linguistic terms, service provision.

An example may best illustrate this latter point. Outsource Inc. provides the detailed technical support for a major computer (PC) manufacturer which has its European manufacturing base in Ireland. A customer in Paris purchases one of these machines and experiences a problem setting up the machine. They dial a local Paris number and are automatically routed to the manufacturer's support facility in Ireland. If the manufacturer is unable to solve the problem themselves they immediately switch the call to Outsource Inc. in Dublin who continue with the diagnosis. If the problem cannot be resolved over the telephone, the caller is told that an engineer will call them within two days. At that stage the call is terminated. The support person in Outsource Inc. then logs an incident report on the call and refers the matter to a resource controller in the same area who will arrange for one of the company's engineers, based locally in Paris, to call on the customer (as a representative of the main manufacturer) having been briefed on the likely nature of the problem and on any likely hardware or software requirements. If the problem is likely to be hardware related (e.g. a failed hard drive) then a parallel logistics report is also logged to ensure that the engineer will be supplied with the appropriate piece of equipment. Outsource Inc. maintains a small equipment dump, typically a small rented unit, in each of the areas supported by the engineers. Throughout this exchange the client assumes that he/she is dealing with a single company. He/she is unaware that his/her call has been switched to another country, has gone through two different companies and has been fixed by a subcontractor.

Discussion

This chapter has outlined a very broad conceptual framework on the nature of contemporary trends in organisational functioning and design. This framework is presented as providing a 'space' within which to place and examine the concept of telework. The view presented is that telework, as a concept, is real and meaningful though not amenable to simple definition. While it is possible to talk of 'telework' as a distinct trend it is essential that this trend be seen in its proper context namely, as a subsidiary issue within the broader study of the changing nature of work organisations in contemporary society. In this regard, the complex nature and impact of telework is diffused across a number of the dimensions presented in the framework. In this way it is not suggested that telework is simply and exclusively a postmodern concept but can be either modern or postmodern or, as in the two organisational cases discussed above, an hybridisation of both forms. In this regard, the modified framework presented in this chapter can be used to chart or locate the seemingly contradictory development of telework initiatives within a definite organisational context. Each of the eleven headings in the framework identifies a relevant research issue within which the role of telework can be explored (see figures 4.2 and 4.3). Taken together, the various headings in the framework offer the potential to integrate past and present research into telework and to guide further research on the topic.

While the adoption and diffusion of telework practices within organisations would appear to be relatively evolutionary and *ad hoc*, it is suggested here that telework, directly or indirectly, impacts upon organisational arrangements in three main ways:

1   to increase centralisation and control;
2   to decentralise and empower; and
3   to facilitate micro-enterprise (the growth of small entrepreneurial firms).

Teleworking which increases centralisation and control can ideally be seen in the substantial growth in off-shore teleservice or back-office companies typical of the Telebed case detailed above. These organisations typically are bureaucratic in nature, focus on standardised data input operations and are clearly modernist in orientation. Telework which decentralises and empowers can be seen in the way that a number of organisations are facilitating and encouraging their core employees to operate from flexible locations with the latest technologies. Such occurrences can be technology and/or strategy led; just as strategy is not always deliberate, but sometimes emergent, so too it is not always determining, but sometimes offers opportunities which shape organisation and work structure.

These decentralising tendencies are partially in evidence in the case of Outsource Inc. detailed above. Organisations of this nature typically lean towards the postmodern side of the framework. It is interesting to note that in the case of both Telebed and Outsource Inc. the issue of networking and network collaboration is equally important. Telework which facilitates micro-enterprise can be seen in the increasing use of independent contractors by both modernist and postmodernist organisations as part of their deliberate business strategy (outsourcing, downsizing, cost reduction, numerical flexibility, etc.). These 'independent contractors' can tender and provide services irrespective of distance and location utilising advanced information and communication technologies. Telecottages are a related development of this tendency. While these forms, which we see as central to the future growth of telework, are presented here as an associated feature or adjunct of the organisational tendencies within both modernist and postmodernist organisational forms, it is possible to see this trend as a reemergence of a premodern discourse (a feudal society based on vassalage and skilled artisans and associated guilds operating under a system of patronage) with premodernity, modernity and postmodernity operating simultaneously in contest (Boje 1995). The elaboration of a third, interlinked premodern dimension to reflect the unique dynamic and independent existence of stand-alone, entrepreneurial homeworkers and the associated development of telecottages is a project requiring attention. If successful, this third dimension would partially get around the obvious limitations of a simple dualistic framework which lends itself too easily to simplistic notions of progress and linearity.

A final comment would appear appropriate as to the nature of the changes discussed in this chapter. Clearly, information and communication technologies have played and will continue to play a significant role in the shaping of organisational geographies, particularly in terms of their facilitation of collaborative work arrangements between geographically dispersed associated and independent organisations. However, it is fair to say that these postmodern/virtual tendencies within organisations, to date at least, have remained firmly within the logic of capitalism. As Kumar suggests, the 'imperatives of profit, power and control seem as predominant now as they have ever been in the history of capitalist industrialism' (1995: 154).

To conclude, this chapter has presented a tentative conceptual framework with a view to locating the issue of 'telework' within the broader ongoing debate on the changing nature of work organisations within the organisational behaviour literature. Building upon and extending the work of Clegg (1990) we suggest that telework should not just be seen as a stage in the inevitable slide towards the virtual organisation but more as an intrinsic and complex feature of changes currently being experienced by both modernist and postmodernist organisational forms.

References

Aglietta, M. (1979) *A Theory of Capitalist Regulation*, London: New Left Books.

Allen, S. and Wolkowitz, C. (1987) *Homeworking. Myths and Realities*, Basingstoke: Macmillan.

Atkinson, J. (1984) 'Manpower Strategies for Flexible Organisations', *Personnel Management*, August.

Bell, D. (1973) *The Coming of Post-Industrial Society*, New York: Basic Books.

Bertin, I and Roberts, S. (1996) 'Telefutures: A Study on Teleworking in Ireland', Dublin: Forbairt and Telecom Eireann.

Blackler, F. (1995) 'Knowledge, Knowledge Work and Organizations: An Overview and Interpretation', *Organization Studies* 16, 6: 1021–46.

Blunt, P. (1989) 'Strategies for Human Resource Development in the Third World', opening address to 'The International Human Resource Development Conference', University of Manchester, 25 June.

Boland, R. and Tenkasi, R. (1995) 'Perspective Making and Perspective Taking in Communities of Knowing', *Organization Science* 6, 4 July.

Boje, D.M. (1995) 'Premodern, Modern and Postmodern: Are We Moving Forwards or Backwards?', paper presented at the 1995 Academy of Management, Vancouver.

Brandt, S. (1983) 'Working at Home: How to Cope with Spatial Design Possibilities Caused by the New Communications Media', *Office Technology and People* 2: 1–13.

Burrell, G. (1988) 'Modernism, Post Modernism and Organizational Analysis 2: The Contribution of Michael Foucault', *Organization Studies* 9, 2: 221–332.

Clegg, S. (1990) *Modern Organizations: Organization Studies in a Postmodern World*, London: Sage.

Cooper, R. and Burrell, G. (1988) 'Modernism, Post Modernism and Organizational Analysis: An Introduction', *Organization Studies* 9, 1: 91–112.

Coulson-Thomas, C. (1991) 'IT and New Forms of Organization for Knowledge Workers: Opportunity and Implementation', *Employee Relations* 13, 4: 22–32.

Crook, S., Pakulski, J. and Waters, M. (1992) *Postmodernization. Change in Advanced Society*, London: Sage.

Davidow, W.H. and Malone, M.S. (1992) *The Virtual Corporation*, New York: Harper and Row.

Drucker, P. (1978) *The Age of Discontinuity*, New York: Harper and Row.

—— (1993) *Post-Capitalist Society*, Oxford: Butterworth-Heinemann.

Galbraith, J. (1967) *The New Industrial State*, Boston: Houghton Mifflin.

Giddens, A. (1990) The Consequences of Modernity, Cambridge: Polity.

Handy, C. (1989). *The Age of Unreason*, Cambridge, MA: Harvard Business School Press.

Harvey, D. (1990) *The Condition of Postmodernity: An Inquiry into the Origins of Cultural Change*, Oxford: Basil Blackwell.

Hassard, J. (1994) 'Postmodern Organizational Analysis: Towards a Conceptual Framework', *Journal of Management Studies* 31, 3: 303–24.

Holti, R. and Stern, E. (1984) *Social Aspects of New Information Technology in the U.K.: A Review of Initiatives in Local Communications*, London: Tavistock/Institute of Human Relations.

Huws, U., Korte, W. and Robinson, S. (1990) *Telework, Towards the Elusive Office*, London: John Wiley.

'Information Society Ireland. Strategy for Action' (1997) Report of Ireland's Information Society Steering Committee, Dublin: Forfas.

Jackson, P.J. (1992) 'Organizational Change: The Role of Telework', Proceedings of Employment Research Unit Annual Conference, Cardiff Business School.

Jameson, F. (1992) *Postmodernism, or, The Cultural Logic of Late Capitalism*, London: Verso.

Kumar, K. (1995) *From Post-Industrial to Postmodern Society. New Theories of the Contemporary World*. Oxford: Basil Blackwell.

Lash, S. and Urry, J. (1987) *The End of Organized Capitalism*, Oxford: Polity.

Miles, R.E. and Snow, C.C. (1992) 'Causes of Failure in Network Organizations', *California Management Review*, Summer: 53–72.

Moorcroft, S. and Bennett, V. (1995) *European Guide to Teleworking: A Framework for Action*, Dublin: European Foundation for the Improvement of Living and Working Conditions.

Nilles, J.M., Carlson, F.R., Gray, P. and Hanneman, G.J. (1976) *The Telecommunications–Transportation Trade-off*, Chichester: Wiley.

Parker, M. (1992) 'postmodern Organizations or Postmodern Organization Theory', *Organization Studies* 13, 1: 1–17.

Piore, M., and Sabel, C. (1984) *The Second Industrial Divide*, New York: Basic Books.

Reed, M. (1996) 'Expert Power and Control in Late Modernity: An Empirical Review and Theoretical Synthesis', *Organisation Studies* 17, 4: 573–97.

Soja, E.W. (1989) *Postmodern Geographies: The Reassertion of Space in Critical Social Theory*, London: Verso.

Stehr, N. (1994) *Knowledge Societies*, London: Sage.

Webster, F. (1995) *Theories of the Information Society*, London: Routledge.

Weick, K. (1995) *Sensemaking in Organisations*, New York: Sage.

5

RETHINKING THE VIRTUAL ORGANISATION

Martin Harris

Introduction

The view that new technology is fundamentally affecting work organisations has been a rich source of controversy and comment over the last fifteen years or so. In the UK, the Economic and Social Research Council (ESRC) has announced a new research programme on 'the virtual society' whose purpose is to investigate:

> the role of electronic technologies over a range of human and social activities and determine the extent to which they are fundamentally affecting the way in which people behave, organise themselves and inter-act with each other.
>
> ESRC (1996)[1]

Many accounts of contemporary restructuring have been influenced by the idea that production has become more 'disorganised' (Lash and Urry 1987). This trend is particularly apparent in organisational theory, where there is a wide-spread belief that we are seeing a paradigm shift away from bureaucracy towards disaggregation and 'the end of organisation' (Lash and Urry 1987; Kanter 1991; Quinn 1992; Handy 1995). This broader context forms the background to the analysis of the virtual organisation in this chapter.

Part 1 of the chapter provides a brief introduction to the debate on the virtual-ity, and identifies two aspects of the debate that deserve further investigation. First, the virtual organisation has been represented as an historically significant paradigm shift. This produces a strong sense of *déjà vu* in the mind of the critical observer, and begs the question of how far the new virtual forms can be seen as a real and significant new departure from existing modes of organising. Second, the debate has been dominated by overtly prescriptive and rationalist interpret-ations, and there is a need for a more robust theorisation of the issues. Part 2 examines more closely the precise ways in which the virtual organisation has been represented as a radically new, discontinous 'paradigm shift'. The argument here is that newly emergent forms of organisation may, broadly speaking, be more 'Fordist' in character than has been acknowledged by proponents of the paradigm shift.

The issue of trust has featured prominently in discussions of innovative 'networked' alternatives to markets and bureaucratic modes of organisation. Part 3 argues that analyses of the virtual organisation are pervaded by a highly generalised 'portmanteau' treatment of trust which underestimates the part played by culture and ethical values within a broad diversity of *extant* organisational forms. Recent empirical work on MITI (the Japanese Ministry of International Trade and Industry), the BBC and the NHS shows that 'market', 'hierarchy' and 'network' forms of organisation may co-exist in the same institutional setting. This suggests that the 'end of organisation' thesis may be radically premature, and that the assumption of a paradigm shift may need to be revised. The concluding part of the chapter offers an alternative theorisation of the virtual organisation which moves decisively away from the existing 'epochal' framework assumed by proponents of the paradigm shift.

Part 1: defining the virtual organisation

Several authors have sought to establish a comprehensive definition of the virtual organisation. Barnatt (1995) identifies virtuality with malleability and transient work patterns. He also argues that the virtual organisation has no identifiable physical form and that its boundaries are defined and limited only by the availability of IT. Barnatt also argues that technology allows the new form to dispense with bureaucratic rules and contractual relations. Davidow and Malone (1992) emphasise the malleable and amorphous form taken by virtual organisations. The boundaries will be ill-defined so that:

> To the outsider it will appear almost edgeless with permeable and continously changing interfaces between company, supplier and customer. From inside the firm will be no less amorphous, with traditional offices, departments and operating divisions constantly reforming according to need. Job responsibilities will regularly shift, as will lines of authority even the very definition of employees will change, as some customers and suppliers begin to spend more time in the company than some of the firms own workers.
>
> (Davidow and Malone 1992: 5–6)

Jackson and Quinn (1996) argue that moves towards the virtual organisation result from 'two mutually supportive developments'. Corporate restructuring (see, for example, Kanter 1989; Quinn 1992) involves changes in the ways in which organisational sub-units and functions are fitted together within the corporation. This can be located in more theoretical work on the ways in which different contractual and control structures may be appropriate for different sub-units

(Ouchi 1979; Williamson 1975; Sako 1992). The second aspect cited is overtly technological and is centred on the potential innovations which take place at the conjunction of technology and organisation. Research on the virtual organisation has recieved renewed stimulus from developments in information and communications technologies (ICTs). ICTs allow temporally or spatially dispersed organisational functions, work teams, or individuals to work on a common project or work task. Teleworking, which is closely associated with homeworking, subcontracting and franchising, has typically been confined to lower-order tasks. Leading commentators are confident, however, that the virtual forms allowed by more advanced communications technologies will include significant numbers of professionals and 'knowledge workers'.[2]

The virtual organisation as a paradigm shift

Accounts of the virtual organisation are invariably concerned with defining the virtual organisation in contradistinction to earlier forms, and they are usually constructed around the assumption that the virtual organisation should be viewed as an emergent new paradigm. A number of prominent themes are present, including the role of information in the creation of new business opportunities, marketisation, debureaucratisation, value chain analysis, moves away from Taylorism, and calls for the moral fabric of the organisation to be overhauled.

Innovation and new business opportunities

Enthusiasts regard the virtual organisation as synonymous with new business opportunities, technological innovation and organisational change. As with earlier developments in the field of information technology, and with currently influential representations of 'cyberspace', proponents of the virtual organisation are concerned with the innovative potential of vastly increased information flows. Information technology is closely associated with improvements in the control and co-ordination of core activities; functional integration, quality levels and responsiveness. A large part of Handy's argument for the virtual organisation (Handy 1995) turns on his conception of organisations as processors of information. Thus he argues that:

> more and more of our economic activity is a churning of information, ideas and intelligence in all their infinite variety . . . an invitation to virtuality.

> (1995: 41)

The pervasive belief is that information can itself be equated with wealth creation and economic progress. Davidow and Malone (1992) treat the move to virtual forms of organisation as an economic necessity, and link it to calls for industrial renewal.

The business-led models of virtuality are as much concerned with efficiency as they are with innovation. Several of the best-known accounts are rooted mechanistic assumptions about the nature of organisations. Thus, Davidow and Malone argue along strictly rationalist lines, that:

> the creation of the virtual corporation will result from linking relevant databases into ever more extensive and integrated networks. The information that we generate often induces and controls the actions of others.
>
> (1992: 64–5)

They also argue, in a similarly rationalist vein, that the provision of timely and accurate information allows the organisation to concentrate on results rather than task supervision:

> bringing the crucial information instantly to the right decision maker and then transmitting the resulting decision through the network just as quickly means that the organisation must organise around outcomes rather than tasks. Success means working to product results.
>
> (1992: 172)

Market rationality and 'friction free capitalism' pervades the writings of leading commentators such as Nicholas Negroponte and Bill Gates. As Jackson (1996) points out, Gates (1995) has argued that the superhighway metaphor is an inappropriate one and that:

> A different metaphor that I think comes closer to describing a lot of the activities that will take place is that of the ultimate market. Markets from trading floors to malls are fundamental to human society, and I believe that this one will eventually be the world's central department store.
>
> (1995: 6)

Cyberspace and virtual working have been associated, in a second strand of thinking, with fragmentation and social atomisation. High-trust relationships between contracting parties are seen as an antidote to this. For Charles Handy, the new virtual forms offer the possibility of establishing new social employer-employee relations based on trust and co-operation. If we are to enjoy the benefits of the virtual organisation we will, he concludes, need to run organisations more on the basis of trust than control. However, Handy is in no doubt that many Western firms remain firmly wedded to the idea that control remains the *sine qua non* for efficiency. He calls for the 'instrumental' contract of employment to be replaced by a 'membership' contract for a smaller core. This emphasis on trust for a core of valued employees is strongly reminiscent of Piore and Sabel (1984) and of comparative work on the more inclusive models of employment developed in Sweden, Japan and Germany.

Virtual organisations, postmodernity and the rejection of Taylorism

The emergence of the new virtual forms is also closely associated with the assumption that late twentieth-century organisations are moving decisively away from Taylorism, scientific management and bureaucracy. Virtuality is associated with new approaches which require responsibility, autonomy, and enterprise. The new subject at work is represented as:

> enterprising; self-regulating; market oriented; productive; autonomous and responsible.
>
> (Brigham and Corbett 1996: 46)

Kanter (1989) claims that 'commitment to organisation' still matters but that managers build commitment by offering 'project opportunities':

> The new loyalty is not to the boss or company, but to projects that actualise a mission, and offer challenge growth and credit for results
>
> (Kanter 1991, quoted in Brigham and Corbett 1996: 49)

The concern with fluidity, responsiveness and less restrictive forms is often equated with the emergence of the postmodern organisation. Brigham and Corbett draw on Clegg's theorisation of the postmodern organisation (Clegg 1990) to argue that the virtual organisation is the archetypal postmodern form:

> These organisational forms become a virtual necessity in order to come to terms with the new external environment organisations are facing; flexiblity and responsiveness are key factors for economic success and only the virtual organisation has the speed and flexiblity to cope with this new external environment.
>
> (Brigham and Corbett 1996: 49).

The above excerpt from Brigham and Corbett contains an important clue as to the underlying nature of the debate on the virtual organisation. The assumption is that a range of external factors make the move towards high-trust virtual organisations imperative. Underlying this assumption is a particular reading of Clegg's depiction of the postmodern organisation as a paradigm shift away from bureaucracy and Taylorism (Brigham and Corbett 1996: 49; Clegg 1990: 272). McGrath and Houlihan (1996; this volume) base their analysis on a reading of Clegg which assumes a similar binary opposition of modern/postmodern organisational forms, but this chapter also incorporates empirical evidence which is not easily squared with the blanket assertion of a paradigm shift away from Taylorism. These authors adopt a much more equivocal reading of virtuality and the postmodern organisation, and they conclude by identifying the emergence of 'hybrid' organisational forms (McGrath and Houlihan 1996: 272).

Summary

The above analysis provided a broad treatment of what has been argued within the debate on the virtual organisation. There are two underlying aspects of the debate that deserve comment at this point. First, the virtual organisation has been represented as an historically significant paradigm shift. This produces a strong sense of *déjà vu* in the mind of the critical observer, and it begs the question of how far the new virtual forms can be seen as a real and significant new development. Second, there has been a preponderance of business-led models whose orientation is overtly prescriptive and rationalist in character. The result has been that the debate is generally undertheorised. The next part of the chapter examines more closely the precise ways in which the virtual organisation has been represented as a radically new, discontinous paradigm shift. It also relates the debate on virtuality to a broader account of contemporary restructuring, and puts the case for further theoretical development.

Part 2: the virtual organisation as a paradigm shift

Proponents of the virtual organisation have not thus far produced a theoretical synthesis which integrates complex changes in technology, markets, institutions and organisations into an overall schema. The virtual organisation concept can, however, be related to a number of earlier attempts to develop a comprehensive account of techno-organisational change. These attempts would include flexible specialisation/post-Fordism, moves towards 'disaggregated' organisational forms, and new production concepts such as lean manufacturing and business process re-engineering. Within these models, market, technological and organisational factors are typically bound together in what Jones has termed a 'tight nexus' (Jones 1990).

Figure 5.1 identifies three key aspects including: the assumption of a paradigm shift; the central role accorded to technology; and 'emancipatory' calls for the ethical/moral fabric of the organisation to be overhauled. The substantive content of each model varies – the key point to note is the ways in which a very broad spectrum of factors are subsumed within the paradigm shift itself. The assumption of an overarching paradigm shift promotes an 'apocalyptic' (or millenarian) view of the historical process (Collingwood 1961) in which new social structures emerge from a sharp disjuncture and old forms are discarded in favour of the new (Kumar 1995; Willcocks and Grint 1997). All of the models cited in Figure 5.1 are designed to operate at a high level of substantive and theoretical generality. One result of this is that they incorporate exceedingly broad definitions of technology which cannot easily be squared with more critical work on the nature of technology and the innovation process. Many researchers regard the very use of the word 'technology' as heavily implicated, symbolically, in the assumption of radical discontinuity with existing modes of production and organisation (see, for example, Smith and Marx 1995; Jackson 1997; Willcocks

PARADIGM SHIFT	ROLE OF TECHNOLOGY	'MORAL FABRIC'
'Second industrial divide' (Sabel and Piore 1984)	Progammable machines allow flexible specialisations	Craft ethos Multi-skilling High-trust relationships
New techno-economic paradigm (Freeman 1993)	ICTs signal end of Fordism and 'hard growth'	'Creative destruction' of old practices
Lean manufacturing (Womack et al. 1990)	Technology signals end of mass production	Consensus at work
BPR and the 'disaggregated organisation' (Quinn 1992)	IT allows control of processes	Control of labour and value chains creates responsive organisational forms
Virtual organisation (Handy 1995)	ICTs allow organisations to be dispersed in time and space	Fragmentation offset by high-trust relationships

Figure 5.1 New organisational paradigms

and Grint 1997; Williams 1997). The assumption of a paradigm shift, juxtaposed with a more or less abstract conception of 'technology' results in an 'oppositional' view of *production systems* – the technical organisational changes under consideration are seen as a 'once-and-for-all' departure in which new and old organisational forms are seen as mutually exclusive.

Several influential critics have argued that the microelectronic revolution does not, in fact, signal a paradigm shift in the underlying structures of industrial capitalism. Kumar draws on the work of Beninger to argue that the impact of microelectronics on systems of production and distribution needs to be understood as part of a longer-run 'control revolution' which has been unfolding since mass-production began to gather pace in the early twentieth-century (Kumar 1995; Beninger 1986). Kumar also notes that the decentralised structures and distributed information systems associated with ICTs are entirely compatible with enhanced managerial control, and with the retention of Taylorism (Kumar 1995: 150–201).

The 'control revolution' thesis is broadly consistent with a range of studies which undermine the argument for an emergent new organisational paradigm. Hyman (1992) argues that the flexible specialisation misunderstands the nature and extent of the changes underway. A number of more detailed studies show that advanced manufacturing technologies do not represent a radical departure from the earlier Fordist organisation of production. Studies carried out by Coriat

(1991), Nolan and O'Donnel (1991), Tomaney (1994) and Smith (1991) all demonstrate the ways in which flexible specialisation needs to be seen as a complement to (and in some cases an extension of) mass-production. For these writers, the new paradigm is very much embedded in the old.[4]

In the United States, 'new wave' management theory tends to sideline the independent influence attributed to technology, whilst maintaining a focus on the disaggregation which has accompanied the restructuring of Western firms in the 1980s and 1990s. Porter's (1980) work on value chains and outsourcing has been a highly influential starting point for many proponents of new wave theory. Recent work by Kanter emphasises functional integration, delayering and cost reduction (Kanter 1991). Quinn's 'Intelligent Enterprise' thesis (Quinn 1992) borrows heavily from both Kanter and Porter. Quinn cites the Nike and Apple companies as paradigm examples of the new 'disaggregated' organisations. These organisations can be seen as 'virtual' in the sense that they are geographically dispersed, heavily reliant on extensive subcontracting networks, and concentrate on certain knowledge-intensive aspects of production.[5]

New wave management thinkers such as Kanter and Quinn advocate organisational transformation, whilst retaining a rationalist and rationalising view of the firm. The widespread tendency for companies to downsize and to outsource what were previously regarded as essential services and functions to subcontractors has been accompanied by profound shifts in the employment relationship. The wide-ranging investigation of employment relationships carried out by Capelli (1995) provides evidence for intensified control, shifts in the basis of the psychological contract, and the subordination of previously sacrosant notions of service to the dictates of competition and individual performance. All of the studies cited above point to a more 'Taylorised' view of late capitalism than is acknowledged by those who view contemporary changes in work and organisation as a paradigm shift. Constance Perin's work on remote working and the moral fabric of the organisation is particularly interesting in this connection.

Perin develops an empirically well-grounded 'symbolic schema' for analysing the problem of remote working and the moral fabric of the organisation (Perin (1991, 1996). The general line of argument is that the organisational possibilities offered by information technology applied to remote working may be blocked by a range of symbolic and political control factors operating within the organisation. Perin's work is focused on salaried professionals and technical employees who are said to enjoy more opportunities for 'self-management' than other white-collar employees (Perin 1991). The central finding is that salaried professionals and their employers were reluctant to adopt more flexible temporal and spatial patterns of work. Thus:

> Employees believed that being absent would be disadvantageous to their careers and employers believed that they could not supervise people out of their presence.
>
> (1991: 259)

Perin suggests that the nineteenth-century 'panopticon' principle of industrial production – based on the surveillance allowed by co-location, co-presence and co-visibility – was 'alive and well'. In this symbolic scheme, authority is 'sustained by co-presence, whilst it is undermined by distance' (1991: 259). In the context of recession, career prospects may be uncertain and Perin observes that professionals (who locate much of their identity in office 'influence') may have good reason to be less than enthusiastic about the 'invisibility' entailed by virtual working. For employees working at home two or three days per week, the 'semiotics of time and space' and the panopticon principle of visibility acted to override:

> the computer logics of asynchronicity and virtual presence, the competence logics of uninterrupted thinking time, and the household logics of self-scheduling to meet nonwork goals.
>
> (1996: 260)

Organisations employing professional and technical specialists are increasingly using highly directive project management models for defining output requirements, budgeting and scheduling. Perin regards these models as 'tools for approximating the Taylorisation of non manufacturing work' (see also Perin, this volume).

Recapitulation

The debate on the virtual organisation has highlighted a number of technological and organisational developments in the organisation of production. This section has developed an alternative reading of these developments based on a number of arguments which can be summarised as follows:

1   the underlying structure of the virtual organisation concept bears a close resemblance to earlier formulations which have been based on a 'tight nexus' of technological, organisational and environmental factors and a reconfiguration of production around innovation rather than efficiency. These formulations assume a paradigm shift in technology and organisation and a historically significant break with Taylorism and mass-production.

2   The argument for a paradigm shift cannot easily be squared with the accounts of contemporary restructuring cited above. The analyses cited indicate that new technologies and organisational forms are firmly embedded in the earlier paradigm. A number of researchers have pointed out the significance of the productivity innovation dilemma and the need for more understanding of firm-specific strategic choices and managerial 'readings' of particular contexts.

3   Some aspects of the virtual organisation debate are closely related to new wave management theories and calls for more 'disaggregated' organisational

forms. However, new wave management theory is embedded in a highly rationalistic discourse of enhanced managerial control. Once again this points to a more Fordist and Taylorist reality of production than is acknowledged by those whose work assumes the existence of a paradigm shift towards high-trust 'networked' organisations.

4   The role of technology may be overstated in discussions of virtuality and disaggregation. Several studies indicate that the core characterisitic of the disaggregated organisation is not the use of technology, but its tendency to outsource and manage suppliers via a more intensive management of value chains (Kanter 1989, 1991; Quinn 1992; Hill *et al.* 1997). This view squares with the late capitalist doctrine of doing 'more with less' and careful management of the 'productivity innovation dilemma' (Clark *et al.* 1985; Hill *et al.* 1997).

5   Perin's work on 'the semiotics of time and space' undermines the view that 'asynchronous' remote working can be regarded as synonymous with emancipation at work.

The above analysis suggests that much of the restructuring which occurred in the 1990s has been, broadly speaking, more Fordist in character than has been acknowledged by proponents of the paradigm shift, who appear to have misconstrued some very basic characteristics of late twentieth-century capitalism.[6]

The evidence indicates that many Western firms *have* been subject to generalised pressures for change. But it has become clear that management are typically faced with a variety of structural options at different levels within the corporation. This is consistent with the extensive literature on technology and firm-specific strategic choices.[7] There may be, however, theoretical reasons for rejecting the assumption of a thoroughgoing paradigm shift which takes us beyond a concern with firm-specific strategic choice.

Part 3: locating the virtual organisation in a broader theoretical context

It would be easy, given arguments laid out above, to propose that proponents of the paradigm shift have misunderstood the essentially neo-Fordist and neo-Taylorist character of the microelectronic revolution. But this underestimates both the complexity and the significance of the developments associated with teleworking and virtuality. It is clearly inadequate, even at the level of description, to argue that 'nothing much has changed'. The debate on the virtual organisation helps us to focus on a number of technological and organisational developments which are real and significant.

One way to progress research in this area would be to call for more work on the organisational processes and interests associated with virtual working. Much of the best empirical work supports the view that there can be no 'one best way' to promote organisational innovation – here we are back on the familiar territory of strategic choice (Child 1972). But there may be good theoretical reasons for a more radical reframing of the debate on the ways in which new organisational forms co-exist with old ones. The bridge to this broader conceptual terrain is provided by recent comparative work on the role of culture and divergent organisational rationalities in explaining how organisations are structured (Fukuyama 1995; Clegg 1990). This work also gives a clue as to how we might productively rethink the issue of trust and its significance for the emergence of new organisational forms.

Ethical norms and the comparative dimension

A common criticism of models based on a paradigm shift is that they offer prescriptions which tend to downplay questions of institutional specificity and the influence of particular national traditions. Much of the best comparative work is centrally concerned with the ways in which radically different ethical values and norms of association serve to underpin a diversity of organisational forms in different societies. As noted above, the imputed paradigm shift in the techno-organisational basis of production is posited on a complete break with the Weberian form. This is in keeping with the focus on smaller and more flexible forms, and with the general tendency towards disaggregation and 'the post-modern turn' observed by leading theorists of postmodernity and organisation (Lash and Urry 1987; Harvey 1989; Clegg 1990; Hassard and Parker 1993; Thompson 1993).

The work of commentators like Coleman (1988), Fukuyama (1995), Granovetter (1985) and Clegg (1990) incorporates two features which are significant for the present discussion of trust and virtuality. First, these authors are concerned with the ways in which organisations and institutions are underpinned by divergent rationalities. The authors show that culture gives rise to a manifold diversity of organisational structures, normative codes, control mechanisms and rationalities which differ radically from those associated with the precepts of Weber and Chandler. Markets, bureaucratic hierarchies and networks all feature as viable alternatives which may be interwoven in different ways. Here the sociohistorical breadth of canvass is much broader than would be implied by the portmanteau concept of 'trust'. Second, and more significant for the debate on the new paradigm, they are concerned with the analysis of *extant* (rather than newly emergent) organisational forms which have deep historical and cultural roots.

Clegg's work on divergent rationalities and the 'cultural turn' in organisational theory

Clegg's analysis starts with the ways in which the diversity of organisational forms (and economic life generally) is culturally and economically 'embedded'. Economics is seen as a necessary, rather than a sufficient, condition for organisational life. Organisational theory based on social and institutional embeddedness implies not just trust, but a much greater diversity of forms than would have been anticipated by Weber, Chandler or Williamson. The examples deployed include the Korean *Chaebol*, Chinese and Italian banking networks, and Japanese *Zaibatzu*.

Clegg's work on the postmodern organisation derives not from the belief that bureaucracy has collapsed or that we are seeing the 'end of organisation' but from the idea that 'the one best way' advocated by Western thinkers has to be abandoned in the light of the plurality described above (Clegg 1990: 158–63).

Paradigm-shift models of industrial renewal are based on the belief that both markets and hierarchies are being superseded by new networked forms of organisation based on high-trust relationships (as with the much-cited example of Benetton and subcontracting networks in the Third Italy). But these models do little to explain the ways in which markets, hierarchies and networks may co-exist as complementary alternatives *within the same institutional setting*. A study of MITI (the highly innovative Japanese Ministry of International Trade and Industry) carried out by Fransman (1990) serves to illustrate this complementarity. Fransman demonstrates that MITI acted as a repository of knowledge but that it differed radically from its Western counterparts. The 'networked' character of its structure and operations derived from forms of collaboration which avoided the duplication of effort associated with market competition. State intervention in the innovation process was also concerned with 'close-to-market' development of new products and processes which departed with Western models of industrial innovation. MITI's organisational structure contained elements of a classic bureaucracy, but the minstry also made use of 'market' and 'network' mechanisms to facilitate the transfer of technological knowledge. The MITI example provides an interesting perspective on the changes underway within both the BBC and the NHS, which continue to depend on bureaucratic structures, whilst attempting to develop both 'market' and 'network' modes of organisation. The MITI example *could* be characterised as a 'high-trust' (or 'networked') organisation – but this results in a highly misleading and restricted view of the organisational form which developed. There is a danger that prescriptions for the networked organisation, sustained by a diffuse and undertheorised 'portmanteau' concept of trust will become the equivalent of a universal 'one best way' for the 1990s. The real issue is not the incidence or absence of 'trust' within organisations, but understanding the ways in which a diversity of organisational forms and modes of control may co-exist in a single institutional setting. Most theorisations of the virtual organisation are silent on the question of how this diversity is possible.

Part 4: further theoretical development

The debate on the virtual organisation has, on occasion, overlapped with analyses of postmodernism (Brigham and Corbett 1996; McGrath and Houlihan, this volume). Most analysts of the postmodern organisation take as their intellectual starting-point the notion of an epoch/epistemology divide. According to this view, the postmodern can act as a signifier either for a *historical periodisation* or as a theoretical prism of understanding through which we view organisations. Hassard writes:

> In the first use, postmodernization as an epoch, the goal is to identify features of the external world that support the hypothesis that society is moving towards a new postmodern era.
>
> (Hassard 1993: 2)

Here the major theme (one that is closely allied with the associated concepts of post-Fordism and post-industrialism) is that:

> the social and economic structures reproduced since the industrial revo-lution are now fragmenting into diverse networks held together by information technology
>
> (Hassard 1993: 3)

Postmodernism as an epistemology reflects developments in post-structuralist philosophy. Thus Hassard argues that:

> Postmodern epistemology suggests that the world is constituted by our shared language and that we can only know the world through particular forms of discourse our language creates. It is argued however, that as our language is continually in flux, meaning is constantly slipping beyond our grasp, and can thus never be lodged within one term. The task of postmodern writing, therefore, is to recognise this elusive nature of lan-guage, but never with the aim of creating a meta-discourse to explain all language forms.
>
> (Hassard, 1993: 3)

The analyses and commentaries reviewed in this Chapter assume that new organisational forms exist in an empirically knowable world. In line with this view, the chapter has concentrated on the ways in which the virtual organisation has been represented as an emprically observable paradigm shift (i.e. an 'epoch' view of the phenomenon observed). This approach provides a useful way into a difficult field of enquiry, but it is apparent that the epoch view has its limitations. The epoch/epistemology divide is useful because it neatly separates the issue of historical change from questions of how we 'read' the organisation. The problem with this approach, as Hassard readily admits, is that the post-structuralist thought 'operates on a high plane of abstraction' and that researchers are faced with the difficult problem of relating the divide to 'real world' research. Research-ing the virtual organisation confronts the social scientist with a complex and contradictory phenomenon in a field of study permeated by reification and prescription. But the virtual organisation concept, like the more populist notion of cyberspace, is characterised by a semantic instability which may render it ultimately resistant to empirical investigation. Here the epistemological view, with its roots in the philosophy of language, can help us to reframe the problem of researching virtuality and the new organisational forms associated with cyberspace. This change in perspective would involve the recognition that our understanding of a changing world, may be as much a matter of aesthetics as it is empirics. Reframing the discussion of virtuality around a more 'aestheticised' view of technological and organisational change immediately draws our attention to the millennial themes pointed out by Kumar and others. What is missing from the debate on virtuality is a recognition of the *symbolic* function of the paradigm shift, with its powerful appeal to a future in which technical development is associated with economic growth and more 'emancipated' forms of work. With this view, the paradigm-shift models depicted in Figure 5.1 may be better seen as *archetypes* rather than as prescriptions for organisational design. Reconceptualising these models around the notion of an archetype is useful because it reminds us of their fundamentally 'ideal-typical' character. They should be viewed as logical constructs whose main value is to signal broad tendencies and movements; their primary function is *not* to provide organisational blueprints in the manner of prescriptive business-led models.

Another useful feature of the archetype view is that it addresses the question of semantic instability. The archetypal view is valuable precisely *because* the precise definitions and meanings are necessarily looser than would be implied by empirical observation. The concern with language associated with the epistemology perspective has an obvious bearing here. Loosely structured characterisations allow the discussion of virtuality to retain a broad appeal to a diverse range of analysts, commentators and publics, each of which may inhabit their own 'language games' and closed systems of meaning. The archetype view captures more readily the 'ideological' aspect implied by the existence of different sociotechnical constituencies (Molina 1990; Howells 1995) whose expectations of the new ICTs are constructed around a variety of mentalities, beliefs and discourses. The concern with discourse is reflected in recent work by Dutton and Guthrie (1991) who argues that the new ICTs are being shaped not according to the logic of a single 'game' or discourse but according to an *ecology of games* inhabited by a very wide range of policy-makers, analysts, commentators and publics. The more familiar notion of technological and organisational *artefacts*, derived from social constructivist approaches, can be combined with the epistemology perspective described above. An artefactual approach allows us to dispense with 'black-box' reified accounts of technology and focuses analysis on the underlying social processes and constructions which form such a vital element in the 'mutual shaping' of technologies and organisations (McLoughlin and Harris 1997; Williams 1997; MacKenzie 1992).

The archetype and artefact view can be usefully combined within an archetype/artefact dichotomy. Elements of this dichotomy are being played not just in the social construction of the virtual organisation, but also in the broader prospect of cyberspace, where 'new' information and commmuncations technologies are being shaped by the beliefs and social practices associated with an extremely broad range of constituents and language 'games'. These technologies appeal to a powerful symbolic logic whose 'real world' lines of development, although as yet unclear, can be expected to produce new sites of social action and engagement. This symbolic logic is well-understood by corporate players like BT and Microsoft who are demonstrably involved not just in the creation of technological artefacts, but also in the creation of meaning. These processes are what gives 'technology' its power to change our lives.

Notes

1 The technical characteristics of the new communication and information technologies (ICTs) exert a seductive influence on the minds of policy-makers and commentators. Twenty years of empirical work on information technology has produced some useful insights into the theoretical status that should be accorded to technology. A key aspect here is that technology provides a certain 'structure of opportunities' but does not in itself determine outcomes or provide ready made solutions to the manifold problems of organisation and control facing those directly concerned with production.

2 This would appear to be the case given recent European and North American policy statements. The European Commission, for example, predicts that the numbers of teleworkers will reach 10 million by the year 2000. The US labour market already contains an estimated 5.5 million teleworkers.

3 These authors also argue that further research will require a more sophisticated view of trust than has been deployed thus far.

4 The volume by McLoughlin and Harris (1997) contains a number of studies which explore the nature and extent of managerial choice and relates Child's concept of strategic choice to a number of issues in technology analysis (see for example Hill, *et al.* 1997). These authors also argue that proponents of the new paradigm misunderstand the nature of the 'productivity innovation dilemma' facing managers.

   Much of the earlier work on the process of technological change has highlighted the ways in which the controls exercised by managers are bound up with the question of strategic choice (Child 1972) – but it has been demonstrated that the question of strategic choice has recieved little or no serious theoretical treatment within models based on the assumption of a paradigm shift (McLoughlin and Harris 1997).

5 Quinn develops a comprehensive range of guidelines and tools for managing the 'productivity innovation dilemma'. Like the latter day proponents of virtuality he also focuses on the problem of maintaining alliances between contracting parties.

6 One problem is the general tendency for commentators to subsume entirely separate levels of analysis in their accounts of the 'virtual corporation'. Restructuring programmes have been driven by mergers and capacity reductions which have altered the shape of whole industries. 'Devolved' forms of managerial control exercised at the level of production may co-exist with increased size and concentration of capacity at the sectoral level. This has been the pattern in a diverse range of industries including electronic capital goods, defence, pharmaceuticals, banking and broadcasting. At this level, the concern has been very much with increased *integration*, rather than fragmentation. The study of corporate structure and innovation carried out by Hill *et al.* (1997) shows that firms have become more concerned with, for example, customer responsiveness, harnessing research and development activities more closely

to the marketing function, and with reducing costs. This study suggests that senior management was concerned not with disaggregation, but with integration. Western firms may be opting for a radical form of *structural* decentralisation which may nevertheless co-exist with cultural norms and allocative procedures which are in fact highly centralised.

7 Buchanan and Boddy, 1983, 1986; McLoughlin and Clark 1995; Child *et al.* 1987; Child and Smith 1987; Clark and Staunton 1989; Loveridge and Pitt 1990; Mansell 1994; McLoughlin and Harris 1997).

References

Barnatt, C. (1995) *Cyberbusiness: Mindsets for a Wired Age*, Chichester: John Wiley.

Barras, R. (1994) 'Interactive Innovation in Financial and Business Services: The Vanguard of the Service Revolution', in Rhodes, E. and Wield, D. (eds) *Implementing New Technologies*, Oxford: Blackwell/NCC.

Beninger, J.R. (1986) *The Control Revolution: Technological and Economic Origins of the Information Society*, Cambridge, MA and London: Harvard University Press.

Brigham, M. and Corbett, M. (1996) 'Trust and the Virtual Organisation: Handy Cyberias', in Jackson, P.J. and Van der Wielen, J. (eds) Proceedings of the Workshop *New International Perspectives on Telework: From Telecommuting to the Virtual Organisation*, London 31 July–2 August 1996, 2, Tilburg, The Netherlands: Tilburg University Press.

Buchanan, D.A. and Boddy, D. (1983) *Organizations in the Computer Age*, Aldershot: Gower.

—— (1986) *Managing New Technology*, Oxford: Gower.

Capelli, P. (1995) 'Rethinking Employment', *British Journal of Industrial Relations* 33, 4: 563–602.

Child, J. (1972) 'Organisation Structure, Environment and Performance: the Role of Strategic Choice', *Sociology* 6, 1: 1–22.

Child, J. and Smith, C. (1987) 'The context and process of organizational transformation – Cadbury Limited in its sector', *Journal of Management Studies* 24, 6.

Child, J., Ganter, H.D. and Keiser, A. (1987) 'Technological Innovation and Organizational Conservatism', in Pennings, J. and Buitendam, A. (eds) Technology as Organizational Innovation, Cambridge, MA: Ballinger.

Clark, K.B., Hayes, R.H. and Lorenz, C. (1985) *The Uneasy Alliance: Managing the Productivity-Innovation Dilemma*, Boston, MA: Harvard Business School Press.

Clark, P. and Staunton, N. (1989) *Innovation in Technology and Organization*, London: Routledge.

Clegg, S.R. (1990) *Modern Organisations*, London: Sage.

Coleman, J.S. (1988) 'Social Capital and the Creation of Human Capital', *American Journal of Sociology* 91, Supplement 395–3120.

Collingwood, R.G. (1961) *The Idea of History*, Oxford: Oxford University Press.

Coriat, B. (1991) 'Technical Flexibility and Mass Production', in Benko, G. and Dunford, M. *Industrial Change and Regional Development*, London: Belhaven.

Davidow, W.H. and Malone, M.S. (1992) *The Virtual Corporation*, London: Harper Business.

Dutton, W.H. and Guthrie, K. (1991) *An Ecology of Games: The Political Construction of Santa Monica's Public Electronic Network*, in Dutton, W.H. and Guthrie, K. (eds) *Information and and the Public Sector*, North Holland: Elsevier Science Publishers.

ESRC (1996) 'The Virtual Society', Research Programme Specification Document, October, ESRC: Swindon.

Fransman, M. (1990) *The Market and Beyond: Cooperation and Competition in Information Technology in the Japanese System*, Cambridge: Cambridge University Press.

Freeman, C., Sharp, M. and Walker, W. (1993) *Technology and the Future of Europe: Global Competition and the Environment in the 1990s*, London: Pinter.

Fukuyama, F. (1995) *Trust: The Social Virtues and the Creation of Prosperity*, New York: Free Press.

Gates, B. (1995) *The Road Ahead*, London: Viking-Penguin.

Granovetter, M. (1985) 'Economic Action and Social Stucture, the Problem of Embeddedness', *American Journal of Sociology* 91: 481–510.

Hammer, M. and Champy, J. (1993) *Reengineering the corporation*, New York: HarperCollins.

Handy, C. (1995) 'Trust and the Virtual Organization', *Harvard Business Review* May–June: 40–50.

Harvey, D. (1989) *The Condition of Postmodernity*, Oxford: Blackwell.

Hassard, J. (1993) 'Postmodernism and Organizational Analysis: An Overview', in Hassard J. and Parker, M. *Postmodernism and Organizations*, London: Sage.

Hassard, J. and Parker, M. (1993) *Postmodernism and Organizations*, London: Sage.

Hill, S., Harris, M. and Martin, R. (1997) 'Flexible Technologies, Markets and the Firm: Strategic Choices and FMS', in McLoughlin, I. and Harris, M. (eds) *Innovation, Organizational Change and Technology*, London: International Thompson Business Press.

Howells, J. (1995) 'A Socio-cognitive Approach to Innovation', *Research Policy* 24: 883–94.

Howells, J. and Hine, J. (1993) *Innovative Banking*, London: Routledge.

Hyman, R. (1992) '*Plus Ça Change*: The theory of Production and the Production of Theory', in Pollert, A. (ed.) *Farewell to Flexibility?* Oxford: Blackwell.

Jackson, P.J. (1996) 'The Virtual Society and the End of Organization: Feeling Our Way in the Dark', Keynote address to the World Wide Web Federal Consortium's Web Masters Workshop, Washington, DC, August.

—— (1997) 'Information Systems as Metaphor, Innovation and the 3 Rs of representation', in McLoughlin, I. and Harris, M. (eds) *Innovation, Organizational Change and Technology*, London: International Thomson Business Press.

Jackson, P.J. and Quinn, J.J (1996) 'Control in the Virtual Organisation', Paper presented to the Management Control Association, Sheffield, 24 May 1996.

Jones, B. (1990) 'New Production Technology and Work Roles: A Paradox of Flexibility Versus Strategic Control?', in Loveridge, R. and Pitt, M. (eds) *The Strategic Management of Technolgogical Innovation*, Chichester: John Wiley.

Kanter, R.M. (1989) *When Giants Learn to Dance*, London: Simon and Schuster.

—— (1991) 'The Future of Bureaucracy and Hierarchy in Organization Theory', in Bourdieu, P. and Coleman, J. (eds) *Social Theory for a Changing Society*, Boulder, Colorado: Westview.

Kumar, K. (1995) *From Post-Industrial to Postmodern Society*, Oxford: Blackwell.

Lash, S. and Urry, J. (1987) *The End of Organized Capitalism*, Oxford: Oxford University Press.

Loveridge, R. and Pitt, M. (1990) *The Strategic Management of Technological Change*, Chichester: John Wiley.

McGrath, P. and Houlihan, M. (1996) 'Conceptualizing Telework: Modern or Postmodern?', in Jackson, P. J. and Van der Wielen, J. (eds) Proceedings of the Workshop *New International Perspectives on Telework: From Telecommuting to the Virtual Organisation*, London, 31 July–2 August 1996, 2, Tilburg, The Netherlands: Tilburg University Press.

MacKenzie, D. (1992) 'Economic and Sociological Explanation of Technical Change', in Coombs, R., Saviotti, P. and Walsh, V. (eds) *Technological Change and Company Strategies*, London: Academic Press.

McLoughlin, I. and Clark, J. (1995) *Technological Change at Work*, Milton Keynes: Open University Press.

McLoughlin, I.P. and Harris, M. (eds) (1997) *Innovation, Organizational Change and Technology*, London: International Thomson Business Press.

Mansell, R. (1994) *Management of Information and Communication Technologies, Emerging Patterns of Control*, London: ASLIB.

Molina, A. (1990) 'Transputers and Transputer-Based Parallel Computers, Sociotechnical Constituencies and the Build-Up of British–European Capabilities in Information Technologies', *Reseach Policy* 19: 309–33.

Negroponte, N. (1995) *Being Digital*, London: Hodder and Stoughton.

Nolan, P. and O'Donnel, K. (1991) 'Restructuring and the Politics of Industrial Renewal, the Limits of Flexible Specialization', in Pollert, A. (ed.) *Farewell to Flexibility?* Oxford: Blackwell.

Ouchi, W.G. (1979) 'A Conceptual Framework for the Design of Organizational Control Mechanisms', *Management Science* 25, 9: 833–48.

Perin, C. (1991) 'The Moral Fabric of the Office: Panoptican Discourse and Schedule Flexibilities', *Research in the Sociology of Organizations* 8: 241–68.

—— (1996) 'Project Management Models as Social, Cultural and Cognitive Systems: Relating Paid and Unpaid Work Schedules', in Jackson P.J., and Van der Wielen, J. (eds) Proceedings of the Workshop *New International Perspectives on Telework: From Telecommuting to the Virtual Organisation*, London, 31 July–2 August 1996, 2, Tilburg, The Netherlands: Tilburg University Press.

Piore, M. and Sabel, C. (1984) *The Second Industrial Divide: Prospects for Prosperity*, New York: Basic Books.

Porter, M.E. (1980) *Competitive Strategy: Techniques for Analysing Industries and Competitors*, New York: The Free Press.

Quinn, J.B. (1992) *The Intelligent Enterprise*, New York, Basic Books.

Rhodes, E. and Wield, D. (eds) (1994) *Implementing New Technologies*, Oxford: Blackwell/NCC.

Sako, M. (1992) *Prices, Quality and Trust: Inter-firm Relations in Britain and Japan*, Cambridge: Cambridge University Press.

Slack, J.D. (1984) 'The Information Society as Ideology', *Media, Culture and Society* 6: 247–56.

Smith, C. (1991) 'From 1960s Automation to Flexible Specialization: a *Déjà Vu* of Techno logical Progress', in Pollert, A. (ed.) *Farewell to Flexibility?* Oxford: Blackwell.

Smith, M.R. and Marx, L. (eds) (1995) *Does Technology Drive History?*, Cambridge, MA: MIT Press.

Thompson, P. (1993) 'Postmodernism: Fatal Distraction', in Hassard, J. and Parker, M. (eds) *Postmodernism and Organization*, London: Sage.

Tomaney, J. (1994) 'A New Paradigm of Work Organization and Technology?', in Amin, A. (ed.) *A Post Fordist Reader*, Oxford: Blackwell.

Willcocks, L. and Grint, K. (1997) 'Re-Inventing the Organization? Towards a Critique of Business Process Re-Engineering', in McLoughlin, I. and Harris, M. *Innovation, Organizational Change and Technology*, London: International Thomson Business Press.

Williams, R. (1997) 'Universal Solutions or Local Contingencies? Tensions and Contradictions in the Mutual Shaping of Technology and Work Organization', in McLoughlin, I. and Harris, M. (1997) *Innovation, Organizational Change and Technology*, London: International Thomson Business Press.

Williamson, O.E. (1975) *Markets, Hierarchies and Trust*, New York: Free Press.

Womack, J.P., Jones, D.T. and Roos, D. (1990) *The Machine that Changed the World*, Oxford: Maxwell Macmillan International.

Part 2

UNDERSTANDING AND MANAGING BOUNDARIES IN TELEWORK

One of the most important recent developments in telework has been those conceptual and theoretical studies that have sought to provide a better illumination of temporal and spatial issues. Early accounts of telework illustrate some relatively naïve assumptions about these. Space was largely looked upon as, first, the 'physical distance' that had to be overcome in travelling (commuting) to work – where this took place in central workplaces – and, second, the 'container' – the walls, rooms, etc. – in which work took place. More recently, approaches have illuminated the fact that time-space structures do not act as passive backdrops to work and family life but are *constitutive* features of what goes on there. As such, the very experience and meaning of work draw heavily on the properties of the contexts involved. Because certain places (the home, the office, etc.) embrace particular sets of symbols and social relations, we need a more informed understanding of the psychological, social and cultural properties these create. This is essential if we are to understand the potential implications of innovations that alter the temporal and spatial structures of social systems.

This is the aim of Part 2 of this book. Drawing on studies undertaken in Austria, Canada, UK and Germany, the authors illustrate how individuals and families have sought to adapt to changes that reconstitute the boundaries between and within work relations and the home.

To introduce this, Martin Kompast and Ina Wagner set out a framework in Chapter 6 which highlights the way temporal, spatial and cultural boundaries are reshaped by innovations in telework. They argue that new temporal and spatial modes of organising demand new ways of managing boundaries between colleagues, clients and private life, and illustrate how the family network is drawn into work relations by teleworking. The authors also develop a gender perspective which illuminates in particular how temporal and spatial practices have traditionally influenced gender roles and lifestyles.

In Chapter 7, Kiran Mirchandani continues this line of analysis in terms of the way in which telework disrupts the divide between what we traditionally understand as the domains of 'work' (so far as it occurs in specially design workplaces) and those of so-called 'non-work' (i.e. the arena dedicated to leisure, the family or activities that are not 'real work'). By renegotiating this divide, Mirchandani shows how homeworkers reconstruct their very notions of 'work' and 'non-work' when social and spatial relations are reconstructed.

Leslie Haddon highlights further issues involved in home-based telework in Chapter 8. He describes the strategies people use to cope with the integration of activities within and outside the home. He focuses especially on the maintenance of boundaries between domestic and work roles. Since teleworking has consequences for the wider context of social relations, he argues that employees and employers have a joint responsibility for managing the demands that these present.

In the final chapter of Part 2, André Büssing explores some conceptual, empirical and theoretical links between teleworking and quality of life. This points to different ways by which we can evaluate the individual's expectations of and feelings towards the physical environment, work content and job security. Büssing examines the social tolerance of telework by looking at such factors as ecology, culture and the humanisation of work. The chapter discusses studies that examined the way in which telework allowed individuals to manage their time in ways that better integrated work, family and social relations. He also contrasts the benefits for quality of life that are achieved through homework with those obtained from collective, centre-based teleworking.

6

TELEWORK

Managing spatial, temporal and cultural boundaries

Martin Kompast and Ina Wagner

Introduction

The term telework covers a whole range of practices and social forms, from home-based work, to part-time commuting between multiple work sites, and mobile work. Each of these variants can be seen as corresponding to a set of connected or layered work spaces, some of them material and immediate, others distributed and virtual.

In this chapter we develop a conceptual framework which builds upon several notions:

- We make use of the notion of space, both as a geographical and a cultural category, for understanding work as grounded in the properties of places. We will try to understand what kind of workplaces are, e.g., a central office, the home, a client site; in which ways these places are structured, furnished, inhabited, designated for particular activities and actors (at the exclusion of others): and connected to other places.
- We also look at the relations between those places and time. Transitions between places often require actors to adapt to different temporal modes; to move, for example, from compressed, fragmented time to sequential, continuous time. Distance work and electronic connections between multiple workplaces change the notion of presence and availability.
- We develop a gender perspective which is informed by feminist theory and grounded in women's experiences of inhabiting/making transitions between places and temporal structures. We use this perspective as a source for criticism of dominant practices and as access to a greater variety of lifestyles.
- We analyse changes of work systems and organisational context as influencing the ways in which spatial, temporal and cultural boundaries are defined and managed, and this within a theoretical framework which is

inspired by research on computer-supported co-operative work (CSCW). Boundary crossings and connections require conscious effort, to actively reconstruct the relations between fragmented and disconnected places, and to build new and meaningful webs of connections. This may have far-reaching consequences for the ways in which people actively, flexibly and reflexively re-form, re-orient and re-combine their actions to fit the exigencies of the work as it unfolds.

The empirical basis of this chapter is a series of investigations into two international computer companies in Austria, TeleCorp and RegComp (Hergge *et al.* 1996; Kompast 1996).[1] Both projects were initiated by an alliance of managers (mainly middle management with some back-up from top executives) and shop stewards, with initial motivations focusing on a mixture of goals: to position themselves as pioneers of distance work arrangements as well as vendors of supporting technology, to officialise and learn from employees' experiences with 'unofficial teleworking', to explore new work systems, and (in the case of shop stewards) to exert control over emerging forms of work and translate the project experiences into a regulatory framework. All participants in the pilots volunteered. While TeleCorp management's attitudes to teleworking was ambivalent and they still hesitate to make more long-term, costly commitments, one of the results of the pilot project at RegComp was a 'tailored' organisational-technical support structure for teleworking employees.

The University was asked specifically to look into their work practices, into the ways that they bridged private and professional lives, into what kind of organisational and technical support was needed, and into the possibilities of developing a regulatory framework covering issues such as working time, ergonomics and security.

The theoretical perspective

The concept of place plays an important role in feminist theory. It helps focus on the specific properties of interaction spaces, their multiple visible and invisible closures, and on the dense, complex and multi-layered connections between people who are not necessarily co-present in space and time (Clement and Wagner 1995). Places are specific settings of interaction; they provide a context for social activities. We can describe places in spatial terms – their location, dimensionality, spatial qualities, their connections to other places and by the ways they are furnished. The ways in which places are 'designed' and inhabited provide a context for activities and social relations. This context can be described in terms of documents and the ways in which they are ordered and made accessible (bookshelves, archives, libraries, databases), of machines, of people, their skills, tasks and particular knowledges, of an organisational history and memory (as stored, for example, in documents and peoples' heads and externalised in the stories they tell).

Ethnographic studies have drawn attention to the relevance of context and to the artful and skilled practices of people that maintain orderliness and workflow (Star 1991; Suchman 1993). In fieldwork in the printing industry Bowers *et al.* (1995) point to some of the activities necessary for ensuring a smooth flow of work, such as prioritising incoming orders, anticipating regular, known-in-advance work, taking account of each other's work, and identifying and allocating interruptible work. Shapiro *et al.* (1997), in their study regarding the practice of landscape architecture, discuss some of the difficulties of making visual judgements that arise from spatial arrangements, arguing: 'One of the reasons behind the clumsiness of the situation is the need for more context. Not all of the montage is visible on the screen, making it necessary to scroll through it as the conversation develops. Moreover, there is a host of related material that is needed but not available' (1997). Both are examples of activities that require a shared sense of the work to be done, including the organisational context in which it takes place, the procedural context of the work as it unfolds, its content context (in the case of visualisations, for example, the context of what they represent and communicate), and the context of previous work. When work is spread out over multiple distributed work sites (each with their own materiality, temporality and embeddedness), close attention has to be paid to the notion of place, context and presence and their relevancy in the creation of 'orderliness' and of mutually aligned interaction (Auramäki *et al.* 1996).

We can see from the relation between place and context that places are not neutral. Haraway (1991) argues that they are places for 'something' (at the exclusion of other things), providing actors with a 'view from somewhere', a special vision. Dorothy Smith (1990) uses this insight in her approach to knowledge, emphasising the possibility to locate and identify positionings as a precondition of knowing. One of her key questions is: 'How does a knower, embodied and situated in a local and particular world, participate in creating a knowledge, transcending particular knowers and particular places?' (1990: 62). A particular 'script' can only be produced at a particular place. Conversely, making sense of distant knowledges (from which the subjects have disappeared) requires a place from where this distant knowledge is retrieved, taken into account, interpreted and acted upon. A place offers a chance to re-introduce subjectivity, it provides a specific vision from and against which knowledge can be examined and positioned in a process of 'siting and sequencing' (Probyn 1990: 184).

Places are connected, they reflect other places and times, and this in different ways, for example, being furnished with memories from those other places, having developed a common history, being situated in a view's distance from each other, being connected by people's migrations and transitions between them, and, more recently, by electronic mail or a shared screen for collaborative work. Some places have been established as enclosed sites, making access difficult and tied to privileges, but most of them are internally regionalised, subdivided into areas that have been designated to specific persons and activities. Issues of power can be addressed in spatial terms, in terms of inclusion, exclusion and confinement, unequal furnishings, and (lack of) connections to other places. In this perspective the relations of power and knowledge are understood as embodied and materialised in the 'material, social, and literary practices of discourse and representation, discipline and resistance' that are to be found in different places (Watson-Verran and Turnbull 1995: 117).

Feminist theorists stress the fundamental ambiguity of places – the struggle of being positioned in places that are not of one's own making and choice (and eventually denigrated as inferior) and the pleasures one may find in living and working there. Elspeth Probyn discusses the home as a locale which is built around women, 'a locale of their own design' (Probyn 1990: 181), which simultaneously reflects patterns of domination and provides women with space for positively negotiating and articulating their identities and relations.

Probyn (1990) also points to the connection of place and time as identifying relations between places, events and the knowledges produced. Also time has to be read 'from somewhere'. Spatial representations of time have a long tradition. They draw attention to the embeddedness of process in place. What is present is located somewhere, and a trajectory in time is often one that connects different places. Hägerstrand's vision of time-geographies offers a starting point for analysing these relations. He developed an ecological model of people's time-space routines which marks individuals' separate and intersecting paths and the domains they cover. His diagrams can be read as micro-topographies of daily life. Hägerstrand's diagrams are more than just a series of templates for tracing trajectories in time and space. What makes them interesting is that they seem to capture simultaneity and conjunctures that 'can easily escape linear language' (Pred 1984: 202). As Gregory argues, the diagrams point to the complex dialectic between presence and absence. What is present, is always mediated by what is absent, each temporal location 'elucidating the dense, complex and multi-layered connections between people who are not copresent in time and/or space' (Gregory 1994: 117). Biography (and, more generally, narrative) are instantiations of these connections in and of time and place.

Feminist theory points to the fact that women's experience of time is often contradictory and ambivalent. There is a conflict between availability (the willingness to 'fill in', when needed) both at work and at home, and setting time apart for oneself or a 'project' (regardless of ad hoc demands). This seems typical of many areas of women's work. We can see, for example, in nursing how computerised care plans interfere with a distinct quality of care which rests upon nurses' often ad hoc availability for comfort and sentimental work. When computerised care plans emphasise the focus on nurses' own pre-planned nursing projects and nurses are seen as setting apart time for specialised activities, irrespective of ad hoc demands, this emphasises the highly professionalised part of this work while neglecting some of its more spontaneous and emotional components (Wagner 1993). There are different temporal orders in different places. While time at work is allocated, measured and constrained, many activities at home (in particular being with children) ask for 'letting time pass' (Becker-Schmidt 1982).

Teleworkers do not only have to make transitions between multiple work sites; they also make extensive use of electronic spaces for communication and work. These spaces are different from the places we are familiar with (Wagner forthcoming). They open up a wide arena for dis-locating and re-embedding knowledges, for eradicating connections to persons and places, for disrupting and reassembling 'narratives' (such as a workflow, a project history, a client relationship). A wider range of temporal modes and horizons becomes available, from synchronous and co-present action to 'extended discourses' between distant locales. This also means that a potentially larger variety of temporal orders mesh and need to be aligned. In contrast to the accelerated but still continuous and step-by-step flow of activities which characterises mechanical regimes, there is a level of immediacy in computer-based action spaces which tends to collapse the interplay of presence and absence. We can for instance observe how computer-based networks change the temporal order in an architectural design office. In a traditional work environment a design is worked out sequentially, step-by-step, in distinct spatially extended places where discussion and overview require the physical movement of persons and plans (Wagner, forthcoming). Electronic space with its fluid time-space boundaries allows us to examine a design 'in the doing', and this by multiple actors from distributed places. As such, electronic media intensify and accentuate the modernistic gesture 'to *disrupt* narrative sequence, to *explode* temporal structure, and to accentuate *simultaneity*' (Gregory 1994: 216; italics in original).

Looking at time-space contextualities in this way allows us to examine the properties of different workplaces and to understand what happens when work becomes spatially and temporarily more distributed, and this not only from the point of view of the organisation but also of the individual who 'moves work' between places.

In particular this chapter will look at:

- issues of context – how telework interrupts context and how people manage to hold available, connect and manipulate various aspects of context;
- connections, closures and regionalisations and their implications for managing boundaries with colleagues, clients and private life, for connecting as well as for keeping places apart;
- practices of time management – how people cope with different temporal regimes, how they deal with issues of presence and accessibility;
- issues of co-operation (and power) – how people balance interdependencies, maintain access to resources, communicate effort and competence.

The cases

When collecting empirical evidence, our main aim was to make this dimension of people's work – the ways in which they actively, flexibly and reflexively re-form, re-orient and re-combine their actions to fit the exigencies of the work as it unfolds – more visible, and to understand how this is facilitated or made difficult by the organisational and technical furnishing of their multiple workplaces. In particular, we looked at the co-operative nature of participants' work, patterns of interdependent activities, practices of assigning tasks, distributing resources, maintaining reciprocal awareness, arriving at shared understandings, and the allocation of functionality between workers and the technologies they use.

The empirical material on which we base our analysis is a series of in-depth interviews with 41 teleworkers (26 from TeleCorp, 15 from RegComp). These teleworkers fall into four different categories:

1   highly qualified sales representatives who have to build and maintain stable relationships with selected business unit clients and co-ordinate the expertise necessary for tailoring and implementing a particular product;
2   systems engineers whose job mainly consists of configuring products, sometimes in co-operation with other companies with complementary interests;
3   service technicians whose work of necessity regularly takes them away from their offices;
4   administrative staff whose job it is to give back office support for several sales representatives.

In the majority of cases participants were interviewed at the beginning of the pilot (in their office), shortly after they had settled into a 'teleworking mode', and then again after a period of experience with teleworking. These later interviews were carried out in their homes and gave opportunity for observations of current practices, including practical demonstrations and simulations of some work processes, as well as interviews with family members. In addition, some interviews with managers and dependent, non-teleworking co-workers were carried out. For this chapter we selected the cases of six participants (two women and four men) to illustrate some of the diversity of contexts and practices associated with teleworking.

Organisational context and work design

Workers in both companies are placed in what we described earlier as performance-intensive settings (Clement and Wagner 1995). Although our firsthand experiences are in the computer sector, there are good reasons to assume that this reflects a more general trend (Quinn and Paquette 1990; Klein and Kraft 1994). These are organisations which expect their employees to develop a high level of self-reliance and self-organisation. As the company provides little support for managing tasks co-operatively, there is a large and unregulated 'market' for the negotiation of resources, co-operation and priorities which is not visible in common descriptions of business processes. People are used to developing and using their own network of support for coping with problems as they arise. The culture of self-organisation and self-reliance is reflected in trends such as output-oriented reward structures (employees are not primarily paid for the time they work but for the results they produce) and the deregulation of (formerly strict) working time arrangements.

Moreover, in service-oriented contexts, as much co-operative work takes place outside the company premises, for example, at a client site, so people have little shared time in the office. This strengthens their dependence on technical support systems such as computer networks and the variety of services provided through them. As much of the most important information is no longer provided by the co-inhabitants of people's offices but by spatially distant partners, people are used to consulting databases and electronic bulletin boards. Technologies are designed and introduced to support the parallel management of tasks at a distance. Protecting and drawing boundaries in such an environment is experienced as cutting oneself off from a multiplicity of only partially knowable and predictable resources.

From this perspective, telework is just an additional, 'logical' step towards spatially and temporally distributed forms of work. It promises further possibilities of reducing technical and organisational overhead costs through intensifying the use of employees' private resources (space, equipment, energy, etc.) on one hand, and through shifting much of the 'invisible' work of communicating, organising and maintaining onto their shoulders on the other hand. We can understand both companies' attempt at increasing their knowledge base for 'micro-managing' the use of skills, technical equipment and office space as part of this strategy. TeleCorp is about to develop a 'desk-sharing' program. While originally the prime motivation was to reduce the need for expensive office space, it is now connected to the idea of flexibly accommodating an increasing number of partially or temporarily employed people.

These trends are related to the notion of the 'flexible firm'. Telework serves as an umbrella for arrangements which increase management's 'flexibility over where and when people work' and at the same time helps to exert control over the regionally dispersed operations (Wagner 1994). This, Joan Greenbaum (1995) argues, 'has meant a shift from central workplaces to organisations that parcel work out to different companies, sub-contractors and individuals working from home'. TeleCorp has started a business re-engineering initiative aimed at defining tasks and procedures and assigning them to different locations.

In addition to this, RegComp pursues a strategy of 'presence in regionally distributed places'. These places (which are spread out all over Europe and managed by one central unit) are occupied by different actors – production centres, partner companies (who act as distributors of RegComp's products), major clients and regional sales representatives (whose job it is to bridge geographical distance by mediating between places and the interests and skills that inhabit them). Parcelling work out to distributed actors is related to a notion of presence as being 'mediated' by subcontractors and individuals who, although visibly connected to RegComp, also have their own local identity.

An additional feature of telework is its relation to a project-based organisation.

Employees in both companies are involved in a variety of projects to which they have to devote time, skill and effort, and this often in different roles and at different levels of intensity. Constance Perin (1996) describes a system of work in which employees experience a wide range of 'project density':

> Each project in its different phases makes different time demands, often according to different schedules. Each project puts employees into different spaces, real and virtual, at their division and section office, the offices they travel to, and at home.
>
> (Perin 1996)

This trend is reflected, for example, in the shifting profile of the sales representative, and this most markedly within RegComp. People whose job it was to sell the company's products developed a continuous service relationship with selected clients. Selling has become a project which requires initial consulting, co-ordinating expert support, providing training, and monitoring. While belonging to the 'core group' (those doing the 'real work') in one project, they might be part of the 'periphery' (contributing a small number of hours and limited expertise) of several other projects. Moreover, projects are tied into larger networks of alliances, partnerships and controlling bodies, representing different patterns of hierarchy and influence:

> Reference groups, steering committees, reviewers, and business unit clients, quality managers, and financial managers are 'satellites' to projects that can increase task congestions, numbers of electronically mediated interactions, and face-to-face meetings.
>
> (Perin 1996)

This strongly reflects the current trend towards 'business process re-engineering' (BPR):

> As part of the re-engineering process, job ladders are now being replaced by different sorts of 'broad banding', clumping jobs into bands that involve a wide range of presumably interchangeable skills and operational responsibilities.
>
> (Greenbaum 1995: 104)

Multiple perspectives

Workers' perspectives on teleworking reflect several basic trends. While some primarily seek to enhance their possibilities of moving flexibly between places, others seek to work longer stretches of uninterrupted time from their home. For a few, aligning work and private life was the main incentive. Some already were 'unofficial telecommuters', mobile workers and/or located in a regionally distant area. They perceived the pilot as an opportunity for officialising their status and improving their technical and organisational infrastructure. Among RegComp's regional sales representatives there were some who used the telework arrangement to move back into their home region (mostly to small villages in the countryside).

Case 1 (TeleCorp)

As part of the administrative support staff, Ms B. works for several sales people in her company. Her main task is the detailed preparation of offers, including price calculations, for a complex product. This requires her to collect technical data concerning the specifically tailored hardware configuration, to determine service charges, to calculate variants and to keep track of negotiated changes. All these activities are co-ordination intensive and, although there is good electronic support (electronic mail, access to various databases and tools), Ms B. is normally involved in ongoing, parallel negotiations with several sales people and has to sequence her tasks flexibly according to changing priorities. One of her prime motivations for working partly at home was the idea of being able to cut herself off from this quite demanding, stressful work environment. Although Ms B. works part time (28 hours), her workload is rarely under 35 hours. Teleworking is made difficult by a variety of technical problems, among them the lack of an ISDN connection which makes working on-line rather cumbersome, so that 'it is most efficient to work at 6 a.m. in the morning or after 10 p.m. in the evening'. Her colleagues find her limited availability when she works at home hard to accept (in particular if she switches off her phone and is only accessible through e-mail). As conflict over her as a 'resource' grew, her permission to participate in the pilot was withdrawn. Ms B. herself would like to extend the periods she works from her home because it leaves her more time for organising her own work.

Case 2 (TeleCorp)

Mr C. is Project Manager and responsible for large application development projects in the financial sector. About 70 per cent of his time is spent with his major client, an insurance company, where he has been given his own office space. The rest of his time he divides between his workplace in the central office and his home. Even before the pilot, Mr C. had started to build his own electronic work environment which would make him independent of place (and of the services of a central office). His main work site is his Thinkpad on which he has installed LAN-Distance Software and Lotus Notes as a project communication environment. He considers this environment very much as his own personal resource and a catastrophic breakdown some time ago cost him almost two months of hard work in re-installing all the software he needed. All relevant documents are stored in his Lotus Notes database, the propagation and communication of document changes is automated. Most of the project-related messages can be found in his two mailboxes (one at each work site) which have not yet been connected. Mr C. feels that direct communication is needed only when his team comes together to develop solutions to a complex problem. He has reorganised his work so that he can concentrate some of it in his home. His teleworking days are Tuesdays and Friday afternoons (plus all the extra time in the evenings and during the weekend). Mr C. installed an automatic time-recording system (Timetrac) on his Thinkpad which he uses to keep track of his own use of time.

Case 3 (TeleCorp)

Ms D. has been in the media as a showcase of a woman who uses technology for combining work with family responsibilities. She has a young child and has just returned from a period of part-time leave to a full-time job. As a marketing representative she was responsible for the acquisition of a major business contract. The detailed planning of this contract could be carried out individually and allowed her to spend some of her three-day/23-hours job at home (plus the unpaid extra time she voluntarily added). Electronic access to both the central office and her major customer is restricted to the host-based environment and this she experiences as workable but not ideal. While her main customer knows her private phone number and can reach her directly at home, all other contacts have up to now been mediated by one of her colleagues who received incoming calls and contacted her whenever he considered it necessary. Ms D.'s return to a full-time occupation has made fluent transition between work and child-care more difficult. While before she felt able to juggle competing demands, she now needs someone to look after her daughter on her teleworking day. Still, being present and sharing the way to kindergarten or the supermarket, for example, with her child, are important for Ms D. and she also considers them an opportunity for focusing on 'restful thinking'. Since longer periods of creative and concentrated work at home are potentially conflicting with her wish to give more attention to her child, she has a tendency to shift those periods to the late evenings.

Case 4 (TeleCorp)

Mr E. lives in a large apartment with his wife and five children. His work site at home is located in a corner of the spacious living room and packed with his laptop and lots of paper documents, a replica of his office. When he works at home, his wife's access to the telephone is limited. But otherwise his presence is not overwhelming. He hardly has time to join in the meals, and very occasionally babysits. Mr E. is currently involved in two projects in the banking sector and responsible for adapting his company's software to the hardware platform and has to do quite a bit of programming and testing. His main co-operation partner was partly transferred from Germany to the US. This is why synchronous communication is only possible in the evenings. At the same time, he has to give support to two geographically distant, smaller software companies and has to help them convert their software. Co-ordination of these multiple work sites is difficult, since their systems are only partially connected and compatible. Although project documentation is supported by Lotus Notes, document transfer from project partners to the central company server often takes up to a whole day. Mr E. can for example configure software from home, but can only test it at the local site. E-mail communication with project partners is not possible, because the local networks are not connected. Mr E. spends 2–3 days a week travelling between Vienna, Linz and Salzburg. One of his main complaints is that the modem connection from his hotel never works and he therefore has to drive to the local branch and ask his private contacts to let him send his messages to the Vienna office. When he arrives back home late at night, the first thing he does is to log onto the LAN and read his mail.

Case 5 (RegComp)

Mr F., a regional sales representative, is responsible for a large number of clients in the west of Austria. RegComp's management found the regional office space he shared with a service technician and a part-time secretary too costly and decided to install a teleworking arrangement for both men in their homes and move the secretary to the Vienna headquarters (where she at present gives distance support for several sales representatives). As neither man was ready to use his home environment for work, Mr F. privately arranged office space for himself on the premises of a company owned by a family member which RegComp agreed to pay for (and which the service technician then decided to use as well). This unofficial 'accidental' arrangement turned out to be quite efficient for both. Mr F.'s family connection makes it possible for him to use the daily support of his sister-in-law (a seamstress) in many small ways. She often delivers his mail or organises his office supplies. One problem is connected to the strict separation between the company's centralised dispatch system (the electronic work environment for service technicians) and Mr F.'s technical infrastructure. As the costs for both systems are accounted for by different organisational units, they are not allowed to share them. Also, Mr F. regrets the loss of local secretarial support which in his view is not replaccable by a distance arrangement.

Case 6 (RegComp)

Mr G. is a young service technician who used the telework pilot project to move back into his home region. He installed his office in a two-room apartment (which RegComp helped him to find and co-finances) from where he is electronically connected to the company's centralised dispatch system through which the distribution of already 'qualified' (diagnosed and prepared) work orders (and supplies of spare parts) and the reporting on completed work are organised. For emergencies the company has rented a small local storage room for spare parts. Service instructions and utilities can be supplied on CDs to clients. These arrangements make Mr G. quite independent from more personalised office support, particularly as his mobile phone allows him spontaneous access to some of his centrally located technician friends, whose advice he can ask. Mr G. built up these unofficial contacts during the period he worked as qualifier within the company's headquarters and recurrent short (two-week) periods in Vienna help him renew these acquaintances. One of Mr G's major complaints is that electronic connections to the company's headquarters are slow and do not permit access to the total electronic environment. He also feels insecure as to how his manager perceives his work from a distance and would appreciate more regular, formalised forms of reporting and feedback.

The properties of places – making connections and transitions

Places of work are not easily interchangeable. Each of the places we studied – the central office, the home, the location of clients and project partners – is a place for particular activities, and connections to other places are not always easily established on one hand, and not always desirable on the other.

The central office is the place where the main technical and organisational support structure is established and where one's internal co-operation partners, including managers, are present, at least part of the time. Teleworkers describe themselves as spatially embedded in a team or circle of colleagues, often in a large office space arrangement. This supports the kind of peripheral awareness (Heath and Luff 1992) of the activities of others which is valued as an important source of information and the opportunity for spontaneous informal contact. It also provides a rich contextuality for work only part of which is electronically stored and accessible. Context is established by the specific combinations of people's ongoing interactions, documents, artefacts and ecology present at particular times in particular locations. Communication is dense in this place. It is a place for *ad hoc* meetings as well as for pre-scheduled working sessions which are used for creating new ideas, solving a pending problem, or finalising a piece of work under pressure. The other side to this is the potentially continuous accessibility for others to make a request, intrude with a piece of information, look for support

How much these activities can be imported into the home does not only depend on the nature of a person's work but on his/her willingness to reorganise by setting apart activities that can be disembedded from the (co-operative) context. Among these separable activities are, for example, those which require high levels of concentration over a longer period of time, those which are of a 'closing-down' character (such as writing memos and notes, calculating proposals, preparing slides), or those which to a large extent are electronically supported. People who make their first move out of a central office environment find it much more difficult to make the (partial) transition to the home as a workplace than those who already are experienced at working independently and on their own (such as service technicians). Also, there is a difference between people who need technical support for a hectic existence between multiple work sites and those who hope for longer stretches of uninterrupted work at home.

Employees' experience of the home as a place of work varies considerably. A crucial difference is how much this place is set apart – separated physically, mentally, electronically – from places outside, as well as from the parts of one's home in which the life of significant others unfolds. Separation and/or connectedness can take on different forms. Some teleworkers want to be connected on-line, to have everything available at their fingertips. They tend to recreate their office environment at home, including paper documents and access to all electronically stored resources. There are of course limitations which are most acutely felt by RegComp's regional sales representatives, for example, the lack of meeting and demonstration facilities. Another interesting feature of the home as a work site is its potential invisibility. RegComp's policy is a strict centralisation of all client contacts. Regional sales representatives and service technicians are not allowed to let clients know their local phone number. The mediating of local presence is in conflict with employees' interest in being more directly accessible. The opposite can be observed in TeleCorp where some teleworkers want to be able to prevent clients from locating the place from where they work. Making one's location invisible can be an attempt at preserving a shelter from uninvited intrusions on the one hand, and at not upsetting conventional expectations of what makes a proper work environment on the other hand.

Common to most of our interviewees is the fact that sheer physical distance between home and office makes a difference. Physical proximity means that the working culture of the office (including the high level of pressure experienced there together with the expectation to be available) potentially reaches into the home. The further away one's home is from the office, the easier it becomes to establish a distinct working culture. The downside to this is the lack of contextual information which seems to be aggravated by physical distance. This is reflected, for example, in people feeling inhibited to approach a colleague with requests from a distance, not knowing how such a request will be received. One of the higher-level managers at TeleCorp is described as someone who uses his working time at home or on the road (where he seemingly has uninterrupted time to think about work to be done by others) to send out all sorts of e-mail messages with requests, assuming that his staff is available for responding immediately (and at the same time not responding timely to requests by his staff for help in a pending and urgent decision). In particular, regional sales representatives, during their frequent trips to RegComp's central location, consciously seek to benefit from the multiple shared information resources a densely populated work environment offers.

Another interesting feature is the regionalisation of the home as a place both for private life and work. This is were we can find the most obvious marks of gender. For almost all the men, although physically close to their family, work at home takes place within well-defined boundaries. When some men use the dining-room table as their preferred work site, this is not to invite children in, but to keep them at a distance, and this is the centre of some of the family's activities. In some cases, people use their home's basement for office space. Then it may happen that the family is not even aware of them being there. The home not only becomes visibly regionalised, but work then takes place in complete isolation (and often under ergonomically unacceptable conditions).Working at home does not mean a mixing of spheres; on the contrary, extra effort has to be made to keep them separate. Some fathers with young children, especially, have therefore decided not to participate in the telework pilot or withdrawn from it. They felt that extending the company's working culture into their homes created stress for their families and opted for a strict separation of incompatible roles (and places).

This may be different for women with young children (such as Ms D.) for whom teleworking offers the option of prolonged presence in the home. Although they too have to find a suitable place within the home for engaging in concentrated work, they seem to activate connections to other places in the home and the local environment much more frequently. These transitions, Ms D. argued, simultaneously add to the quality of her life (she is present when her daughter needs her, she uses short time-slots in between for doing small things with her) and heighten conflict between competing demands.

In addition to the central office and the home as work sites, many teleworkers have to visit their clients and some of them spend a considerable part of their working week there. These are clearly 'places of priority', where one should be most of the time, since this is where contracts are negotiated and settled and the main *raison d'être* is established. Our interviewees enter these places as visitors (in the particular role of a systems expert and/or vendor) and in some cases are assigned a temporary office. Depending on the particular arrangements, they find themselves in a position of power (as providers of expertise and resources) or dependency. Here physical distance is important. Distance not only increases the time spent travelling, for instance, for while a nearby client can easily be invited to the company's demonstration facilities, lack of local access to a place for displaying technically sophisticated equipment turns sales representatives from hosts into their clients' guests. Curiously, RegComp with its policy of 'mediated local presence' in regionally distributed work sites and partner companies does not systematically exploit the advantages of physical proximity. In many cases the location of its regional sales representatives and service technicians is only loosely connected to where their major clients are. Management from a distant centre seems to have priority over local anchors.

Practices of transition between these multiple places vary. Documents are either transferred electronically, carried as files in one's laptop, or printed out and stored in one's briefcase. Practices depend on a person's task, the quality of electronic connections and personal preferences. In particular, electronic connections to client sites are partial and unstable. In the majority of cases e-mail connections still do not exist, in some cases a shared local work space for a particular project has been built, but transfer and updating of documents is slow. The main technology for communication is still the telephone. In those cases in which the telephone has to be shared with the family, it is perceived as intrusive; work-related calls become mixed up with private calls, children have to be told not to pick up the phone when daddy works at home and friends told not to call at certain times of the day. A second telephone line helps disentangle both spheres. On the other hand, practices reflect the company's policy. In RegComp all major support (including telephone contact) is centralised. A good example is Mr F.'s secretary who moved from the small regional office to the company's head-quarters where her responsibilities were extended. She still knows some of Mr F.'s major clients, but in many cases local knowledge has not been built up or cannot be maintained. Support for distance work in these cases becomes, of necessity, impersonal.

A particular type of boundary transgression can be observed when family members start taking over jobs that normally would have been provided by the company. Examples are Mr A.'s wife who translates documents into English and Ms B.'s son who takes care of computer breakdowns. Mr F. has privately organ-ised his local office environment (for himself and a service technician) and uses his sister-in-law's daily support in many small ways. Related to these practices are fantasies of independence from the company's resources, e.g. Mr C. who has built his own electronic work environment. The spatial and temporal arrange-ment of work for some of RegComp's sales representatives, although they are on a regular payroll, already resembles that of a consultant or subcontractor.

Presence, availability and attuning temporal orders

The quality of time and time-management practices differ from place to place. The office is characterised by the continuous presence of others, a presence which can be both helpful and intrusive. Events tend to 'roll over you' and there is a culture of marking things as urgent in order to get attention. Respondents complain about the nearly total lack of time autonomy. They feel that only part of their working day is free (from meetings, *ad hoc* calls and requests, the need to jump into the car for a spontaneous client visit) for doing things in one's preferred temporal order. The pattern that emerges is one of work which is largely carried out individually and sequentially and is distributed, but with frequent need for alignments (e.g. handing over documents to others, synchronous co-operative work in team sessions). The examples point to an increasing compression of time and there is some evidence of a shift from sequential work flows to a technology-supported, more simultaneous and parallel order of activities and functions. High workloads and a culture of immediacy make it difficult for all employees (with the exception of RegComp's regional sales representatives and service technicians) to establish regular patterns of teleworking which would allow them to, for example, work for several days from home. In particular, within TeleCorp home-based work is often restricted to 'border times' such as mornings and evenings or the weekend (and even vacation time).

Time at home is perceived as sequential and uninterrupted. The need for an immediate response to work-related demands is clearly diminished. Time at home is also characterised as 'buffer time', as providing the opportunity to clear an unfinished job. In particular, evenings (when children are in bed) are described as times for undisturbed (and therefore 'efficient') work. However, the flow of work can come to an halt, when at some point the input of another person would be needed to be able to continue. This, together with technical transmission problems, makes working time at home potentially less fluent (e.g. Ms B. found that she would need detailed checklists of unfinished items if she worked on particular tasks at home). While this seems to be a major problem for TeleCorp's employees, most of whom have made their first step out of the central office environment, RegComp's mobile, regional workforce have already adjusted to a more self-contained mode of arranging their work.

Many perceived problems of time management relate to presence and, associated with it, accessibility and availability. Some people contrast the constant demands on their *ad hoc* availability in the central office environment with their limited accessibility when working at home (although there is a permanent telephone connection). This 'in-office "absence" or mobility is a chronic condition of managers and employees alike' and 'secretaries and administrative staff report difficulty in locating them [in-office staff] sometimes' (Perin 1996). Within TeleCorp, absence connected with telework arouses distrust (less so of management than of one's colleagues). This is reflected in the difficulties of teleworking employees to flexibilise the boundaries between private and work activities. Instead of making use of the opportunities for more fluent transitions between both spheres, they tend to reproduce traditional temporal patterns of work when at home. Also, when teleworking, their presence at last-minute meetings cannot be guaranteed. Ms B. describes an incident when she jumped into the car to drive to an urgent meeting and this turned out to be less urgent than it had appeared.

High project densities and a culture of immediacy aggravate problems of presence and availability. In particular, in (gendered) power relationships, presence is not always substitutable by electronic accessibility. People tend to expect the continuous visible presence of others. This creates particular problems for the administrative staff among the telecommuters who are expected to act as a continuous back-up system to others whose work practices have a high level of immediacy and reactivity. Ms B. is in such a position and looked at telework as a possibility of temporarily retreating from *ad hoc* demands. During her telework days she made deliberate use of her limited availability when at home for serialising tasks her colleagues expected her to focus on in parallel (to the extent that she did not respond immediately to phone-calls and e-mail messages). Her case exemplifies the differences of work cultures, between an overly hectic, communication-dense environment with little respect for people's private arrangements, and one which draws much firmer spatial, temporal and social boundaries around individual workplaces.

Related to this is the handling of temporal conflict. In the home, different temporal modes meet – the rhythm of work (which has been carried over from one's office environment), the temporal order of the home (which may vary considerably during the day), and the times which are dominated by the technicalities of networking. Flexible adjustments between these orders are not only made difficult by technological insufficiencies. The possibility for such adjustments also depends on power relationships, e.g. the boss who calls for an urgent meeting, a client whose request intrudes upon the weekend, or the ability to impose one's own time regime on the family (e.g. Mr E. who first reads his e-mail when he comes home late at night). As a result, work and the temporal modes connected with it, start to pervade the private sphere.

Absence from the office also restricts managers' access to people's work. How to make visible to managers that time at home has in fact been spent working seems only part of the problem. Managers' practices of assessing work are often tacit and intuitive, based on a (potentially misleading) feeling for persons and context. As distance restricts implicit contextual information, managers at Reg-Comp argue, negative aspects such as a client's complaint or the failure to meet a deadline come to the foreground and are more (and in some cases disproportionally) relevant in assessing people's work.

A final and related point is that of practices of regulating and documenting working time at home. While in both companies the men use teleworking for working longer hours (and this partly in a more convenient environment) and making more efficient use of 'buffer time' at home, the women tend to use it for accommodating work to their family responsibilities (less time for commuting, more opportunity for fluent transitions between work and family). One major problem of timing work at home is that external temporal patterns (although partly internalised) are missing or become weaker with increasing (spatial and temporal) distance. In particular, the starting and end points become blurred and, as a consequence, work assumes a dominant presence. There are some attempts at documenting working time (mainly to satisfy legal requirements) but not all work related activities are accounted for. Either people do not want to face the fact that they work too much or they already know that their overtime exceeds legally defined limits. Private life and work being spatially close makes it more difficult to regulate the dominant temporality of an unfinished job or urgent request.

Empirical evidence does not support the assumption that teleworking gives people more freedom and autonomy in bridging private and professional lives; on the contrary, 'the private sphere seems to be increasingly dominated by the exigencies and logic of work, but this in ways that are partially "masked" and not transparent, leaving the illusion of autonomy, flexibility and individual option open' (Hergge et al. 1996: 30).

Separating and inter-connecting communication spaces

In this chapter we ask how our findings about places, temporal orders and boundaries can be used for developing an appropriate organisational and technical environment. We found different patterns of work systems at TeleCorp and RegComp that need to be accounted for. These can be located on a continuum, with work practices embedded in and nourished by a rich context based on presence at one end, and a more self-contained and only partially connected environment at the other end. Work at TeleCorp resembles more the former. It is mainly project based. Although much of it is carried out individually, sequentially and distributed among multiple actors and work sites, at the same time it is embedded into a communication-dense environment, vulnerable to frequent interruptions and interspersed with episodes of intense synchronous co-operative work in small teams. This reflects a culture of work which is performance intensive and highly 'reactive' and a nature of tasks for which solutions often are not a 'a simple one-to-one relation, but a fuzzy complex of many-to-many relations. In such situations, it is not surprising that discussion, experience and intuition are valued' (Auramäki *et al.* 1996). Such an environment presents people with difficulties over and above those of establishing more regular patterns of working at home. Maintaining a smooth flow of work when at home becomes a major problem, both in terms of coping with high project densities (and therefore communication requirements) and of accessing the 'market' of informal resources needed. Employees at RegComp experience the reverse problem. Having already established more independent patterns of work, they have to invest in building informal (local and distant) networks of support.

Individual needs and preferences add to this diversity. While some people want to carry their fully equipped office with them and there is no longer a distinct place and time for everything, others want to disrupt continuity and to preserve the distinct quality of different work sites. Those who engage in highly communicative and mobile forms of working are less dependent on immediate and reliable electronic access to a complete work environment than those who continuously use a great variety of electronic documents stored in different networks. Needs such as setting time apart and disconnecting places, or being continuously available and having immediate access, cannot be satisfied by one and the same organisational-technical solution.

Both companies have reacted in different ways to this diversity. At TeleCorp, although initiated from the top, the pilot project was not systematically used for framing a consistent technical-organisational umbrella. This is visible in a variety of experimental, partly individually tailored solutions, with the result that not all participants have access to the same electronic and communicative environment. From the start, however, RegComp provided all participants with a homogenous electronic environment and a highly centralised support structure.

Among the potentially useful technology for supporting distance work are:

- file-sharing tools that support transmitting and working on shared documents;
- screen-sharing tools with audio/video function that support synchronous co-operative work;
- time and project management tools that support accessibility and give an overview of the current state of work;
- newsgroups and electronic talk tools that support the informal sharing of information and resources;
- security tools, filter and translation assistants which support the selected access and integration of external partners into the company's electronic environment.

Although many of these tools exist, not all of them have yet been made generally available and integrated. While access to and the handing over of shared artefacts seems quite well supported in both companies, project management activities such as scheduling and distributing work (with the exception of Reg-Comp's dispatch system) are still difficult to cope with when at home. Even more problematic is the handling of those *ad hoc* requests and urgencies at a distance which not only require an intensive exchange but some shared feeling for the situation. Working from home is potentially less fluent since the nature of these demands is their unpredictability. Communication in general is made difficult by the lack of ISDN connections (which makes working on-line extremely vulnerable to interruptions) and by the lack of connections between messaging systems. Certain software solutions that people have built up locally (such as a Lotus Notes project environment within TeleCorp) and find immensely useful, turn out to be restrictive as soon as they need to make transitions and connections.

The telephone remains the major communication medium when people work from home. These connections (including fax) need to be improved so that the handling of incoming calls is optimised. Practices vary and at TeleCorp employees can regulate telephone contacts pretty much at their discretion. Some choose to be directly accessible to those who dial their office phone number (and appreciate the fact that the caller cannot identify the place from which they speak), others prefer the mediation of a central switchboard, make frequent use of their voice box, or ask their secretary or a colleague to act as intermediaries. Most prefer to have one single phone number for all phone contacts, and only some have regionalised their phone connections depending on who calls and where they are. At RegComp there is only one centralised solution available and the company insists on this single entry point (at the exclusion of individual external lines). However, while the internal distribution of incoming calls, including their referral to people's homes is well supported, it is not possible to refer a call back from the home (when the line is occupied or no one answers) to the internal net of the company. This will require building (preferably individually programmable) connections between the internal net (which forms an end node) and outside (home) nodes.

Although electronic environments provide the possibility of immediate contact, there is always the option of closing this point of entry into one's private work environment (e.g. not reading e-mail). A lot of conflict revolves around these issues of presence and accessibility in cases of *ad hoc* demands (whose acuteness is difficult to assess, particularly from a distance). This is aggravated by the fact that working from home is vulnerable to suspicion. Some of this could be helped by providing a simple response function which tells outside callers if and for how long a person is 'out'. Interestingly, this will erase some of the distinct qualities of the home as a work site by introducing more formalised and businesslike ways of solving the 'problem of managing and balancing social and work calls, and of creating understandings, for example, about when they [the teleworking women] were more easily accessible for both purposes' (Haddon 1996).

One of our central observations is that, contrary to the wish of some to preserve private communication spaces, electronic support for teleworking favours centralised technical solutions in the form of a central entry point into the totality of a company's electronic environment. Two different examples illustrate this point. RegComp has backed up its regionalisation strategy by developing a centralised dispatch system. Service technicians such as Mr G. are tied in multiple ways into this system. Work orders are 'qualified' (that means diagnosed, and an appropriate solution suggested) in the central office and distributed from there. Mr G. connects his laptop via Datex P to the central server and prints out his order forms on which he reports on work completed when he returns from his client visits. Spare parts are regularly dispatched to his regional base where he has hired a small storage room. RegComp's service technicians do not have access to the company's total electronic environment (and feel excluded for this reason). Also, the organisational support of RegComp's regional sales representative has been centralised, with one centrally located, specific support group responsible for case handling. In this case the central filtering of interactions between distributed employees is given priority over the possible advantages of more intimate local knowledge of particular clients (which, for example, a locally situated secretary might accumulate).

In TeleCorp the spatial distribution of work over multiple sites makes the disadvantages of individualised PC-based LANs much more acutely felt; and this not only from the perspective of management but also from one's co-workers. For example, this system makes connecting different document systems difficult and means that individual discipline in updating and maintenance has to be high. When employees use their laptop as their main working tool, where they store their own work documents, this results in a highly regionalised communication space which is no longer routinely updated and accessible from everywhere. When in addition these employees are frequently absent from the central office, informal *ad hoc* arrangements are no longer sufficient for creating shared and timely attuned electronic spaces. In one of the two pilot units this resulted in pressure to install a central server within the local PC network (with its comfortable software) which offered the advantage of making accessible and visible to all others regularly updated versions of the work of those absent.

Conclusions

In her account of a woman teleworker in rural Norway who runs her own business from her kitchen table, Ann-Jorunn Berg (1996) uses the cyborg metaphor (Haraway 1991) for explaining how 'technology becomes the glue that keeps various aspects of her life together'. She claims that technology has become a natural part of her environment and her activities. Similarly, it can be argued that the electronic work environments described above become an integral part of the multiple work sites that they connect and partially transform, thereby erasing some of their distinctness.

Still, the amalgams of persons and machines we found at different places are far from harmoniously aligned, as we can see from the numerous instances of people refusing to have their homes totally invaded by work-related realities, and those of people who fight for a smooth, noiseless integration. Also, temporal-spatial arrangements clearly reflect power relations. We saw this in the example of administrative staff who have to flexibly adapt to changing conditions and demands and whose physical absence from the central office is not accepted; or of men who impose their working presence on their families. We also found symbolic the aspects of gender in the attempts to find a place and time for everything.

Our main observations can be summarised as follows:

- As places are not interchangeable and electronic networks can only partially replace context (as provided by the specific combinations of people's ongoing interactions, documents, artefacts and ecology present at particular times in particular places), teleworking arrangements support work systems that minimise the need for *ad hoc* co-operations and alignments. At the same time, certain aspects of work (in particular the many support functions which help maintain a smooth flow of work) are 'privatised' and made invisible.
- The corresponding organisational form is a regionally distributed network of business units managed from central headquarters, with teleworkers acting in consultant or subcontractor roles, with a focus on mediating between places and the skills and interests that inhabit them.
- This spatial and temporal distribution of work and people increases the tendency towards providing a central entry point to the company's internal electronic and communication environments (including telephone connections). Central filtering of teleworkers' work and of their interactions with clients is given priority over the possible advantages of local accessibility and knowledge. This also reflects some of the control dilemmas that arise when the possibilities for 'tacit monitoring' offered by co-presence and a rich context are diminished and communications as well as documents have to be handled at a distance.

- The spatial proximity of work and private life does not 'automatically' facilitate fluent transitions between both spheres. The dominant temporality of work is carried into the home and extra effort has to be made to establish and maintain boundaries.

- Working at home is individualised and hard to fit into traditional regulatory frameworks. Among the most pressing problems are: establishing stable temporal work patterns, regulating accessibility and preserving the continuity of informal relationships, making one's work visible and accountable, establishing 'good' practices of documenting, updating, and sharing. While some of this can be supported by a rich (and tailorable) electronic information and communication environment, there is also a need for developing practices of articulation and alignment which take account of distance and limited presence.

Notes

1 The study at TeleCorp was carried out by a team of researchers affiliated with the Abteilung für CSCW.

References

Auramäki, E., Robinson, M., Aaltonen, A., Kovalainen, M., Liinamaa, A. and Tuuna-Väiska, T. (1996) 'Paperwork at 78 k.p.h', *Proceedings CSCW'96*.

Becker-Schmidt, R. (1982) 'Lebenserfahrung und Fabrikarbeit: Psychosoziale Bedeutungsdimensionen Industrieller Tätigkeit', *Kölner Zeitschrift für Soziologie und Sozialpsychologie*, Special Issue 24: 297–312.

Berg, A.-J. (1996) 'Karoline and the Cyborgs: The Naturalisation of a Technical Object', Paper presented at the COST A4 and GRANITE Workshop *The Shaping of Gender and Information Technology in Everyday Life*, Amsterdam.

Bowers, J., Button, G. and Sharrock, W. (1995) 'Workflow from Within and Without: Technology and Cooperative Work', in H. Marmolin, Y. Sundblad and K. Schmidt (eds) *Proceedings of the Fourth European Conference on Computer-Supported Cooperative Work ECSCW'95*, Dordrecht: Kluwer Academic Publishers: 51–66.

Clement, A. and Wagner, I. (1995) 'Fragmented Exchange. Disarticulation and the Need for Regionalised Communication Spaces', in H. Marmolin, Y. Sundblad and K. Schmidt (eds) *Proceedings of the Fourth European Conference on Computer-Supported Cooperative Work ECSCW'95*, Dordrecht: Kluwer Academic Publishers: 33–49.

Greenbaum, J. (1995) *Windows on the Workplace. Computers, Jobs, and the Organization of Office Work in the Late 20th Century*, New York: Monthly Review Press.

Gregory, D. (1994) *Geographical Imaginations*, Cambridge, MA: Blackwell.

Haddon, L. (1996) 'The Dynamics of Information and Communication Technologies and Gender', Paper presented at the COST A4 and GRANITE Workshop *The Shaping of Gender and Information Technology in Everyday Life*, Amsterdam.

Hägerstrand, T. (1975) 'Space, Time and Human Condition', in A. Karlqvist (ed.) *Dynamic Allocation of Urban Space*, Farnborough: Saxon House.

Haraway, D. (1991) *Siminas, Cyborgs, and Women*, New York: Routledge.

Heath, C. and Luff, P. (1992) 'Collaboration and Control. Crisis Management and Multimedia Technology in London Underground Control Rooms', *Computer Supported Cooperative Work. An International Journal* 1, 2: 69–94.

Hergge, R., Kolm, P., Kompast, M., Steinhardt, G. and Wagner, I. (1996) 'Alternierende Telearbeit bei IBM', Forschungsbericht zu einem Pilotversuch 'Alternating Telework at IBM', Research Paper of a Pilot Study, Wien.

Hirschhorn, L. and Farquhar, K. (1985) 'Productivity, Technology and the Decline of the Autonomous Professional', *Office Technology and People* 2: 245–65.

Klein, H.K. and Kraft, P. (1994) 'Social Control and Social Contract in Networking. Total Quality Management and the Control of Work in the United States', *Computer Supported Cooperative Work. An International Journal* 2, 1–2: 89–108.

Kompast, M. (1996) 'Working From Home' und 'Telework bei HP Austria', Zwischenbericht zu einem Pilotversuch, Institut für Gestaltungs- und Wirkungsforschung der TU, Wien.

Perin, C. (1996) *The Part-Week Telecommuting Option in Telia Research and its Organizational and Managerial Implications*, unpublished Project Report.

Pred, A. (1984) 'Place as historically contingent process: structuration theory and the time-geography of becoming places', *Annals of the Association of American Geographers* 74: 279–97.

Probyn, E. (1990) 'Travels in the Postmodern: Making Sense of the Local', in L.J. Nicolson (ed.) *Feminism/Postmodernism*, New York: Routledge.

Quinn, J.B. and Paquette, P.C. (1990) 'Technology in Services. Creating Organizational Revolutions', *Sloan Management Review*,Winter: 67–78.

Shapiro, D., Mogensen, P. and Büscher, M. (1997) 'Lancaster Landscape Architecture Design Scenarios', in I. Wagner (ed.) *DESARTE First Phase Project Overview*, Technische Universität Wien.

Smith, D.E. (1990) 'The Social Organisation of Textual Reality', in D.E. Smith (ed.) *The Conceptual Properties of Power. A Feminist Sociology of Knowledge*, Boston: Northeastern University Press.

Star, S.L. (1991) 'Invisible Work and Silenced Dialogues in Knowledge Representation', in I. Eriksson, B. Kitchenham and K. Tijdens (eds) *Women, Work and Computerization*, Amsterdam: North Holland.

Suchman, L. (1993) 'Do Categories Have Politics? The Language/Action Perspective Reconsidered', in G. De Michelis, C. Simone and K. Schmidt (eds) *Proceedings of the Third European Conference on Computer-Supported Cooperative Work ECSCW'93*, Dordrecht: Kluwer Academic Publishers: 1–14.

Wagner, I. (1993) 'Women's Voice, The Case of Nursing Information Systems', *AI and Society* 7, 4: 295–310.

—— (1994) 'Networking Actors and Organisations', *Computer Supported Cooperative Work. An International Journal* 2, 1–2: 5–20.

—— (forthcoming) 'Boundary Confusions and Embeddings: Aesthetic Production in Electronic Terrains', Paper for the ENACT Workshop in Hamburg, 21–23 August 1996.

Watson-Verran, H. and Turnbull, D. (1995) 'Knowledge Systems as Assemblages of Local Knowledge', in S. Jasanoff, G.E. Markle, J.C. Petersen and T. Pinch (eds) *Handbook of Science and Technology Studies*, London: Sage.

7

NO LONGER A STRUGGLE?

Teleworkers' reconstruction of the work–non-work boundary

Kiran Mirchandani

Introduction

This chapter focuses on professional home-based telework. Qualitative interviews were conducted with women and men working at home in Canada. I begin with a brief overview of telework within the Canadian context, and of the methodology followed for this study. The chapter then focuses on the ways in which teleworkers organise their paid work activities within the home. By working at home these workers disrupt the boundary between 'work' and 'non-work' which is conventionally constructed as a physical distinction between workplace and home. Teleworkers stress the inaccuracy of the assumption that the workplace is the domain of 'work', while the home is the domain of 'non-work'. They develop extremely efficient ways of working within the home, and refer to what they do as 'real work'. Teleworkers plan their work to a great degree and measure their work through outcomes. In this way, they define 'real work' in terms of planning and measurement, rather than in terms of location. They argue that many of the activities that are currently paid for in the office setting (such as informal interactions) are in fact 'non-work'. In addition, the office environment (part of the 'public sphere' which is associated with 'work') is constructed as a less appropriate environment for effective 'real work' compared to the private sphere of the home.

This reconstruction of the work–nonwork boundary (in terms of planning and measurement rather than location) has significant gender implications, primarily because women continue to assume most of the responsibility for so-called 'non-work' activities such as child-care and housework. It would seem that teleworkers are well placed to recognise that just as the workplace is not always a domain of work, the home is frequently not a domain of 'non-work;' the relabelling of home-based domestic responsibilities as more than 'non-work' would allow for the recognition of the importance of these activities. While teleworkers plan and measure their household activities in ways similar to their paid work they do *not*, surprisingly, move towards the definition of these activities as work. They often parallel their domestic work and child-care to the 'breaks' that are taken within the office environment. While both female and male teleworkers are involved in housework and child-care, I argue that they are wary of defining these activities as work primarily because they continue to be located within organisational cultures within which any concern for their families would effectively de-legitimise their paid work. Future policy on telework should, accordingly, situate the work arrangement within the cultures of organisations, rather than assuming that by working at home employees will automatically be able to reduce the conflict between their work and family responsibilities.

Telework in the Canadian context

According to the 1991 Census, 1.1 million members of the employed labour force in Canada work at home. This constitutes eight per cent of the workforce and includes farm workers, self-employer entrepreneurs, pieceworkers and home-based salaried professionals (Siroonian 1993: 16). The 'Survey of Work Arrangements' (Statistics Canada 1991) attempted to measure the number of wage and salary workers at home (self employed and farm workers were excluded). It revealed that 600,000 employees work some or all of their scheduled hours at home. This represents six per cent of the total number of salaried workers in Canada. It should be noted, however, that this estimate includes overtime work at home (that is, individuals who work a full office-based week and do additional work at home) (Siroonian 1993: 50). Another study, the 1991 Gallup poll showed that twenty-three per cent (or 2 million) of the Canadian working population work at home. Out of these, three per cent (or 260,000) are salaried employees who spend part or all of their workdays at home in lieu of a traditional office (Orser and Foster 1992: 70).

It can be seen that national data collection agencies often adopt different definitions of telework. As a result, not only is the Canadian data on telework dated, but it is also not comparable, allowing for little verification through replication. Indeed, more effective information on telework can be discerned from small-scale case studies (Tippin 1994; Tessier and Lapointe 1994; Mirchandani 1996) even though these case studies do not allow for the computation of national estimates of the numbers of teleworkers in Canada. Information on telework in Canada has also been exchanged at conferences such as 'Towards the Virtual Organisation: Implications for Social and Organisational Change' (1994) and 'Telework '94' (1994). These conferences suggest that the debate on telework in Canada differs from that in the United States in that it is not as strongly situated within issues such as energy conservation, transportation difficulties or pollution. Rather, telework in Canada is often considered in the context of the global restructuring of the economy; as such, the concerns of organised labour unions which point to the potential for telework to lead to work intensification, lower employee protection and greater health and safety hazards are often included in discussions of telework.

Methodology for present study

Open-ended qualitative interviews were conducted in 1993 and 1994 with thirty female and twenty male teleworkers in Ontario and Quebec. Two strategies were used to generate the sample of teleworkers. First, 'criteria sampling' was used where individuals who met certain predetermined criteria were included in the sample (Patton 1990: 176; Miles and Huberman 1994: 28). The use of criteria sampling served to ensure that similar manifestations of the phenomena were being compared. The teleworkers interviewed were all salaried employees and did professional or managerial work at home in lieu of, rather than in addition to, office-based work. These individuals moved from working in an office to working at home without any corresponding change in their job functions or employment contracts. Some continued to work in an office part of the week, while others who were completely home based had worked in an office in the past. This allowed respondents to compare their experiences of working at home and working at a central office. The fact that teleworkers worked in occupations where most of their colleagues continued to be office based also allowed them to reflect upon the effects on their work of their physical remoteness from the central work site.

To generate a heterogeneous set of individuals who met these criteria, a 'snowball sampling' method was used (Patton 1990: 176). In order to initiate the snowball, I contacted individuals in companies that I knew had telework programmes, as well as distributing flyers to friends and colleagues about my search for teleworkers. I also placed advertisements in newspapers and magazines. Interviews were conducted in Ottawa, Montreal and Toronto. Interviews were taped and transcribed verbatim. A qualitative analysis programme (The Ethnograph) was used to assist in the data analysis.

While all individuals in the sample met the criteria discussed above, there are several important differences within the sample. Teleworkers interviewed worked within a wide variety of organisations (one-third in the public sector and two-thirds in the private sector). Individuals from eighteen different organisations were interviewed. Teleworkers in the present sample were clustered in four main occupational categories – Management (Business Managers, Project Managers); Business, Finance and Administration (Auditors, Researchers); Natural and Applied Sciences (Computer Programmers, Systems Analysts); and Sales and Service (Marketing Representatives, Sales Representatives). More women were in Business, Finance and Administration occupations while more men were in Managerial and/or Natural and Applied Science occupations. Across the occupational and demographic diversity within the sample, however, trends can be identified in the ways in which teleworking women and men define and organise their work and non-work activities. These trends are the focus of this chapter.

It should be noted that the individuals in the present study differ on many important race and class dimensions from 'homeworkers' (or pieceworkers) and the experiences of working at home reported in this chapter are not generalisable to this latter group of workers.

The boundary between work and non-work

Ronco and Peattie argue that 'much of what we see as . . . work has to do with drawing boundaries' (1983: 10). Only by contrasting 'working' with other activities such as 'fooling around', 'being unemployed' or 'participating in a hobby' does the concept of 'work' have meaning (Ronco and Peattie 1983: 12).

The concept of work is most frequently understood in contemporary Western society in terms of two overlapping boundaries: payment and location. As Daniels notes, in modern industrialised society, 'the most common understanding of the essential characteristic of work is that it is something for which we get paid' (Daniels 1987: 403; Dunnette 1973: 1). The association between work and economic remuneration is accompanied by the construction of the public sphere as a domain of production, where one *is paid* for work, and the private sphere as a domain of consumption, where one *pays for* food, clothing and shelter (Lozano 1989: 104; Mirchandani 1996).

Feminist theorists have focused on the ways in which this definition of 'work' is fundamentally gendered. They critique the gender blindness of the association of work with the public sphere, stressing that the construction of the private domain as a sphere of leisure represents the male experience of the home. This construction fails to reveal the ways in which the home can be a site of work for many women. As Mackenzie notes, 'work in the home, the place associated with leisure, is not seen as real work' (1986: 88; Rose 1993; Massey 1991). Feminist theorists also focus on the fact that much of women's domestic work in the private sphere in fact plays an integral role in supporting 'paid work' activities. As Luxton notes, domestic work is 'indispensable labour that converts the wages of the paid worker into the means of subsistence for the entire household and that replenishes the labour power of household members' (Luxton 1980: 18; Armstrong and Armstrong 1990; Rosenberg 1990).

It can be seen that teleworkers' experiences can provide a unique challenge to traditional definitions of work. For almost all the teleworkers in the present sample, work at home is an entirely voluntary arrangement; several in fact had to actively lobby their employers for months to introduce telework. Both the women and men mention multiple reasons for wanting to work at home; most often, however, they say that they want to gain greater control over their work environment, increase work productivity, manage family responsibilities with less stress, and save on their commute times. These workers, therefore, do not believe that the current physical division between the workplace (as a site of paid work) and home (as a site of non-work) is an effective way to organise their lives. As one man says, for example, 'it makes no sense for people to drive through some great misty void to arrive into a canyon [the office] with other people who have also left themselves behind . . . [and to] reverse the whole process at the end of the day'. (Interviewee 11)

By working at home, teleworkers eliminate the physical distance between their 'work' and 'non-work'. At the same time, they recreate the division between work and non-work on a daily basis. The following sections outline the ways in which teleworkers reconstruct the notions of work and non-work while they do paid work within the private sphere of their homes.

Teleworkers' reconstruction of 'work' and 'non-work'

Rather than identifying 'work' in terms of location, teleworkers define 'real work' in terms of the method in which activities are conducted. They argue that 'real work' can be conducted outside the 'public' sphere of the workplace; in fact, the private domain provides a better environment for 'real work' than the workplace. In addition, teleworkers stress that much of what is currently paid for within the public sphere is in fact 'non-work'.

Defining 'real work'

Drucker argues that we are in the midst of a shift from a capitalist to a 'post-capitalist society' (1993: 1), in which knowledge will be the basic economic resource (1993: 3). The leading members of this 'knowledge society' are 'knowledge workers' (1993: 8), and the greatest challenge facing post-capitalist society is enhancing the productivity of knowledge workers (1993: 83). To overcome this challenge, Drucker writes that, first, 'workers must be required to take responsibility for their own productivity and to *exercise control* over it' (1993: 92; emphasis in the original), and second, 'the results [of work] have to be clearly specified, if productivity is to be achieved' (1993: 85).

Wadel, in a similar vein, identifies two characteristics of activities that are not recognised as work. First, the time spent on these activities seems to be sporadic, and seems less planned compared to the activities recognised as work. Second, the time and effort spent on there activities cannot be clearly defined in terms of the product they produce (1979: 379).

Drucker's and Wadel's analyses coincide with the two central principles through which teleworkers organise their paid work activities and distinguish these activities from their non-work. First, they plan and exercise control over their work, and, second they evaluate their work in terms of measurable work output. Through these principles teleworkers define the characteristics required for doing good work, or 'real work'. Real work epitomises ideal work in the post-capitalist society; and teleworkers are, in Drucker's terms, the 'knowledge workers' who are its 'leading social group' (1993: 8).

'Real work' as planned work

Both female and male teleworkers spend considerable time and energy in planning their work, in terms of a) the organisation of their work activities and b) the scheduling of their work times.

A) The organisation of work activities

Teleworkers are examples of what Thompson characterises as workers with 'responsible autonomy' who 'effectively control themselves' rather than needing to be overtly controlled (1983: 153). One way in which teleworkers control their work output is by planning their work activities. They divide these activities into 'tasks' to be completed and designate specific days or times for these tasks. As one woman says:

> I have assigned certain times of my week that have become very distinct times for me to do a particular task. Like Monday is my paperwork day so I don't make any sales calls on Mondays ... [this scheduling] allows you to be a lot more firm in your commitments to people in terms of sharing communications and access to information.
>
> (Interviewee 42)

Another way in which teleworkers plan their work activities is by making lists or work plans. As one woman puts it, she 'works off lists' (Interviewee 14). A male teleworker says:

> I always work from a book which is a running work plan. Everything I do or say or listen to is all written down ... every item becomes an action ... in the morning I go through the [book] and I look at the [undone items] – I either write them again or I do them'.
>
> (Interviewee 27)

Through such planning, teleworkers believe that they do their paid work activities in the most effective manner possible. As one man puts it 'I'm getting a heck of a lot accomplished ... I've got everything lined up to work on so I know exactly what I'm going to do' (Interviewee 35).

B) The Scheduling of work times

Another way in which teleworkers plan their work is by organising their work schedules. They exercise control over their schedules by designating specific times for interactions with colleagues, again so that they can work most effectively. Teleworkers, for example, say:

> [with telework] work got better for everyone because rather than having those dreadful *ad hoc* meetings . . . it required a bit more discipline of everyone to say, 'OK, at one o'clock . . . I'll find B. and we'll phone you at home'.
>
> (Male interviewee 11)

> the thing is that *I* choose my interruptions like [if] I've got to talk to somebody it's usually me who decides to phone them after I've finished a block of work . . . That will not likely have happened at [the office]. Somebody would have come by.
>
> (Female interviewee 18)

Perman, in her study of the value workers place on non-monetary aspects of their jobs, finds that workers place a high value on having control over their work schedules (1991: 169). Both female and male teleworkers, it can be seen, do place a high value on having this control; they believe that the ability to plan their work schedule in this manner allows them to work most effectively.

'Real work' as measurable work

Traditionally work has been defined in terms of the times within which it is done, rather than output. As Wadel argues, the folk (or lay) concept of work is that it is a set of activities which one is paid for and does at a specific place (workplace) and at specific times (working hours) (1979: 368–9). Working out of the traditional office environment teleworkers believe that criteria other than visibility should be used to judge work. As one man says:

> you're supposed to work from 9 to 5 [but] that is not what it's about. You have to get used to the mind-set – there is something to be accomplished . . . within a certain time frame . . . and the only important thing is whether or not it gets accomplished . . . the hours you work, what you do . . . isn't relevant.
>
> (Interviewee 10)

Wharton studies the impact of flexible work schedules on women in residential real-estate sales. She argues that although women are attracted to real-estate sales because of the flexibility it offers, this flexibility often requires longer work hours since work income is dependent on hard work and high productivity (Wharton 1994: 196). In a similar manner, teleworkers' greater control over their work, in conjunction with the assessment of their work by measurable output, often leads them to do overtime work. More than a third of the teleworkers in the study attribute their high productivity to the fact that they work more than forty hours per week. One woman calls this 'teleworkaholism' where 'you become a junkie, you become so productive' (Interviewee 43). Another man says that with telework:

some people might start putting in an awful lot of hours . . . it's like giving a . . . hospital shelf [full of drugs] to a drug addict. If someone's a workaholic . . . you open the barrier even wider for him [*sic*] to work every night [and] weekends.

(Interviewee 49)

For some teleworkers, however, the measurement of work by output can some-times reduce the amount of overtime work that they do. One woman says that she does less overtime work because on telework days, 'I fit eight hours into an eight-hour day' (Interviewee 37). A man similarly says that with telework, 'I'm not being frustrated in the evening because of not being able to accomplish what I needed to accomplish during the day and having to bring it home' (Interviewee 1).

Through planning and measuring their work by outputs rather than presence in the workplace, teleworkers believe that they are effective workers. As one woman says, 'the more they want to see your face . . . the less real work you do' (Interviewee 46). 'Real work' is, in this manner, defined as work which can be measured by outcomes and which is judged in terms of tasks completed rather than time spent. In addition, real work is work that is planned and for which workers have control over their work activities and interruptions. Both female and male teleworkers argue that the home provides the ideal setting for real work, thus disrupting the equivalence between work and the public sphere. In addition, teleworkers exclude much of what is currently paid (such as chit-chat) within the office setting from definitions of real work.

The 'non-work' in the office

Drucker argues that productivity in a post-capitalist society requires 'the elimin-ation of whatever activities . . . do not contribute to performance' (1993: 90). Workers should scrutinise each of their job tasks and ask whether they contribute to their performance (1993: 91). If a task does not enhance performance, Druck-er suggests, 'the procedure or operation must be considered a "chore", rather than "work"' (1993: 91). Teleworkers follow Drucker's prescription; putting each of their job tasks into question they sieve out any activities that do not enhance their work performance and label these as 'non-work'.

One activity teleworkers consistently excluded from the definition of work is social interaction at the office. Perman, in her study of the value workers place on non-monetary characteristics of their jobs, finds that talking to co-workers is evaluated 'more as a job burden than as a job advantage' (1991: 171). Tele-workers, both female and male, clearly and emphatically stress that such activities are not work. Teleworkers say:

There are so many distractions that happen in the office that are not viewed as being distractions in corporate business. It's the social part of business. It gets defined as the social part of doing business when it's really just a waste of time ... the only way you can really achieve productivity enlargements is by having people work longer ... or by doing less chit-chat'.

(Male interviewee 11)

In the office ... if you saw a movie last night you'd go to your neighbour and say, 'Did you happen to see that movie last night?' And then you get carried away in a conversation that can last sometimes an hour. Then somebody will decide, well let's go for a coffee break, these fifteen minute coffee breaks get stretched into thirty minutes. The house is nice and quiet.

(Female interviewee 17)

Wadel suggests that such social interactions may be considered 'non-work' for several reasons. One reason is that 'the formal organisation can fulfil its goals, it is held, without these activities' (Wadel 1979: 373). Accordingly, teleworkers do not see a direct link between social interactions and their measurable work outputs:

When I go back to the office there's a lot of wasted time ... I find there's so many interruptions at work. They say, 'Well this is productive use of our time'. I'm not so sure about that – a lot of that stuff is just chit-chat ... I mean is it something that me [*sic*] as an employer would want to pay for? I don't think so. I think there's a lot of time wasted in the existing corporate structure that is considered work that really isn't.

(Male interviewee 44)

At the office ... if you worked five hours you did a good day, you know you have your colleagues coming in, you have phone calls, people pass in front of your office [and say] 'Hi, did you watch that program yesterday or something happened to my mother'. So there's that chit-chat that I don't have at home ... I'm putting [in] a good seven-and-a-half hours a day at home which I was not doing [at the office].

(Female interviewee 9)

Another reason social interactions are defined as non-work is that they are often not planned. They occur on an *ad hoc*, sporadic basis, or happen 'in the natural course of events'. (Wadel 1979: 374, 379). As one teleworking man says:

You'll think twice before calling somebody and start just chatting about the office politics ... but if the person is right there, you want to take a break, you want to stretch your legs, start talking to the person beside you. It's amazing the amount of time that's wasted with that.

(Interviewee 49)

Aside from such social interactions being identified as a 'waste', teleworkers also say that being available for consultation does not always lead to efficient work. One woman says:

> When you're right there they're more apt to check their little problem out with you and your peer and the next person. [When I'm at home] they have to phone me . . . what that really does for the company is it helps people make better decisions on who they're going to get input from and how frequently they're going to interrupt you'.
>
> (Interviewee 38)

Social interactions are not only linked to inefficient work, but are also seen to place constant emotional demands on employees. One man says:

> You're not five minutes in . . . your office . . . somebody . . . is going to see you there and they're going to want to tell you how rotten the week has been or dump all the problems that they've had in their life [onto you] . . . after you've been dumped on a couple of times during the morning while [you're] trying to have your cup of coffee, it can't help but influence what kind of day you're going to have.
>
> (Interviewee 01)

Women more than men mention that their proximity to their peers is often abused when they are at the central work site, heightening the fragmentation in their work. Sheppard notes that the fact that women are seen to be more accessible or 'person oriented' can sometimes affect their career mobility (1992: 158). Women are conscious of this and say:

> I don't get any of [what I classify as my work] done [at the office]. People want to ask me questions . . . my boss wants to talk to me . . . people walk by and they ask you a question they could have just as easily found out themselves.
>
> (Interviewee 46)

> It's very difficult when you're trying to [work] and you have people popping in and out of your office all the time. [I also often] had oddball requests to design menus, invitations . . . [now] I can concentrate on my real job.
>
> (Interviewee 34)

Not only are informal interactions defined as non-work, but sometimes so are meetings. As one woman says:

> I really really try to avoid meetings because it's a plague in this milieu.

People are always [saying], 'Let's meet, let's do lunch'. I really don't like that because I think really a lot of the time it's a waste of time.

(Interviewee 16)

The environment itself fosters such fragmentary work:

in the office sometimes there's such a frenzy . . . because I'm across from the secretary and across from the printer and next to the boss . . . I can't focus, I can't concentrate.

(Female interviewee 28)

These activities are not part of 'real work' since they do not always relate in a direct way to outcome and occur on an *ad hoc* basis. In arguing that 'work' is not, in fact, all activities that are currently remunerated, teleworkers propose a definition of 'work' that is not based on its location in the public sphere.

Household labour: the anomaly

In these ways, teleworkers disrupt conventional equivalencies between 'work' and location, and instead define 'real work' as activities which can be clearly measured and planned. While they work at home teleworkers continually plan and measure not only the activities that they do as part of their jobs, but also their domestic work and child-care. Women remain overwhelmingly responsible for household work in Canada (Pierson 1995: 13); the construction of these activities as not part of (and therefore less important than) 'real work' therefore has gendered implications.

Feminist theorists identify a need for a more inclusive definition of work – one which is more 'ample and generous' (Smith 1987: 165) and which would include women's domestic, volunteer and invisible work (Wadel 1979: 412; Daniels 1987: 403). It would seem that teleworkers are well situated to begin to recognise the 'workful' (DeVault 1991: 228) nature of these activities, and challenge their conventional definition as 'non-work'. However, despite their common site of domestic and paid work, teleworkers make little move towards thinking of their domestic work as work, and in fact are careful to differentiate such activities from their 'real work'. This construction of domestic work is discussed in the next section of the chapter, followed by analyses of why teleworkers (both female and male) may be reluctant to define their household work as real work.

Planning and measuring domestic work

Ninety per cent of the individuals interviewed for the present study are married and two-thirds have children. A little more than a third of the married teleworkers perceive their domestic responsibilities to be shared with their spouses. For the remainder of the married respondents, women assume primary responsibility for domestic work. There are considerable differences in the types of domestic tasks female and male teleworkers do. In particular, women remain responsible for integrating children's needs into their paid work schedules. Very few of the women in the sample undertake child-care while they are doing paid work, however, almost all of the mothers are responsible for making childcare arrangements and for organising their paid work around the timings of these arrangements.

Teleworkers, both female and male, place great value on the ability to control their work and non-work schedules, and some intersperse their paid work and domestic work activities. Like their 'real work' activities, teleworkers attempt to plan and measure their domestic work and child-care. Much of the stress of balancing work and family, teleworkers note, is due to the fact that office-based work does not allow them to plan their domestic work and child-care. As one woman says:

> When I take a break, I can . . . do a load of laundry . . . I can sweep the floor . . . supper is no longer a struggle either . . . [Before I started to telework] when I'd walk in the door, I'd hear, 'What's for supper?' My coat wouldn't even be off. But now, I usually put chicken in the oven or whatever just before I leave to pick up [my daughter] so it is ready [for dinner time].
>
> (Interviewee 34)

Planning their household responsibilities involves organising their domestic work and child-care activities as well as co-ordinating the scheduling of paid work and domestic work times. Teleworkers say:

> It's nice to be able to cook lunch for my kids . . . when they come home from school . . . I make myself two or three coffees in the morning and work through my lunch so I can take off an hour when my kids come home from school.
>
> (Male interviewee 24)

> Originally I used to go to a playgroup on Tuesday and Thursday mornings and then I would work in the afternoon [and evening] . . . I did that for a while and I found it wasn't as effective working in the afternoon, so I flipped it [and worked mornings and evenings instead].
>
> (Female interviewee 40)

Teleworkers note that through such scheduling of household activities and times, they get the measurable benefit of greater leisure time at weekends. As one woman says:

> It's at the point now where I can say that my whole day I have control of and it's smooth . . . I don't do my spring cleaning in the middle of the

day . . . but I do enough to keep . . . on top of everything . . . whereas before the whole weekend you just kind of dreaded because you'd have to do it all . . . I actually wake up on Saturday morning and we have hockey, I can sit and read the newspaper.

(Interviewee 07)

Household work as 'non-work'

Despite these attempts to plan and measure their domestic work and child-care activities, teleworkers clearly and emphatically define these activities as 'non-work'. The primary way in which teleworkers define domestic work as 'non-work' is by referring to such domestic work as a 'break'. As one woman says, 'I like to be able to do a wash and vacuum . . . sometimes I just need a break . . . it's kind of relaxing because you can accomplish that and you can get your mind off of work' (Interviewee 21). One man talks about tasks such as shovelling snow, mowing the lawn or washing the truck in this manner, 'I usually do [these tasks] before I work . . . Or I may mix the two . . . if it's snowing then I'll work and if it stops snowing I'll go out and clean it. Then I'll come back in and do some work – it gives me a break' (Interviewee 31).

Teleworking women more often than men refer to their domestic work as 'non-work'. This is presumably because more women are responsible for domestic work and child-care. However, it is also likely to be related to the continuous need for teleworkers to legitimise their paid work so that it is recognised as 'work' (see Mirchandani 1996). Feminist theorists such as Daniels note that women themselves often do not see domestic work as 'work' requiring effort. Given that the work of a homemaker is private, it lacks validation (Daniels 1987: 405; also Lozano 1989: 121–2). This confirms 'women's own sense that much of [this work] ought to be offered spontaneously' and that the knowledge required for such activities should be 'natural for women' (Daniels 1987: 407, 410; DeVault 1991). For example, teleworkers frequently draw parallels between the 'breaks' they take at home to do housework, and the 'spontaneous' and 'natural' social interactions with their colleagues in the office. As one woman says, 'I [sometimes] throw in a load of laundry . . . but I'm sure I waste a lot less time at home than I do at the office chatting' (Interviewee 06). Domestic work is compared to breaks in the workplace, and therefore characterised as non-work. The reasons that teleworkers feel the need to underplay the workful nature of household tasks is discussed in the following section.

Organisational cultures: supporting the exclusion of household labour

Teleworkers, while working at home, continue to be located within a specific organisational culture. Mills defines organisational culture as 'consisting simultaneously of a structured set of rules in which behaviour is bounded and of a process, or outcome, resulting from the particular character of the rule-bound behaviour of the actors involved' (1989 30). Two manifestations of the gendered organisational culture can be discerned in teleworkers' experiences; first is the necessity to be completely engrossed in the work process and second is the assumption that family concerns are always secondary to work concerns (Mills and Murgatroyd 1991: 78–90).

Mills and Murgatroyd argue that office or professional work occurs within a gendered organisational culture and 'the rules of this particular game involve appearing to be detached, logical, unemotional and absorbed in the work process' (1991: 78). This is, as Acker notes, the assumption that paid work has 'first claim on the worker' (1992b: 255; Ferree 1990: 873). Both female and male teleworkers perceive their employers to have demonstrated a high degree of 'trust' in them by allowing them to work at home; given this trust they have an obligation to follow the 'rules' of 'the game' (Mills and Murgatroyd 1991: 78). As Perin argues, 'to compensate for their invisibility and the distrust that accompanies it [teleworkers are] . . . expected to justify their organisational value through deliverables' (1991: 256). Teleworkers say:

> I am responsible enough to follow through on my end of the requirements . . . people are trusting me with the fact that I am serious about my work. Otherwise I think that I would be taking advantage of the system.
>
> (Female interviewee 30)

> it's very dependent on who you work for . . . trusting you sufficiently to see that you actually can work away on your own and produce . . . results'.
>
> (Male interviewee 4)

Mills and Murgatroyd write that men in particular are often expected to demonstrate a dedication to the organisation that can only be achieved with the aid of a wife (1991: 80). Accordingly, teleworking men say, 'the company owns more of you than you own of the company. There is an expectation that you put in twelve hours a day, or sixteen hours a day' (Interviewee 23); and 'I only get paid for seven-and-a-half hours a day, but I haven't worked only a seven and-a-half hour day in years' (Interviewee 24).

Teleworking women, although to a lesser extent than the men, also perceive the requirement for a high level of organisational commitment.

Related to the assumption that workers will be completely absorbed in the work process is the 'expectation that family life comes second to the organisation' (Mills and Murgatroyd 1991: 80). Teleworkers say that they have to continually 'discipline themselves' to focus on their paid work while they are at home and to ensure that work needs are given priority over their families. Teleworkers say:

> Discipline . . . [is] forcing myself to [say], OK, let's go work. You're in a

home environment, we're not conditioned to associate that with work. [We] associate that with leisure and pleasure and housework . . . not with office work. It [requires] discipline to [say] let's go down and work.

(Male interviewee 31)

They [my employers] trust me and know I'm not going to get peanut butter all over their records because my kids have been playing on the dining room table [where I work].

(Female interviewee 41)

I'm probably a good individual to [telework]. My manager [knows that I'm not] . . . out doing my grocery shopping or something when I'm supposed to be working.

(Female interviewee 37)

Mills and Murgatroyd note that 'the added power of the hidden aspects of gender rules is that they often stand for something else, for example, being detached is valued at one level as a male trait, but at another level as a necessary professional act' (1991: 79). The worker who does 'real work', which excludes domestic work, invisible and emotional work, and social and informal interaction, can only, in the abstract, be the male worker (Acker 1992a: 568). As Tancred notes, work 'is defined in terms of *men's* modal experience rather than women's dominant work experience' (1995: 12, emphasis in original).

Implications for telework policy

Telework programmes are often introduced in response to studies which indicate that employees experience significant conflict between their 'work' and 'non-work' or family lives. The Conference Board of Canada, for example, conducted a survey of four hundred corporations and found that sixty per cent of employees expressed difficulty in balancing their work and family demands (Alvi 1992). In the context of the widespread prevalence of work–family conflict, telework is seen to provide employees with some flexibility to reconstruct the boundaries between their work and non-work lives, and to reduce the conflict associated with conventional definitions of this boundary in terms of physical distinctions between workplace and home. This chapter reveals, however, that while telework does provide both women and men with the flexibility to relieve some of the work–family stress associated with office-based work, it does not address the organisational devaluation of household responsibilities which is at the root of the cause of work–family conflict.

Teleworkers challenge conventional boundaries between work and non-work within which 'work' is constructed as paid activity that occurs in a public work-place and 'non-work' is seen as unpaid activity that occurs in the home. Instead these workers argue that what is 'real work' should not be decided on the basis of location, but on how well the activity is planned and results in measurable output.

Within this framework, teleworkers relabel much of the informal interaction that occurs within the workplace as non-work. It would seem that teleworkers would also be able to relabel much of their planned and measurable domestic activity as work. By doing this, they would be able to address the source of much of the stress they experience with office-based work in balancing their work and family demands. They do not, however, do this, primarily because they continue to be located within specific organisational cultures which reinforce the hierarchy between work (which is assumed to have 'first claim on the worker' (Acker 1992b: 225) and non-work (which is conceptualised as a secondary concern). In forming telework policy, therefore, work-at-home programmes should be seen not as ends in themselves but rather as tools which allow for the rethinking of these assumptions and norms which shape the cultures of contemporary organisations.

Acknowledgement

I would like to thank Dr Peta Tancred for her guidance throughout this research project.

References

Acker, J. (1992a) 'Gendered Institutions: From Sex Roles to Gendered Institutions', *Contemporary Sociology* 21, 5: 565–95.

—— (1992b) 'Gendering Organisational Theory', in A.J. Mills and P. Tancred (eds) *Gendering Organisational Analysis*, New Park: Sage.

Alvi, S. (1992) 'Perspectives on the Public Sector/Private Sector Interaction', Boston University Work and Family Roundtable, 14–16 October, Montreal.

Armstrong, P. and Armstrong, H. (1990) *Theorising Women's Work*, Toronto: Garamond Press.

Daniels, A.K. (1987) 'Invisible Work', *Social Problems* 34, 5: 403–15.

DeVault, M.L. (1991) *Feeding the Family: The Social Organisation of Caring as Gendered Work*, Chicago: University of Chicago Press.

Drucker, P. (1993) *Post-Capitalist Society*, New York: Harper Business.

Dunnette, M.D. (1973) *Work and Nonwork in the Year 2001*, Monterey: Brooks Cole Publishers Company.

Ferree, M.M. (1990) 'Beyond Separate Spheres: Feminism and Family Research', *Journal of Marriage and the Family* 52, November. 866–84.

Finch, J. (1983) *Married to the Job: Wives' Incorporation in Men's Work*, London: George Allen and Unwin.

Harvey, D. (1989) *The Condition of Postmodernity: An Enquiry into the Origins of Social Change*, Oxford: Basil Blackwell.

Lozano, B. (1989) 'Bringing Work Home', in *The Invisible Workforce: Transforming American Business with Outside and Home-Based Workers*, New York: The Free Press.

Luxton, M. (1980) *More than a Labour of Love*, Toronto: The Women's Press.

Mackenzie, S. (1986) 'Women's Responses to Economic Restructuring: Changing Gender, Changing Space', in R. Hamilton and M. Barrett (eds) *The Politics of Diversity*, London: Verso.

Massey, D. (1991) 'Flexible Sexism', *Environment and Planning D: Society and Space* 9: 31–57.

Miles, M.B. and Huberman, A.M. (1994) *Qualitative Data Analysis: An Expanded Sourcebook*, 2nd edition, Newbury Park: Sage.

Mills, A.J. (1989) 'Gender, Sexuality and Organisation Theory', in J. Hearn, D.L. Sheppard, P. Tancred-Sheriff and G. Burrell (eds) *The Sexuality of Organisation*, Newbury Park: Sage.

Mills, A.J. (1992) 'Organisation, Gender and Culture', in A. J. Mills and P. Tancred (eds) *Gendering Organisational Analysis*, New Park: Sage.

Mills, A.J. and Murgatroyd, S.J. (1991) *Organisational Rules: A Framework for Understanding Organisational Action*, Milton Keynes: Open University Press.

Mirchandani, K. (1996) 'Living in the Office: Telework and its Critical Reflection of the Public–Private Dichotomy', unpublished doctoral dissertation, Department of Sociology, McGill University, Montreal.

Orser, B. and Foster, M. (1992) 'Home Enterprise: Canadians and Home-Based Work', prepared for the home-based Business Project Committee, February.

Patton, M.Q. (1990) *Qualitative Evaluation and Research Methods*, 2nd edition, Newbury Park: Sage.

Perin, C. (1991) 'The Moral Fabric of the Office: Panopticon Discourse and Schedule Flexibility', *Research in the Sociology of Organisations* 8: 241–68.

Perman, L. (1991) *The Other Side of the Coin: the Nonmonetary Characteristics of Jobs*, New York: Garland Press.

Pierson, R.R. (1995) 'The Politics of the Domestic Sphere', in R.R Pierson and M. Cohen (eds) *Canadian Women's Issues, Vol.II – Bold Visions*, Toronto: James Lorimer and Co.

Ronco, W. and Peattie, L. (1983) *Making Work: Self Created Jobs in Participatory Organisations*, New York: Plenum Press.

Rose, G. (1993) *Feminism and Geography*, New York: Polity Press.

Rosenberg, H. (1990) 'The Home is a Workplace: Hazards, Stress and Pollutants in the Household', in M. Luxton (ed.) *Through the Kitchen Window*, 2nd edition, Toronto: Garamond Press.

Sheppard, D. (1992) 'Women Managers' Perceptions of Gender and Organisational Life', in A.J. Mills and P. Tancred (eds) *Gendering Organisational Analysis*, Newbury Park: Sage.

Siroonian, J. (1993) 'Work Arrangements', Analytical Report No. 6. Ottawa: Statistics Canada.

Smith, D.E. (1987) *The Everyday World as Problematic*, Toronto: University of Toronto Press.

Statistics Canada (1991) 'Survey of Work Arrangements', Cat. 71–535, No. 6. November.

—— (1995) *The Daily*, Tuesday 1 June.

Tancred, P. (1995) 'Women's Work: A Challenge to the Sociology of Work', *Gender, Work and Organisation* 2, 1: 11–20.

'Telework '94 – Télétravail' 94, (1994) Symposium Proceedings, 14 and 15 November, Toronto, Canada.

Tessier, A.M. and Lapointe, F. (1994) 'Telework at Home: An Evaluation of a Pilot Project at Employment and Immigration Canada', Centre for Information Technology Innovation (CITI), Laval, March.

Thompson, P. (1983) *The Nature of Work*, London: MacMillan Press.

Tippin, D. (1994) 'Control Processes in Distance Work Situations: The Case of Satellite Offices', Paper presented at the Canadian Sociology and Anthropology Association Annual Meetings, Calgary, June.

'Towards the Virtual Workplace: Implications for Social and Organisational Change' (1994) Conference organised by Industry Canada, University of Toronto, 4 November.

Wadel, C. (1979) 'The Hidden Work of Everyday Life', in S. Wallman (ed.) *Social Anthropology of Work*, London: Academic Press.

Wharton, C.S. (1994) 'Finding Time for the "Second Shift" ': The Impact of Flexible Work Schedules on Women's Double Days', *Gender and Society* 8, 2: 189–205.

8

THE EXPERIENCE OF TELEWORKING

A view from the home

Leslie Haddon

Introduction

In 1992/3 an in-depth study of twenty teleworking households in the UK was conducted as part of a longer term project organised by Professor Roger Silverstone and funded by PICT, a programme within one of the British research councils. The aim of that project, based originally at Brunel University and later at Sussex University, was to examine the experience of Information and Communication Technologies (ICTs) in the home.

The first Sussex study was of teleworkers, who were chosen to explore the relationship between home and paid work in a situation where the boundaries between them were being challenged in a particularly dramatic form. An additional advantage of focusing on this group was that it could build on the authors' previous empirical research (Haddon 1991, 1992b; Haddon and Lewis 1994). It is worth emphasising that some of the insights from this study apply to many more workers who use their home partially as a work base (e.g. mobile workers), who bring some of their work home after leaving offices, or who allow themselves to be contactable at home for work purposes. Some of the results of this case study are reported elsewhere (Haddon 1992b; Haddon and Silverstone 1992, 1994) the most detailed report being Haddon and Silverstone (1994).

The importance of technology

Given that telework has frequently been picked out as emerging out of the information society, it is worth asking just how important is the actual technology for this mode of working. It was clear from this study (and others) that there are some forms of telework where ICTs can play an essential role: for example, for teleworkers programming a distant mainframe computer via a modem, for analysing data using software packages, or for mediating computer conferences. Such teleworkers, often but not always employees, could now bring their essential tools home – they were no longer tied to work because of the need to access a centralised facility. However, these types of telework appear to be relatively few in comparison to work involving text production, or clerical or professional forms of administration: for example, secretarial word processing, report writers or accounting. For these teleworkers, predominantly self-employed, ICTs make the work easier and quicker and they offer some new options. Indeed, they have become more essential given clients' expectations about the speed of production or their desire for electronic output. Yet this work could have taken place in the past without the aid of new ICTs. In fact, in our sample, both an editor and an abstract writer had worked for nearly 20 years at home, only starting to use new telecoms and electronic technology as they appeared in the 1970s and 1980s. Before this the only technologies they used were the typewriter and the basic phone. These examples represent forms of professional and clerical work – not captured in literature on traditional manufacturing homework – which have always been conducted at home by a few.

In between these two sets of teleworkers are those for whom ICTs are more than just a facilitator because of the magnitude of the task and the time pressures involved. For these, mostly but not exclusively self-employed, ICTs make telework more of a feasible option. Examples for our study included an executive managing director, a publisher trading in international book rights, and various consultants producing substantial reports and packages at short notice. In these cases communication was a significant element in their work, or else they were producing major texts in a short time span which required a professional appearance. The existence of ICTs which provide the kind of personalised technological back-up that they might expect in an office had made teleworking viable.

In sum, there are different degrees to which technology is a facilitator of telework, with one key variable being employment status. But even where ICTs have been relatively more important for conducting the telework, it is important to appreciate that they act as an enabling force rather than a driving one. For companies, the social–economic factors driving telework such as the need to reduce building overheads or to retain staff have already been well documented in the telework literature. Equally, it is mainly social considerations which shape individuals' decisions to telework, as we will see below.

If telework appears at this moment to be attracting more attention in this country and elsewhere, this is as much a result of social causes as changes in technology. Such causes include a greater awareness of this option, the fact that working at home has become more acceptable to employers or clients, the rise of teleworker organisations offering various kinds of support and – more negatively – the massive restructuring of companies in the recession which for some means telework is the only alternative to unemployment or early retirement.

The heterogeneity of telework

Telework is by no means a unitary phenomenon. It is important to underline at the outset the fact that the circumstances of teleworkers vary greatly and hence so does their experience and evaluation of this mode of work. In fact, asking current or past teleworkers whether telework is, overall, a 'good' or 'bad' thing would probably produce as wide a range of responses as asking people to evaluate work in general.

First, they have different reasons for taking up teleworking. This study and past research suggest that domestic reasons would appear to predominate, especially for women. But this can include being at home, perhaps reducing working hours, to be more available for children as well as using telework to escape from the purely domestic role, perhaps as a stepping stone to office work. Alternatively, the decision to telework can be prompted by work or work-related considerations: to avoid commuting, as a reaction to problems experienced in offices, as part of a decision to embrace a more entrepreneurial role, as a consequence of re-dundancy when there is little chance of being employed again because of age. So telework can be a positive choice, perhaps a lifestyle choice. Or it can simply be the best option open, one chosen with ambivalence, and with at best a partial commitment. It can be 'choice' with varying degrees of voluntariness.

If we consider the route into telework as a career trajectory, the question of where people are coming from, as well as their reasons for taking that path, are also a consideration. For example, it makes a difference to suddenly switch from full-time office work to teleworking compared to coming from the domestic role of housewife or husband. The organisation of the day and the expectations of one's social networks are different and have to change in different ways to accommodate this mode of work. In addition, the status of the work is different in different households – ranging from being the equivalent of a full-time office job to being a means to earn a little extra money for the family. And lastly, the control which teleworkers have over the timing, pace and amount of work varies – for both professional and clerical teleworkers.

The dynamics of telework

Domestic life has its own rhythms and routines, its temporal and spatial patterns, its shared values and rules as well as its domestic conflicts. These all shape how teleworking can enter the home and whether and how it can be accommodated. Hence, although the arrival of telework can have a bearing on those domestic patterns, telework also has itself to be adjusted to fit in with home life.

But this is not just a question of establishing a teleworking pattern once and for all. Both telework and domestic life have their own dynamics. Telework can change in terms of such matters as its content, the necessity for contactability, the balance of work inside and outside the home, the spatial requirements of work and the times when work has to take place. In households, the fact that children are born and grow up introduces constantly changing demands on domestic space and time. Relationships also change, with tensions, conflicts, the negotiation of new ways of organising household life, the break-up of households and the formation of new ones. There is also material change, with the acquisition of new homes and hence opportunities for new spatial arrangements.

The consequence of these dynamics is that the experience of telework changes. It can take place at different times in different places. At times it can become more stressful, as new problems constantly emerge – at other times it can be easier to accommodate. As a result, we can talk of telework trajectories not just into the home but into telework careers over time. Indeed, after longer or shorter periods, some give up this mode of working and return to office-based work or else cease to be part of the labour force – thereby establishing trajectories out of telework. In other words, the decision to telework should not be seen as being final. Teleworking is a provisional, sometimes temporary, commitment to a working arrangement. For some people telework is indeed the final stage in their career while for others teleworking is only a stage in their lives, an option like taking a career break, or the decision of many mothers to work part time while the children are young and return to full-time working later.

Time and space

One of the great benefits that advocates of this mode of working seize upon is the flexibility it offers to teleworkers. Yet any temporal flexibility which telework may offer is in practice constrained by social factors. First, there are the demands of work. These include the requirement of employees to co-ordinate activities with others who are working core hours in an office or the need to be contactable at certain times. Our case study revealed instances of managers regularly having to face crises at times not of their own choosing, and of clerical and professional self-employed teleworkers working longer hours than they would have liked because of rush jobs, the need to bring new products to market, consultancy deadlines, or short-term notice of work.

At the same time, teleworkers often experience pressures to synchronise their non-work with others both inside and outside the home. In our study, those female clerical teleworkers, and some professionals, who could not afford to pay for child-care could often only work when the children were not around or when their partners could look after them. In cases where young children were present this meant working in the evenings and at weekends. Or some teleworkers tried to keep weekends free to retain a place in the community – since that was when social activities were most likely to occur. In addition, many teleworkers preferred to stick to the approximate times that they used to work to in offices because this routine helped their self-discipline.

As regards actual strategies for organising time, key patterns emerged. In one, work was relatively more imposed upon domestic life and, if necessary, household routines had to be adjusted. For example, many employees on telework schemes continued to work in the day and so that time was blocked out for work: they did not suddenly take on more domestic tasks by virtue of being home nor did they make themselves totally accessible to others in the household. Alternatively, the demands of work meant it took place outside traditional office hours – but again, work took precedence. This appeared to be a more masculine style, but one also adopted by some women, particularly professional employees. In contrast, a more common female pattern, especially clear where the telework was part time, involved fitting work into domestic rhythms, fitting it in around the times when the children or partners were absent and hence not making demands, or fitting it in between other domestic responsibilities.

In terms of when work takes place, the pattern whereby telework was imposed on home life was more often associated with virtually no change from core office hours. There was perhaps just a little more flexibility than flexitime offers, which is often useful for child management. The contrasting pattern involved working non-standard hours – either when work was fragmented and fitted in and/or performed in the evenings or at weekends. For those working long hours, of course, prioritising work meant working both the core day and evening and weekend work.

Turning now to questions of space, social constraints also affect the location of telework. Although regular commitments to visit one or more work sites may limit teleworkers' choice of where they would want to live, of far more significance is domestic inertia. Our teleworkers were established in houses, were part of communities, their children had friends at local schools and they had partners whose own work commitments had to be considered. In our sample, only one household, where both partners teleworked, was considering relocating to the South of France. On the whole, the flexibility offered by telework does not lead people to radically relocate and de-camp to the countryside.

The location of telework within homes was also constrained by domestic considerations. A common image of teleworking is one where telework is conducted in a home office, and, hence, work-related ICTs are based in a separate, defined work space. This did happen to an extent, although it was more likely in the case of professional teleworkers because they tended to have bigger homes. But even professional teleworkers and certainly clerical ones often operated in a shared space: in multi-purpose rooms, guests rooms, dining rooms, often bedrooms, caravans and even in kitchens. The point is that both work and, especially, children made competing demands on space. Because these demands changed over time, as work changed, as children grew older, telework sometimes had to move around the house, at one point taking place in a dining room, at another in a bedroom, at another, if a larger house was acquired, in a study. Such constraints on space became significant for the teleworker's scope for impression management, for creating an image of their telework both to other household members and to outsiders. This included constraints on the manner in which they could display their technology as a means to identify with high-tech images of telework.

Maintaining boundaries between home and work

Making time and finding space for telework involves some negotiation within households – albeit negotiation where some household members may well be able to mobilise more power than others. In particular, teleworkers have the problem of boundary maintenance: to greater or lesser extents, they need to separate work and home life and prevent their mutual interference. This works on a number of levels. For example, some teleworkers became self-acknowledged workaholics as the proximity of work that they enjoyed was just too tempting. For others work used to 'hang over them' because it was so near at hand, sometimes visible while the home felt less like a home – with teleworkers choosing to spend more time in their gardens or take weekend breaks to 'get away'. These were perhaps more extreme strategies, but the general, in part psychological, dilemma still had to be faced and managed by those introducing work into their homes.

One important level at which boundary maintenance operates involves creating rules and understandings about the accessibility of teleworkers to other household members or contactability for either work or social purposes. In our study, ICTs could sometimes help to manage the latter. For example, both incoming work and social phone-calls could be directed to certain time spots, or to different phones. Some teleworkers also used the answerphone, and to some extent the fax, to control the timing of communication, taking and responding to different types of message when it suited them. This allowed them better to control interruptions – from work or social calls – according to whatever task is at hand.

Another dimension of boundary maintenance involved impression management: being able to convey to outsiders – clients, employers and others contacted in the course of work – the image of being in a workplace. This often meant regulating how telephones were answered and who could answer them under what conditions. It could also mean regulating the sound regime of the home in general or at least the spaces in proximity to telework – so that domestic noise neither interfered with work nor created the wrong impression to outsiders.

The final example of boundary maintenance involved stipulating whether and when different household members could have access to work-related ICTs. There were sometimes tensions, for example, over the use of computers by children where teleworkers feared it might damage the hard- or software. And certainly, access to shared PCs by others in the household was likely to take second priority to the teleworker's own use. Similarly, use of a single phone-line could lead to conflicts over the way domestic calls blocked the line and hindered incoming work calls. Any rules about use could be either accepted or flouted. Alternatively, for some teleworkers, especially employees where equipment is supplied by employers or professional self-employed workers, the solution was to avoid sharing ICT resources and instead acquire a second (or third) computer dedicated to work or one or more extra phone-lines specifically for work.

Teleworking and others

Clearly teleworking has a bearing on and is affected by a range of social relation-ships within the household. In the research the responses of other household members, particularly partners, also had to be taken into account. This was because others in the house could support, or alternatively resist, telework in a variety of ways. They were sometimes enrolled in the actual work itself. Partners could support telework in practical terms, by taking over child-care or keeping children away from the teleworker, enforcing boundaries and regulations. This appeared to be far more significant, for example, than doing more to help with routine domestic tasks: telework apparently made little difference to the gendered division of labour in most teleworking households.

In addition, partners and sometimes children could literally help with the work. Sometimes this assistance as auxiliary labour involved no particular help with the actual technology of production: it might, for instance, involve picking up and delivering work material or acting as a sounding board for ideas. But sometimes others in the household did take part in the production process, either, in the case of male partners usually, acting as a technical support or else using ICTs and developing new computer and telephone skills.

Finally, social networks outside the home could play a role in supporting tele-work. Most often such support had no bearing on actual technologies: it might be in the form of networks to help take on some of the workload, provide additional child-care back-up or simply provide social contact to overcome any sense of isolation. But that support also included networks which, like partners, could provide technical advice and assistance relating to the teleworker's technologies.

Implications

This review of the Sussex research first examined the influence of technology on the development of telework. While ICTs enable some forms of telework and facilitate others this mode of working is not some automatic product of a new information age – its growth, or certainly its greater visibility, reflects wider social, cultural and economic developments and considerations.

The heterogeneity of telework demonstrated here serves to question some media and futurological stereotypes, be they utopian or dystopian. The sheer variety of trajectories into telework and the status and control over that work underline the fact that it can be experienced in different ways by a wide range of people for different reasons. This must make us reflect on assumptions that only people with certain psychological orientations are suitable for or take up this kind of work.

For those who would manage company telework schemes it should be clear that some aspects of telework are simply beyond the control of managers because the household has its own dynamics. There are various domestic reasons, as well as career decisions, which lead people to take on telework at one stage and give it up at another. This also means that when organisers of telework schemes calculate the use of future office space, equipment needs etc. they would need to ask what difference it makes if telework is regarded as being transitional, and they can therefore expect a certain proportion of their teleworkforce to want to return to the office. As for those giving advice on self-employment at home, they need to think not just about how to handle the trajectory into telework, but also the trajectories through it and sometimes out of it. A more general observation is that future scenarios of teleworking are misleading if they suggest any secular trend whereby teleworking jobs replace on-site jobs. If teleworking is transitional for many, the picture is rendered far more complex. Teleworking is no longer simply displacing traditional office-based work. Instead, it is an option open to more and more people as a component in their work career.

Finally, this review has covered a number of points about the issues facing teleworkers. It is clear that despite popular images there are limits to the flexibility offered by telework, both in terms of time and space. All teleworkers have somehow to confront the issue of managing the boundaries between work and home, an issue which appears again and again in a number of guises, and some teleworkers manage it better than others. But here we need also to appreciate the fact that they are not isolated individuals but live in social contexts with others, both inside and outside the home, whose support (or resistance) has a bearing on the whole experience.

References

Haddon, L. (1991) *Disability and Telework*, British Telecom Laboratories, Martlesham.

Haddon, L. (1992a), *Clerical Teleworking - How it Affects Family Life*, British Telecom, Martlesham.

Haddon, L. (1992b) 'Telework, Gender and Information and Communication Technologies: A Report on Research in Progress', unpublished paper given at the workshop 'The Gender-Technology Relation: Contemporary Theory and Research', Brunel University, 21 September.

Haddon, L. and Lewis, S. (1994) 'The Experience of Teleworking: An Annotated Review', *International Journal of Human Resource Management* 5, 1: 193–223.

Haddon, L. and Silverstone, R. (1992), 'Information and Communication Technologies in the Home: The Case of Teleworking', *Working Paper 17*, SPRU/CICT, University of Sussex.

—— (1993) *Teleworking in the 1990s: A View from the Home*, SPRU/CICT Report Series, No. 10, University of Sussex, August.

—— (1994) 'Telework and the Changing Relationship of Home and Work' in Mansell, R. (ed.) *Management of Information and Communication Technologies: Emerging Patterns of Control*, London: Aslib. Also in Heap, N. *et al.* (1995) (eds) *Information Technology and Society: A Reader*, London: Sage.

9

TELEWORKING AND QUALITY OF LIFE

André Büssing

Teleworking and teleco-operation

The era of teleworking started during the 1980s. Early projects and experiments with teleworking were run, for example, in the printing industry, with female workers performing low-skilled text processing and datatyping (for Germany, see, for example, Goldmann and Richter 1991; Huws *et al.* 1990). Over the years teleworking facilities rapidly became cheaper and, therefore, teleworking started to become attractive in a variety of different areas of work with low-skilled as well as high-skilled jobs (see Handy and Mokhtarian 1996; Nilles 1994). However, the cost of hardware and software is just one aspect; other aspects about the attractiveness of installing teleworking programmes are concerned with diverse financial and non-financial reasons. For example, we find 'hard' arguments like real-estate, energy and labour costs, as well as 'soft' arguments like binding of high-qualified employees to the organisation, higher concentration on work or control over working time etc.

Nowadays in most segments of service and production teleworking has been introduced and is growing. Besides service areas such as consulting, care, marketing and trade, we find teleworking in insurance and banking companies, in the electronic industry and increasingly in traditional industrial production, as, for example, the automobile industry (see Godehardt 1994; Huws *et al.* 1990). Moreover, teleworking becomes more and more a part of the growing new type of boundary-less and virtual organisation (see for example, Campbell 1996; Picot *et al.* 1996). These organisations use telematics not only for the purposes of teleworking, they also employ advanced information and communication technologies in order to establish new forms of networking organisations and new divisions of labour (see Littek and Charles 1995).

In this modern perspective of organisations teleworking becomes part of a larger frame which can be called *teleco-operation*. It is defined as a type of production which is supported by information and communication media, and which is based on a new division of labour between bearers of tasks, organisational units and organisations at different locations (see Reichwald and Möslein 1996). Besides teleworking, the concept of teleco-operation also comprises *telemanagement* (i.e. co-ordination of media-dislocated tasks) and *teleservices* (e.g. tele-consulting, -marketing, -medicine, -learning, -engineering, -banking and -shopping).

Organisational forms of teleworking can be structured according to four aspects: location, time, technical devices and contract (see Büssing 1997a; Büssing and Aumann 1997a; Kordey and Korte 1996; Reichwald and Möslein 1996; and see Figure 9.1). The *location* determines whether teleworking is performed at home, in neighbourhood offices, satellite offices, telecentres, telecottages etc., or is mobile (e.g. management, craftsmen, sales staff in the field). The *time* regulates whether teleworking is done permanently (home-based telework) or alternates between home and central office. The use of technical devices varies between *on-line* operation (e.g. data is exchanged via ISDN) and *off-line* operation (e.g. tape, disk, CD-ROM). Many different *forms of contracts*, from regular salaried employment to self-employment, are applied to teleworking.

Because of the many different forms of teleworking it is difficult to make reliable estimations of its dissemination. This does not only hold true for Europe – and Germany in particular – it is well-known internationally. One of the clear facts is that today teleworking is much more widespread in the US than in Europe, and we find peculiarities in different countries with respect to its organisation due to the cultural, societal, geographical and economic context.

Therefore, results about the occurrence of teleworking differ considerably

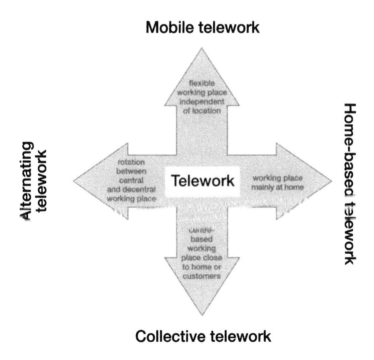

Figure 9.1 Organisational forms of teleworking

between the sources of data, not least of the frequent differences in the definition of teleworking used.

In 1993, more than 6.6 million of the US workforce was teleworking, with a strongly increasing tendency (see Korte *et al.* 1994). The New York consultancy, Link Resources, which has conducted regular surveys in the US since 1986, registered some 8 million telecommuters working at least two days a week at home. A further 9.2 million use teleworking as a source of additional income (see Rane 1995). Note, however, that these data are based on a wide definition of telework.

In Europe and particularly in Germany teleworking is not as widespread and common compared to the US, although the necessary facilities are widely available (see Godehardt 1994; Qvortrup 1995). However, the tendency towards a broader application of teleworking in service as well as in industrial organisations is strong, and we can expect teleworking to become a major feature of work organisation in many European companies in the near future.

The type of teleworking which is dominant in most countries is the alternating of telework between home and organisation (see Figure 9.1), i.e. telecommuters stay at home for three or four days a week and work in the central office for the remaining time. Currently, the organisation of teleworking in neighbourhood, satellite office, telecentre facilities, etc. remains less prevalent (see Aicholzer 1996; Büssing and Aumann 1997b). In this chapter we look at these two segments of teleworking: telecommuters (alternating teleworkers and home-based teleworkers) and collective teleworking in neighbourhood, satellite offices or telecentres. Therefore, neither self-employed teleworkers nor organisational employees who do their overtime work at home are, by definition, telecommuters, and thus they will not be considered here.

Social and private life under teleworking

Quality of life and teleworking in its larger context

Quality of life is a global evaluative term that summarises a person's reactions to the expectations in his or her life. Quality of life is based on different contexts for human activity, for example, satisfaction with the physical environment, satisfaction with work, and feelings of economic security and political involvement (Van Sell and Jacobs 1994: 81; see also Figure 9.2).

Each of these different contexts is central to a different discipline, level and unit of analysis. We have to consider economics, ecology, sociology, psychology, etc., macro-, meso- and micro-level, as well as, for example, society, community, family, the workplace, and the individual employee. In the following we refer to models etablished by Van Sell and Jacobs (1994) and Büssing and Aumann (1996a). Both models integrate theory and research on teleworking by referring to different disciplines, levels and units of analysis (for other classification systems of teleworking which integrate different disciplines, levels and units of analysis see,

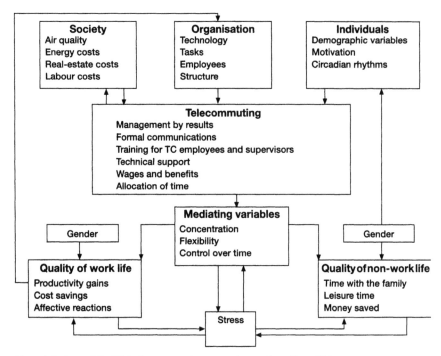

Figure 9.2 A model of links between telecommuting and quality of life
Source: after Van Sell and Jacobs 1994

for example, Ramsover 1985, or Chapman, Sheehy, Heywood, Dooley and Collins 1995). The model of 'links between telecommuting and quality of life' proposed by Van Sell and Jacobs is non-recursive and shows that the use of telecommuting depends on three things:

> societal limitations and costs, aspects of organisations, and the readiness of individuals to become telecommuters. The feedback arrow shows that telecommuting programs affect societal limitations and costs. The success of telecommuting is greatly affected by the employer's management of the telecommuting program and by the telecommuter's allocation of time. The influence of telecommuting on the individual's quality of life appears to be explained by the telecommuter's improved concentration, flexibility, and control over time. The dependent variable, quality of life, is divided into quality of life at work and away from work. Gender appears to moderate the impact of telecommuting on work and non-work life, while telecommuting programs appear to affect telecommuter's stress level.
>
> (1994: 82)

Social tolerance of teleworking

With their concept of social tolerance of teleworking Büssing and Aumann (1996a) relate to the quality of life as well as to results of technology research. In their concept, social tolerance adopts a basic perspective and becomes an intersection between the facets of:

- ecology
- constitution and democracy
- culture
- economy
- humanisation of work.

Social tolerance of teleworking with respect to ecology

Teleworking has to be studied with respect to its ecological chances and risks. *Chances* could be a protection of natural resources (energy), traffic reduction, the saving of space and the improvement of air quality. However, the potential environmental benefits are controversial. For example, some researchers predict a substitution of commuter traffic by an overcompensation through increasing traffic during leisure time. *Risks* could, for example, result from increasing computer production and problems with the disposal of toxic material or from radiation through wireless telephone and mobile radio communication.

Social tolerance of teleworking with respect to constitution and democracy

Social tolerance of teleworking with respect to constitution and democracy is a wide area which is beyond the limits of this contribution. Only some aspects will be mentioned here. With respect to teleworking we have to consider questions like the inviolability of the home, the potential for equal rights and rights of minorities. The inviolability of the home conflicts with the duty of the employer to care and control for an ergonomic design of the working place (e.g. VDU). On the one hand teleworking can be a way to create a new deregulated labour market (e.g. outsourcing of jobs into self-employment), on the other hand it offers opportunities to, for example, integrate people into the labour market who are handicapped or who are obliged to care for parents, children or relatives.

Social tolerance of teleworking with respect to culture

Again, the social tolerance of teleworking with respect to culture is a broad field; we will restrict this aspect to the potential for making use of cultural opportunities. Teleworking offers autonomy and latitudes with regard to work and leisure time which increase the potential for cultural activities, because the opening hours and the crowding of cultural institutions are no longer barriers, and needs for culture can be met more spontaneously.

Social tolerance of teleworking with respect to economy

The position of economic issues in the teleworking debate is diverse. This stems largely from the different economic views taken. So far teleworking has mostly been dealt with from a microeconomic point of view: productivity gains and cost savings by the companies and money saved by the teleworkers. However, the social tolerance of teleworking with respect to economy demands a macro-economic addition to grasp its global and long-term effects. These effects are determined, for example, by the public and private telematic infrastructure, by national and global competition and position of companies, by the access to labour markets, by the availability and development of qualification on all levels, by quantities and qualities of health care and social support.

Social tolerance of teleworking with respect to the humanisation of work

For the purposes of work and organisational psychology *humanisation of work* as the fifth aspect of the social tolerance of teleworking is of main interest. This fifth aspect is also closely related to some aspects of quality of life and non-work life. According to Hacker (1985) and Ulich (1994) human work design comprises four criteria:

* *Freedom from harm* (i.e. no physical or psychophysical harm);
* *Freedom from impairment* (i.e. psychosocial well-being at the working place);
* *Reasonableness* (i.e. compatibility with norms and values with respect to job design and job content);
* *Health and personality enhancement* (i.e. chances for health and personality development at work, namely the development of cognitive and procedural skills, as well as social and metacognitive skills; health and personality enhancement should lead to a transfer between work and non-work; see also Frese and Zapf 1994).

In the following, an overview on some of the results concerning these four criteria of human work design (according to Büssing and Aumann 1996b) will be given:

Freedom from harm The living space of teleworkers often does not offer adequate working conditions (size of rooms, lighting, disturbances, equipment). Rarely workplaces at home are designed in accordance with ergonomic guidelines. Rather, telecommuters themselves are required to design their workplace without ergonomic know-how and appropriate instructions (see Huws *et al.* 1990; Katz and Duel 1990; Wedde 1994).

Freedom from impairment Teleworking leads to contrary effects with respect to quality and satisfaction with private life. On the one hand it affects family time positively and supports the simultaneousness and compatibility of job and family activities (see Garhammer 1995); on the other hand the blending of work and private life leads to stress and role conflicts (see Hall 1990; Huws 1984; Shamir 1992). This effect will be heightened under conditions of working times that are inappropriate for family concerns (see Goldmann and Richter 1992; Van Sell and Jacobs 1994). Moreover, teleworking which is not performed in a dependent employment status often leads to overstrain and self-exploitation. A lack of opportunity for social comparison of teleworkers constitutes an additional breeding ground for this effect (see Katz and Duell 1990). However, teleworking also contributes to stress reduction as in the case of stand-by duties which can be designed more agreeably from home (see Wedde 1994), or by reducing working and the associated stress situations (Gray *et al.* 1993).

Reasonableness Teleworking is experienced as reasonable by the majority of persons concerned, since this form of work can be incorporated into individual and family concerns, which is not easily feasible for other forms of work such as part-time work, for instance (see Büssing *et al.* 1996; Goldmann and Richter 1991, 1992; Garhammer 1994; Glaser and Glaser 1995; Van Sell and Jacobs 1994). In particular, for persons suffering from restricted mobility (because of personal handicaps, social obligations like caring for the elderly or raising children) teleworking offers an alternative to unemployment or interruption of employment. Still, one must remain sceptical towards teleworking that neither conforms with occupational training standards nor with the employee's level of occupational qualifications. The question of how far reasonableness can be evaluated only against the background of complicated access to labour markets and restricted life concerns is yet to be answered.

Personality enhancement The variety of tasks and activities of decentralised teleworking frequently is less diversified and characterised by lower autonomy than corresponding centralised work (see Büssing *et al.* 1996; Katz and Duell 1990). Often only routinised and clearly circumscribed tasks with little need for communication are found in teleworking, which may constitute a dequalifying aspect. Teleworking usually implies increased flexibility and sometimes also increases in autonomy. Flexibility and autonomy facilitate personal competences such as time management, self-organisation and independence. However, social competences demanded in situations like teamworking, communication and social conflicts are neglected, especially in decentralised and isolated home-based teleworking. An important aspect of personality enhancement is the opportunity for career development. Up to now, teleworking has made it more difficult to progress in terms of one's career. Progress has been impeded by factors such as: foreclosure because of being a teleworker, and because of being less informed about organisational structures, organisational life and career paths. A different assessment of teleworking and its career opportunities may come about in the wake of the globalisation of information and computer work and the dissolution of traditional structures in companies. Here, new competences and qualifications are demanded, and a new information and knowledge management will be established that telecommuters may well deal with in a better and quicker fashion than employees in traditional work forms (see Tung and Turban 1996).

Quality of non-work life under teleworking

Little research exists about the impacts of teleworking on the quality of life away from work. This is an amazing fact given that workers in teleworking programmes are supposed to be motivated by goals outside work. Some data does exist on the impact of teleworking on time for family and leisure activities, and on money saved. Moreover, according to the literature, gender, and especially gender-related obligations, may be a moderator of the relationship between teleworking and the quality of life outside of work, as well as at work (see Figure 9.2).

The quality of non-work life on the level of the individual worker can be described by variables like satisfaction, motivation, well-being, enhancement of skills, feelings of competence, control and so forth. However, the individual perspective is restricted and cannot embrace the system dynamics of the quality of non-work life of teleworkers. Rather, impacts of teleworking should be investigated in their system context, i.e. in consideration of family, partnership and non-work living arrangements.

To gain an understanding of this important argument the working time of teleworkers can serve as a good example because working time is probably the most important positive aspect for teleworking in Germany (see Büssing and Aumann 1996c) and elsewhere (see Mayer-List 1995; Qvortrup 1995; Van Sell and Jacobs 1994). Teleworking is regularly associated with individual freedom for family and leisure time. Although this seems obvious from an individual point of view it is in fact quite often not the case, and it is hidden by two circumstances. First, by the fact that most studies concentrate on working hours of the teleworking person and not on working hours of couples, families or – more generally – social systems. Therefore, the nominal gain in freedom for family and leisure time is quite often outweighed by indispensable obligations which are not compensated for in the social system. Second, the duration of working time is the focus in most studies instead of switching attention to the position and distribution of working time. Taking into account the working time patterns of couples and families, instead of individual telecommuters, one has to consider a deregulation of traditional working time patterns in many areas of work, i.e. the deregulation of working hours. Therefore, all types of shift-work, weekend and night-time work characterise the time pattern of a family system.

Moreover, a growing flexibility of working time schedules is another reason for position and distribution to have become more important. As a result, position and distribution determine the degree of common social time through the number of unsocial hours that have to be worked in families (for the same argument with respect to working time see Büssing 1997b).

A major shortcoming of research on the quality of non-work life for telecommuters is the fact that the impacts that work and other areas of life have on each other are not considered. The research has focused primarily on the effects of work on leisure time activities and on family life. Little research has been carried out that investigates how teleworking affects the interrelation between work and non-work domains of life. And these mutual interdependencies are most significant for the quality of life in both domains. From the literature on work and leisure we know that unidirectional influences between the two areas of life and their additive and cumulative effects are not sufficient to explain the link between work and non-work, and quite often are misleading not only from the scientific point of view but also from the subjective concepts of workers and employees (see Büssing 1995). Rather, one should study the interaction between the two areas of life and the underlying impacts to reach a valid understanding of this complex phenomenon (e.g. Büssing 1992; Zedeck 1992).

Teleworking, family and leisure: examples for mutual interdependencies and their impact on the quality of life

Teleworking at IBM Germany

The accompanying study by Glaser and Glaser (1995) on decentralised workplaces outside the headquarters at IBM Germany is based on interview data from 38 respondents. From the total 56 teleworkers at IBM Stuttgart all female employees (13) participated; the interviewed 25 male employees were randomly chosen, yet they represented the distribution across all IBM plants in the Stuttgart area. There were gender-specific differences in age in this sample. Male employees at an average age of 43.6 years were significantly older than their female colleagues with an average age of 34.9 years. With the exception of two persons (5.3 per cent), the teleworkers lived with a partner, two thirds of whom contributed to the household income. Three quarters of the teleworkers had to take care of children, with 29 per cent caring for two or more children. The central tasks for teleworkers were programming in the broadest sense (50 per cent), systems maintenance and surveillance (39.5 per cent) and training/service for software users (34.2 per cent).[1]

Teleworkers exhibit a high level of education: 57.9 per cent had university or polytechnic degrees, particularly in mathematics, engineering, physics, economics. One half of the remaining 42.1 per cent stemmed from crafts or technical occupations (electricians, toolmakers, mechanics and so on), the other half from business or trade. On average, teleworkers had been working for 12.8 months (ranging from 3 to 36 months) at decentralised workplaces. The majority of teleworkers (73.7 per cent) worked full time with 42.6 hours on average. 26.3 per cent worked part time with 28.7 per cent hours on average. Of the part-timers, 70 per cent were women (and 54 per cent of women were working part time).

Further, 42 per cent worked up to one day, 32 per cent more than one day and up to two-and-a-half days and 18 per cent worked three to five days at home. Shift-working was performed by 8 per cent of the teleworkers. While more than half (65 per cent) of the male teleworkers predominantly work hourly up to max-imally two days at home, 66 per cent of the women work at least two, and up to five days at home. The gender-specific distribution of working times between centralised and decentralised activities becomes even clearer if one considers the duration of working times, since two-thirds of part-timers are women (the female teleworkers at IBM work more often at home than in the company, whereas male teleworkers spend more working time in the company than at their work places at home). Nearly all respondents (95 per cent) mentioned a typical weekly dis-tribution of centralised and decentralised working times, which means that there are typical days on which people will work at home and at the company. Of those interviewed, 75 per cent of the teleworkers are satisfied with this distri-bution, while 15 per cent would like to work more at home; the remaining 10 per cent wanted, for example, more flexibility, more work in the evenings and daily change between work at home and in the company. The teleworkers chose a typical distribution of the relatively flexible and autonomously arrangeable working times at home (70 per cent). Although this distribution differs from the one respondents used when working in the company, a clear structure of working times seems to be important to most of the teleworkers. The individual design of working times may also explain why only one-half of teleworkers experienced a higher degree of self-discipline just because of their autonomy in working time design.

Time for partnership, family and leisure

The study shows that teleworkers did not spend more time with their families, partners or on their private lives as a whole. However, they were able to choose the right time for attending to their families and to take part in family life in a better way. An interesting result with respect to the use of time is the fact that about 60 per cent report to be able to receive visitors more spontaneously.

Participating in family life

More than 50 per cent of the teleworkers clearly state that they can participate better in the lives of their children. At the same time they complain about being increasingly involved in rows among the children and about the need to educate the children not to speak to them continually (40 per cent). The assumption that home-based working leads to a better understanding of education as a form of work was not supported. For 70 per cent of respondents this is irrelevant and only 13 per cent agree to the assumption. More time-intensive participation in family life is, however, also associated with a negative aspect: some 30 per cent of respondents, in particular the home-based teleworkers, miss having a break from the family and a sense of partnership in the company, and for some respondents continuous contact with family members appeared to be more than enough.

Impacts of family on work and vice versa

A frequent effect of home-based teleworking is that job stress is carried into the family and partnership. Nevertheless, the fact that the family develops more understanding for the work is seen as a positive feature of home-based work. Nearly a quarter of respondents report problems with relaxing from work when they were at home, so that a neglect of family and partnership (18.4 per cent) or a neglect of private contacts and hobbies (24 per cent) was the consequence. About a third of respondents reported that they were disturbed by family members. At least 21 per cent of teleworkers are interrupted by tasks for the family that emerge on short notice and leave little time to react ('Oh-could-you-quickly' tasks). Only in 34 per cent of cases did interruptions at short notice not occur.

Multiple loads and compatibility of work and family

An important result of the IBM study is the fact that neither men nor women perceive a double load through work and family, which is surprising as, particularly for female teleworkers, multiple loads through co-ordination of work, family, children and household work was assumed (see Büssing and Aumann 1996d; Fischer et al. 1993; Goldmann and Richter 1991; Handy and Mokhtarian 1996). Glaser and Glaser (1995) suggest that the female teleworkers at IBM are not faced with a serious dilemma: they do not have to decide in favour of paid employment in teleworking or unemployment; they rather decide on whether to work centralised or decentralised. Since teleworking is not perceived as more stressful than centralised work, there are no particular multiple loads. To what extent this argument is compatible with the problems of compatibility of work and family concerns mentioned above remains unclear. Still, 84 per cent of the female respondents with children report they telecommuted in order to settle the problem of taking care of their children in a better way. Only 33 per cent of the mothers would want to work at home irrespective of the question of taking care of children.

Isolation through home-based work

Although teleworking at IBM is not exclusively homebased and considerable time is spent in the company, feelings of isolation emerge in some teleworkers (18.4 per cent). More than half of the respondents (60 per cent) report that incidents of achievement cannot be shared spontaneously with somebody else and some (40 per cent) mention that they often miss someone to talk to.

Teleworking compared to centralised work under different working time schedules

The study by Garhammer (1994, 1995) surveyed 1,545 persons, 489 of which were employees with normal working time schedules and 1,056 working 'flexible' hours. Apart from the group of employees working normal time, four groups were formed for analysis:

- home-based teleworkers
- well-known flexible non-standard working time schedules (persons in shift-work or weekend work)
- 'time pioneers' consisting of higher municipal employees, employees working in the fields of training and education, freelancers and the self-employed
- employees from three working time projects in the manufacturing and service industry.

Nearly all of the 27 teleworkers are women, 50 per cent of whom have children. The group of teleworkers consists of 12 freelancers from all over Germany, two employees of Hewlett-Packard and 13 free contractors working in the field of data collection for a large market research institute (Gesellschaft für Konsumforschung Nürnberg). The women were teleworking for a relatively short period of time, more than half of them for less than three years.

On average the teleworkers worked 21.8 hours at home and 12.9 hours away from home. Of the female teleworkers, 89 per cent reported broad autonomy with respect to the position of working time, of these, only 12 female teleworkers (44 per cent) had a say in scheduling tasks.

Time for partnership, family and leisure

In comparison with the group of employees with normal working times, the traditional shift-work group, weekend workers and time pioneers, female teleworkers (as well as employees with normal working times) report the lowest time difficulties and spend more time with family and friends than the other groups. Thus, in comparison with other working time groups, teleworkers on average spend an additional 1.45 hours exclusively with their children. Teleworkers have slightly less spare time than employees in normal working time schedules, although they work more than one hour less on average. The reason lies in household obligations, which are 1.7 hours higher for teleworkers each day than for employees with normal working times. Teleworkers emerge from the comparison of different working time regulations as clearly the most satisfied group with respect to participation in public life. Also with respect to everyday life at home and with children, teleworkers appear relatively satisfied, but the organisation of everyday life under the condition of normal working times and taking care of children under the condition of flexible working time models does seem comparatively better or more easily feasible than in teleworking.

Participation in family life

On the basis of his study, Garhammer (1994) characterises teleworking as a family-friendly solution. The hallmark of family friendliness is attributed to teleworking because (a) employees can spend more time on taking care of children and (b) it allows an adaptation of working times to family and individual needs. Consequently, teleworkers are affected by only minor time difficulties.

Impacts of family on work and vice versa

Despite the overall positively perceived time sovereignty, 84 per cent of respondents still see their private life affected with by occasional time pressures of tasks. Garhammer's study shows that time sovereignty makes an individual design of life possible. Thus, the group of teleworkers displayed a strong mixture of work and leisure activities, i.e. leisure activities do not have to be restricted to the period between 6 p.m. and 12 p.m. as demanded when working normal times; instead an almost equal distribution of private activities during the course of the day emerges. Time sovereignty in connection with locally independent work seemingly leads to new work and leisure rhythms, which presumably correspond considerably more to individual needs and requirements than externally determined working and leisure times. However, 40 per cent of the teleworkers miss the clearly separated private sphere under the condition of home-based flexible teleworking, and at least 25 per cent believe they cannot work at home without interruption. The availability for children is evaluated positively as a family- and children-friendly solution, yet at the same time it is associated with negative effects on the work in the sense that teleworkers complain that maintaining concentration while working is made more difficult.

Multiple loads and compatibility of work and family

For 89 per cent of respondents the compatibility of work and family in teleworking is feasible. Teleworking seems to be particularly suited to mothers with children of school age up to 15 years. Those with children of that age especially made complaints about role conflicts between work and family – first, because there are inadequate facilities for taking care of children in that age group, and second, leisure and family activities are concentrated on the weekend and third, the time schedules of companies and schools often collide. Therefore an essential aspect with regard to compatibility of work and family was identified in 'time sovereignty'. This was the case with large sections of the sample of teleworkers in the survey. Autonomy over the design of working time appears to be used for offsetting job stress through flexible times, for relaxation or reducing the time pressure that emerges during the process of harmonising work and family, and by attaining a favourable fit between the time demands of those spheres of life.

Isolation through home-based work

In Garhammer's (1994) study the female home-based employees remained involved in the social networks of the company by alternating with forms of telework. Still, one-third of respondents reported negative experiences relating to having too little contact outside the home, and at least one-fifth missed social contacts at work.

Teleworking of women in the insurance business

The study by Büssing *et al.* (1996) is an evaluation study of two pilot projects in the insurance business (Allianz Lebensversicherung AG and Württembergische Versicherungs AG) focusing on teleworking with women during and after parental leave. Using interviews and questionnaires for the collection of data concerning both personal and work situations, eleven teleworkers, and two control groups with nine women re-entering the job after parental leave and ten women presently on parental leave, were investigated. The teleworkers were employed on a temporary and part-time basis. They were still on parental leave or had just started working again after a shortened period for parental leave. Those women re-entering their jobs did so after maternity leave, parental leave or the shortened parental leave, and worked 4-day weeks on a part-time basis (with the exception of one person working full time). Women on parental leave interrupted their employment for the period of parental leave. The average age for the teleworkers was 31 years (ranging from 24 to 39 years). The women have one or two children, with the majority of women on parental leave having two children. The children's age (5.1 years) for women re-entering the job was higher on average than those of teleworkers (2.3 years) and women on parental leave (2.7 years). Taking care of children is done by women on parental leave themselves, while the teleworking women take care of their children themselves for one part of the time, while the other is covered by partners, relatives or day-care mothers. The children of women re-entering the job are taken care of by relatives or kindergartens.

The educational level of the total sample is high: 50 per cent of participants finished secondary education or a specified secondary education, and one-third of the women either held diplomas from occupational training institutions (business studies) or had graduated (mathematics, informatics, teaching, economics). On average, the participants have been employed for 10 years and 9 months for the present company. Previous task fields of the women can be divided evenly into the categories of high-skilled clerical work and administration (in departments of the insurance companies dealing, for example, with accidents, automobile insurance policies) and the organisation of data processing (data and programme analysis, programming, testing).

Impacts of family on teleworking and vice versa

Looking at the subjectively perceived relationship of work and leisure, tele-workers show no particular role conflicts between the two spheres of life. The neutrality and strict independence of both spheres is denied; still, segmentation is considered as a compensatory strategy for stress. The teleworkers used segmenta-tion of both spheres of life selectively and in a differentiated way for the reduction of undesired influences between work and leisure.

Multiple loads and compatibility of teleworking and family

The study makes clear that teleworking for working women may present a favourable alternative for harmonising work and family demands. The female teleworkers were able to establish a temporal fit between household, family and job demands more easily than women re-entering the job. The teleworking women were able to adapt both job demands to individual and family concerns and vice versa. This bilateral adaptation to work and private demands occurs during the typical course of a day, just as it occurs in the case of special situations and unforseeable incidents. The female teleworkers often design their working times complementing those of their husbands or partners, and adapt to circum-stances in their families by flexible teleworking times, so that multiple loads can be avoided more effectively. In contrast, everyday life with women re-entering the job is dominated by the rhythm of work; individual and family needs are adapted to work; only in exceptional situations are work and private demands tuned to each other.

Isolation through home-based telework

As expected, work contacts decrease in teleworking. In particular, informal and private communication was affected, which obviously could not be carried out adequately via phone or electronic media. The loss of social contacts cannot totally be attributed to decentralised teleworking, as women re-entering the job also reported a reduction in the amount and frequency of social contacts in the company. Reasons can be found in (a) part-time employment which leaves less room for a constant flow of information and for informal communication, and (b) in the circumstance of family obligations, because little children make it more difficult to attend extraorganisational meetings which often followed work. Yet certain forms of organisation of alternating teleworking seem to alleviate the problem of the loss of social contacts, for example, by institutionalising centralised hours of attendance.

Collective teleworking: advantages for quality of life ?

The results from studies on home-based and alternating forms of teleworking give an impression both of their advantages and shortcomings for quality of life. Major advantages of these two forms of teleworking from the individual and family point of view seem to be the increase in flexibility and autonomy with respect to time, the related benefits for family and leisure activities and obligations, the increase in fit between demands from work and non-work, and, of course, the reduction in stress from commuting. However, results also reveal noticeable shortcomings. Most of them are correlated with the co-operative and social nature of work and the fact that home-oriented teleworking does not offer too many chances for complete task performance, face-to-face communication, informal exchange of information, use of social competencies and skills, and so forth.

Critics of these unfavourable aspects of home-oriented teleworking agree on the advantages of collective forms of teleworking, like neighbourhood and satellite offices, telecentres or telecottages, etc., to overcome many of the risks for quality of life (see Aicholzer 1996; Bagley *et al.* 1994; Baitsch *et al.* 1991; Büssing and Aumann 1997b; OFFNET Project Team 1995). The relevant gains from collective forms of teleworking can be summarised with the following points:

- periods of social isolation from home-oriented teleworking can be avoided;
- the co-operative nature of working tasks can be taken into account for work design;
- social competencies can be used in daily face-to-face communication with colleagues and customers;
- flow of information at work, particularly the informal informational supply, is kept up;
- (symbolic) boundaries between work and non-work which are useful to avoid too much spillover between work and private life (through deprivatisation of home, overcrowding and so forth) will not be broken down;
- decentralisation, flexibilisation, and the neighbourhood of collective teleworking places establish family friendly working conditions;
- collective teleworking also allows closer and more direct contact with customers;
- nearby collective teleworking contributes to a reduction of commuting and, therefore, stress;
- technological infrastructure, equipment and work design usually are superior; this allows and supports the performance of more sophisticated and complex working tasks;
- telematic equipment can be used more intensively, economically and ecologically;
- technical functioning of infrastructure and equipment can be more easily

assured; in case of defects, breakdowns, etc., technological know-how for repair is readily available;

- legal aspects like queries with respect to liability as well as work, health and safety protection can be more easily and effectively regulated and controlled for.

Results from a survey of 5,347 persons in five European countries by Empirica (see Korte *et al.*1994) reveal a marked interest in this organisation of teleworking. While 47 per cent of the Spanish participants state their interest, fewer, but still around one-third, of the participants from the other European countries (England, France, Germany, Italy) show an interest in collective teleworking. Contrary to this subjective demand, an amazing reserve against collective teleworking in European companies is revealed by the same study. Among the 2,507 companies which took part in this study only 6–7 per cent say that collective teleworking is an attractive new form of work organisation. (i.e. there are only slight differences between England, France, Germany, Italy, Spain). Most companies prefer – at least, to some extent – home-based or alternating forms, and they particularly like the self-employment status of teleworkers independent of the organisational form of teleworking.

What could be the reason for these large differences between the demand from individuals and companies? Companies might be afraid of the economical and organisational costs and necessary investments on the one hand, and disappointed by the long-term return for these investments on the other hand. It is obvious that most of the costs of collective teleworking are up to the companies while many of the costs of home-based and alternating teleworking (e.g. rooms, telecommunication infrastructure, extras) are on the teleworkers' side. This – at least at first glance – favourable calculation for organisations and companies with respect to alternating telework was understood as a major factor limiting innovations with regard to telecentres (see Aicholzer 1996; OFFNET Project Team 1995).

However, information from the unfortunately few publications (see Aicholzer 1996; Bagley *et al.* 1994; Büssing and Aumann 1997b; Godehardt 1994; International Labour Office 1990; Kordey and Korte 1996), and from the rapidly growing number of websites on projects, point at a growth and potential for collective forms of teleworking all over the world. Quite well-known projects are for example: 'Telecommuting in the San Francisco Bay Area' (Fay 1996), 'Australian Rural Telecentres Association',[2] 'Strategic Development Scheme 1993–94 of the Powys County Council in Wales',[3] the initiative 'TeleCottage Wales',[4] telecentre projects in Austria,[5] and telecentre projects in Germany (see Büssing and Aumann 1997b; Technologie-Transferzentrale Schleswig-Holstein 1996; Technologie Transfer Trier GmbH 1997).

Many of these projects in collective teleworking are politically motivated and go back to public, private, community and state initiatives. They aim, for example, at the development of rural or economically weak regions by taking advantage of the overall and societal benefits of collective forms of teleworking, e.g. use of 'gentle technologies', reduction of traffic, use of regional labour markets, installation of modern teleinfrastructures, the setting up of family-friendly working places. Therefore, it seems that many of today's projects in collective teleworking in some way or another support quality of life in the broad sense defined above.

Conclusions and perspectives

With respect to quality of life, teleworking opens up a whole string of new options for companies and their employees. These options are multifaceted. Besides the different areas of economy, ecology, culture and so forth we have to consider chances and risks on the different levels of the individuals, their families and social groups, as well as on the level of their workplaces, companies and markets. And moreover, we have argued that these different areas and levels interact, and that effects on a single, or individual level, cannot validly be generalised to a system level, for example, a family. The discussion and evaluation of teleworking so far suffers from short-circuit arguments which do not account for this complexity with respect to quality of life and the social tolerance of teleworking as proposed in the concepts by Van Sell and Jacobs (1994) and Büssing and Aumann (1996a).

This chapter is dedicated to the quality of life of teleworking and to the social tolerance of its conditions and outcomes in the interface between work and non-work, in particular of teleworking, family and private life. It restricts the focus to the forms which are most common today, i.e. to home-based and alternating teleworking, and it compares these two with merits and problems with regard to quality of life of collective forms of teleworking. For home-based and alternating teleworking the results from the literature and the results from our studies show two sides of the coin and depict gains, losses and the ambivalence of the teleworkers. Quality of life as well as social tolerance of teleworking are improved on the one hand and impaired in some aspects on the other. For example, we find a better overall fit and more specifically an improved synchronisation between family obligations and work requirements – especially for women – reduced stress because of reduced working, more autonomy for working time regulations, and so on. However, because the fit between work and family is largely due to the decision of the teleworker, one easily can imagine the 'golden cage' the teleworker is caught in when he or she is faced with the impacts of his or her decisions and acting on the systems level of the family.

Another detriment to the quality of life of the home-based and alternating form of teleworking is due to the co-operative and social nature of work. While teleworkers gain flexibility and autonomy to improve the quality of their private and family lives, at the same time they are faced with little participation in the co-operative and social life of the organisation. They lack face-to-face communication, experience of social competencies, and the informal flow of information, and they need to be much more self-organised and self-motivated without support from colleagues and superiors. From the scarce empirical research on the quality of life and teleworking so far it is hard to tell what will be the long-term outcomes and consequences with respect to well-being, stress, gains and losses in time, money, qualification and so forth.

In direct comparison, forms of collective teleworking seem to avoid many of the detrimental effects on the quality of life under home-based and alternating telework. However, it would be a superficial argument to valuate collective teleworking generally as a superior organisational form. The suitability of and the choice for a specific form of teleworking depends very much upon pre-conditions like individual and family circumstances, the situation of work and organisation, and upon the tasks. Moreover, a decision for or against a form of teleworking under the criteria of quality of life cannot be independent of the period of one's personal and social development, i.e. while during certain phases of life – for example, during the phase of founding a family – it might be very useful to do home-based telework, in many other periods collective teleworking will be much more appropriate.

The rapid change of working life continues and with it new forms of work like teleworking not only gain in attractiveness, but also they are increasingly offered to people who, unfortunately, are not yet ready for the new message. Telework in particular is associated with high hopes, yet hardly anyone today knows exactly what future work with a large proportion of teleworkers will look like or ought to look like. Only one thing seems to be certain, that 'reality will cut through' and that the rules according to which future work will be designed cannot be deduced from rules of the past. The various forms of telework may develop into new and interesting options if they are linked with differential work design and work organisation regarding the conflicting relationship between work, family and leisure. Something really must be done to prepare people for this new form of work in their families, schools and occupations, making clear the options, challenges and risks for their working biographies and their social security.

Acknowledgement

Thanks are due to Sandra Aumann, Thomas Bissels and Kenija von Malm for their helpful assistance in preparing this paper.

Notes

1 The broad fields of activities lead to multiple answers. Therefore, the responses add up to more than 100 per cent (Glaser and Glaser 1995).
2 http://www.netc.net.au/telecentres.html;http://netspot.com.au/oltc/olcs/case32.htm
3 http://www.telecentres.com/tcjmsup.htm
4 http://www.telecottages.org/
5 For example, http://obelix.soe.oeaw.ac.at/telework/

References

Aicholzer, G. (1996) 'Telework centres: a desirable social innovation without future?', in P.J. Jackson and J. van der Wielen (eds) Proceedings of the Workshop *New International Perspectives on Telework: From Telecommuting to the Virtual Organisation*, London 31 July–2 August 1996, 2, Tilburg, The Netherlands: Tilburg University Press.

Bagley, M.N., Mannering, J.S. and Mokhtarian, P.L. (1994) *Telecommuting Centers and Related Concepts: A Review of Practice*, University of Calfornia: Davis Institute of Transportation Studies.

Baitsch, C., Katz, C., Spinas, P. and Ulich, E. (1991) *Computerunterstützte Büroarbeit. Ein Leitfaden für Organisation und Gestaltung* [Computer Supported Office Work. A Manual for Organizing and Design], Zürich, Verlag der Fachvereine.

Büssing, A. (ed.) (1992) *Arbeit und Freizeit* [Work and Leisure]. *Themenheft der Zeitschrift für Arbeits- und Organisationspsychologie*, 36.

—— (1995) 'Work and leisure in health care. A study of subjective concepts', in Hagberg, M., Hofmann, F., Stößel, U. and Westlander, G. (eds), *Occupational Health for Health Care Workers*, Landsberg am Lech: Ecomed.

—— (1997a) 'Telearbeit' [Teleworking], in D. Frey, C. Graf Hoyos and D. Stahlberg (eds), *Lehrbuch der Arbeits-und Organisationspsychologie* [Textbook of work and organizational psychology], Göttingen, Verlag für Angewandte Psychologie.

—— (1997b) 'Working time scheduling and the relation between work and leisure', in G. Bosch, D. Meulders and F. Michon (eds), *Working Time: New Issues, New Norms, New Measures*, London: Routledge.

Büssing, A. and Aumann, S. (1996a) *Sozialverträglichkeit von Telearbeit* [Social Tolerance of Teleworking] (Report No. 35) München, Technical University, Chair of Psychology.

—— (1996b) 'Telearbeit aus Arbeitspsychologischer Sicht. Untersuchung von Telearbeit anhand von Kriterien Humaner Arbeit' [Teleworking from a Work Psychology Perspective. Evaluation of Teleworking Using Criteria of Humanized Work], *Arbeit. Zeitschrift für Arbeitsforschung, Arbeitsgestaltung und Arbeitspolitik* 5: 133–53.

—— (1996c) 'Telearbeit und Arbeitszeitgestaltung' [Teleworking and Working Time Design], *WSI-Mitteilungen* 49: 450–8.

—— (1996d) 'Telearbeit und das Verhältnis von Betrieb, Familie und Freizeit: Eine aktuelle Bestandsaufnahme' [Teleworking and the Relationship between Company, Family and Leisure. A Review], *Zeitschrift für Arbeitswissenschaft* 50: 225–32.

—— (1997a) *Telearbeit. Analyse, Bewertung und Gestaltung ortsungebundener Arbei* [Telework. Analysis, Evaluation, and Design], Göttingen, Verlag für Angewandte Psychologie.

—— (1997b) *Telezentren im Bayerischen Raum. Organisationsanalyse von Kollektiver Telearbeit in Telezentren* [Telecentres in Bavaria. Organisational analysis of collective teleworking], Report No. 38, München, Technical University, Chair of Psychology.

Büssing, A., Kunst, R. and Michel, S. (1996) *Qualifikationsanforderungen, Berufliche Qualifizierung und Mehrfachbelastung unter Telearbeit. Eine Quasi-Experimentelle Untersuchung von Telearbeiterinnen im Erziehungsurlaub* [Qualificational Demands, Qualification and Multiple Work Load under Teleworking. A Quasi-Experimental Study of Teleworking Women on Parental Leave], Report No. 31, München, Technical University, Chair of Psychology.

Campbell, A. (1996) 'Creating the virtual organisation and managing the distributed workforce', in P.J. Jackson and J. van der Wielen (eds) Proceedings of the Workshop *New International Perspectives on Telework: From Telecommuting to the Virtual Organisation*, London 31 July–2 August 1996, 2, Tilburg, The Netherlands: Tilburg University Press.

Chapman, A.J., Sheehy, N.P., Heywood, S., Dooley, B. and Collins, S.C. (1995) 'The organizational implications of teleworking', in C.L. Cooper and I.T. Robertson (eds) *International Review of Industrial and Organizational Psychology*, Chichester: Wiley and Sons.

EITO (European Information Technology Observatory) (1996) Mainz, Eggebrecht.

Fay, N. (1996) 'Telecommuting in the San Francisco Bay Area: a case study of two regional telecommuting programms', in P.J. Jackson and J. van der Wielen (eds) Proceedings of the Workshop *New International Perspectives on Telework: From Telecommuting to the Virtual Organisation*, London 31 July–2 August 1996, 2, Tilburg, The Netherlands: Tilburg University Press.

Fischer, U., Späker, G. and Weißbach, H.-J. (in collaboration with J. Beyer) (1993) *Neue Entwicklungen bei der sozialen Gestaltung von Telearbeit* [New Developments of the Social Design of Telework], Informationen zur Technologiepolitik und zur Humanisierung der Arbeit No. 18, Düsseldorf: DGB-Bundesvorstand.

Frese, M. and Zapf, D. (1994) 'Action as the Core of Work of Psychology: A German Approach', in H.C. Triandis, M.D. Dunette and L.M. Hough (eds) *Handbook of Industrial and Organizational Psychology*, Palo Alto: Consulting Psychologists Press.

Garhammer, M. (1994) *Balanceakt Zeit. Auswirkungen flexibler Arbeitszeiten auf Alltag, Freizeit und Familie* [Balancing Act Time. Influences on Everyday Life, Leisure and Family], Berlin: Sigma.

—— (1995) 'Sozialverträglichkeit von Arbeitszeiten. Soziologische Überlegungen und Ergebnisse der Zeitbudgetforschung' [Social Tolerance of Working Time Design. Sociological Considerations and Results from Time Budget Research], in A. Büssing and H. Seifert (eds) *Sozialverträgliche Arbeitszeitgestaltung* [Social tolerance of working time design], München: Hampp.

Glaser, W.R. and Glaser, M.O. (1995) *Telearbeit in der Praxis. Psychologische Erfahrungen mit außerbetrieblichen Arbeitsstätten bei der IBM Deutschland GmbH* [Teleworking in Praxis. Psychological Experiences with Decentralised Workplaces at IBM Germany GmbH], Neuwied, Luchterhand.

Godehardt, B. (1994) *Telearbeit. Rahmenbedingungen und Potentiale,* [Telework. Conditions and Potentials], Opladen, Westdeutscher Verlag.

Goldmann, M. and Richter, G. (1991) *Beruf und Familie endlich vereinbar? Teleheimarbeit von Frauen* [Job and Family Finally Compatible? Home-Based Telework of Women], Dortmund: Montana Druck- und Verlagsgesellschaft mbH.

—— (1992) *Teleheimarbeit von Frauen. Betriebliche Flexibilisierungsstrategien und das Interesse von Frauen an Vereinbarkeit von Beruf und Familie* [Home-Based Telework of Women. Flexibilisation Strategies of Companies and the Interests of Women in the Compatibility of Work and Family], Dortmund, Ministerium für die Gleichstellung von Frau und Mann des Landes Nordrheinwestfalen.

Gray, M., Hodson, N. and Gordon, G. (1993) *Teleworking Explained*, Chichester: Wiley.

Hacker, W. (1985) 'Activity – A fruitful concept in industrial psychology', in M. Frese and J. Sabini (eds) *Goal Directed Behavior: The Concept of Action in Psychology*, 262–84. Hillsdale, NJ: Erlbaum.

Hall, D.T. (1990) 'Telecommuting and the management of work–home boundaries', in *Paradigms Revised: Annual Review of Communications and Society*, 177–208. Institute for Information Studies, Nashville, TN: Northern Telecom Inc. and Queenstown, MD, Aspen Institute.

Handy, S.L. and Mokhtarian, P.L. (1996) 'The future of telecommuting', *Futures* 28, 3: 227–40.

Huws, U. (1984) *The New Homeworkers: New Technology and the Changing Location of White-Collar Work*, London: Low Pay Unit.

Huws, U., Korte, W.B. and Robinson, S. (1990) *Telework: Towards the Elusive Office*, Chichester: Wiley.

International Labour Office (ILO) (1990) *Telework*, Conditions of Work Digest Series, Vol. 9, No. 1.

Katz, C. and Duell, W. (1990) 'Individuelle Telearbeit für Männer. Chance für Neue Geschlechterrollen?' [Individual Telework for Men. Chances for New Gender Roles?], in F. Frei and I. Udris (eds), *Das Bild der Arbeit* [The picture of work], 302–14. Berne: Huber.

Kordey, N. and Korte, W.B. (1996) *Telearbeit Erfolgreich Realisieren* [Teleworking Successfully Realised], Stuttgart: Vieweg.

Korte, W.B., Kordey, N. and Robinson, S. (1994) *Telework Penetration, Potential and Practice in Europe*, TELDET Report No. 11 (also referred to as Empirica (TELDET Project) 1994.

Littek, W. and Charles, T. (eds) (1995) *The New Division of Labour*, Berlin: de Gruyter.

Mayer-List, I. (1995) 'Möchten Sie in diesem Büro arbeiten?' [Would you like to work in this office?], *SZ Magazin*, 44, 3 November: 36–44.

Nilles, J.M. (1994) *Making Telecommuting Happen. A Guide for Telemanagers and Telecommuters*, New York: Van Nostrand Reinhold.

OFFNET Project Team (1995) *Networked European Neighbourhood Offices: An Evaluation of the Neighbourhood Office Model of Teleworking*, Project report to the commission of the European Communities, Vienna: Austrian Academy of Sciences/ITA.

Picot, A., Reichwald, R. and Wigand, R.T. (1996) *Die Grenzenlose Unternehmung* [The boundaryless organisation], Wiesbaden: Gabler.

Qvortrup, L. (1995) *Telework: The Trend Towards Networking*. CCS, Odense University, Denmark. UCRL: http://www.icbl.hw.ac.uk/telep/resource/LarsTelework.html

Ramsover, R.M. (1985) *Telecommuting: The Organizational and Behavioral Effects of Working at Home*, Michigan: UMI Research Press.

Rane, A. (1995) *Home Office Market Update*, Link Resources Corporation, New York.

Reichwald, R. and Möslein, K. (1996) 'Telearbeit und Telekooperation' [Telework and teleco-operation], in H.-J. Bullinger and H.J. Warnecke (eds) *Neue Organisationsformen im Unternehmen – Ein Handbuch für das Moderne Management* [New Forms of Organisation of Firms – A Handbook for the Modern Management], 691–708. Berlin: Springer.

Shamir, B. (1992) 'Home: The perfect workplace?', in S. Zedeck (ed.) *Work, Families, and Organizations*, 272–311. San Francisco: Jossey-Bass Publishers.

Technologie Transfer Trier GmbH (1997) *Telearbeit in Rheinland-Pfalz* [Telework in Rheinland Pfalz] http://www.rpl.de

Technologie-Transferzentrale Schleswig-Holstein (1996) *Projekt Telearbeit in Schleswig-Holstein* [Project Telework in Schleswig-Holstein]: http://tisch.ttz-sh.de/ta/

Tung, L.-L. and Turban, E. (1996) 'Information technology as an enabler of telecommuting', *International Journal of Information Management* 16: 103–17.

Ulich, E. (1994) *Arbeitspsychologie* [Work psychology], Stuttgart: Schäffer-Poeschel.

Van Sell, M. and Jacobs, S.M. (1994) 'Telecommuting and quality of life: A review of the literature and model for research', *Telematics and Informatics* 11: 81–95.

Wedde, P. (1994) *Telearbeit. Handbuch für Arbeitnehmer, Betriebsräte und Anwender* [Telework. Handbook for Employees, Works Council and User], Köln: Bund.

Zedeck. S. (1992) 'Exploring the domain of work and family concerns', in S. Zedeck (ed.) *Work, Families, and Organizations*, 1–32. San Francisco: Jossey-Bass Publishers.

Part 3

INTEGRATIVE FRAMEWORKS FOR TELEWORKING

Much has been said about the issues teleworking raises for a whole range of matters in organisational and social life. Until recently, however, little has been written to suggest how we can understand the role for, and manage the transition to, telework in a reasonably systematic way. The contributors to Part 3 seek to address this. Each illustrates ways in which teleworking issues can be integrated into broader areas of social planning and organisational change.

Alistair Campbell and Charles Grantham in Chapter 10 concentrate on the management of intellectual capital. They point out that the spatial and temporal distribution of modern organisations, and their reliance on the creation and cultivation of their knowledge base for competitive advantage, demand new ways of managing the informational and human resources of enterprises. This involves combining 'technical perspectives' – such as the ability to access data – with 'business perspectives' – the questions of utility and added-value. To illustrate how this can be done in a distributed environment, the authors introduce the methodology of the 'Organisational Assessment System' (OAS). This, they suggest, helps to assess the readiness of an organisation to move into distributed working and identifies needs – such as for skills and knowledge – that are required if the arrangement is to meet its business objectives.

The integration of teleworking into 'service management' jobs is the focus of chapter 11 by Scott Johnson. Those people who work directly with the customer – such as consultants and sales people – are, Johnson argues, ideally placed to take advantage of teleworking support. He discusses a framework for integrating teleworking into service management, with the aim of enhancing the delivery of services – for example, through better relationship-building with customers thanks to an improved allocation of service workers' time. He points out that effective implementation of teleworking in service jobs must address several important factors, such as the effects of teleworking on customer behaviour.

In Chapter 12 Lois and Benjamin Goldman address the way broader social issues can be combined with teleworking developments, particularly where these take place in urban areas. They argue that city planners have an important role to play if teleworking is to bring advantages to cities as a whole, rather than simply benefiting individual teleworkers and their companies. The authors show that because planners provide a longer term and more socially inclusive perspective, they are well-placed to identify and integrate a wider range of issues that relate to quality of life and economic development in cities.

The integration of teleworking with broader social issues is also the concern of Chapter 13 by Ann Brewer and David Hensher. According to these authors, commuting behaviour is strongly associated with changes in work practices. They develop a framework for the study of travel behaviour by examining it in the context of the organisation of work. In doing so they develop links between travel behaviour and such issues as the human resource orientation of companies (for example, supervision and reward mechanisms) and work arrangements (such as compressed work weeks, telework, and so on).

Koji Sato and Wendy Spinks in Chapter 14 focus on the possible contribution of teleworking to crisis management. This draws on experiences following the earthquake which stuck Kobe in Japan in 1995. They outline the results of a survey regarding the extent of earthquake damage and the disruption this caused to normal life – especially work and commuting routines. This also describes the role teleworking played in dealing with the disruption. The authors point out that the lessons learned from this can be integrated into disaster planning to help achieve a better response to future situations.

In the final chapter of Part 3, Paul Jackson illustrates how teleworking ideas were used as a perspective in a 'non-teleworking' organisation to frame a process of organisational analysis and learning. In the case he describes, possibilities for spatial reorganisation were identified that addressed specific problems and opportunities faced by the organisation.

10

ORGANISATIONAL ASSESSMENT IN THE DISTRIBUTED WORK ENVIRONMENT

Using measures of intellectual capital in the planning process

Alistair Campbell and Charles Grantham

Introduction

Distributed work, describing one of the most rapidly growing workplace and organisational trends, has as many definitions as there are people studying or practising it. Distributed work can be defined as work activity conducted by groups or teams of people separated from each other in time and space, with advanced communication technologies being used to co-ordinate the work processes taking place. Distributed work is concerned with the central or core business function of the enterprise, and as such the outsourcing of support functions to external agents should not be classified as distributed work. Irrespective of the exact definition employed, distributed work includes workers, managers and the technology that enables them to complete tasks at a distance from each other (Grantham and Nichols 1993). The extent of this phenomenon is hard to measure. Estimates of teleworking in the US vary from a conservative figure of 4.47 million persons (ISDW 1996) to a high of 7.0 million (Raur 1995). The European Union has set a goal of having 20 million teleworkers in Europe by 2002.

For some organisations, the virtual office is the most radical form of distributed work replacing the fixed location office with a mobile workforce linked only by technology. The virtual office faces change at every turn, from information systems support for the new workforce, to management and career development skills for individual employees. Yet the virtual office is only one of the growing number of forms of distributed work. Distributed work is a workplace phenomenon that can be classified according to where workers are in time and space. Figure 10.1 describes the arrangement of the virtual work place.

The advantages of distributed work appear to include increased productivity

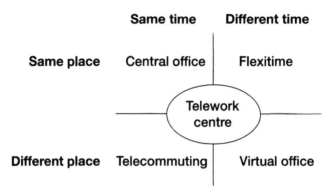

Figure 10.1 Virtual workplace arrangements

(Hesse and Grantham 1991) and worker satisfaction, reduced commuting time and transportation-related environmental stress, and decreased corporate overhead expenses (Pratt 1993; Di Martino and Wirth 1990; Kraut 1987; Kraut 1989; Olson 1987). Studies also suggest that the challenges successful distributed work programmes must overcome include worker isolation, the need for new ways to monitor performance, the need for new organisational structures and norms to ensure maximum return on the distributed work investment (Grantham 1996b).

The technology that makes remote work possible is becoming more sophisticated every day. At its most basic, distributed work relies on telephone and electronic mail connections supplemented with fax communication. Desktop videoconferencing tools are bringing technology to the home-based distributed worker. More sophisticated, and expensive, videoconferencing, satellite and collaborative work systems can enhance communication between home offices and neighbourhood or satellite centres. Groupware applications make it possible for remotely located workers to work simultaneously on the same computer-based projects (LaPlant 1993; Holtham 1992; Ishii *et al.* 1994; Finholt and Sproull 1990). IBM's acquisition of Lotus Development Corporation and the purchase of Collabra Software by Netscape Communications are indicative of the growing popularity and importance of groupware programs in the corporate application market. Telepresence systems combine groupware applications with videoconferencing tools to simulate the collaborative environment of working together at the same time and place.

Intellectual capital

The management practices that create the next generation of business organisations will be knowledge based. Business performance will not only be assessed by financial performance, but will also be measured in terms of intellectual assets and the ability to create and apply new ideas in the marketplace. The result of this is that a new model of organisational functioning is required to effectively manage the creation and use of intellectual capital; current management theories are becoming inadequate for these new spatially and temporally distributed organisations. Business leaders and thinkers are struggling to understand the organising principles of these new organisations.

Intellectual capital is a concept that has grown in popularity over the past few years. Organisations have come to find the more traditional ways of managing assets wanting, when the market value of companies begins to significantly exceed their component replacement costs (Brooking 1996). John Kenneth Galbraith first used the term *intellectual capital* in 1969 (Feiwal 1975). Galbraith believed that this form of capital was more than just a static asset, having a dynamic component which added value in its application to business need. Definitional arguments aside, Galbraith managed to focus new attention on the value of intangible assets in organisations.

Intellectual capital is not just the data or the information that resides in files, databases and papers. Information, intelligence, knowledge and, finally, wisdom are related but take on different values with increasing scope and context. Therefore, knowledge can be created from information, when that information is applied to solving a problem within the context of a business operation. Information contained in this paper for example has a value, but has even greater value when it is adapted to solving a financial management problem. It then becomes knowledge.

Many definitions are currently being proposed for this complex concept. Tom Stewart defines intellectual capital as the intangible assets of skill, knowledge and information that have been formalised, captured and leveraged to produce a higher-valued asset. There are three principles that drive the need to manage knowledge. First, the value of intellectual assets exceeds by many times the value of balance sheet assets. Second, intellectual capital is the raw material from which financial results are achieved. Finally, managers distinguish between different types of intellectual capital (Stewart 1994). Organisations such as Skandia Group, Dow Chemical, Hughes Aircraft, Equitable Life and Canadian Imperial Bank of Commerce are beginning to formalise how they specify, account for and manage this asset. In fact, many US Big Six accounting firms are beginning to integrate intellectual capital into their service operations. Ernst and Young, Andersen and Price Waterhouse have established research and development projects to explore the evolution of intellectual capital management.

Probably the most cogent view of intellectual capital has been developed at Skandia Group through the leadership of Leif Edvinsson, Corporate Director Intellectual Capital. The Skandia Group have created a model describing the principal building blocks that combine to form the company's intellectual capital (Skandia Group 1995). The model is illustrated in Figure 10.2.

Human capital is the source of innovation and renewal, providing information, insight, and ideas. Schultz defines human capital as:

> The decisive factors of production in improving the welfare of poor people are not space, energy, and cropland; the decisive factors are the

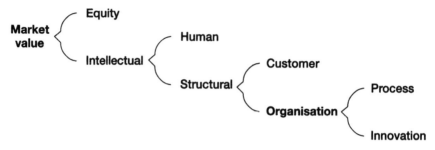

Figure 10.2 Skandia's model of intellectual capital

improvement in population quality and advances in knowledge. These advancements can be augmented by appropriate investment in human capital.

(Schultz 1981)

A company's human capital base is composed of four individual characteristics (Hudson 1993):

1 genetic inheritance
2 formal education
3 life experience
4 social psychological attitudes about life and business.

Human capital is the engine of creation in an enterprise ranging from the R&D laboratory to face-to-face customer interaction. It is where the capacity of the firm is formed and moulded. Human capital is not a subset of intellectual capital, but the storehouse of it, the capacity for it and its limiting factor. In fact, some commentators believe that the shortage of human capital will be the limiting factor in enterprise expansion in the next century (Coates 1995).

Structural capital is the non-human element that supports human capital. Structural capital is defined as the sum of the strategy, structure, systems and processes that enables an organisation to produce and deliver products to customers. It is an enabler of performance, promoting the continuous application of knowledge to business. It also is a cultural ethos that promotes learning and sharing of those learning experiences (Senge 1990). The most effective way to manage this element of capital is through examining information flows in and around an organisation. These information flows are the distribution channel of applied knowledge from the firm to the customer. Structural capital is arguably of greater importance, as it remains with the company, and it can be used time and again. Structural capital can amplify the value or subtract from human capital (Skandia Group 1995).

Structural capital includes customer capital and organisational capital. *Customer capital* is the knowledge of channels, customer preferences, trends and competitive intelligence. Customer satisfaction is measured in terms of demands customers make on the firm for products and services. These demands then feed back into the organisation via human and structural capital mechanisms and appear as changes in distribution channels and service levels. Without human or structural capital a firm cannot receive added-value from customer capital. When internal human capital reaches its own limit, the only effective tactic to increase overall intellectual capital is to tap into the customer base to discover new preferences, changes and applications. Market position can present competitive advantage (Porter 1985). 'Distinctive competency' or uniqueness of the firm (Prahalad and Hamel 1990) is rooted in customer expectations. This suggests therefore, that part of an organisation's customer capital lies outside management's direct control, and in fact is held by its customers.

Organisational capital contains the 'systematised, structured and packaged competencies and systems for converting the company's innovative strength and value-creating work processes' (Skandia Group 1995). Organisational capital enables faster and more effective sharing of knowledge through making it more accessible to users. Enhanced future earnings capabilities will be realised as the competence and experience can be multiplied or leveraged through increased internal or external co-operation (Skandia Group 1995). The Skandia model stresses both structural and organisational capital and, by inference, management's ability to capture, analyse and exploit intellectual capital. Conventional industrial business models are built on the assumption of a central controlling authority of assets as a means of measuring the value of the enterprise. Skandia's organisational emphasis follows this business model. An alternative is to place more importance on measurements of customer capital. In the emerging Internet commerce business model it is argued that value lies in the interaction between companies and their customers (Hagel and Armstrong 1997). Data about customer preferences and behaviour is therefore a key differentiator. An approach to managing intellectual capital that is more 'net centric', placing key value-added on customer relations, is more closely related to an emerging business model than the Skandia approach.

Managing intellectual capital

As more and more of the value-adding business process becomes the creation and delivery of intellectual capital, the focus of organisational leaders must shift away from cost containment of hard assets. The major organisational issue to be addressed by communities, educational institutions and business planners for the next decade, is how to manage the development and stewardship of intellectual capital.

Managing intellectual capital combines information resources with human resources. Information resources are made up of databases, telecommunication networks and interface engines. Human resources add value to information by setting the context of the business activity ('How do we do it?'), generating meaning ('What does it mean to us and the customer?') and understanding purpose ('Why do we do this anyway?'). Leaders cannot take for granted that employees will either answer these questions, or for that matter even care about them.

This differentiation in value-adding mechanisms results in the creation of a conflict in management agendas. People with technical responsibilities tend to focus on one set of measures, priorities and world views; while those given the responsibility of human resource management tend to see things from a business perspective. In researching the development of intellectual capital accounting procedures and implementation plans, two opposing orientations to these issues have been identified; the *technical perspective* and the *business perspective* (Jacoby 1995). First, the basic technical perspective is that value is added through connectivity (Michalski 1995). The greater access to data sources, the higher the volume of electronic mail and the more ease of use of the computer, all combine to contribute to the valuation of intellectual capital. This perspective results in the expenditure of financial assets to bring more power to the desktop, implement Executive Decision Systems (eds) and connect databases through applications such as Lotus Notes. However, being connected to datasources does not mean that data or knowledge can be extracted and applied in a business setting. The technical perspective places a premium on activity. It is an engineering perspective.

The basic *business perspective* is based on application utility (Dyson 1996). Having a large library without a librarian who can help interpret specific information needs is next to worthless. Creativity and performance in action carry a premium. This is the softer side of the intellectual capital equation, and what makes most managers nervous. Their problem is how to structure a budget to increase the application utility of their firm. Having employees with numerous degrees or qualifications is of limited value, unless they also have the skills to apply this knowledge. This overall contrast shows up in terms of comparing design (business perspective) to engineering (technical perspective). These are not mutually exclusive concepts or activities. However, the central issue facing managers is how to deal with the conceptual shift in decision-making from the perspective of engineering to that of design.

Integrating these two seemingly divergent perspectives is required for the management of intellectual capital. This integration will come through increased education in the workplace, which is effectively an intellectual capital creation process in itself. Peter Drucker explains the logic behind this contention. In brief, a transformation of our very social structure is underway, which is currently being experienced in both business and education. This social transformation coupled with transformation of businesses has come together in the development of intellectual capital management as a focus of current management science (Drucker 1994).

What then, are the necessary and sufficient conditions for the specification of a more comprehensive management model? The current accepted definitions of intellectual capital, begin by defining a group of basic categories of intellectual capital reservoirs. This approach, however, appears to be inadequate to explain differences in market valuation and replacement cost of enterprises. As this gap between replacement cost and market valuation increases it becomes necessary to better understand where, and how, intellectual capital is created so we can develop the tools and techniques to help us maximise firm valuation. Recent economic thinking has begun to point out the critical nature of this issue. A recent quote from Gary Becker, the 1992 Nobel Laureate highlights this:

> Human capital is as much a part of the wealth of nations as are factories, housing, machinery, and other physical capital. In fact, economists *estimate* that human capital accounts for much more than half of all the wealth in the U.S. and other economically advanced nations.
>
> (Becker 1996; [our emphasis])

It appears that a sufficient model would move the analysis to a higher level of measurement – from merely nominal to ratios. This refined model also needs to specify elements of intellectual capital, and organisational effectiveness by extension, in terms of core business processes of knowledge-based enterprises, not technical-based functions. Another necessary condition is the inclusion of environmental or external elements which impact the enterprise. Large organisations invariably have a hierarchical dimension to their structure that affects the flow of intellectual capital. Finally, a necessary and sufficient management model operates in a way that promotes clear communication within all parts of the organisation and can be easily grasped by managers.

Intellectual capital management will become more and more important in the life of organisations as they see a need to better manage all asset bases (Sterns 1994). Intellectual capital is coming to be understood as a necessary supplement to traditional financial management for knowledge-based organisations (Brooking 1996; Bontis 1995). Intellectual capital needs to be measured to enable assessment of its real value to the firm. Organisations can be characterised in many ways, with the conventional approach using financial models. These models, however, are less relevant in information-intensive environments. Typical financial management focuses on 'hard assets' which can be translated into interchangeable terms such as dollars, units of inventory or other physical entities (Quinn 1992). There is a category of assets owned by firms which is closely related to intellectual capital. These assets are usually referred to as 'intellectual property assets'. For example, patents, copyrights, trade and service marks are intellectual property that can be valued and carried on the books. There is concern however that an additional category of 'soft assets' such as intellectual capital, or goodwill, have gone unmeasured or only estimated in the roughest of terms. The result of this is great difficulty in measuring and managing the intangible assets of skill and knowledge, which are the chief ingredients of the new economy (Bontis 1995).

The proposition remains that new models of organisational functioning are needed and intellectual capital has a high potential for being a basis for the development of these new models. Many contemporary management consultants are trying to do this. 'Organisational learning' (Senge 1990); 'Business Re-engineering' (Hammer and Champy 1993) and 'Organisational architecture' (Nadler 1987) are a few of the theories that have been proposed. The use of financial models in defining organisational processes has already been mentioned, whilst other approaches have adopted a sociotechnical perspective (Cummings 1986). All these different approaches however, have difficulty in capturing a complete, systemic 'picture' or 'image' of the organisation (Morgan 1986). There appears to be, therefore, rationale for developing advanced ways of thinking about how the firm functions. Dur and Bots (1991) offer three cogent reasons:

1   Organisations develop over long time spans and much knowledge about functioning is tacit knowledge, not reflected in past financial records.
2   Organisations allow for many vantage-points – which are continually negotiated.
3   Organisations often grow rapidly so that no one individual can have a reliable picture of the entire organisation at any one time.

The current business environment changes so rapidly, with a larger span of control, that the old ways of analysing organisations have reached their limits of utility as the theory underlying intellectual capital illustrates. Organisations process information to manage uncertainty and puzzling situations. The way in which they manage the flow of information can indicate the relative health of large, formal, complex organisations. The study of information flows can extend to an organisational analysis model of measurable information flow patterns that can be used to depict the use of intellectual capital in large organisations.

The organisation analysis system

The Institute for the Study of Distributed Work (ISDW) has developed a methodology for assessing the state of organisational health of any large, complex, human organisation (Grantham 1993; Grantham and Nichols 1993; Grantham and Nichols 1995; Grantham 1996a). The Organisational Assessment System (OAS) is designed to help managers make decisions about whether or not their organisation is ready to move into the distributed work environment. The OAS allows a preliminary assessment of the capacity and performance of an organisation's intellectual capital management process. The OAS can also be used by an organisational development consultant to produce specific statements of what needs to be put into place (including knowledge and capabilities) to enable people to accomplish business process objectives.

The OAS has been developed from the existing literature on organisational analysis, drawing principally on the work of Beer (1985), Bennett (1987), Daft and Lengel (1986), Forrester (1961), Kotter (1978), Miller and Miller (1991), Morgan (1986) and Tuft (1990) and from the science of systematics (Bennett 1987). The OAS has been developed as an alternative to more conventional ways of assessing organisational effectiveness. Most analytic systems are based on sociological perspectives of structure, whereas the OAS is based on a social psychological perspective of process (Bennett 1987). In the OAS, structure refers to relatively stable patterns of interaction between people in organisations that persist over time and give rise to the creation of status and power hierarchies. As these hierarchies disappear in distributed work organisations, perspectives more suited to dynamic interactions among members of organisations are more relevant to analysing and solving ongoing business planning issues.

Systematics differs from more typical general systems theory or operational research in that it focuses on the study of patterns of process which repeat themselves over and over again. For example, the study of any situation begins with a question like 'What are we looking at?' or 'What am I trying to understand?' The universality of this questioning process is called the MONAD in systematics and is a single-term system, or method of analysis. Systematics then is a collection of these universal means of analysing processes in natural systems, with large, complex, human organisations being among these systems. Bennett's constructions are a number of multiple-termed systems. They range from the single-termed MONAD to a twelve-termed system called a DOCEDAD. Each of these termed systems has a quality to it which is associated with the logical type of problem it is suited to study (Bennett 1987). The OAS employs a five-term system as the most appropriate cognitive structure to use when analysing an organisation's ability or inability to realise its purpose and potential. Five-term systems refer to realisation of potential whereas others discussed elsewhere, such as a six-term system, refer to issues of harmony across organisational boundaries (Grantham and Nichols 1995).

Each of the five factors in the systematics theory can be defined in terms of a central business process question which the organisation needs to satisfactorily answer in order to realise its true potential. The OAS takes each of these five terms and translates them into operational factors that focus on one of these key business process questions. Each of these questions are then in turn translated into a series of indicators which, when rated and summated, create quantifiable scales that indicate relative appropriate organisational functioning. Table 10.1 shows the correlation of these key business questions to Bennett's five-term factors and Table 10.2 describes the element of the OAS and the associated indicator items.

The OAS methodology is therefore based on a five-factor model which looks at information systems, human resources, customer relations, planning capability and leadership as they support distributed work. Each factor is measured by a set of indicators ranked on a five-point Likert scale and weighted to reflect the

Table 10.1 Definition of business factors

Business process question	Systematics factor	Factor
What are we talking about?	Uniqueness	Systems
What are we sure of?	Lower nature	Leadership
What is possible for us?	Higher nature	Personnel
What will the environment help and oppose?	Nourishment	Planning
What is becoming necessary?	Mastery	Site

relative importance of each indicator. Summary measures of indicators are used for diagnosis and planning.

The OAS was developed as an organisational planning tool built upon solid organisational theory. The current direction has been to extend the organisational model (i.e. five process factors) into the area of intellectual capital management. Returning to the five-factor model at the level of individual item indicators and performing an analytic factor analysis, has created a subset of the OAS which measures intellectual capital. The result is another set of OAS factors that assess an organisation's human, structural and customer capital. In a sense, this has linked the theoretical literature of both organisational assessment and intellectual capital management. If in fact these two approaches towards planning and development of organisations are linked at a conceptual level, then it should be possible to see some correlation in the results of measuring an organisation's effectiveness.

The use of the organisational analysis system in planning distributed working

A large international software company (known here as SoftCo) bought a European subsidiary organisation. They realised that they would need to learn more about remote working to manage the acquisition adequately. In addition, the company was having trouble attracting top talent to its headquarters north of Silicon Valley. As a result of these two elements, the company decided to open a remote facility within Silicon Valley that would show them how distributed working could be integrated into the company's operations. The centre would be used to attract new employees, whilst maintaining morale and increasing productivity among workers who were tired of commuting to headquarters. The company leased new space and began an aggressive renovation and move-in plan without completing an assessment of the technological and management impacts of the distributed environment they were creating. In short, planning was lacking.

Management and worker resistance to the programme made it clear that creating a remote work space takes more than buying a building, setting up some computers, and letting people work from home. For this organisation, accustomed to highly informal, decentralised, personal ways of work, distributed work

Table 10.2 Elements of the OAS

Factor	Operational definition	Number of indicators
Systems	Information systems capabilities and functioning to support distributed work	15 items
Leadership/ direction	Capacity of organisational leadership to motivate employees, measure results and assess ongoing operations for variance control	18 items
Personnel	Capabilities of human resources, adequacy of training and continuous learning procedures	13 items
Planning	Degree of sensitivity to anticipate challenges to organisations, changes in market and speed to incorporate changes in operations	14 items
Site	Infrastructure to support interaction with customers	11 items

represented a fundamental change in the company's culture, work processes and morale. The company delayed full roll-out of the new facility until it could assign a full-time project manager to the project. Though only a few hundred employees were moving, all 2,000 of the company's workers were affected by the move, and responsibilities for it were spread over several departments. The project manager ensured a central source of consistent communication between departments, provided realistic timetables that co-ordinated the needs of all affected workers, and made sure that appropriate training and support were in place before the move.

External management consultants were brought in to help the project manager because of a shortage of human resources. The responsibilities of the consultant were to:

1   Develop policies and procedures for the new remote facility.
2   Develop selection criteria to determine who would work in the new facility.
3   Develop assessment methods for measuring performance and cost benefits in the new facility.
4   Provide training and education to employees and their managers.
5   Define and install the right hardware, software and networking capabilities for workers at all levels in the new facility.

These steps were designed after an organisational analysis was completed. Results of the OAS showed that the company had relatively weak support for customer service, planning and personnel. This is illustrated in Figure 10.3.

Based on the normed OAS database, any indicator below rating 3.0 usually portends significant organisation effectiveness issues. This type of profile is not unusual for a high-tech, rapid growth enterprise, which is focused on creating technology tools for its customers. These companies see themselves as the 'experts', so they tend not to listen for customer input. These technology

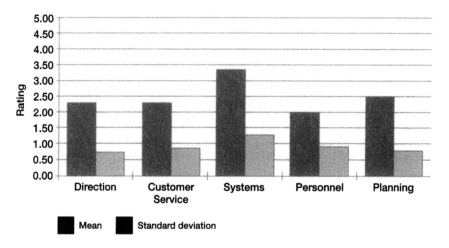

Figure 10.3 SoftCo OAS results

companies move on instinct and see human assets as commodities to be pur-
chased on the open market. The OAS results were verified by the on-site experience of the external consultants given the very reasons they were brought into the
company. Noting the apparent correlation between the standard OAS and the
new model of intellectual capital, previously attained data was reviewed to conduct
a historical comparison of companies that had been examined using the OAS.
Table 10.3 compares the average percentile scores on the OAS with SoftCo scores.

It is quite apparent in this comparison that SoftCo has significant organisational issues. The company has below average success scores (25 per cent and
over) on three critical business indicators: Customer service, Personnel and Planning. This then raised the question of how these indicators related to the use
of intellectual capital within the organisation. After calculating the intellectual
capital scales from the OAS, a similar pattern was identified in the data. This is
illustrated in Figure 10.4.

Again, using the database as a normative standard, factors with a rating of less
than 2.50 indicate areas for further attention. The results suggest that SoftCo is

Table 10.3 Comparative OAS analysis

	Average score (%)	SoftCo score (%)	Difference (%)
Direction	62	46	16
Customer service	76	49	27
Systems	63	71	−8
Personnel	68	43	25
Planning	76	50	26

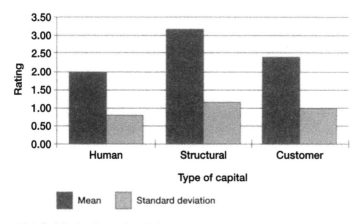

Figure 10.4 SoftCo intellectual capital

relatively deficient in human capital. This indicates that the company is not building human capital, and in fact is consuming it at a greater rate than it is being
replaced. This is borne out by SoftCo's problem in attracting and keeping high-
talent people. Second, the results show a deficit in customer capital. This is especially critical for long-term sustainability of organisations in the high-tech field.

The outcomes and implications of the analysis for SoftCo were fairly dramatic.
Within 60 days of completing the OAS and informing management of the
results, SoftCo cancelled its attempt at moving into the distributed work world.
The project was called off citing a lack of adequate resources and too much time
pressure to complete a critical product release. The failure to provide alternative
working locations also began to result in difficulties hiring key talent. The resulting lack of sufficient engineering staff only exacerbated existing product development problems. In fact one key executive took a position with the company
only after being provided with a personal chauffeur to drive him the 70 miles to
and from work each day.

In the long term there are many issues to be resolved. The OAS and intellectual capital analysis is only a diagnostic. It is not a complete description of the
underlying etiology of the organisational issues. It can, however, highlight underlying issues, before they become openly apparent. After another two product
development cycles (approximately 12 months in total), SoftCo began experiencing very difficult times. Products failed to ship on time, the software was
prone to bugs and competitors began to steal market share. All of these factors
culminated in a major management shake-up, resulting in the replacement of
the CEO and several key executives. The board of directors stepped in to take
control and attempted to right some of the problems. All these actions were, in
reality, predictable a year in advance.

Conclusion

There are three major implications for business planning which can be drawn from the SoftCo case study. First, there clearly is a need for planning integration using a tool like the OAS. Planning is a multi-disciplinary effort by definition, but what is required is a reliable means to compare multiple perspectives of the organisation. In doing this, planners can begin to conduct 'what if' sensitivity analysis and develop a clearer understanding of what factors impact each other. In the case of SoftCo, executives could have, over time, begun to see what impact lack of customer sensitivity had on product development cycles.

Second, the case study shows that more emphasis needs to be placed on using measures of intellectual capital in organisations where assets literally 'walk out the door every night'. Certainly intellectual capital analysis supports, and is correlated with, more traditional ways of making diagnoses and assessments as an input to the planning process. Finally, both methods of analysis show the importance of customer relationships in the rapidly changing world of software development. In fact, some industry commentators are now saying that the driving force in this sector was technology prowess in the 1970s, business acumen in the 1980s and will be customer service in the 1990s as the Internet removes intermediaries, bringing makers and users of technology into direct contact.

Managers must move forward in developing their own capacity to learn. Successful organisations will be characterised by the qualities of their leaders. Leaders must first strive to develop their own intellectual capital before they can hope to institutionalise the process (Hudson 1993). It is to be hoped that managers and leaders can take the idea of a hierarchy of responsibility and use it as a yardstick to manage their time. Development of intellectual capital requires more of 'doing the right things' than doing 'things right'. Learning comes through trying, failing and trying again. It is the key task of leadership to first develop themselves and then construct an organisational climate which encourages others to do the same.

There is obviously much more work to be done with the theoretical proposal of managing intellectual capital. The application of this model was in the Information Technology sector, because the change factors apparent in the business environment make it paramount for the industry to quickly address them. These pressures necessitate rapid change in management models and times of rapid change open possibilities for experimenting with new ways of knowing and working.

The overall conclusion is that the coming pre-eminence of intellectual capital as a value-adding element in modern enterprises requires the conscious development of a new way of viewing the workplace. The shift from 'hard asset' management to enterprises based on intellectual capital requires an integration of technical and business perspectives. The OAS model is proposed as meeting the necessary and sufficient conditions for a model of intellectual capital that can be adapted to the strategic management of large service-based organisations.

Furthermore, the OAS is general enough to permit comparisons across industry segments such as heath-care and financial services. Investment decisions can then be based on uniform criteria at a macroeconomic level.

References

Becker, G.S. (1996) 'Human capital: One investment where America is ahead', *Business Week*, 11 March: 8.

Beer, S. (1985) *Diagnosing the System for Organizations*, New York: John Wiley.

Bennett, J.G. (1987) *The Dramatic Universe Vol. II*, Charles Town, WV, Claymont.

Bontis, N. (1995) 'Organizational learning and leadership', ASAC Conference, Windsor, Ontario.

Brooking, A. (1996) *Intellectual Capital: Core Assets for the Third Millennium Enterprise*, New York: International Thomson Business Press.

Coates, J. (1995) 'Work and pay in the 21st century: an impending crisis', *Employment Relations Today*, Spring: 17–22.

Cummings, T.G. (1986) 'A concluding note: future directions of sociotechnical theory and research', *Journal of Applied Behavioral Science*, 22, 3: 355–60.

Daft, R.L. and Lengel, R.H. (1986) 'Organizational information requirements: Media richness and structural design', *Management Science*, 32, 5: 554–71.

Di Martino, V. and Wirth, L. (1990) 'Telework: A new way of working and living', *International Labour Review* 129, 5: 529–54.

Drucker, P. (1994) 'The Age of Social Transformation', *Atlantic Monthly*, November: 53–80.

Dur, R.C.J. and Bots, P.W.G. (1991) 'Dynamic modeling of organizations using task/actor simulation', Proceedings of the Second International Working Conference on Dynamic Modeling of Information Systems, Washington, DC, 18–19 July: 15–35.

Dyson, E. (1996) 'Intellectual property on the net release 2.0', *Release 1.0* 1–96: 1–14.

Feiwal, G.R. (1975) *The Intellectual Capital of Michael Kalecki: A Study in Economic Theory and Policy*, Knoxville: The University of Tennessee Press.

Finholt, T. and Sproull, L.S. (1990) 'Electronic groups at work' *Organization Science* 1, 1: 41–65.

Forrester, J.W. (1961) *Industrial Dynamics*, Cambridge, MA: MIT Press.

Grantham, C.E. (1993) 'Visualization of information flows: virtual reality as an organizational modeling technique', in Wexelblat, A. (ed.) *SoftWhere: Applications of Virtual Reality*, New York: Academic Press.

—— (1996a) 'Design principles for the virtual workplace', Proceedings of the ACM SIG on Computer Personnel Research, Denver, CO: 21–38.

—— (1996b) 'Working in a virtual place: a case study of distributed work', Proceedings of the ACM SIG on Computer Personnel Research, Denver, CO: 38–52.

Grantham, C.E. and Nichols, L.D. (1993) *The Digital Workplace: Designing Groupware Platforms*, New York: Van Nostrand-Reinhold.

—— (1995) 'The digital workplace', *Annual Review of Communication* 48: 963–74.

Hagel, J. and Armstrong, A. (1997) *Net Gain*, Boston: Harvard Business School Press.

Hammer, M. and Champy, J. (1993) *Reengineering the Corporation: A Manifesto for Business Revolution*, London: Nicholas Brearley Publishing.

Hesse, B. and Grantham, C.E. (1991) 'Electronically distributed work communities:

implications for research on telework', *Electronic networking: Research Applications and Policy* 1, 1: 4–17.

Holtham, C. (1992) 'Improving the performance of workgroups through Information Technology', Lotus Corporation Working Paper on Groupware, Lotus Corporation, MA.

Hudson, W.J. (1993) *Intellectual Capital: How to Build It, Enhance It, Use It*, New York: John Wiley and Sons.

Ishii, H., Minoru, K. and Kazuho, A. (1994) 'Iterative design of seamless collaboration media', *Communications of the ACM* 37, 8: 83–97.

Jacoby, W.E. (1995) 'Strategic information systems planning and implementation in the US financial services industry', Ph.D. thesis, University of London.

Kotter, J. (1978) *Organizational Dynamics: Diagnosis and Intervention*, Reading, MA: Addison-Wesley.

Kraut, R.E. (1987) 'Predicting the use of technology: The case of telework', in Kraut, R.E. (ed.) *Technology and the Transformation of White-collar Work*, Hillsdale, NJ: Lawrence Erlbaum.

—— (1989) 'Telecommuting: The trade-offs of home work', *Journal of Communication* 39, 3: 19–47.

LaPlante, A. (1993) 'Teleconfrontationing', *Forbes ASAP*, Summer: 110–26.

Michalski, J. (1995) 'The economics of connectivity', *Release 1.0*, 12–95: 1–9.

Miller, J.G. and Miller, J.L. (1991) 'A living systems analysis of organizational pathology', *Behavioral Science* 36: 239–52.

Morgan, G. (1986) *Images of Organizations*, Beverly Hills, CA: Sage Publications.

Nadler, D. (1987) 'The effective management of organizational change', in Lorsch, J.W. (ed.) *Handbook of Organizational Behavior*, Englewood Cliffs, NJ: Prentice-Hall.

Olson, M.H. (1987) 'Telework: practical experience and future prospects,' in Kraut, R.E. (ed.) *Technology and the Transformation of White-collar Work*, Hillsdale, NJ: Lawrence Erlbaum.

Porter, M.E. (1985) *Competitive Advantage: Creating and Sustaining Superior Performance*, New York: Free Press.

Prahalad, C.K. and Hamel, G. (1990) 'Core competence of the corporation', *Harvard Business Review* 68, 3: 79–83.

Pratt, J.H. (1993) 'Myths and realities of working at home: characteristics of home-based business owners and telecommuters', National Information Technical Service, Springfield, VA.

Quinn, J.B 1992) *Intelligent Enterprise: A Knowledge and Service Based Paradigm for Industry*, New York: The Free Press.

Kane, A. (1995) '1995 Home Office market update', LINK Resources Inc, New York, NY.

Schultz, T. W. (1981) *Investing in people: The economics of population quality*, Berkeley and Los Angeles, CA: University of California.

Senge, P. (1990) *The Fifth Discipline : The Art and Practice of the Learning Organization*, New York: Doubleday.

Skandia Group (1995) 'Intellectual capital value creating processes', Supplement to 1995 Annual Report.

Sterns, N. (1994) 'Emerging trends in health care finance', *Journal of Health Care Insurance*, 21, 2: 1–10.

Stewart, T.A. (1994) 'Managing your company's most valuable asset: intellectual capital', *Fortune*, 3 October: 28–33.

Tuft, E.R. (1990) *Envisioning Information*, Cheshire, CT: Graphics Press.

11

TELEWORKING SERVICE MANAGEMENT

Issues for an integrated framework

Scott A. Johnson

Introduction

Over the last twenty years, the emergent work trends of teleworking and service management have evolved in parallel although developed from differing philosophy. Teleport development has tended to take a systems perspective, with a focus on how organisations can improve internal work processes and reduce costs through structural redesign and technological support. Teleworking employees' jobs are physically changed, in terms of location, personal interaction, reporting procedures, direct supervision, etc. Service management considers the role of individuals and their behaviour toward affecting external customer perceptions of quality; thus, the emphasis is on employees who have contact with customers, supported through redesign of their job functions and methods of supervision. Customer contact employees themselves may be psychologically changed due to expanded responsibilities. Although the perspectives behind these two work approaches may be different (systematic and structural versus individual and interpersonal), teleport and service management may be quite complementary, such that each adds value to the operations of the other and to the organisation as a whole.

The success of each approach depends largely on the willingness and ability of employees to embrace the work philosophy and work within the system; this has been acknowledged and empirically proven in service management, and needs to be recognised in teleport. Due to their changed roles within the organisation, teleworkers and contact employees are each presented with increased opportunities for autonomous decision-making and behaviour. As these employees become more independent and remote from the organisation, direct forms of supervision become inadequate. Managers must become aware of factors which critically influence the employees' behaviour.

Customer service jobs have been described as ideal for teleworking

185

environments, so it is likely that the number of customer contact employees (teleworking contact employees) working away from the traditional collective office will increase. The structural and system features of a teleworking environment will help to reinforce the service management attributes of employee empowerment, discretion and control in serving customers. When teleworking contact employees are inclined to exhibit positive behaviour, the combined effects of teleworking and service management will result in success for the customer and the organisation. However, when they are inclined to exhibit negative behaviour, these same combined effects will enable teleworking contact employees to potentially do more harm to customers and the organisation than would the separate effects of either teleworking or service management. In such extreme cases, damage to customer and organisation interests would be exacerbated by an integrated teleworking service management approach.

Although teleworking and service management are well-established topics and have many common objectives, they have not been systematically and effectively integrated in the management literature. The purpose of this chapter is to discuss an integrated framework for viewing teleworking service management and some important factors of which organisations must be aware in order to effectively implement it. These factors include management challenges, characteristics of teleworking contact employee jobs and potential behaviourial consequences of teleworking service management.

Teleworking service management

Teleport is defined as work carried out in a location which is remote from central offices or production facilities (Wright and Oldford 1993). Teleworkers have little or no ongoing personal contact with co-workers or supervisors, and are linked to the organisation through technology (telephone, computer, fax, e-mail, voice-mail, pager, etc.) For the purposes of this discussion, the term teleport shall encompass these and all other forms of remote work such as telecommuting, virtual office, distance work and flexiplace.

The US business sector has increasingly shifted from a goods-focused economy to a service-focused economy over the last twenty-five years (Bowen 1990). Among the factors influencing this shift have been automation of manufacturing, transformation of office work by continuously improving information technology, and increased frequency of support services outsourcing. This service focus encourages a transition in management philosophy from the traditional corporation with a perceived tangible infrastructure to a virtual corporation or network organisation consisting of webs of relationships (Grönroos 1994; Gummesson 1994). The concept of service management incorporates several core values emphasising customer satisfaction, service employee satisfaction, and customer service employee interaction that are relevant to teleworking management. This includes the synchronisation of human input and technology, combining service personnel, physical resources, systems and customers, to deliver the service and create customer value (Grönroos 1994; Gummesson 1994). Service management takes a systems view that requires all elements of the service system to act in co-ordinated ways to produce service excellence (Schneider 1994).

The service management paradigm holds that every member of an organisation is responsible for customer satisfaction. Through a triangle of service relationships, the organisation makes promises to customers (through external communication), and then must enable its frontline customer contact employees to keep these promises, by providing training, resources and support (Zeithaml and Bitner 1995). Virtual work processes such as teleworking may be an effective tool for service delivery if they are well received and supported by customers, employees and the organisation. Teleworking employees can play pivotal roles in this service triangle, because they have the most potential to influence customers directly, and control communication between customers and the organisation.

The initial development of the service management and teleworking philosophies seemed to have emphasised different fundamental concepts. Service management focused primarily on the importance of the customer. Teleworking was driven chiefly by organisational concerns (cost reductions, productivity gains, regulatory compliance, etc.); Bowen and Schneider (1988) state that management theories emerging outside of marketing, which generically prescribe models of organisational functioning such as teleworking, ignore not only service but the customer as well. From a perspective of economic exchange, service management was more of a 'bottom-up' approach starting with the customer, and teleworking was a 'top-down' redesign planned by the organisation. The individual employees who would be involved in delivering this service to customers, or be the ones actually working remotely away from the office, were an afterthought or assumption taken for granted. Schneider (1994) suggests that because service employees had been generally poorly paid and near the bottom of the organisation, there was a tendency to disregard their feelings or effect on customers. Personnel holding customer contact jobs have been frequently among the least educated employees in companies, possibly lacking language, interpersonal or other skills to serve customers effectively (Zeithaml et al. 1988).

More recent research findings and company experience, especially over the last fifteen years, has reinforced the importance of the individual service employee. This heightened recognition of employees has been more prevalent in the service management philosophy, due to their demonstrated influence on customers. Teleworking management seems to mainly consider employees with regard to their attitudes toward teleworking, productivity changes and supervisory concerns; these are still issues largely directed internally toward the organisation. With the proliferation of teleworking jobs involving customer contact, it is hoped that management will more carefully consider the pivotal impact that teleworkers have on external customer satisfaction. It is important to study an integrated framework of teleworking service management in order to gain increased understanding of the potential benefits and consequences associated with teleworkers' roles.

In the service management literature, employee influences on customer satisfaction are emphasised as crucial. The integration of telecommuting with service management research must identify and measure the effects of telecommuting service management on employee behaviour in dealing with customers. Teleworking contact employees cannot simply be regarded as mechanisms for service delivery. These employees have accurate perceptions of customers' perceptions of service quality, and can also accurately identify the service delivery and human resources management issues that would enhance customer satisfaction (Schneider and Bowen 1995). Effective teleworking service management design should explicitly include these contact employees as the crucial link between organisations and customers, and examine the effects of teleworking on customer-focused behaviour. Substantial evidence has shown that the attitudes and perceptions of customer contact employees have a significant impact upon customer perceptions of an organisation's service quality (Bowen and Schneider 1985; Parasuraman 1987; Schneider and Bowen 1985; Tornow and Wiley 1990; Zeithaml and Bitner 1995). Such findings reinforce the basic premise of internal marketing, that satisfied employees will lead to satisfied customers (Brown *et al.* 1994). Such internal development of personnel includes both an attitude management aspect and a communications aspect (Grönroos 1994). More organisations are recognising that in order to realise organisational performance gains from satisfied customers, they must first manage the internal processes and situational factors that lead to satisfied employees. Thus, the role of the supervisor in a customer service environment takes on increased importance: no longer simply managing employees, but ultimately affecting external customer satisfaction.

Although considerable research attention is being paid to the management of customer and employee interactions in service encounters (Brown *et al.* 1994), relatively few studies have examined the influence of organisational factors such as teleworking on employee service behaviour. The linkage of organisational strategy to human resources practices affects customer service and support (Rousseau 1995). This alignment of human resources management systems and service quality strategies, under the paradigm of service management, will continue to be a challenge for all organisations during this decade (Dyer and Holder 1988). Teleworking service management involving customer-focused human resource management may also enhance organisational competitiveness (Schneider 1994). This is the thrust of the service management philosophy, and a critical consideration for managing customer service employees in a teleworking environment.

The practice of teleworking, but even more so predictions of its future success, have outpaced precise investigation into this phenomenon. Possibly this is due to the intuitive simplicity of transforming traditional office jobs into teleworking jobs. This could be especially true with regard to service management. Researchers have suggested that teleworking is eminently suitable for jobs that deal with intangibles: service-based rather than production-based; knowledge, rather than craftsmanship; information, rather than raw materials; networking, rather than physical facilities. Positions described as ideal for teleworking include those with extensive customer interaction, such as sales, customer service and insurance claims representatives (Flanagan 1993). As such, teleworking could be regarded as a tool for service delivery that achieves benefits for the organisation, employee and customer. Teleworking programmes implemented in part to improve customer interaction in terms of sales, service and support, have shown some positive results in the US. After implementation, AT&T saw a 15 per cent increase in customer contact during its first 18 months, while Dun and Bradstreet's sales productivity increased by nearly 30 per cent (Oglivie 1994). IBM teleworkers have reported spending 95 per cent of business hours on customer calls since being able to work away from the traditional office structure; similar results have been experienced by Aetna Life and Casualty, Arthur Andersen and Co., Ernst and Young, and Pacific Bell (Flanagan 1993). An exploratory study of nearly 300 American teleworking contact employees noted that customer relationships were all perceived to have been positively influenced by teleport.

However, other teleworking researchers have suggested the opposite, that teleworking is best suited for independent, routine tasks that do not involve a high level of social or professional interaction (Richter and Meshulam 1993). This may imply long-term challenges for some teleworkers in dealing with customers. Thus, the wholesale adaptation of service jobs to a teleworking environment may not be as straightforward as popularly accepted. There are enough elements of compatibility and complementary support between teleworking and service management to promote more investigation, and dissenting views might help persuade companies to proceed with more deliberation and forethought regarding the critical issues.

The challenges of managing teleworking contact employees

The simple service management equation that satisfied employees lead to satisfied customers has more complex components. Service employees' attitudes and perceptions may be influenced by a variety of factors, from individual mood to customer relationships; many of these are not controllable by the organisation. The most influential factor that is controllable may be the organisation's human resources management (HRM) policies and procedures. Organisations in which employees describe the HRM practices under which they work in more positive terms have customers who report they receive superior service quality. One large facet of such HRM practices is supervision, which provides employees with feedback on performance, establishes rewards and shares information (Schneider 1994).

Just as the role of the employee takes on increased significance in a teleworking service environment, so does the role of the teleworking supervisor. Teleworking contact employees who are empowered with more autonomy, control and discretion may seem to suggest a need for less supervision, but other factors such as removal from the office infrastructure, elimination of the social support network and fragmentation of the internal corporate culture emphasise the crucial link played by the supervisor between the teleworking contact employee and the organisation. As the teleworking contact employee comes to embody the organisation to the customer, it is likely that the supervisor fulfils this role for the teleworking contact employee. The teleworking contact employee's supervisor doesn't necessarily need more or less supervisory skills, but a different set of skills entirely.

Supervision

Service organisations typically use two types of formal supervisory controls, namely output and process (behaviour), to direct employees toward attainment of desired organisational objectives. Output controls direct employees by specifying output goals and standards, while leaving the choice of methods and procedures to the employees themselves. Output control has been suggested as more appropriate for a teleworking environment. Researchers consistently recommend the use of objective outcome criteria such as hours worked, tasks completed and finished product (Hamilton 1987). Management by walking around doesn't work in a teleworking environment. Supervisors can't observe teleworkers' attendance, attitude and appearance of working hard; personality and style are no longer as important in managerial evaluations. US companies like Ernst and Young have installed more objective measures and compensate people based on their output, rather than their input (Ogilvie 1994). However, to the extent that service employees believe that the attainment of output goals is beyond their control, they may experience feelings of loss of control and come to resent output control (Challagalla and Shervani 1996).

Behavioural, or process, control directs employees by specifying the methods and procedures to be adopted in performing tasks. The task complexity, high input uncertainty, and employee–customer task interdependence of many service encounters make it difficult to specify in advance how teleworking contact employees are to behave in the unpredictable range of circumstances that may arise (Bowen and Schneider 1988). The authors contend that behavioural control in a global sense may not be feasible, and only output control may be appropriate.

Teleworkers in general may not welcome any form of supervisory control which they may perceive as a trade-off with their own sense of control over the service environment and customer relationships. Due to the boundary-spanning nature of their roles, teleworking contact employees are more likely to be dissatisfied with managerial attempts at direct control than are non-teleworking contact employees. Teleworkers may view supervisory controls as signalling a lack of trust and decrease in empowerment to perform their jobs. Ramaswami (1996) found that service employees behave in dysfunctional ways when they are subject to both output and behavioural controls. In a service environment remote from direct supervisory observation, there exist many possibilities for teleworkers to act in ways which further their personal interests but are harmful to long-term organisational performance. For example, teleworkers may act to violate customer privacy for personal gain where service encounters or record-keeping transactions occur at an unsupervised location (Jensen 1993).

Bowen and Schneider (1988) conclude that the major challenge to service management organisations is that each contact employee is relatively uncontrollable; instead, management must take control of the situational variables influencing employees to provide them with implicit direction. For example, supervisors at Intel who discover employee output below objectives will go out to observe what the teleworker is doing and learn whether the results are due to a phenomenon of a specific situation, or whether there is a problem with that particular teleworker (Taylor 1994). In addition to enhanced feedback, communication, evaluation and relationship building, the supervisor must encourage employee commitment in an environment more conducive to a control strategy of management, one lacking the structural and sociocultural support systems of the office workplace. Bowen and Schneider (1988) advocate that service organisations holistically design all their sub-systems to create an environment permeated with cues about the organisation's emphasis on the delivery of service and acceptable means for providing it. Employee behaviour is then controlled by this service climate, culture, image, atmospherics, or ethic. The separation of the teleworking environment from the office core makes it difficult to reinforce a service culture as teleworkers are no longer physically embedded in these central repositories of beliefs and values, and may feel increasingly isolated from the organisation and fall outside the informal network and socialisation process (Kurland 1994). To combat this problem, some companies are increasing the amount of face-to-face meetings, social gatherings and communication in general among supervisors and teleworkers (O'Connell 1996). US accounting firm Ernst and Young has tried to sustain its corporate culture and provide a new social structure in its teleworking environment through constant communication, training, career counselling and team-forming (Ogilvie 1994). Even the creation of an 'electronic water cooler', such as a network bulletin board or chat room, can help to give teleworkers a frame of reference with fellow employees and reinforce a sense of organisational culture that may otherwise fragment (Kurland 1994).

Employee development and performance evaluation

Although high level management tends to assume that teleworking results in increased overall satisfaction and thus is desired by the vast majority of employees, decision-makers sometimes neglect to take into account specific aspects of the job, work environment, or characteristics of individual employees that may differentially cause dissatisfaction. In fact, prior studies have shown that negative consequences generally aren't considered at the organisational level beyond a vague notion that 'some employees may not function as well in the less structured work-at-home environment.' (Ramsower 1985). The existing teleworking literature constantly refers to the negative possibility that employees might become invisible, or 'out of sight, out of mind', with regard to organisational development, promotion, rewards, etc. Duxbury and Haines (1991) found that some employees felt strongly that teleworking would impede their professional development and threaten career opportunities. Olson and Primps (1984) noted that teleworkers believed that working at home would adversely affect their chances for promotion. This presents a challenge for the teleworking supervisor with regard to teleworker morale and motivation.

Operationally, management of service employees may be negatively impacted by supervisory fears of not being able to closely observe and monitor employees. In general, experts suggest that teleworking supervisors learn to more effectively manage outcomes. In a service context, this might hinder performance appraisal if outcomes are difficult criteria by which to measure the quality of delivery processes, relationship building and customer satisfaction. Such appraisal must be based on operations as a process, viewed as a series of activities carried out through customer interaction (Kullven and Mattsson 1994). One implication is that supervisors may need to rely more on culture and climate than formal, obtrusive control mechanisms to manage service employee behaviours (Bowen 1990), but this can be challenging in a teleworking environment. Another consideration is that organisations increase control through initial staffing for the teleworking positions, or by socialisation and training for the existing employees (also a potentially formidable task with remote employees) (Bowen and Schneider 1985).

Although employee satisfaction is critical to the long-term effectiveness of any performance appraisal system, it has received relatively little attention. Employee attitudes toward the fairness and acceptability of the system may determine the ultimate success of performance appraisal (Dobbins et al. 1990), and will predict how willing they are to 'buy into' the goals which they are expected to meet (Harris 1988). Performance appraisal may be as important for HRM reasons (e.g. making promotion decisions, employee feedback and development, administrative decision-making, programme evaluation, documentation) as it is for customer satisfaction (providing a feedback mechanism for perceptions of employee satisfaction or dissatisfaction with organisational policies and procedures, working conditions, etc.)

Research on teleworking has generally ignored the role that performance appraisal systems (and teleworker acceptance of those systems) play in affecting teleworking productivity and satisfaction (Hartman et al. 1991). This seems to be an area where more investigation is needed. Management appraisal researchers such as Judge and Farris (1993) suggested that traditional approaches to performance appraisal may be inadequate when the work of employees is unobserved, while Dobbins et al. (1990) found that subordinates will not receive informal feedback when they are not closely monitored and so will need more information from a formal performance appraisal system to evaluate the acceptability of their performance (perhaps lacking a social comparison frame of reference). Thus, the authors found that characteristics of performance appraisal that provide more information and reduce uncertainty were more positively related to appraisal satisfaction. Greenberg (1986) also noted the importance of rater familiarity with rate performance as a positive influence on employee perceptions of fairness with the performance appraisal system.

Perceptions of being isolated and 'out of sight, out of mind' suggest that teleworking employees will be concerned with how their performance is evaluated and which criteria are fairer: work-related behaviours or outcomes. Employees may react negatively to outcome-based evaluations if they feel they are influenced by factors beyond their control. Such sensitivity could be exacerbated when employees feel that raters can't observe potential barriers to performance that might exist, or when the influence of the customer on the service encounter outcome isn't taken into account.

Zeithaml and Bitner (1995) note that in companies where customer satisfaction in every encounter is a goal, there is often a need to adjust the performance criteria from a total emphasis on productivity data and hard numbers to other means of assessing performance. Current research in service management suggests that output control alone may be insufficient when employees are delivering a highly intangible service; customers increasingly rely on employee behaviour as tangible, physical evidence for defining the reality of the service (Bowen and Schneider 1985). In many service organisations, output control systems may be inappropriate or insufficient for measuring employee performance relating to provision of quality service because they overlook key aspects of job performance that customers factor into service quality perceptions (Zeithaml et al. 1988). Thus, evidence suggests that teleworking employees would be more satisfied with rating criteria that considered their controllable, but unobservable, behavioural outputs as well as the more uncontrollable, but observable, objective outcomes. Teleworking contact employees are more likely to perceive a combination of behavioural-based and output-based performance evaluation criteria as fairer than output-based performance evaluation criteria alone, due to the potential influence of uncontrollable system factors.

Tansik (1990) presents guidelines that might apply to employees in a teleworking environment, when employees have a high level of self-control over the work process, and there is a high degree of customer induced uncertainty concerning the desired output. Tansik suggests that there is a significant problem in establishing rigorous, quantifiable goals for that output and advocates that evaluation criteria should be based on system effectiveness rather than efficiency measures. Tansik's system factors include customer satisfaction, and the question might be raised: is this a result of the organisational system over which the employee has little control, or the teleworking service sub-system which the employee to a large degree creates and controls?

Fairness perceptions and psychological contracts

There is ample evidence that fairness matters in service encounters, especially in terms of employees' perceptions of fairness regarding the organisation and the supervisor (Clemmer 1993). Fairness in the workplace is a better predictor of customer service behaviours and co-operation than job satisfaction and employees who perceive a fair relationship with their employer are more likely to go beyond typical role-prescribed behaviour in providing service to both external and internal customers (Organ 1994). Such fairness perceptions can be examined in the global context of employees' psychological contracts. Psychological contracts are derived from employees' perceived reciprocal expectations and obligations of their organisations not explicitly stated in the employment contract (Robinson *et al.* 1994). Psychological contracts are intact when employees perceive that employers have upheld their promises and obligations, and contracts are breached when employees perceive that such promises and obligations have been broken and that their contributions to the organisation have not been adequately reciprocated (Morrison and Robinson 1997). Employees' cognitive assessment of the status of their psychological contract leads to evaluations of outcome fairness, or distributive justice. Research has shown that when these contracts are intact, i.e., when both parties have upheld their ends, employees perceive fairness in their relationship or interactions with supervisors or the organisation (Rousseau 1995). Such perceptions have been found to cognitively influence employee behaviour.

The implications for managing teleworking contact employees' fairness perceptions are profound. In a remote work environment, the fairness of outcomes may be the only criteria by which these employees can judge the intentions of the supervisor and organisation. There is less opportunity to assess fairness of interaction or procedures, because they are less visible. The perceived fairness of supervisors' decisions and organisational policies significantly influences employee behaviour. A key factor of these fairness perceptions is whether the organisation has kept the promises that the employee perceives it has made; such perceived promises may relate to supervisory support, accurate performance evaluations, and opportunities for career development and advancement. The inability for direct supervisory observation, lack of social referent comparisons with co-workers, and external influence of customers compounds the challenges for supervisors in upholding these perceived promises. It may not be satisfactory for the supervisor to devise alternative methods for achieving the organisation's HRM objectives in a teleworking environment; rather, it is more important to understand what the teleworking contact employee expects from the organisation. Employees' cognitive assessments of 'broken promises' are likely to be stronger influences on their behaviour in a teleworking environment lacking cues for structural reinforcement and deterrence from the organisation.

Characteristics of teleworking contact employee jobs

Teleworking contact employees' fairness perceptions derived from their psychological contracts influence their motivation to behave in a certain manner; this behaviour is facilitated by certain characteristics of their teleworking contact roles. Employees who work in positions which involve frequent contact with external customers typically have roles and responsibilities distinct from internally positioned employees who are 'buffered' from external customers. Contact employees are described as being 'on-stage' or on the front lines in dealing with customers, compared with non-contact employees who are 'back-stage' or behind the scenes in supporting roles; both kinds of roles (direct support and indirect support) contribute to effective customer service and satisfaction, but it is contact employees who bridge the gap in the strategic value chain between the organisation's 'production' focus and the customers' 'consumption' focus. In high-contact settings, contact employees help to reinforce prospective customers' positive expectations and to reduce their sense of uncertainty or risk, by relaying realistic information about the actual service (Kingman-Brundage *et al.* 1995) in ways that the organisation cannot. As such, contact employees have influence over customer satisfaction beyond the quality of the organisation's outputs, and may be more difficult to closely supervise when working on the front lines. In many service organisations, contact employees are more likely to practice self-management and have entrepreneurial-type responsibilities. There is not a supervisor physically present in the teleworker–customer dyad who can exercise ongoing, immediate quality control; teleworkers are essentially acting alone (Bowen and Schneider 1988). This combination of influence and autonomy affords teleworking contact employees a degree of discretion in their behavioural choices, derived from the unique attributes of their roles: boundary spanning, control and empowerment.

Boundary spanning

Teleworking contact employees span the boundary between the internal organisation and external customers, delivering organisational products and services to customers, and transmitting customer requests and feedback back to the organisation. They are likely to be both physically and psychologically remote from the organisation and closer to the customers they serve. Many teleworking customer service workers have remarked that they are more responsive to customers' needs and feelings when stationed in their own homes (Piskurich 1996). Companies like Lotus Development Corp. and IBM have implemented teleworking programmes with stated objectives to put employees closer to customers and increase their interaction time (O'Connell 1996). Schneider and Bowen (1995) note two important roles these teleworkers play for the organisation: as impression managers their behaviour affects customers' perceptions of service quality; and as gatekeepers of information they provide the organisation with insights into customer attitudes, competitor information and ideas for service quality improvements, while they provide customers with 'inside' information about the organisation itself. Thus, these employees can embody the organisation to customers, and they are often the best or only source of customer data to the organisation (Bitner *et al.* 1994). Boundary-spanning teleworkers may become even more powerful if the information they control is vital for organisational survival (Aldrich and Herker 1977).

Teleworkers' boundary-spanning roles are more sensitive to ideas of management behavioural control. Restrictions on employee behaviour might hinder the effectiveness of information flow and employees' abilities to deal with situational customer factors. The boundary-spanning roles themselves offer a degree of autonomy to teleworkers by virtue of their proximity to customers and shielding from management eyes; this is often enhanced with management policies designed to empower contact employees to serve customers. In an era of increased competition, flattened organisational hierarchies and shrinking layers of middle management, organisations frequently empower teleworking contact employees with more formal decision-making authority, to complement the informal power and control they have over customer service encounters.

Control

It is important for the organisation to control every individual service encounter to enhance overall customer perceptions of service quality, and focus on the controllable elements at the point of interaction that may influence customer evaluations (Bitner *et al.* 1990). However, it may not be clear who is most in control of a service encounter in a teleworking environment: the organisation, the customer or the teleworking contact employee. If the contact employee does gain more control (either real or perceived) over the service encounter in a teleworking environment, can the organisation and customer work within this framework to ensure effective service delivery? Evidence suggests that customers like to be in control (Rafaeli 1989). It is logical that customers could perceive teleworking as decreasing the complexity and structural differentiation of the service delivery process from the organisational service provider's perspective (Mills 1985). By perceptually removing the presence of the organisational monolith, customers may come to regard the teleworking service encounter as being on a more level playing field: a one-on-one interaction on equal footing with the teleworking contact employee. Teleworking contact employees also may rely more on the customer as 'co-producer' of the service delivery without the constant physical and cultural reinforcement of organisational support. At the same time, however, the customer may become paradoxically more dependent on the individual teleworker, with the service encounter truly facilitated by the employee's work preparation. In that case, control is shifted from the customer to the employee.

Studies have found that contact employees are genuinely proud of their roles and abilities to service customers (Bitner *et al.* 1994), and a partial source of that pride is employees' control over their jobs, which they perceive as encompassing service encounters (Alpander 1991; Rafaeli 1989). Bitner *et al.* (1994) noted that service employees feel especially frustrated when they cannot control the service encounter enough to recover from a service failure or adjust the system to accommodate a customer need. Having control enables employees to take appropriate action to create customer satisfaction (Bitner *et al.* 1990). When service employees perceive that they can act flexibly in problem situations, their perceived control increases and performance improves (Zeithaml *et al.* 1988). Even in the absence of service failures, employees may, in fact, increase their control of teleworking service encounters if they are better able to ignore, reject, react to and educate the customer, overact, and physically control the customer (Weatherly and Tansik 1993). Without close, direct supervision, such control methods may be more easily enacted by teleworking contact employees. This would decrease the control of the customer as well as that of the supervisor, whether or not there has been a service failure. Bateson (1985) noted that employees' need for control is intrinsically motivating, and the organisation must find ways to balance their need for control with operational efficiency, which may require control-oriented operating procedures and environment.

Empowerment

Bowen and Lawler (1992) noted that empowerment is a common issue among most excellent service organisations. Empowerment means sharing power, information, rewards and knowledge with the actual employees who conduct the service encounters. It can enable employees to provide quicker on-line responses to customer needs and to dissatisfied customers (Bowen and Lawler 1992). It can also help service employees to recover from service failures and delight customers by exceeding their expectations (Bowen and Lawler 1995). Alpander (1991) suggests that empowerment may be successful because it helps employees fulfil their need to control the work they are doing, and to influence a situation or another individual's thinking, attitude or behaviour.

When managed effectively, empowered teleworkers can achieve gains for the organisation and customers, such as improving service delivery efficiency and contributing productive ideas. However, there is caution that empowerment can only be successful when employees and management trust each other (Berry 1995). In customer-focused organisations, the ability of management to develop and preserve long-term, trusting relationships with employees is a critical component of their long-run success (Strutton *et al.* 1993). The organisation must be able to trust employees to act on the customer's behalf and not abuse their position in the service management process. Teleworkers, from a distance, must be able to trust that the organisation is working on their behalf and not pursuing its own political agendas. Berry (1995) points out that managers will not give power to employees without trust, and employees will not accept it without trusting management's intentions. The issue of power and control in the hands of empowered teleworkers can worry managers who fear that the employees will give away too much to customers. In reality, contact employees have a natural degree of power and control over customer service encounters, whether or not there are well-designed, systematically implemented organisational practices and procedures of empowerment. This power and control may be augmented by the remote and autonomous nature of teleworking.

Front-line teleworking contact employees manage themselves to a significant degree in creating value for their customers. Although the best teleworking contact employees will be empowered self-leaders, at the same time empowerment may not be right for everyone. Teleworkers will react positively to empowerment if they have strong needs to grow and to deepen and test their abilities (Bowen and Lawler 1992). Teleworking doesn't simply empower employees because they are physically separated from the office infrastructure. In fact, it doesn't necessarily even make employees more autonomous unless they are given the power to make decisions on their own, the knowledge necessary to help the customer by themselves, the ability to design and attain their own rewards, and information of how they contribute to overall organisational results (Schneider and Bowen 1995). The organisation's teleworking structures, practices and policies must clearly show employees that they are empowered to deal effectively with customers (Bowen and Lawler 1995). Effective service management requires the active management of both the empowerment process and the overall service delivery system. Many empowerment programmes fail when they focus on power without also redistributing organisational information, knowledge and rewards for service performance that balances organisational and customer interests. Contact employees may receive formal power to act as 'customer advocates', doing whatever it takes to please customers, but may not receive the necessary training to act as responsible business people (Bowen and Lawler 1995). This might even lead to creative rule breaking by contact employees, which can cause major problems for the organisation.

Potential consequences of teleworking service management

The complementary natures of telework and service management offer potential for organisational success through integration of the two approaches. Many of the process improvement objectives of telework are aligned with the customer-focused objectives of service management. However, the organisation must be careful to consider the role played by teleworking contact employees, and the expectations they may have. Teleworking service management can enable motivated employees to exhibit exceptional levels of customer service and positive behaviour toward the organisation, or it can enable de-motivated employees to exhibit some dysfunctional behaviours toward customers and the organisation. Such dysfunctional behaviours are made even more insidious by the remote nature of telework, because they may not be detected immediately; by the time they are detected, irreparable damage may have been done to customer relationships and the organisation's image and profitability.

Discretionary service behaviour

There potentially exist many types of behaviours that teleworking contact employees may choose to exhibit but that are not easily regulated, measured or monitored. These employees may have more personal control or discretion over the type and extent of behaviour they exhibit, as well as how, when, where, and at whom the behaviour is directed. These behaviours are uniquely influenced by teleworkers' roles as boundary spanners: the teleworking contact employee may mediate the organisation–customer exchange to the extent that internal organisational members never work directly with external customers. In this context, teleworkers have discretion regarding their behavioural output; in a sense, they are free to choose from a menu of service behaviours when working with customers. These service behaviours are based on teleworkers' individual choice, judgement, latitude or ability to make responsible decisions – in effect, they are 'discretionary'. Such discretionary service behaviours are more difficult for organisations to manage (or even to be aware of), and could have a more profound impact on organisational effectiveness than monitored employee behaviours (Blancero and Johnson 1997).

Teleworking contact employees who perceive an intact psychological contract with their organisation and a sense of fairness may be inclined to exhibit positive discretionary behaviours, i.e. do things to help both customers and the organisation whether or not it is explicitly part of their job. Teleworkers who perceive a breached psychological contract with the organisation may choose to remedy this unfairness by exhibiting negative discretionary service.

By nature of their boundary-spanning, empowered job roles, teleworking contact employees will be more likely to direct retaliatory discretionary service behaviour toward external customers, even in response to perceived internal injustice, with the intent of hurting the organisation. In a customer service context, teleworkers usually have more discretion and control over external structural job characteristics and interpersonal relationships than they have over internal job characteristics and relationships. That is, they may be free to exhibit both functional and dysfunctional behaviours externally (in terms of impact to the customer and/or the organisation) than they would be inside the organisation (due to direct supervision, organisational culture, work group norms, written regulations and policies, etc.). When teleworkers need to 'voice' their remedy or retaliation to perceived internally generated inequities, they are more likely to direct their behaviours (which are likely to be negative) externally in many situations for several reasons (Blancero et al. 1996).

Teleworkers directly influence and, to an extent, control external customer relationships, whereas the same employees may feel relatively powerless, anonymous or ineffectual in an organisationally dominated relationship. Robinson *et al.* (1994) note that employees may perceive themselves as powerless to effect change in their employers' behaviour, and thus may simply adjust their own perceived obligations in order to redress the situation. In this case, contact employees are likely to believe that externally directed discretionary service behaviours will have more of an impact on 'redressing' the situation, because they can be more easily targeted, observed, measured and controlled than internally directed behaviours.

In one sense, these discretionary service behaviours may be viewed as an outlet for teleworkers expressing appreciation or co-operation (positive) or retaliation (negative), depending upon the nature of the antecedents. Negative discretionary service behaviours detract from the work-related output of employees, and may include escape from work, defiance, resistance to authority, aggression and revenge (Blancero and Johnson 1997). This could result in teleworkers' destructive behaviour, damaging organisational profitability as well as customer satisfaction. Greenberg's (1990) research suggests that employees who perceive organisational inequity may either react with aggressive acts or attempt to adjust the balance of resources in their favour. In seeking to retaliate against perceived outcome unfairness by the organisation, teleworking contact employees may resort to such negative activities as sabotage of organisational equipment, providing intentionally damaged or inferior products or services to customers, or misrepresenting the organisation in such a way as to have a negative impact on both organisation and customers. Negative behaviours may also involve the exercise of discretion by employees who have not been empowered to do so by the organisation, or the use of criteria in exercising discretion that are unacceptable to the organisation. Ashforth and Lee (1990) describe discretionary defensive behaviours that may be directed toward customers, such as over conforming (working to rules), passing the buck, and playing dumb. Bitner *et al.* (1990) cite possible examples of discretionary service behaviour such as profanity, yelling and rudeness. Such negatively intended behaviour detracts from the work-related output of agents, would likely result in major losses of customer satisfaction and resultant decreases in organisational profitability, both short and long term. Organisational reputations regarding customer service are very difficult to repair once they are damaged.

'Tele-shirking'

The remote work environment and technological support enjoyed by teleworking contact employees also provides them with the potential to exhibit negative behaviour in the form of shirking their job responsibilities. Instead of teleworking, there may be 'tele-shirking'. Tele-shirkers may take advantage of a lack of direct observation to dupe their supervisors into believing they are actually working, while simultaneously avoiding contact with their customers. Research has shown that contact employees use a variety of discretionary tactics to control their encounters with customers, including ignoring, avoiding, stalling and distracting them, and exerting physical control over elements of the service environment (Ashforth and Lee 1990; Rafaeli 1989; Shamir 1980; Weatherly and Tansik 1993). In a teleworking environment, employees may invoke electronic options to achieve these negative behaviours, for example, sending all incoming calls to voice-mail; not answering a page or fax; or manipulating a computer program to falsify on-line productivity counts. Teleworkers may also take excessive amounts of time to return calls from customers or respond to requests from supervisors. Tele-shirking may not be an ideal long-term situation for a teleworking contact employee seeking to retaliate against the organisation, because of outcome performance measurements that are likely to reveal inactivity; however, teleworkers may still do a considerable amount of damage to the organisation's image and customer relationships, by shifting blame for poor performance to the organisation, in the eyes of the customer.

Imbalanced relationships

Teleworking contact employees must manage relationships with their customers and their organisation. The organisation must also manage its relationships with employees and customers; in a teleworking environment, this may require the organisation to manage its customer relationships through its employees. However, as previously noted, teleworking contact employees move physically and psychologically away from the organisation (as represented by the office structure and interaction with supervisors and co-workers) while moving virtually closer along these lines to customers. The teleworkers may tend to lose their identity and connection with a fragmented corporate culture (Kurland 1994). In lieu of organisational social structures, teleworking contact employees may seek to compensate by networking and socialising with customers. An alternative perspective of employee–customer relationships suggests that customers may serve as substitutes for leadership of the contact employees (Schneider and Bowen 1995), which may be especially applicable in a remotely supervised teleworking environment. This combination of relational forces presents the opportunity for teleworking contact employees to establish stronger relationships with customers than with the organisation. When used positively, such relationships may result in increased customer loyalty and satisfaction. However, there also exists the potential for abuse of the close employee–customer relationship. Negatively motivated teleworkers may conceivably collaborate with like-minded customers to deceive or defraud the organisation, or could even form a partnership with customers in competition with the organisation.

In a well-managed teleworking service environment, the relationships among the organisation, the employees and the customers should be balanced as much as possible. The ideal service encounter balances the customer and employee needs for control with the customer and organisational needs for efficiency. No single relationship (organisation–employee, employee–customer, customer–organisation) can dominate the service delivery process for the organisation to be completely successful over the long term. All three parties should have input into the design of the service delivery process, and this would include input into the teleworking service management process as well. Balanced input and agreement among the parties can help to satisfy their respective needs. Schneider and Bowen (1995) noted that agreement between perceptions of management's desired flexibility, employees' desired flexibility, and customers' desired flexibility resulted in greater employee satisfaction and better customer-reported service quality. Potential teleworking contact employees who are resistant to change or threatened by the loss of status and tradition associated with the central office may become more receptive to working remotely if they are made to feel that their input is valued and they are involved in helping to design the new teleworking programmes.

Summary and conclusion

This chapter discusses an integrated framework of teleworking and service management. The rationale for such an integrated approach and its potential benefits are apparent in both the research being done in each of these areas and in practical application by US companies like AT&T, Bell Atlantic, IBM, Hewlett-Packard and MCI (Blodgett 1995; Ditlea 1995; Jensen 1993; Piskurich 1996). However, less apparent and less well investigated are the organisational challenges and potential behavioural consequences associated with management of teleworking contact employees. These employees are moving physically and psychologically away from the organisation and closer to their customers. Characteristics of teleworking service jobs such as boundary spanning, empowerment and control over service encounters enhance employees' autonomy and discretion. Supervisors can no longer rely on direct methods of employee observation, control and evaluation. Instead, supervisors must be able to understand and manage the organisational factors that influence teleworking contact employees' behaviour. Employee perceptions of fairness underlie much of their motivation and behaviour. Supervisors need to take steps to ensure that their decisions are perceived as fair; they must find ways to convey the fairness of decision processes and communication as well, not an easy task in a remote work environment. One way to learn more about individual employees' fairness perceptions is to become aware of their psychological contracts, the promises they believe the organisation has made to them. The management of employees' fairness perceptions and psychological contracts is controllable by the organisation, through its HRM programmes. Without a thorough understanding of these elements, there is no guarantee that teleworking contact employees won't exhibit negative behaviours that are detrimental to customer perceptions of service quality and organisational profitability.

The implementation of a teleworking environment for service delivery is a balancing act among the organisation, employee and customer. First, the needs of each party must be considered. The organisation may need to use flexible work arrangements to recruit and retain the best service workers, addressing their personal as well as work needs by becoming a preferred employer (Zeithaml and Bitner 1995). Not all contact employees may be equally productive in a teleworking environment. There may be certain customer situations where employees with stronger social needs could be effective in building relationships with customers but less so in working independently away from the office social structure. Organisations should also consider differential customer needs for either relationship-based or transactional service encounters when making staffing decisions. Customer satisfaction may be enhanced through more personalised attention, and the flexibility of teleworking could allow employees to allocate time as needed to different customers. Yet not all customers want the efficiency and predictability of a service to be jeopardised by a personalisation strategy. According to Surprenant and Solomon (1987), all forms of service personalisation by employees do not necessarily result in more positive evaluations by customers of the service offered. Quality customer service is viewed as customers receiving the level of service they desire; this entails service employees being sensitive to customer wishes (George and Jones 1991). Organisations shouldn't assume that all customers want or need empowered teleworking contact employees who may feel closer to them.

There is no solid evidence that teleworking productivity increases remain permanent over time, so other factors may be necessary reinforcers to ensure service quality. The service encounter can be standardised to some extent by the influence of the organisational climate and culture on the delivery employee; but the encounters will not be homogeneous, based on decreased influence of the organisation and the increased influence of employee and customer characteristics. Because the teleworking contact employees and customers can build closer relationships, it is likely that this employee–customer interaction will characterise the nature of the teleworking service delivery process more than the organisation–employee or supervisor–employee interaction. Regardless of how the teleworking service process is developed, the bottom line is that the teleworking environment must produce a seamless service encounter for the customer.

To be effectively integrated in a service management framework, teleworking must aid in effective recruitment, eliminate role ambiguity and role conflict, capitalise on good employee–technology job fit, provide appropriate HRM systems and enhance empowerment and teamwork (Zeithaml et al. 1988). The organisation must fully balance its reasons for using teleworking service management in the first place. The right reasons are driven by employee and customer needs before organisational needs such as cost reduction and regulatory compliance. Teleworking is not an end in itself, and should not be viewed as an organisational panacea (Whiting 1995). It can be a tool for improving service delivery and must be aligned with customer-driven service designs and standards while strongly considering employee factors. The study of virtual work environments must extend beyond internal management issues in order to assess its full potential as a tool for achieving organisational goals. Since the nature of teleworking makes it well suited for service delivery, the research must focus externally to include the effects of teleworking on the customer as well as the organisation and employee.

References

Aldrich, H. and Herker, D. (1977) 'Boundary spanning roles and organization structure', *Academy of Management Review* 2: 217–30.

Alpander, G.C. (1991) 'Developing managers' ability to empower employees', *Journal Management* 10, 3: 13–24.

Ashforth, B.E. and Lee, R.T. (1990) 'Defensive behavior in organizations: a preliminary model' *Human Relations* 43: 621–48.

Bateson, J.E.G. (1985) 'Perceived control and the service encounter', in J.A. Czepiel, M.R. Solomon and C.F. Suprenant (eds) *The Service Encounter: Managing Employee/Customer Interaction in Service Businesses*, Lexington, MA: D.C. Heath and Co.

Berry, L.L. (1995) *On Great Service: A Framework for Action*, New York: The Free Press.

Bettencourt, L.A. and Brown, S.W. (1996) 'Customer-contact employees: relationships among workplace fairness, job satisfaction and prosocial behaviors', unpublished doctoral dissertation, Arizona State University.

Bitner, M.J., Booms, B. and Tetrault, M. (1990) 'The service encounter: diagnosing favorable and unfavorable incidents', *Journal of Marketing* 54: 71–84

Bitner, M.J., Booms, B. and Mohr, L. (1994) 'Critical service encounters: the employee's viewpoint', *Journal of Marketing* 58: 95–106.

Blancero, D. and Johnson, S.A. (1997) 'Customer service employees and discretionary service behavior: a psychological contract model', Paper presented at Academy of Management Conference, Boston, MA.

Blancero, D. Johnson, S.A., and Lakshman, C. (1996) 'Psychological contracts and fairness: the effect of violations on customer service behavior', *Journal of Market-Focused Management* 1: 47–61.

Blodgett, M. (1995) 'Mobile work force boosts MCI sales' *Computerworld* 29, 48: 16.

Bowen, D.E. (1990) 'Interdisciplinary study of service: some progress, some prospects', *Journal of Business Research* 20, 1: 71–9.

Bowen, D.E. and Lawler, E.E. (1992) 'The empowerment of service workers: what, why, how, and when', *Sloan Management Review*, Spring: 31–9.

—— (1995) 'Empowering service employees', *Sloan Management Review*, Summer: 73–84.

Bowen, D.E. and Schneider, B. (1985) 'Boundary spanning role employees and the service encounter: some guidelines for management and research', in J.A. Czepiel, M.R. Solomon, and C.F. Suprenant (eds) *The Service Encounter: Managing Employee/Customer Interaction in Service Businesses*, Lexington, MA: D. C. Heath and Co.

—— (1988) 'Services marketing and management: implications for organizational behavior', in L.L. Cummings and B.M. Staw (eds) *Research in Organizational Behavior*, , Greenwich, CT: JAI Press.

Brown, S.W., Fisk, R.P., and Bitner, M.J. (1994) 'The development and emergence of services marketing thought', *International Journal of Service Industry Management* 5, 1: 21–48.

Challagalla, G.N. and Shervani, T.A. (1996) 'Dimensions and types of supervisory control: effects on salesperson performance and satisfaction', *Journal of Marketing* 60, 1: 89–105.

Clemmer, E.C. (1993) 'An investigation into the relationship of fairness and customer satisfaction with services', in R. Cropanzano (ed.) *Justice in the Workplace: Approaching Fairness in Human Resources Management*, Hillsdale, NJ: Lawrence Erlbaum Associates.

Ditlea, S. (1995) 'Home is where the office is', *Nation's Business* 83, 11: 41–4.

Dobbins, G.H., Cardy, R.L., and Platz-Vieno, S. (1990) 'A contingency approach to appraisal satisfaction: an initial investigation of organizational variables and appraisal characteristics', *Journal of Management* 16, 3: 619–32.

Duxbury, L. and Haines, G.H. (1991) 'Predicting alternative work arrangements from salient attitudes: a study of decision makers in the public sector', *Journal of Business Research* 23: 83–97.

Dyer, L. and Holder, G.W. (1988) 'A strategic perspective on human resource management', in L. Dyer (ed.) *Human Resource Management: Evolving Roles and Responsibilities*, Washington, DC: BNA.

Flanagan, P. (1993) 'Here come the "road warriors"', *Management Review* 82, 9: 36–40.

George, J.M. and Jones, G.R. (1991) 'Towards an understanding of customer service quality', *Journal of Managerial Issues* 3: 220–38.

Greenberg, J. (1986) 'Determinants of perceived fairness of performance evaluations', *Journal of Applied Psychology* 71, 2: 340–2.

—— (1990) 'Employee theft as a reaction to underpayment inequity: the hidden cost of pay cuts', *Journal of Applied Psychology* 75: 561–8.

Grönroos, C. (1994) 'From scientific management to service management: a management perspective for the age of service competition', *International Journal of Service Industry Management* 5, 1: 5–20.

Hamilton, C.A. (1987) 'Telecommuting', *Personnel Journal*: 91–101.

Harris, C. (1988) 'A comparison of employee attitudes toward two performance appraisal systems', *Public Personnel Management* 17, 4: 443–55.

Hartman, R.I., Stoner, C.R. and Arora, R. (1991) 'An investigation of selected variables affecting telecommuting productivity and satisfaction', *Journal of Business and Psychology*: 207–24.

Jensen, J.A. (1993) 'Telecommuting: revolution of the revolution', *Credit World 81, 6: 24–6*.

Judge, T.A., and Farris, G.R. (1993) 'Social context of performance evaluation decisions', *Academy of Management Journal* 36, 1: 80–105.

Kingman-Brundage, J., George, W.R., and Bowen, D.E. (1995) 'Service logic: achieving service system integration', *International Journal of Service Industry Management* 6, 4: 20–39.

Kullven, H. and Mattsson, J. (1994) 'A management control model based on the customer service process', *International Journal of Service Industry Management* 5, 3: 14–25.

Kurland, N.B. (1994) 'Ethics on line: social and ethical implications of telecommuting', Paper presented at the GTE Lectureship Program in Technology and Ethics, Marymount University, Arlington, VA.

Mills, P.K. (1985) 'The control mechanisms of employees at the encounter of service organizations', in J.A. Czepiel, M.R. Solomon and C.F. Suprenant (eds) *The Encounter: Managing Employee/Customer Interaction in Service Businesses*, Lexington, MA:D.C. Heath and Co.

Mohr, L. and Bitner, M.J. (1995) 'The role of employee effort in satisfaction with service transactions', *Journal of Business Research* 32: 239–52.

Morrison, E.W. and Robinson, S.L. (1997) 'When employees feel betrayed: a model of how psychological contract violation develops', *Academy of Management Review* 22: 226–56.

O'Connell, S.E. (1996) 'The virtual workplace moves at warp speed', *HRMagazine* 41, 3: 50–3.

Ogilvie, H. (1994) 'This old office', *Journal of Business Strategy* 15, 5: 26–30.

Olson, M.H. and Primps, S.B. (1984) 'Working at home with computers: work and non-work issues', *Journal of Social Issues* 40: 97–112.

Organ, D.W. (1994) 'Personality and organizational citizenship behavior', *Journal of Management* 20, 2: 465–78.

Parasuraman, A. (1987) 'Customer-oriented corporate cultures are crucial to services marketing success', *Journal of Services Marketing* 1, 1: 39–46.

Piskurich, G.M. (1996) 'Making telecommuting work', *Training and Development* 50, 2: 20–7.

Rafaeli, A. (1989) 'When cashiers meet customers: an analysis of the role of supermarket cashiers', *Academy of Management Journal* 32: 245–73.

Ramaswami, S.N. (1996) 'Marketing controls and dysfunctional employee behavior: a test of traditional and contingency theory postulates', *Journal of Marketing* 60, 2: 105–20.

Ramsower, R.M. (1985) *Telecommuting: The Organizational and Behavioral Effects of Working at Home*, Ann Arbor, MI: University of Michigan Research Press.

Richter, J. and Meshulam, I. (1993) 'Telework at home: the home and the organization perspective', *Human Systems Management* 12: 193–203.

Robinson, S.L., Kraatz, M.S. and Rousseau, D.M. (1994) 'Changing obligations and the psychological contract: a longitudinal study', *Academy of Management Journal* 37, 1: 137–52.

Rousseau, D.M. (1995) *Psychological Contracts in Organizations : Understanding Written and Unwritten Agreements*, Thousand Oaks, CA: SAGE Publications.

Schneider, B. (1994) 'HRM – a service perspective: towards a customer-focused HRM', *International Journal of Service Industry Management* 5, 1: 64–76.

Schneider, B. and Bowen, D.E. (1985) 'Employee and customer perceptions of service in banks: replication and extension', *Journal of Applied Psychology* 70, 3: 423–33.

—— (1995) *Winning the Service Game*, Boston: Harvard University Press.

Shamir, B. (1980) 'Between service and servility: Role conflict in subordinate service roles', *Human Relations* 33: 741–56.

Strutton, D., Pelton, L.E. and Lumpkin, J.R. (1993) 'The relationship between psychological climate and salesperson–sales manager trust in organizations', *Journal of Personal Selling and Sales Management* 13, 4: 1–14.

Surprenant, C.F. and Solomon, M.R. (1987) 'Predictability and personalization in the service encounter', *Journal of Marketing* 51: 86–96.

Tansik, D.A. (1990) 'Managing human resource issues for high-contact service personnel', in D.E. Bowen, R.B. Chase and T.G. Cummings (eds) *Service Management Effectiveness*, San Francisco: Jossey-Bass.

Taylor, T.C. (1994) 'Going mobile', *Sales and Marketing Management* 146, 5: 94–101.

Tornow, W. and Wiley, J. (1990) 'Service quality and management practices: a look at employee attitudes, customer satisfaction, and bottom-line consequences', *Human Resource Planning* 11, 2. 105 16.

Weatherly, K. and Tansik, D. (1993) 'Tactics used by customer-contact workers: effects of role stress, boundary spanning, and control', *International Journal of Service Industry Management* 4, 3: 4–17.

Whiting, V. (1995) 'Telecommuting: an organizational panacea?' Symposium presented at the 36th Annual Western Academy of Management Conference, San Diego, CA.

Wright, P.C. and Oldford, A. (1993) 'Telecommuting and employee effectiveness: career and managerial issues', *International Journal of Career Management* 5, 1: 4–9.

Zeithaml, V.A. and Bitner, M.J. (1995) *Services Marketing*, Chicago: McGraw-Hill.

Zeithaml, V.A., Berry, L.L. and Parasuraman, A. (1988) 'Communication and control processes in the delivery of service quality', *Journal of Marketing* 52: 35–48.

12

PLANNING FOR TELEWORK

Lois M. Goldman and Benjamin A. Goldman

Introduction: the role of planners

If more widespread telework is to bring benefits to urban areas, an important role must be played by city planners. A strong planning approach is required here because, without deliberate attention to broader social objectives, the potential benefits of telework are too often realised only by private individuals and corporations. A planner's fundamental responsibility, in contrast, is to identify long-term goals for a city and the steps needed to achieve them (Bettman 1928). Planners seek to maximise the efficient use of public resources, reduce the inequalities of imperfect market competition for public goods and services and provide forums for broadening public discussion of policy choices. Hence planners have an important and fundamental interest in helping cities plan for the potentially profound effects that this new information technology could have on the quality of urban life and work.

Transportation planners have in fact been interested in telework since the 1970s because of its potential to reduce the costs of traffic congestion, energy use, air pollution, and transportation infrastructure. Yet a variety of other effects of telework – positive and negative, direct and indirect – have risen to the forefront of planners' concerns today. Telework could provide important employment opportunities and higher incomes for the urban poor, for example, but it could also exacerbate decentralisation and urban sprawl. Telework will clearly become an increasingly important issue for city planners if the practice grows as dramatically as is projected. Jack Nilles, for example, who coined the phrase 'telecommute' in 1973, estimates that as many as 50 million Americans will be telecommuting from home or from an off-site telework centre by the year 2030 (Nilles 1991).

The work of planning professionals is integral to achieving the more complex advantages and avoiding the more dire social costs of these revolutionary new work technologies. This chapter reviews what planners in the United States are currently doing to help cities adjust to and influence the effects of telework. It then presents a series of recommendations for overcoming various obstacles to

207

more effective telework planning in the future. Finally, it examines the significant potential of telework centres to direct benefits of telework to city residents and communities that the marketplace for new information technologies would otherwise bypass.

Telework planning in practice

Planners in federal, state and local governments, as well as in private organisations are involved in a variety of initiatives involving telework. Telework is seen as an important tool for reducing air pollution and traffic congestion, providing emergency relief, and improving worker productivity.

Federal government agencies operate several telework centres, and allow almost any interested federal employee to telecommute from home. The US government hopes for 60,000 federal teleworkers, or 3 per cent of its workforce, in the near future (US General Services Administration 1995). A wide variety of prominent national policies, involving, for example, climate change, transportation planning and government efficiency, highlight incentives for telework.

Several state governments are beginning to subsidise telecommunications infrastructure programmes to lay the technological foundations for future telework. Transportation planners in state governments are starting to include telework in models that predict reduction in pollution and traffic congestion from various traffic mitigation measures. Demonstration projects in the states of California, Washington, Utah and Florida, for example, have shown significant improvements in air quality, commuting time and worker productivity.

To date, the widest implementation of telework planning at the local level has been for natural and man-made emergencies. California's geological instability, for example, has led that state to the incorporation of telework in earthquake response plans (Edge Work Group Computing Report 1995). The federal government, with donated equipment from AT&T, temporarily opened several telework centres in Oklahoma City following the 1995 bombing of a federal building there, and many corporations expanded their telework programmes in Atlanta during the 1996 Olympics.

While these public sector initiatives are promising, the private sector accounts for most of the US growth in telework. Employers in the aerospace, pharmaceuticals, travel, software, banking and other industries have telework programmes. Two-thirds of 'Fortune 1,000' companies have telework programmes, largely because of anticipated savings and productivity gains (Goldman 1995).

Overcoming barriers to telework

Several barriers are preventing planners, and the public sector more generally, from integrating telework into many more policy areas than those now taking place. Policy revisions are needed for zoning regulations to allow working at home, for tax laws to give employers and employees incentives to telecommute, for public investments in telework-related infrastructures, and for combating market-based inequities in the distribution of telecommunications infrastructure. Our suggestions in these areas are intended to engage the planning profession more fully in capturing the benefits and ameliorating the negative aspects of telework.

City and town planners need to revise outdated or unreasonably restrictive zoning regulations on homework. An American Planning Association survey found that 'many of the changes in the nature of the workplace have occurred so rapidly that local zoning regulations have not caught up with them' (Herbers 1986). Chicago, for example, had zoning ordinances until the 1980s that banned 'the installation of any mechanical or electrical equipment customarily incident to the practice of a profession', making it a technical violation of the zoning code to own a home computer or fax machine. To make matters worse, in many cases the self-policing nature of American zoning laws (regulations are enforced only when neighbours complain), inequitably discriminates against homework or favours more traditional work-at-home jobs. Appropriate zoning for telework would allow homeowners to combine state-of-the-art telecommunications connections with other design elements conducive to a homework environment. A suburban Lynwood Illinois development, for example, accommodates homeworkers with 'dual zoning' that allows for a residence in front and a business structure at the back of each one-acre lot (Butler 1988). Revising commercial and residential zoning regulations to reflect current telework practises will not only encourage teleworking, but will also be likely to enhance property values significantly (Mokhtarian 1995).

Telework would also get a boost from tax laws that allow home office deductions for teleworkers and tax credits for employers with teleworkers. In 1993, the US Supreme Court severely curtailed the availability of home office deductions (*Commissioner* v. *Soliman* (1993) 113 S. Ct. 701) by denying them to an anaesthesiologist on the grounds that his home was not his primary place of business, despite the fact that the three hospitals where he worked did not provide an office for him to prepare bills, use the telephone, or review patient records (*New Jersey Law Journal* 1993). Federal bills to liberalise eligibility rules for home office deductions, as well as employer tax credits for home- and centre-based teleworkers have been proposed but not enacted as of this writing (see Congressional Information Service 1995; Gillis 1996). Other tax reforms are also needed: private employers should receive tax incentives for leasing telework centre work stations in distressed neighbourhoods, for training workers for telework centre employment and for hiring former public assistance recipients into telework positions.

On the spending side, incorporating telecommunications infrastructure development into the American process of city master plans would enable planners to help communities better accommodate telework and overcome major problems associated with traditional telecommunications development. City master plans have historically provided an important avenue for public participation in determining the future shape of urban infrastructures. Telecommunications infrastructure development, on the other hand, has primarily been the result of private, supply-side approaches (as in 'build-it-and-they-will-come'). Most researchers in the field conclude that this market approach has failed to accommodate the many more job functions that could be done remotely with faster and more reliable telecommunications connections (US Department of Transportation 1993). Demand-driven planning, such as that which occurs with city master plans, in contrast, would provide ongoing opportunities for diverse users, providers and other community interests to influence decisions in a more timely and forward-looking manner. Cornell University and the California-based non-profit Center for the New West, for example, have developed such a demand-driven approach to telecommunications planning that encourages policy-makers, business and community leaders and residents to make proactive requests for needed services from telecommunications providers, rather than limiting public decision-making input to accepting or rejecting provider-initiated proposals (Center for the New West 1995).

Without government intervention, locational advantages from telework – along with all other telecommunications technologies – will continue to concentrate in more affluent white neighbourhoods in the US, exacerbating economic and social inequities. The geographic distribution of new telecommunications infrastructure is significant to planning, because this infrastructure inequality has the potential to contribute substantially to an area's economic downfall. As William J. Mitchell states in *City of Bits*:

> If the value of real estate in the traditional urban fabric is determined by location, location, location (as property pundits never tire of repeating), then the value of a network connection is bandwidth, bandwidth, bandwidth. Accessibility is redefined; tapping directly into a broadband data highway is like being on Main Street, but a low baud-rate connection puts you out in the boonies . . . The bondage of bandwidth is displacing the tyranny of distance, and a new economy of land use and transportation is emerging.

> (1995: 17)

Several cities and states have developed telecommunications infrastructures that try to level access to employment opportunities. While some of these projects include telework as a stated goal, most undertake telecommunications modernisation as a way to attract and retain businesses, needed services, government access, or libraries.

Teleport development is perhaps the most visible and widespread effort. A teleport is a facility that provides a variety of advanced communications services including satellite connections and ISDN lines that local businesses can plug into. The first teleport in the United States opened on Staten Island in New York City in 1983. Since then, over 100 US cities have sponsored teleports, often in partnership with private investors. Teleports are developed to keep jobs in an area, to attract new businesses, to provide modern telecommunications infrastructure, and to revitalise economically depressed areas (Schmandt *et al.* 1989). It is unclear, however, whether teleports offer cities a form of locational advantage, or if they simply offer businesses a way to bypass existing telecommunications infrastructures (Graham 1992). This is precisely the kind of infrastructure development that would benefit from more demand-driven approaches to policy formation, implementation and evaluation.

Bringing telework to the city

The development of multi-purpose telework centres, especially in high-density residential areas, is a logical telework mode for cities to promote. Within the context of a demand-driven approach to their development, telework centres provide an excellent example of a convenient way for cities to overcome many of the obstacles that prevent effective telework planning. Unlike teleports, which are primarily the product of supply-side technology development, the development of telework centres responds to a mix of market and community demands. They have great potential to enhance economic competitiveness while revitalising distressed communities, and providing employment possibilities and welfare improvements for poorer city residents.

Multi-purpose telework centres are the urban equivalent of earlier European telecottages that began in 1985 in Scandinavia and spread quickly throughout Europe. Telecottages are small, mostly rural, multi-service facilities equipped with work stations and advanced telecommunications. Rather than serving geographically isolated rural areas, in contrast, US telework centres offer access and the promise of community revitalisation to economically isolated inner-city residents. They provide 'a robust model for success in remote work facilities', according to scholars Bagley, Mannering and Mokhtarian (1994).

When located in low-income, city-centre neighbourhoods, multi-purpose telework centres offer much more than a direct increase in employment opportunities. They can act as stable anchor tenants in a failing building or struggling section of a central business district, attracting pedestrian traffic and auxiliary businesses, and thereby improving safety. They can also provide access to a wide variety of services. The US General Accounting Office (1995: 24), for example, recommends co-locating federal, state and local government personnel in order to provide one-stop advice about public assistance, immigration, naturalisation and passport services, as well as related programmes regarding educational and job training opportunities, access to affordable housing and crime prevention. Community-based multi-purpose telework centres should also offer child-care facilities, and telemedicine or medical clinics.

The costs of such facilities are moderate relative to their potential impact. In a study of eight private-sector telework centres by Bagley, *et al.* (1994), start-up investments ranged from $120,000 to $425,000 dollars, with monthly operating expenses in the range of $6,600 to $18,900 dollars. Monthly median rent for a work station was only $100, ranging from nought to $850 depending on the centre and tenant. Government funding for telework centres subsidised 30 per cent to 100 per cent of start-up costs, with the expectation that they would soon become self-sufficient. At a minimum, the telework component of these centres includes very basic equipment, such as telephones, paper and pencil, computers and modems. Jobs such as telemarketer, hotel reservationist, word-processor and data entry clerk are obvious candidates for such remote site work, along with necessary supervisory staff.

Employers benefit from this arrangement with property cost savings and improved productivity after a period of initial training and acclimatisation. Productivity improvements can result from tapping under-utilised labour markets, and from several advantages for employees from telework centres, such as easy commutes and on-site child-care. Several studies document 10 per cent to 30 per cent gains in productivity from telework (Fleming 1989). Ultimately, success at such centres depends upon the ability to attract and retain private firms, especially small companies. Small business tenants are important because so much US employment growth occurs in companies with fewer than fifty employees. In addition to the financial incentives discussed, small businesses that work with government agencies would benefit from the close proximity of agency personnel using nearby work stations.

Telework centres located in low-income residential areas may prove to be an important link in the successful transition from dependence on public assistance to financial independence for many poor citizens. Ten million out of the thirteen million Americans on public assistance are being required to work in order to continue receiving government subsidies as a result of recent welfare reform initiatives (Office of Management and Budget 1996). These attempts at reform will meet with only limited success without innovative ways to increase educational and employment opportunities for welfare recipients, many of whom lack basic skills, reliable transportation and affordable day care for their children. Often, public transportation into the central business district from these areas is inconvenient and expensive, making jobs downtown difficult to obtain and keep. Telework centres would help overcome these barriers to productive employment. Telework centres offer jobs within the neighbourhood that often pay more and provide greater security than entry-level jobs in retail stores or restaurants.

Home-based telework, on the other hand, is relatively impractical in many inner-city areas for a variety of physical and sociological reasons. Apartments are often too small to have a dedicated work space, and burglary rates are often high, making companies unwilling to locate equipment in these homes. Daytime conditions may not be conducive to working because of noise or other distractions. While telework centres solve these problems, there are still other concerns associated with working conditions at these centres. Labour unions, for example, feel threatened by the potential for teleworkers to be hired as contractors rather than employees, adding pressure to the growing US trend toward contract work, which now comprises 10 per cent to 15 per cent of the US workforce (Coates

1992). US employers are not required to provide social security contributions, workers' compensation payments, or fringe benefits such as health insurance to contract or contingent workers. Remote site workers in the urban telework centres may be particularly vulnerable to such inferior employment status. To counteract this problem, potential telework centre employer tenants could be screened for commitments to liveable wages, benefits and employee career advancement.

Planning for telework's double edge

Investment in telecommunications technology and telework centres to facilitate telework is a double-edged sword. Widespread telework could drain cities of jobs, revenues and vitality by freeing companies and employees from the need to be close to the central business district. With proper planning, however, telework could divert new employment and educational opportunities to cities. Advanced urban telecommunications infrastructure can also provide locational advantages for urban areas hoping to attract and retain technologically sensitive businesses.

Technological approaches such as improving telecommunications infrastructure will not encourage telework in an urban area by itself. Technology can influence social change, but it rarely determines it. Most private demands for investments to upgrade telecommunications infrastructure come from the most sophisticated users who are pushing the limits of existing technology. Public investments, however, are needed for the least sophisticated users, in order to meet policy goals such as reducing government dependency and promoting community revitalisation.

The role of city planners *vis-à-vis* telework is to propose ways to use the public powers of regulation and taxation to secure the most benefits from telework arrangements for cities and their residents. Without the input of planning professionals, the benefits of telework will flow primarily towards suburban and rural areas, bypassing cities altogether. Deliberate planning of the kind described in this chapter is required for telework to aid urban economic development, rather than merely robbing cities of the best and the brightest workers.

References

Bagley, M., Mannering J.S. and Mohktarian, P.L. (1994) *Telecommuting Centers and Related Concepts: A Review of Practice*, Davis, CA: University of California Institute of Transportation Studies, Research Report UCD-ITS-RR-94-4.

Bettman, A. (1928), 'The Relationship of the Functions and Powers of the City Planning Commission to the Legislative, Executive, and Administrative Departments of City Government' *Papers and Discussions by the Twentieth National Conference on City Planning*: 142–59.

Butler J.C. (1988), Local Zoning Ordinances: Governing Home Occupations', in

K. Christensen (ed.) *The New Era of Home-Based Work: Directions and Policies*: Boulder, CO: Westview Press.

Center for the New West (1995) 'Smart Communities', draft version No. 2, Ontario, CA: Cornell University.

Coates, V.T. (1992) 'The Future of Information Technology', *Annals of the American Academy of Political and Social Science*, 522, July: 45–56.

Congressional Information Service, (1995) (Abstracts) *CIS/Index to Publications of the United States Congress*, Bethesda, MD: Congressional Information Service, Vol. 26, No. 12, December: 52.

Edge Work Group Computing Report (1995) 'Internet Access: Pacific Bell Puts Telecommuting Guide on the Net', *IAC Newsletter, Database*, 6, 283, 23 October.

Fleming, L. (1989) *The One Minute Commuter* Davis, CA: Acacia Books.

Gillis, D. (1996) Legislative Aide to Congressman Barney Frank (telephone conversation and fax) 18 March.

Goldman, E. (1995) 'Execs Believe Telecommuting Benefits Employers', New York, NY: Spector and Associates Press Release, 23 October.

Graham, S.D.N. (1992) 'The Role of Cities in Telecommunications Development', *Telecommunications Policy* 16, 3: 187–93.

Herbers, J. (1986) 'Rising Cottage Industry Stirring Concern in U.S.', *The New York Times*, 13 May: A18.

Mitchell, W.J. (1995) *City of Bits*, Cambridge, MA: The MIT Press.

Mokhtarian, P.L. (1991) 'Telecommuting and Travel: State of the Practice, State of the Art', *Transportation* 18, 3: 319–42.

—— (1995) 'Telecommunications in Urban Planning: Selected North American Examples', prepared for the Habitat II Global Workshop on Transport and Communication for Urban Development, Singapore, 3–5 July, 1995, Davis, CA: University of California Transportation Center Institute of Transportation Studies.

New Jersey Law Journal (1993) 'Taxation', *New Jersey Law Journal*, 18 January: 52.

Nilles, Jack M. (1991) 'Telecommuting and Urban Sprawl: Mitigator or Inciter?', *Transportation* 18, 3: 411–32.

Office of Management and Budget (1996) Budget Supplement, in *Budget of the United States Government, Fiscal Year 1997*, Washington, DC: Executive Office of the President of the United States: Chapters 7 and 8.

Schmandt, Jurgen, Williams, Frederick, and Wilson, Robert H. (1989) *Telecommunications Policy and Economic Development: The New State Role*, New York, NY: Praeger.

U.S. Department of Transportation (1993) *Transportation Implications of Telecommuting*, Washington, DC: U.S. Government Printing Office, April.

U.S. General Services Administration. Office of Workplace Initiatives (1995) *Interim Report: Federal Interagency Telecommuting Centers*, Washington, DC: U.S. Government Printing Office, March.

13

FLEXIBLE WORK AND TRAVEL BEHAVIOUR

A research framework

Ann M. Brewer and David A. Hensher

Background: the changing spatial and temporal dimension of work activity

Reflecting on the 1960s and 1970s reveals an era characterised by a rigidity of working hours, a predominance of full-time employment, one-worker households and an employer requirement to have people physically located at their place of work. This era preceded fax, mobile phones, computer networks and electronic mail. The absence of information technology and telecommunications was offset by the predominance of central business districts in providing employment opportunities. Against this context, relatively low personal incomes, location- and labour-intensive work practices worked well to assist the case for substantial public transport services (especially rail-based in the larger urban areas).

The 'on-line work community' emerged during the 1980s and expanded dramatically in the 1990s, as information and telecommunication technology produced a new set of opportunities and constraints leading to a new order in the labour market. At the same time, there has been a growing desire and ability for people to purchase increasing levels of mobility in order to increase access to an ever-expanding choice set of activities. The flexibility of automobility has provided the nucleus of technology to satisfy the travel preferences of the population for commuting and non-commuting activity (Hensher 1993). With increased access to information and telecommunications technology (mobile phones, fax, e-mail, etc.) and the geographic dispersal of workplaces, it is no longer necessary for all work activities to be physically located at the main employment location.

A forerunner of this new order in Australia was the increased participation of women in the workforce, part time and full time (Table 13.1) and significant microeconomic reform (award restructuring, enterprise bargaining, downsizing), all of which have heavily impacted men's participation rates. In line with these

Table 13.1 Australian labour force participation and work schedules

(i) Workforce participation rates by age for males and females (%)

Age	Male				Female			
	1975	1990	1993	1995	1975	1990	1993	1995
15–19	59	61	54	58	56	59	54	60
20–24	91	90	88	88	65	79	76	78
25–34	97	95	93	93	47	67	65	69
35–44	97	95	93	93	52	73	72	72
45–54	94	90	89	89	45	61	65	68
55–59	88	75	74	74	30	33	37	40
60–64	71	51	48	47	16	16	13	17
65+	17	9	9	10	4	2	2	3
Total	81	76	74	74	42	53	52	54

Source: ABS Cat. 6203

(ii) Hours worked by employed persons ('000)

Weekly hours worked	Male			Female married			Female not married			Female total		
	1975	1982	1995	1975	1982	1995	1975	1982	1995	1975	1982	1995
0	182	213	303	69	79	180	31	50	87	99	128	267
1–15	208*	130	284	444*	288	402	123*	128	277	567	416	680
16–29		225	337		289	461		98	201		386	662
30–34	138	299	347	123	121	217	38	83	130	161	204	347
35–39	423	617	677	188	196	313	163	195	249	351	390	561
40	1563	1177	810	363	255	246	290	289	195	653	543	441
41–44	497*	252	247	57*	38	70	53*	50	58	110*	88	128
45–48		359	446		35	91		35	69		70	160
49+	758	753	1238	62	82	192	28	46	109	90	128	301
Total	3769	4025	4689	1306	1383	2172	726	974	1375	2030	2353	3547

Source: ABS Cat. 6203
* In 1975, the age ranges 1–15 and 16–29 were combined. Likewise for ranges 41–44 and 45–48.

(iii) Average weekly hours worked by employment category, 1975–95

August	Average weekly hours worked					
	Full-time workers		Part-time workers		Weighted average	
	Males	Females	Males	Females	Males	Females
1975	42.2	38.2	15.9	16.3	41.2	31.0
1985	41.3	37.7	16.2	15.8	39.8	29.5
1992	43.0	39.2	14.9	15.6	40.0	29.0
1995	44.0	39.7	15.6	16.0	40.9	29.6

Source: ABS Cat. 6203

trends, there has been a significant change in work attitudes with both employers and workers prepared to participate in more flexible forms of work organisation and arrangements characterised by part-time and contract work. With the support of labour unions, alternative work schedules are increasingly offered to employees giving greater scope for both extending the actual hours of business operation and defining work hours, the work 'week', as well as the location of work activity.

In Australia, there is a long-term trend to shorter standard weekly, annual and lifelong working times (Dawkins and Barker 1987) with a mix of polarised and redistributed reductions in working time. The reduction in working time is not a uniform trend. Polarisation involves continuation of long work hours for some and few work hours for others; redistribution involves shorter working hours which are widespread on a sufficient scale to counteract job loss, leading to a society enriched by the spread of 'liberated time' (Tracy and Lever-Tracy 1991). This increasing heterogeneity away from a classical work schedule has produced a significant change in the composition of the workforce with respect to age, gender and education.

Transport

Despite the fact that very little has been quantified, there is an expanding literature which suggests the potential causal linkages between alternative organisational structure, work organisation, flexible work arrangements, travel behaviour and environmental impact. The importance of these relationships is highlighted by increasing evidence that the greatest potential for reducing greenhouse gas emissions and local air pollution due to the automobile, in particular and all passenger transport in general, is through improvements in automobile technology and flexible work arrangements. The latter is defined spatially and temporally in its most broadest sense (Hensher 1993). Although each unit of automobile technology is contributing less pollution in the 1990s than in previous decades, the ever-increasing number of cars on the roads and the growth in annual kilometres travelled means that improvements in air quality are likely to be short lived (Hensher et al. 1995). One important way to address this significant problem is to investigate travel behaviour associated with commuting and the implications of substitution of non-commuting travel activity for 'saved' commuting activity under alternative work practices. The majority of these journeys are by car with a decline in public transport usage (Table 13.2).

Commuting behaviour is associated strongly with changing work practices producing a shift in commuting (and non-commuting) behaviour. As work practices are becoming more flexible and information based, and urban decentralisation continues with jobs following people, the radially biased high-density public transport corridors are losing their growth opportunities (even though preserving in many instances their patronage). While public transport is more frequently used to travel into city centres, the average duration of the journey length is

Table 13.2 Urban travel activity in Australia, 1971–91

Year	Bus passengers (millions)	Bus pkm* ('000 million)	Train/tram passengers (millions)	Train/ tram pkm ('000 million)	Car trips (millions)	Car pkm ('000 million)	Truck tonne kms ('000 million)
1971	763	3.5	565	7.32	8,912	66.5	9.14
1972	756	3.51	508	6.61	9,217	69.9	9.69
1973	772	3.66	484	6.23	9,456	71.8	10.27
1974	788	3.8	484	6.30	10,049	76.3	11.05
1975	793	3.89	464	6.02	10,594	80.4	12.75
1976	784	3.91	453	5.96	10,863	82.5	13.64
1977	784	3.97	443	5.85	11,340	87.9	14.43
1978	779	4	430	5.70	11,729	90.9	15.95
1979	777	4.06	427	5.67	11,935	92.5	17.37
1980	791	4.19	447	6.13	12,057	93.1	18.41
1981	791	4.16	457	6.29	12,232	94.5	19.88
1982	800	4.19	465	6.46	12,936	99.9	20.80
1983	810	4.17	454	6.30	12,953	100.1	21.87
1984	821	4.15	455	6.36	13,483	104.2	24.23
1985	851	4.26	463	6.44	14,198	113.9	25.41
1986	873	4.34	493	6.97	14,703	117.8	27.15
1987	896	4.43	505	7.19	15,053	123.3	29.28
1988	926	4.51	524	7.47	15,621	131.3	31.82
1989	963	4.76	537	7.67	16,318	137.2	33.50
1990	966	4.75	519	7.47	16,717	140.5	34.08
1991	993	4.87	523	7.52	16,553	139.1	34.08

Source: Cosgrove and Gargett 1992
* Passenger kilometres

longer, acting as a deterrent rather than an incentive. It is too early to predict whether increased labour market flexibility will work against the future of public transport, especially modes of transport which require a relatively dense corridor of movement activity to be economically and environmentally sustainable.

Golob (University of California, also Irvine – in personal communication) suggests that telecommuting monitored in California could reduce vehicle kilometres by as much as 10 per cent. In an Australian study, this is indicated by over four trips per day and 70 kilometres (RTA 1994). The implications of these trends for greenhouse gas emissions and air quality are ambiguous and need careful assessment (Nilles 1991). The ambiguity is in part due to the relationship between commuting and non-commuting travel activity, the interrelationships between activities of household members, (particularly but not exclusively in the case of workers) and the suburbanisation of workplaces. The last opens up opportunities for deeper suburbanisation of residential location given the phenomenon of time budgeting. To take a real example, a two-worker household with children at different schools:

Currently one worker has a multi-purpose city commute of 20 kilometres one way, dropping off a child at school *en route* to the regular workplace. The other worker has a part-time job within 4 kilometres from home, uses a bus and starts at 10.00 a.m., finishing at 1.00 p.m. The other child is driven to a local bus stop to catch a school bus (the trip is 12 kilometres one way). Suppose the full-time employee opts for a 4-day working week, taking every Friday off and working 10 hours each day. They no longer take the child to school because they leave too early and get home too late. The first child now catches a local bus 5 days per week. The commute to the city now has a lower vehicle occupancy for much of the trip. On the day off the amount of driving is less but the number of trips (hence cold and hot starts) is double that of the commute, even though total kilometres have reduced a little. The part-time worker takes the car for the 3 hours on the other worker's day off, instead of using the bus. The opportunity to telecommute for two days for the full-time worker subsequently is used to justify a residential location change further from the city, which increases vehicle kilometres per trip but reduces the number of commuting kilometres for this person. The part-time worker, however, has a longer commute and now requires a second car. The children have to be driven to school.

There is a lot of activity substitution occurring, with some of the change being emission friendly, while other changes are emission unfriendly. The above example illustrates the response possibilities which need to be accounted for in determining the net impact of changing the spatial and temporal opportunities for work activities.

Flexible work arrangements

Telecommuting, compressed work weeks and flexible working hours are all evolving flexible work arrangements (Pratt 1994).

Telecommuting

Telecommuting involves working from a remote office site which is typically the employee's home or a satellite 'telework' centre near or in residential areas fully equipped with appropriate telecommunications equipment and services, and which can serve employees of single or multiple firms, co-located on the basis of geography rather than business function (US Department of Transportation 1993). While these centres are not widespread in Australia they are increasing elsewhere, notably in the USA (US Department of Transportation 1993). Close to eight million people in the USA are estimated to telecommute, typically spending 1 or 2 days per week working from home, with one-third being contract workers.

The opportunity to telecommute depends on how work is defined and structured. It need not be technology-based at all but simply involve paperwork, reading, or thinking (Mokhtarian 1991). Telecommuting defined in a transportation context means a reduction in either the number of commute trips for a home-based worker or in the distance travelled to work for a telecentre worker (Handy and Mokhtarian 1995). Activities that define telecommuting and non-telecommuting are difficult to distinguish when taking into account work-related trips such as visiting clients or customers or contract workers working at home.

Compressed work week (CWW)

CWW is an arrangement whereby workers attend the place of employment on fewer but longer work days to compensate for the lost time, e.g. four 12-hour days. CWW has a direct effect on reducing commuting.

Flexible work hours

Flexible work hours provide workers with the opportunity to control their starting and finishing times on any work day usually within a prescribed bandwidth, e.g. 7.30 a.m. to 6.30 p.m. Flexible work hours assist workers in avoiding peak commuting times but have a small effect on reducing commuting unless combined with a CWW.

The empirical context of flexible work arrangements in Australia

The use of flexible work arrangements, such as telecommuting, CWW and flexible work hours, is not widely used in Australian organisations. There exists a diversity of experience with alternative work arrangements and attitudes towards the idea. In 1994 a major travel study in six capital cities in Australia (Sydney, Melbourne, Adelaide, Brisbane, Canberra and Perth) was undertaken (Hensher 1996). Existing work arrangements of a sample of 850 commuters were investigated, including questions on company policy, telecommuting, CWWs, spatial and temporal working profiles, and reasons for not participating in flexible work arrangements. The survey responses are summarised in Tables 13.3, 13.4 and 13.5.

The profiles of company policy, work arrangements and nature of constraints, either self imposed or directed by an organisation (in Tables 13.3–13.5), suggest that the take-up rate of flexible working hours – spatially and temporally – is very high indeed where the opportunity for such work practices exists. However the ratio of CWW and flexitime to telecommuting is 3:1. The frequency of CWW and flexitime over a 15-day period increases strongly whereas the incidence of telecommuting falls sharply.

In another Australian study conducted in the same time period, telecommuters reported improved productivity, organisational skill, concentration and focus as well as enhanced self-esteem and confidence. They also experienced fewer distractions, interruptions, felt less stressed and experienced reduced travelling time and cost (RTA 1994).

Table 13.3 Company policy on alternative work arrangements

Company policy	Incidence (%)
No flexible arrangements	61.5
Self employed	0.7
Other conditions	1.5
Telecommute	1.8
Telecommute and other	0.1
Flexitime	16.3
Flexitime and other	0.4
Flexitime and telecommuting	2.1
Flexitime, telecommute and self employed	0.1
Flexitime, telecommute and other	0.2
Compressed work week	7.1
Compressed work week and other	0.2
Compressed work week and telecommute	0.3
Compressed work week and flexitime	5.0
Compressed work week, flexitime and other	0.1
Compressed work week, telecommute and flexitime	2.6

Table 13.4 Current work arrangements for commuters

Work arrangements	Incidence (%)	Less than 5 days/mth (%)	6–10 days/ mth (%)	11–15 days/mth (%)	More than 15 days/mth (%)
No flexible arrangements	70.4				
Telecommuter	3.4	80.0	10.0	2.5	7.5
Flexitime	18.1				
Compressed work week	8.1	2.0	1.0	10.0	87.0

For those commuters who do not use CWW (Table 13.5), constraints imposed by corporate policy or lack of (including inappropriate job structure) are high (71.9 per cent) compared to lack of worker interest at 28.1 per cent. For those commuters who do not use telecommuting (Table 13.5), constraints imposed by corporate policy or lack of (including inappropriate job structure or poor resources) are high (96 per cent) compared to lack of worker interest at 4.0 per cent. Table 13.5 suggests that a closer look at corporate policy, work organisation and the role of managers within a hierarchy needs to be investigated in more detail through case studies.

Broadening the picture: critical linkages

The opportunities for flexible work arrangements will be determined by the benefits and problems perceived by employers and workers, the way work is structured, the desire and characteristics of the potential telecommuter, HRM

Table 13.5 Reasons for not working a compressed workweek or telecommuting

Reason	Incidence (%)
Compressed Work Week	
I do not want to work extra hours some days	13.3
The company policy does not apply to me	57.1
My workload and coverage of the week prevents this	11.7
Job responsibilities cannot be compressed	3.1
Self-employment/casual employment	5.1
Other reasons (many individual)	9.7
Total	100
Telecommuting	
Supervisor makes it difficult	1.2
I prefer social and professional interaction in office	3.6
I cannot get motivated away from the office	0.4
I do not have the facilities to work at home	18.1
The type of work I do is not suited to it	74.1
Not company policy	2.6
Total	100

policies and, most importantly, the attitude of immediate supervisors. As information technology makes work and customer activities more location independent, flexible work arrangements may prove a greater incentive for employers to introduce flexibility measures. In Australia there has been an urgent call from the government for better managed enterprises to provide greater organisational flexibility and improved employee relations (Karpin Report 1995). Intense competition and increased labour costs have placed pressure on management and unions to raise productivity, increase flexibility and quality of outputs (Porter 1990). Flexible work arrangements are one way of addressing these initiatives providing management is prepared to engage in cross-functional skilling, manage commitment and design technology (Brewer 1993, 1994, 1995; Harrison 1994). Individual work arrangements are influenced by the internal constraints of organisations such as organisational structure and managerial policies, including human resource management, work organisation and external constraints such as union policies and agreements. The research to date does not address these issues in an integrating manner.

Further, there has been very little work on the actual linkage between flexible work organisation, work hour arrangements and travel behaviour, especially in terms of accounting for the relationship between an employee and the managerial hierarchy which lead to a range of incentives and constraints on opportunities to take up work practices which can aid in more efficient travel patterns from the perspective of ecologically sustainable development (ESD). The extent to which employers and employees support these possibilities varies widely. The matching of employer and employee support for flexible work policies is not necessarily strong within the one organisation; and where it does exist it is often not encouraged by managers throughout the hierarchy. Thus the translation from corporate policy to implementation of flexibility in work arrangements cannot be assured.

While the link between flexible work arrangements, work organisation and efficient travel patterns from the perspective of ESD has been deduced, little research exists focusing on this linkage taking into account the complexity of managerial hierarchy. There are organisational and institutional (managerial and union) constraints in providing various work arrangements as a direct incentive for employees. Managerial and union ideologies may contradict attempts by one or the other to introduce flexibility into work organisation and schedules. The type of flexible work arrangement in place will reflect organisational and institutional factors as well as market ones. It is important to develop a better understanding of how these factors influence HRM practices and how these influence employee commuting activity and consequently non-commuting travel activity. HRM practices in different market and/or industry segments may be a significant predictor of work redesign and pattern of travel behaviour, spilling over to environmental impact.

While there are a few studies (e.g. Mahmassani and Chen 1992; Mahmassani *et al.* 1993) which have looked at the role of the employer in influencing the employees' opportunities to participate in more flexible work arrangements in the interests of improving road traffic levels, the focus has been on either simple workplace rules such as management's tolerance for lateness or the availability of flexible working hours. *There is no research which has developed a formal conceptual framework to enable us to analytically model the causal structures between the employee and the managerial hierarchy (encompassing work design) that impose limitations for the employee to exercise options in the interests of ESD.* It is important to understand both the sets of constraints and incentives that potentially modify travel behaviour in the interests of reducing environmental degradation.

To this end, a structural equation system with latent segmentation and a set of discrete choice models offers an appealing framework within which to investigate the causal linkages between organisational structure, work organisation, work arrangements and employee travel behaviour responses, such as frequency of commuting trips and consequent non commuting trips due to relaxing a constraint on the number of commuting trips. Within such a framework, a number of propositions which have not been evaluated in any formal sense, all of which impact directly or indirectly on travel behaviour and environmental pollution, can be tested. These include:

1 Flexible work arrangements will reduce levels of traffic congestion and automobile emissions.
2 Flexible work arrangements change peoples' travel patterns especially in non-work trips partially negating the benefits of other policies to reduce greenhouse gas emissions and local air pollution.

3   Organisations with flexible forms of work organisation are more likely to consider alternative forms of work hours.
4   Organisations that rely on a rigid (narrowly specialised) internal labour market for regulating work organisation are more likely to adhere to conventional forms of work organisation than those operating on broadened (broadly specialised) internal labour markets.
5   Organisations that are HRM-orientated are more likely to engage in flexible work arrangements.
6   Organisations that are using strategies other than cost (i.e. quality, variety, service) are more likely to engage in workplace reform.
7   Organisations that operate in international markets are more likely to adopt workplace redesign (i.e. learn more quickly about alternative work practices).

The research framework

To address these propositions, a number of issues need to be understood within organisational contexts.

Flexible work arrangements

Flexible work arrangements are an alternative or non-traditional way of working and include telecommuting, CWW, remote working, flexible hours and home-working. Most of these arrangements entail working remotely or altering hours of work, such as working fewer days for longer hours. Although an increased adoption of flexible working arrangements reduces greenhouse gas emissions, employees may be inclined to make use of cars for non-work trips (Allen and Hawes 1979) or travelling to satellite offices, partially or completely negating the environmental benefit. To date there have been no systematic 'causality' investigations of this type in Australia or elsewhere. Data from the California State Employee Telecommute Pilot Project and an analogous investigation in The Netherlands suggest that telecommuting has the potential to reduce the number of non-work-related trips by as much as 17 per cent and peak hour travel up to 26 per cent (Gray, Hodson and Gordon 1993) over the next 10 years.

Work organisation

Work organisation is defined as the interrelationship of work tasks, employees and workplace routines. Providing opportunities for flexible work arrangements necessitates work reorganisation (i.e. redesign). To date, flexible work arrangements have been introduced with little consideration for their relevance to existing work organisation. Introducing flexibility into the work organisation impacts working patterns among employees, skill levels and retention, performance and productivity, recruitment and selection, training, employee health, autonomy and commitment. The impact spills over to the domestic obligations of an employee and the overall profile of travel activity of a household.

Employee commitment

Introducing flexible work arrangements is a form of organisational change. Central to processes of organisational change is a reliance by management on employee commitment, which assumes that employees will respond favourably to changes introduced into the workplace. Consequently, many organisational change programmes, such as total quality management and business process re-engineering, fail because they proceed without acknowledging the preferences of the internal labour market, even when some form of consultation may have occurred.

The labour market is an important influence in all of this. In Australia, primary and secondary labour markets are more amorphous in the wake of massive organisational restructuring over the last decade. In line with this trend, the impact of trade unions in terms of labour–management relations is changing with implications for workplace reform. Unions, for example, are interested in shorter working hours without sacrificing wages nor limiting employment opportunities (*Australian Financial Review* 1997). The industrial relations systems throughout Australia are being subjected to market pressures leading to the need to respond to more flexible forms of working including the nature of work assignments and responsibilities, promotion systems, work scheduling, staffing levels, compensation and incentive payments (Capelli and McKersie 1987). The *internal* labour market literature suggests that groups of rules conform logically and that it is not possible for management to adopt (and adjust) work practices at random (Osterman 1987). The internal labour market today assumes increased skill versatility, commitment and hence responsiveness, amongst employees requiring higher levels of training. A high level of employee responsiveness is essential for the effectiveness of flexible work arrangements. Employees with low levels of skill and autonomy tend to resist change by subverting the change process (Clegg and Dunkerley 1980; Cousins 1987).

In Australia and elsewhere, there is an urgent need to intensify research and debate about how the labour process manifests itself within work organisations and how different outcomes create a range of environmental externalities such as levels of traffic congestion. In particular, researchers need to look more critically at the continuing effects of 'Taylorism' through re-engineering work processes on both the quality of output and working life amongst employees. Traditional methods of management, such as the threat of discipline or dismissal, are not as legitimate in today's context. Increasingly, employers are seeking incentives to manage the responsiveness of the internal labour market, in terms of effort and commitment, to reach higher degrees of skill flexibility and productivity. Flexible work arrangements provide one indicator of employee responsiveness. For example, employees usually have more discretion in how they respond to flexible work arrangements in terms of increased work responsibility and autonomy. Commitment occurs when levels of skill, discretion and autonomy are raised. An expected outcome of commitment is an internalisation of managerial expectations and increased work satisfaction (Brewer 1994). Satisfaction is considered to be an attitude which results from a balancing and summation of many specific likes and dislikes experienced in work. Work satisfaction manifests itself in both an evaluation of the job and of the employing organisation as contributing appropriately to addressing employee preferences (Bullock 1952).

Organisational structure

Organisational structure can be represented by two key dimensions – decentralisation and formalisation. Co-ordination is an important aspect in delegating work responsibility to the lowest reaches of the organisational hierarchy. Bennis (1966) argues that the more professionalised the organisational hierarchy, the greater the tendency towards decentralised decision-making. Decentralisation is an organisational characteristic reflected in the amount of discretion delegated to lower level employees. It is the extent to which employees are assigned tasks and provided with the freedom to implement them without impediment by senior management (Hage and Aiken 1990). A related dimension of decentralisation is the provision of participative decision-making processes. Participation is related to the extent of decentralisation and provides people with a sense of control and partnership in the organisation. Participation is viewed as the capacity of employees to influence a process of joint decision-making between themselves and management, especially in decisions that have future effects on their work. 'Psychological participation' is the amount of influence that employees perceive themselves to possess (Vroom 1960). The level of participation in a workplace reflects the extent to which managers value people's efforts and investment, and this in turn influences employee responsiveness. A clearer understanding is required of the role of management at various levels in an organisation (i.e. the hierarchy of management) in imposing different types of constraints (or relaxing such constraints) to prevent or encourage employees to participate in spatial and temporal work arrangements which are more conducive to reducing levels of transport-induced emissions

Formalisation refers to the extent to which a set of rules and procedures exist to deal with decision-making and work practices (Hall 1982). Decentralisation and formalisation can co-exist in organisations particularly in public sector organisations (Blau 1970). However, highly formalised organisations may inhibit the introduction of innovative or flexible work practices and redesign.

Human resource (HR) orientation

Flexible work arrangements and work reorganisation are examples of progressive HR practices which rely on an innovative orientation by management towards employee attitudes and performance (Damanpour and Evan 1984; Johns 1993). An examination of the innovation literature suggests that a number of broad contextual factors are related to the adoption of HR innovations, including organisational size, structural characteristics, employee commitment and external conditions such as labour relations and market forces (Hall 1982; Pierce and Delbecq 1977).

Shifts in social demographics have already made 'diversity' a significant dimension of human resource management. As labour markets become more diverse, a more disparate mix of attitudes with regard to flexible work arrangements emerges. The most dramatic change is in the increase in the number of women entering the workforce under different work schedules (number of hours, number of days per week). Restructuring work and work schedules provides an opportunity for employees to modify their commuting behaviour. A further impact on flexible work arrangements is household lifestyle and life cycle. There is research evidence that employees in the United States prefer working in flexible working arrangements (Brinton 1983; Economides, Reek and Schuh 1989). For example, dual-career families and single-household heads feel the tension in cycling the demands of workplace and home. A better understanding of how these influences act to determine opportunities for employees to participate in flexible work arrangements and hence travel behaviour is a justifiable area of urgent research.

A consequence of this development is the increase in the number of multi-worker households producing residential location choice behaviour which may be very different from that of traditional single-worker families. With multiple workers and diversified spatial workplaces the residential location choice set is expanded. As a response toward the 'diversity' trend, many organisations are introducing flexible work arrangements as a way of addressing employees' diverse interests. Becoming 'family friendly' is one example of providing employees with an incentive to work in flexible arrangements. The history of flexible work arrangements is too short to make a well-informed judgement about its prospects. It raises important questions about *jobs–family balance* as well as the social and personal benefits of degrees of spatial separation.

Organisational size has been shown to be positively associated with the adoption of innovations (e.g. Moch and Morse 1977). With regard to HR management, larger organisations in workforce terms tend to adopt different practices compared to smaller organisations (Lawler, Mohrman and Leford 1992). Workforce diversity, primarily in terms of skill, may also stimulate an innovative HR orientation (Meyer and Goes 1988). Training participation, both formal and informal, is an important correlate of HR orientation (Schuler and MacMillan 1984).

An overview of the key components, as detailed above, is given in Figure 13.1.

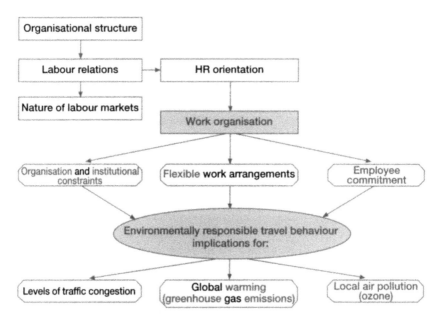

Figure 13.1 Schematic overview of the major potential causal linkages

Formulating key linkages

An empirical interpretation of Figure 13.1 is shown in Figure 13.2 as an example of one possible set of testable hypotheses in respect to four endogenous variables, two of which are discrete and two are continuous – HR orientation (discrete), work arrangements (discrete), employee commitment and travel behaviour response. Figure 13.2 tests the hypothesis that HR orientation directly impacts on work arrangements and the latter conditions employee commitment and travel behaviour response. In turn, travel behaviour response influences employee commitment which itself contributes to work arrangement outcomes where a choice exists. Regardless of employee commitment, the arrangement of work can directly impact on travel behaviour. The direct causal links between HR orientation and travel behaviour (H_6) and employee commitment (H_4) add further information on the contributing role of direct linkages to the overall propensity to engage in specific travel behaviour. The first variable is determined by the organisation, the third and fourth by the employee and the second variable is a mixture of employer and employee determination.

A well-established method for evaluating the strength of these causal linkages is the method of co-variance structures. Browne (1982) presents an outline of this approach.

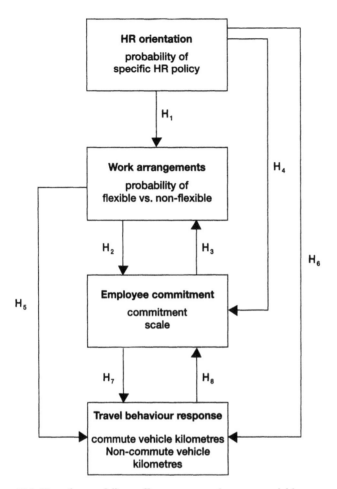

Figure 13.2 Hypotheses of direct effects among endogenous variables

Establishing a research agenda

There is little evidence of a strategic approach towards the integration of human resource policy and 'organisational citizenship' (Brewer 1994). Tele-commuting can provide a pay-back to both business and the community by saving on travel through reducing journeys to and from work and travel time. This chapter sets out a broad framework within which a better understanding of the role of organisational structure, human resource management policy, work organisation and arrangements and travel behaviour responses can be attained.

The linkages between employer and employee decision-making have not been examined sufficiently rigorously to date in respect of opportunities for greater flexibility in work practices both spatially and temporally. A clearer understanding of the forces both motivating and constraining employee responses is essential in the assessment of opportunities for commuters to adjust their commuting and non-commuting travel behaviour in contributing to improvements in global warming and air quality.

There is evidence from the human resource management literature to suggest that where initiatives like alternative work scheduling are introduced, they face indifference or hostility from middle managers (*Australian Financial Review* 1997). Brewer and Hensher (1997) develop a framework within which multiple agents (managers, supervisors and workers) make discrete choices in respect of a common objective – the determination of participation in distributed work, including the opportunities and constraints associated with telecommuting. Ideas in discrete choice theory and game theory are integrated to define a set of choice experiments in which employees and employers interact in arriving at a choice path in a distributed work context.

To this end, a better understanding will be gained with regard to:

- the role of flexible work arrangements in modifying traffic behaviour;
- how environmentally responsible travel behaviour has implications for traffic congestion, global warming and local air pollution;
- whether management issues constitute the major barrier against greater support of flexible work arrangements in work organisations;
- how an awareness of such barriers will assist in reducing them and increasing the likelihood of adoption of flexible work arrangements;
- how flexible work arrangements can modify the efficiency of work organisation and enhance the quality of working life for employees, and how flexible working arrangements lead to an acknowledgement of workplace diversity and its relationship to employee commitment.

The fundamental need is for more empirical information and data on flexible work arrangements, both spatially and temporally, and its implications for travel behaviour. It is important to study the interactions between agents rather than assume their independence. Interactions between an employer and an employee are part of everyday working life and represent a complex process in organisational decision making. Other complex interactions concern those between an employee and the members of their household. Two interactions of particular interest are between the travel-related work preferences of an employee and the work practices policy of an employer, and between employees in multi-worker households (Brewer and Hensher 1997).

Potentially, there are rich opportunities for researchers and policy-makers to look at the role of organisational structure, human resource management policy, work organisation and arrangements and travel behaviour responses in a fresh and stimulating way. The task, however, is formidable. Simply collecting data and modelling it is going to take considerable time and ingenuity. It is one thing to achieve this but the difficulty is adjusting for elusive decision-making processes on a whole array of assumptions underlying organisational structure, human resource management policy, work organisation and arrangements.

References

Allen, R.F. and Hawes, D.K. (1979) 'Attitudes toward work, leisure and the four-day workweek', *Human Resource Management* 18, 5: 10.

Australian Financial Review (1997) 'Despite the gains, bosses find homework a pain', 6 January: 1, 4.

Bennis, W.G. (1966) *Changing Organisations*, New York: McGraw-Hill.

Blau, P. (1970) 'Decentralisation in bureaucracies', in M.N. Zald (ed.) *Power in Organisations*, Nashville: Vanderbilt: 79–82.

Brewer, A.M. (1993) *Managing for Employee Commitment*, Melbourne: Longman.

—— (1994) *The Responsive Employee: The Road Towards Organisational Citizenship*, Sydney: Allen and Unwin.

—— (1995) *Change Management: Strategies for Australian Organisations*, Sydney: Allen and Unwin.

Brewer, A.M. and Hensher, D.A. (1997) 'Distributed Work and Travel Behaviour: The Dynamics of Interactive Agency Choices between Employers and Employees', Eighth Meeting of the International Association of Travel Behaviour Research, Texas, USA.

Brinton, R.D. (1983) 'Effectiveness of the 12-hour shift', *Personnel Journal* 62: 393–8.

Browne, M.W. (1982) 'Covariance structures', in D.M. Hawkins (ed.) *Topics in Multivariate Analysis*, Cambridge: Cambridge University Press: 72–141.

Bullock, R.P. (1952) *Social Factors Related to Job Satisfaction: A Technique for the Measurement of Job Satisfaction*, Bureau of Business Research, Ohio State University, Columbus, Ohio.

Capelli, P. and McKersie, R. (1987) 'Management strategy and the redesign of work rules', *Journal of Management Studies* 24, 5: 441–61.

Clegg, S. and Dunkerley, D. (1980) *Organisation, Class and Control*, London: Routledge.

Cousins, C. (1987) *Controlling State Welfare: A Sociology of State Welfare Work and Organisation*, New York: St Martin's Press.

Damanpour, F. and Evan, W.M. (1984) 'Organisational innovation and performance: the problem of organisational lag', *Administrative Science Quarterly* 29: 392–409.

Dawkins, P. and Barker, M. (1987) 'Working time in Australia: research evidence', Report prepared for the Department of Health, Housing, Local Government, and Community Services, March.

Economides, U., Reek, D.N. and Schuh, A.J. (1980) 'Longer days and shorter weeks improve productivity', *Personnel Administration* 34: 12–14.

Gray, M., Hodson, N. and Gordon, G. (1993) *Teleworking Explained*, New York: John Wiley.

Hage, J. and Aiken, M. (1990) 'Routine technology, social structure and organisational goals', *Administrative Science Quarterly* 14: 366–76.

Hall, R.H. (1982) *Organisations: Structure and Process* (2nd edn) Englewood Cliffs, NJ: Prentice Hall.

Handy, S.L. and Mokhtarian, P.L. (1995) 'Planning for telecommuting: measurement and policy', *Journal of American Planning Association* 61, 1: 99–111.

Harrison, B. (1994) 'The dark side of flexible production', *National Productivity Review* 13: 479, 501.

Hensher, D. (1993) 'Socially and environmentally appropriate urban futures for the motor car', *Transportation* 20, 1: 1–19.

—— (1996) 'An integrated approach to modelling the impact on urban travel behaviour of strategies to reduce greenhouse gas emissions', in D. Hensher, J. King and T. Oum (eds) *World Transport Research, Vol. 1 – Travel Behaviour*, Oxford: Pergamon Press: 271–88.

Hensher, D., Stone, C., Westerman, H. and Raimond, T. (1995) *Roads in the Community: The Urban Context*, Unpublished Report.

Johns, G. (1993) 'Constraints in the adoption of psychology-based personnel practices: lessons from organisational innovation', *Personnel Psychology* 42: 727–86.

Karpin Report (1995) *Enterprising Nation*, Report of the Industry Task Force on Leadership and Management Skills.

Lawler, E.E., Mohrman, S.A. and Leford, G.E. (1992) *Employee Involvement And Total Quality Management: Practices And Results In Fortune 1000 Companies*, San Francisco, CA: Jossey-Bass.

Mahmassani, H.S. and Chen, P.S.T. (1992) 'Comparative assessment of origin-based and en route real-time information under alternative user behaviour rules', *Transportation Research Record* 1306: 69–81.

Mahmassani, H.S., Caplice, C.G. and Walton, C.M. (1990) 'Characteristics of urban commuter behaviour: switching propensity and use of information', *Transportation Research Record* 1285: 57–69.

Mahmassani, H., Yen, J., Herman, R. and Sullivan, M. (1993) 'Employee attitudes and stated preferences toward telecommuting: an exploratory analysis', *Transportation Research Record* 1413: 31–42.

Meyer, A.D. and Goes, J.B. (1988) 'Organisational assimilation of innovations: a multilevel contextual analysis', *Academy of Management Journal* 31: 897–923.

Moch, M.K. and Morse, E.G. (1977) 'Size, centralisation and organisational adoption of innovations', *American Sociological Review* 42: 716–25.

Mokhtarian, P.L. (1991) 'Telecommuting and travel: state of practice, state of the art', *Transportation* 18: 319–42.

Nilles, J.M. (1991) 'Telecommuting and urban dispersal: mitigator or inciter?', *Transportation* 18, 4: 411–32.

Osterman, P. (1987) 'Choice of employment systems in internal labour markets', *Industrial Relations* 26, 1: 46–67.

Pierce, J.L. and Delbecq, A.L. (1977) 'Organisational structure, individual attitudes, and innovation', *Academy of Management Review* 2: 27–37.

Porter, M.E. (1990) *The Competitive Advantage of Nations*, New York: The Free Press.

Pratt, J.H. (1994) 'Characteristics of Telecommuters', Transportation Research Board, 73rd Annual Meeting, Washington, DC.

RTA Teleworking Pilot Project (1994) *Teleworking: A Flexible Opportunity*, Roads and Traffic Authority NSW.

Schuler, R. and MacMillan, I (1984) 'Gaining competitive advantage through human resource management practices', *Human Resource Management* 23: 241–55.

Tracy, N. and Lever-Tracy, C. (1991) 'The longer working week in Australia – working time experiences and preferences of men', *Labour and Industry* 4, 1: 71–94.

US Department of Transportation (1993) *Transportation Implications of Telecommuting*, Washington, DC, April.

Vroom, V.H. (1960) *Some Personality Determinants of the Effects of Participation*, Englewood Cliffs: Prentice Hall.

14

TELEWORK AND CRISIS MANAGEMENT IN JAPAN

Koji Sato and Wendy A. Spinks

Introduction

The concept of telework has received a great deal of international attention in recent years motivated by a variety of issues: travel reduction; energy conservation; air quality improvement; balancing the demands of job and family; reduction of health-care costs through reduction of stress and sick-leave utilisation; broadening employment opportunities for mobility-limited sectors of society (including the disabled, elderly and homemakers); competitive recruitment and retention of the best workers; improved productivity and customer service (such as through extended hours of availability); improving the balance between jobs and housing, including supporting regional economic development by bringing the work to the workers in underdeveloped regions; and emergency preparedness/disaster response.

The devastating Great Hanshin Earthquake which struck Kobe and the surrounding region in the early hours of 17 January 1995 threw into sharp relief the terrifying nature of a direct earthquake hit on a large urban area and the weakness of a high-tech modern city when its communications infrastructure, transportation infrastructure and lifelines are severed. By analysing the results of a survey on companies and employees in the four central wards of Kobe on changes in commuting and work patterns after the earthquake, as well as the level of computer and communication technology usage in conjunction with metropolitan traffic census data, this chapter will focus on the crisis management implications of telework. The first section begins with an outline of the Kobe survey results. The second section then discusses transportation problems which might be expected to occur in Greater Tokyo based on the Kobe results and commute-related statistical data. Finally, the chapter concludes with a brief review of recent policy developments for telework in Japan.

Outline of survey results

Survey objectives and methodology

The Survey on Changes in Commute and Work Patterns after the Great Hanshin Earthquake was commissioned by the Japanese Ministry of Posts and Telecommunications Research Institute and conducted by the International Flexwork Forum's Telework Centre Disaster Response Research Group. The survey consisted of two instruments, one for companies, the other for full-time white-collar employees in the four wards of Kobe which suffered the most damage from the earthquake, namely Chuo, Nada, Higashi Nada and Nagata. Two hundred company surveys and one thousand employee surveys were distributed, the corporate mailing list being compiled randomly from the Kobe Chamber of Commerce's list of members in the four relevant wards, excluding factories. Each company was also asked to distribute five employee surveys in-house. The surveys were mailed on 9 October 1995 with stamped, addressed envelopes for return by 23 October 1995. The response rate for the company surveys was 16.5 per cent (33) and 11.3 per cent (113) for the employees' surveys. A cross-analysis of the data was conducted using the statistical analysis software package SPSSX. Owing to the small sample size, however, no significant results were obtained. As a result, the survey data was analysed using mainly simple descriptive statistics.

Outline of corporate results

Extent of earthquake damage

Regarding the extent of damage to office premises, 21.2 per cent of corporate respondents cited 'totally destroyed' and a further 33.3 per cent 'half destroyed', indicating that more than half of the corporate respondents had experienced some damage to their office premises. Turning to transportation access, 75.8 per cent cited 'no access' and 24.2 per cent 'partial access', these survey results confirming the virtual paralysis of transportation services in Kobe following the earthquake. As for the repair time required for office premises, 'more than one month' was the most frequently cited response (33.3 per cent), followed by 'still unrepaired' (15.2 per cent), indicating that approximately half of the corporate respondents experienced a slowdown or standstill in business activity in excess of one month, and that as of October when the survey was distributed, the office premises of one company in seven were still in a damaged state. Concerning the restoration of transportation services, 84.8 per cent cited 'more than one month'.

Worker contact following the earthquake

The most frequently cited response for initial contact with workers was 'several days later' (69.7 per cent), followed by 'one week later' (21.2 per cent) and 'day of the earthquake' (6.1 per cent). It is clear from these results that companies were unable to determine their employees' situations until several days after the earthquake. Moreover, the fact that fully one-fifth of companies were only able to contact workers a week later suggests that it took even longer to restore business functions. This highlights the importance of establishing an emergency contact system not only in order to contact workers but to maintain business functions. The main form of contact cited was 'by telephone' (90.9 per cent), followed by 'staff came in person' (42.4 per cent) and 'other staff visited' (39.4 per cent). It should be noted, however, that contact by telephone was possible only because, the telephone lines were operational despite a certain amount of overloading. Trying to establish contact in times of emergency by sending around corporate staff or having the workers themselves coming in runs the risk of adding to local confusion, and as such remains problematic in terms of appropriate disaster response.

Business use of communications technologies

Corporate respondents cited 100 per cent pre-earthquake business use of 'conventional telephones', 90.9 per cent 'facsimiles', 51.5 per cent 'mobile telephones', and 48.5 per cent 'computers (including e-mail)'. As of October 1995, when the survey was implemented, 100 per cent cited both conventional telephones and facsimiles, 75.8 per cent mobile phones, and 57.6 per cent computers, indicating an increase in post-earthquake mobile phone and computer usage, especially of the former. Regarding usefulness in the immediate aftermath of the earthquake, 78.8 per cent cited 'mobile telephones', followed by 66.7 per cent for 'conventional telephones', and 48.5 per cent 'facsimiles'. These results highlight the usefulness of mobile telephones in times of disaster, such as earthquakes (see Table 14.1).

Available work options

Regarding the types of work options available before the earthquake, 'direct customer servicing' was the most frequently cited (33.3 per cent), followed by

Table 14.1 Business use of communications technologies

	Conventional telephones	Mobile phones	Personal computers	Facsimiles	Others
Pre-earthquake	33	17	16	30	4
	100.0	51.5	48.5	90.9	12.1
Aftermath of	22	26	2	16	3
earthquake	66.7	78.8	6.1	48.5	9.1
October 1995	33	25	19	33	3
	100.0	75.8	57.6	100.0	9.1

'discretionary work' (18.2 per cent), and 'flexitime' (15.2 per cent). As of October 1995, when the survey was conducted, the relevant responses were 'direct customer servicing' (33.3 per cent), followed by 'flexitime' (21.2 per cent), and 'discretionary work' (18.2 per cent). While the number of corporate respondents citing 'flexitime' showed a slight increase, there is very little evidence of other work options being introduced. No company used satellite offices or home-based telework either before or after the Great Hanshin Earthquake, suggesting that virtually no company considered using information telecommunications as a means of a substitution for physical commutes. Looking at the commute measures applied in the immediate aftermath of the earthquake, 63.6 per cent corporate respondents cited 'home standby', followed by 30.3 per cent for 'mobile work', 27.3 per cent for 'staying at office' and 'discretionary work', 21.2 per cent for 'hotel room reservations' and 'flexitime', 18.2 per cent for 'bus charters', and 15.2 per cent for 'satellite offices'. Regarding whether these measures were formal or informal, 48.5 per cent cited 'formal measures', 30.3 per cent 'supervisor discretion', and 21.2 per cent 'both'.

Corporate crisis management

More than half of the companies surveyed (54.5 per cent) had no crisis management manual in place before the earthquake. Of those with manuals, 33.3 per cent cited 'Yes, no earthquake scenario', and 12.2 per cent cited 'Yes, including an earthquake scenario'. This means that approximately only one company in ten had some form of crisis management manual covering the possibility of an earthquake. Asked whether these crisis management manuals were useful in the immediate aftermath of the earthquake, 46.7 per cent cited 'somewhat useful', 20.0 per cent either 'uncertain' or 'not very useful', and 13.3 per cent 'no use at all'. These results demonstrate a clear division in corporate assessments of their crisis management manuals. Regarding the need to review crisis management manuals, 39.4 per cent cited 'partial review', and 30.3 per cent 'thorough review', indicating that some 70 per cent of companies saw a need to review their manuals. As to the emphasis of such a review process, 43.5 per cent cited 'swift assessment of events', 30.4 per cent 'worker safety', and 17.4 per cent 'maintaining business functions'.

Outline of employee results

Extent of earthquake damage

Regarding the extent of damage to homes, 35.4 per cent of employee respondents cited 'half destroyed', and a further 8.0 per cent 'totally destroyed'. The most frequently cited response for home repair time was 'more than one month' (42.9 per cent), followed by 'still unrepaired' (36.7 per cent). Turning to office premises, 36.3 per cent cited 'half destroyed', and a further 8.8 per cent 'totally destroyed'.

236

The most frequently cited response for office premises repair time was 'more than one month' (56.9 per cent). Regarding transportation access, 61.9 per cent cited 'no access', and 32.7 per cent 'partial access', indicating that more than 90 per cent of those surveyed suffered some form of damage to transportation access. As for transportation repair time, 59.7 per cent cited 'more than one month', 23.4 per cent 'one month', and 7.5 per cent 'two weeks'.

Corporate contact after the earthquake

The most frequently cited response for initial contact with employers was 'several days later' (53.1 per cent), followed by 'day of the earthquake' (46.0 per cent). It is clear from these results that more than half of the employees surveyed were unable to contact their office until several days after the earthquake. The main form of contact cited was 'by telephone' (74.3 per cent), followed by 'went myself in person' (27.4 per cent).

Initial visit to work

When asked when did they first consider going to work, 47.8 per cent answered 'day of the earthquake', followed by 'several days later' (42.5 per cent), and 'one week later' (6.2 per cent), indicating that almost half considered going in on the actual day of the earthquake. When queried on when they actually visited work, however, 51.3 per cent replied 'several days later', followed by 'day of the earthquake' (27.4 per cent), and 'one week later' (10.6 per cent). The mode of transport used for that initial visit was 'own car' (33.6 per cent), followed by 'on foot' (31.0 per cent), 'train' (18.6 per cent), 'bicycle' (15.9 per cent), 'bus' (11.5 per cent), and 'subway' (9.7 per cent).

Individual business use of communications technologies

Of the individual respondents, 96.5 per cent cited pre-earthquake business use of 'conventional telephones', 61.9 per cent 'facsimiles', and 18.6 per cent 'computers (including e-mail)', with only 5.3 per cent citing 'mobile telephones'. As of October 1995, when the survey was implemented, 96.5 per cent cited conventional telephones, 73.5 per cent facsimiles, 23.9 per cent computers, and 15.9 per cent mobile phones, representing an increase in the post-earthquake usage of mobile phones and facsimiles (see Table 14.2).

Commute methods

Pre-earthquake commute methods cited were 'train' (66.4 per cent), 'bus' (21.2 per cent), 'subway' (17.7 per cent), 'own car' (14.2 per cent), and 'on foot' (8.8 per cent). Main commute methods up until transportation infrastructure was restored were 'on foot' (35.4 per cent), followed by 'train' and 'own car' (31.9 per cent

Table 14.2 Individual use of communications technologies for business

	Conventional telephones	Mobile phones	Personal computers	Facsimiles	Others
Pre-earthquake	109	6	21	70	4
	96.5	5.3	18.6	61.9	3.5
October 1995	109	18	27	83	6
	96.5	15.9	23.9	73.5	5.3

each), 'bus' (27.4 per cent), and 'subway' and 'bicycle' (16.8 per cent each). As the next section will show, despite the large-scale damage to Kobe's transportation infrastructure, employees were able to respond by walking or cycling to work because commuter distances in Kobe are not so considerable. As of October 1995, when the survey was conducted, commute patterns had almost returned to pre-earthquake conditions with 65.5 per cent citing 'train', 21.2 per cent 'bus', 18.6 per cent 'subway', 10.6 per cent 'own car', 8.8 per cent 'on foot', and 3.5 per cent 'bicycle' (see Table 14.3).

Commute time

The most prevalent pre-earthquake commute time (one way) was '30–59 minutes', which was cited by 56.6 per cent of employees, followed by 'less than 30 minutes' (20.4 per cent), and '60–89 minutes' (19.5 per cent). As can be seen, more than three quarters of the respondents cited one-way commutes of less than 60 minutes, no respondent citing 'more than 120 minutes'. Commute time and distance in the Kobe region are considerably less than in Greater Tokyo. Regarding one-way commute time before the full restoration of transportation services, 30.1 per cent cited 'more than 120 minutes', followed by '90–119 minutes' (29.2 per cent), and '60–89 minutes' (24.8 per cent). Immediately following the earthquake, the share of respondents with commutes under 60 minutes fell to 15.1 per cent. These results show that even in areas such as Kobe where commutes are shorter than Greater Tokyo, post-earthquake damage to the transportation infrastructure forces many people into long commutes. As of October

Table 14.3 Change in commute methods

	Train	Subway	Bus	Own car	Bicycle	On foot
Pre-earthquake	75	20	24	16	2	10
	66.4	17.7	21.2	14.2	1.8	8.8
Aftermath of	36	19	31	36	19	40
earthquake	31.9	16.8	27.4	31.9	16.8	35.4
October 1995	74	21	24	12	4	10
	65.5	18.6	21.2	10.6	3.5	8.8

1995, when the survey was conducted, 54.9 per cent cited commute time of '30–59 minutes', followed by '60–89 minutes' (22.1 per cent), 'less than 30 minutes' (14.2 per cent), and '90–119 minutes' (6.2 per cent). This shows that some 70 per cent of those surveyed have returned to a one-way commute of less than 60 minutes, indicating almost a full return to pre-earthquake patterns (see Table 14.4).

Implications of the Great Hanshin Earthquake for Greater Tokyo

A statistical view of commutes in Greater Tokyo

Metropolitan traffic census

According to the *Metropolitan Traffic Census: Greater Tokyo Version* (Japan Transport Economics Research Centre 1992a), the total number of business and school commuters carried on public transport such as rail and bus in the entirety of Greater Tokyo in 1990 was approximately 9.47 million. This figure is clearly the largest in Japan, being approximately 2.2 times that of Greater Kinki (Osaka and the surrounding region) and over 8.9 times that of Greater Chukyo (Nagoya and the surrounding region) (see Table 14.5).

Table 14.4 Change in commute hours

	Less than 30 minutes	30–59 minutes	60–89 minutes	90–119 minutes	More than 120 minutes
Pre-earthquake	23	64	22	4	0
	20.4	56.6	19.5	3.5	0.0
Aftermath of earthquake	8	9	28	33	34
	7.1	8.0	24.8	29.2	30.1
October 1995	16	62	25	7	0
	14.2	54.9	22.1	6.2	0.0

Table 14.5 Number of commuters in the metropolitan regions

	Business commuter	School commuter	Total
Greater Tokyo	7,000,027	2,469,723	9,469,750
	73.9	26.1	100.0
Greater Kinki	3,052,004	1,162,028	4,215,032
	72.4	27.6	100.0
Greater Chukyo	634,396	428,325	1,062,721
	59.7	40.3	100.0

Elsewhere, 53.1 per cent (3.72 million people) have commutes longer than 20 kilometres (or 12.0 miles) in Greater Tokyo. In particular, people with commutes in excess of 30 kilometres in Greater Tokyo amount to 30.7 per cent or just under one-third of all commuters (2.15 million), a fact which attests to the extremely high prevalence of long-distance commutes. Greater Tokyo is also in a class of its own regarding commute hours in metropolitan regions with 58.9 per cent (4.12 million) of all commuters travelling 60 minutes or longer in Greater Tokyo.

Potential transportation problems in Greater Tokyo

The Great Hanshin Earthquake, as seen through the results of the Kobe survey, clearly shows that, the severing of commuter and other means of transportation and the destruction of office premises and housing brought urban functions to a temporary standstill and significantly impaired economic activity in the southern section of Hyogo Prefecture around the City of Kobe. It is also clear that the impact of this damage was extremely serious and prolonged.

The scale of damage suffered in the Great Hanshin Earthquake is depicted in Figure 14.1, it being evident that buildings, roads, rail and port facilities all suffered grave damage. Using the Kobe survey results on commuting and work activity, this section will consider potential transportation problems in Greater Tokyo should a similar earthquake strike.

1   Even in areas such as Kobe, where short-distance commuters account for more than 70.0 per cent of all commuters and there is a large proportion of those who can commute on foot, it took companies several days before they could account for their employees following the earthquake. This suggests that it would take companies much more time and effort to account for their employees in areas such as Greater Tokyo, where long-distance commuters predominate. If Greater Tokyo were to suffer a direct earthquake destroying the public transportation system, there is an extremely strong possibility, even in an optimistic scenario, that corporate and government functions in Greater Tokyo would be brought to a standstill for several weeks or even months. Should such a situation occur, the direct and indirect impact on the entire Japanese economy and the world economy would be immeasurable.

2   Because the majority of commuters in Kobe were short-distance commuters, it was physically possible for workers to walk more than three hours along the railroad tracks to get to work. In Greater Tokyo with its obligatory long travel times and distances, however, a huge number of commuters would experience extreme difficulty in getting to work if public transportation links were severed. Additionally, there were many areas left in the southern section of Hyogo Prefecture around Kobe where phone lines remained operational. The growing use of mobile phones also played a part in making it possible to contact workers and business associates. Should the communications

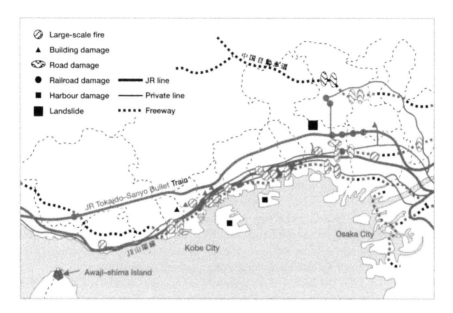

Figure14.1 Types of damage caused by the Great Hanshin Earthquake. Source: *Chosa-Kiho*, no. 123, p. 6, March 1995

infrastructure suffer serious damage in Greater Tokyo, national and local government networks as well as bank and other on-line networks would cease to function.

3   The predominance of short-distance commuters in Kobe is probably one reason why no satellite offices or home-based telework programmes were established. In areas such as Greater Tokyo where residential sprawl has led to long commute hours and distances, conventional work patterns do not offer a tenable response in the event of disasters such as earthquakes. Moreover, it is quite likely that the response applied in Kobe of having workers on standby at home would be meaningless in Tokyo. If there is one lesson the Great Hanshin Earthquake has imparted it is the need to seriously examine using computer and communications technology to substitute for commuting (telework) and the decentralisation of office functions.

4   By continuing to concentrate core management functions in a single place, companies risk having their entire operations brought to a standstill by the destruction of the public transportation infrastructure and lifelines, even if their own office premises escape unscathed. As the preceding results from the Kobe survey clearly show, one company in five suffered total destruction of office premises and a further one company in three semi-destruction. Corporate activity suffered substantially following the earthquake, often taking more than one month to recover. This undoubtedly points to the need for the decentralisation of business functions as a key issue in crisis management.

241

Bearing in mind also that more than half of the companies surveyed had no crisis management manual, there are still many unresolved issues concerning corporate response to emergency situations. US approaches to the question of crisis management strongly emphasise maintaining business functions, a position Japanese companies would do well to follow.

Concluding remarks

The need for telework responses

Should Greater Tokyo with its concentration of information and core management functions be hit, not only Japan but the world at large would feel the impact. It is also true that the vast majority of small and medium-sized enterprises are totally unprepared for such an event. Concrete responses are urgently required, including building stronger cities for disaster prevention, planning crisis management responses and duplicating communications networks.

Not only did the US Federal Emergency Management Agency (FEMA) play a crucial role in responding to the 1994 Northridge Earthquake in Greater Los Angeles, it also took the initiative in promoting office decentralisation by setting up federally sponsored disaster-response telework centres in the Northridge area. The fact that FEMA-led disaster-response telework centres were up and running less than one month after the 1994 Northridge Earthquake is a reflection of the ongoing private and public sector involvement in telework projects in the United States. This means that they were quick to realise the potential of telework and office decentralisation in managing disaster-induced crises. Japan also needs to grasp quickly that the decentralisation of offices and employees is a useful means of crisis management.

To that end, both the public and private sectors need to promote the routine decentralisation of office functions by recognising the vital impact of using communications technologies to substitute for commuter travel and introducing 'telework' which obviates the need for physical displacement. Mainly home-based telework proved extremely effective following the Northridge Earthquake in maintaining business functions and alleviating traffic congestion. Japan also needs to consider telework not only as a means of decentralising office functions, but as a central feature of future crisis responses. This will require, however, some form of public support and a heightened awareness on the part of corporate management.

Public sector initiatives

The national government of Japan is finally taking the initiative in promoting telework. Until recently, the private sector took the lead in implementing telework programmes (sometimes with public sector partners), whereas in the US the reverse is true. Although telework is not as common in Japan as other industrialised nations, a recent survey by the Satellite Office Association of Japan (1997) estimates the number of regular (once or more a week), white-collar salaried teleworkers at 680,000 or 4 per cent of all white-collar salaried workers in Japan. Telework is, therefore, not a negligible force and the recent jump in computer and network use in Japan will boost this number further.

The 'Telework Centre Research Committee Report: Emerging New Work-styles in the Age of Multi-Media' (April 1995) by the Ministry of Posts and Telecommunications (MPT) was a first step towards promoting office decentral-isation in Japan as a disaster-response strategy. This has been followed up with the establishment in 1996 of a Telework Council jointly sponsored by the MPT and the Ministry of Labour. The Council brought together corporate leaders and telework experts to explore avenues for the greater corporate use of telework. A report has been published along with introductory guidelines. Japan's first ever Telework Day was held in May 1997 and several private sector pilots have resulted as well as the first ever public sector telework pilot in Japan undertaken by the MPT.

Acknowledgements

The research for this paper was conducted with the financial support of the Institute for Posts and Telecommunications Policy at the Ministry of Posts and Telecommunications. An earlier version of this paper was presented at the 'Session on Topics in Transportation Statistics and Analysis' of the Western Regional Science Association's 35th Annual Meeting in Napa, California, between 25 and 29 February 1996. The authors have benefited from discussions with Kingsley E. Haynes, George Mason University, and Patricia L. Mokhtarian, University of California at Davis, and from the comments of T.J. Kim, University of Illinois, and several participants at the WRSA's 35th Annual Meeting.

References

Bagley, M.N., Mannering, J.S. and Mokhtarian, P.L.(1994) 'Telecommuting Centers and Related Concepts: A Review of Practice', Research Report No, UCD-ITS-94-4, prepared by the University of California, Davis, Institute of Transportation Studies, for the California Department of Transportation, Office of Traffic Improvement, Sacramento, CA.

Japan Transport Economics Research Centre (1992a), *The Metropolitan Traffic Census: Great Tokyo Version*, Japan Transport Economics Research Centre. (In Japanese.)

—— (1992b) *The Metropolitan Traffic Census: Great Kinki Version*, Japan Transport Economics Research Centre. (In Japanese.)

Ministry of Construction (1995) The 1995 Construction White Paper, Printing Bureau of the Ministry of Finance, Tokyo. (In Japanese.)

Ministry of Posts and Telecommunications (1995) 'Telework Centre Research Committee Report: Emerging New Workstyles in the Age of Multi-Media', Ministry of Posts and Telecommunications. (In Japanese.)

Mokhtarian, P.L. (1991a) 'Telecommuting and travel: State of the practice, state of the art', *Transportation* 18, 4: 319–42.

—— (1991b) *Defining telecommuting*, Transportation Research Record 1305: 273–81.

Mokhtarian, P.L. and Sato, K. (1994) 'A comparison of the policy, social, and cultural contexts for telecommuting in Japan and the United States', *Social Science Computer Review* 12, 4: 641–58.

Mokhtarian, P.L., Salomon, I., Saxena, S., Sampath, S., Cheung, P., Le, K. and Bagley, M. (1996) 'Adoption of telecommuting in two California State Agencies', Research Report No. UCD-ITS-RR-96–5, Institute of Transportation Studies, University of California, Davis.

Satellite Office Association of Japan (1997) *A Report on the Survey of Telework Population in Japan* (A Summary) (1996 edn), Tokyo.

Sato, K. (1995a) 'Recent policy developments in telework centers in Japan after the Great Hanshin Earthquake', Paper presented at the Telecommuting Advisory Council National Conference, Long Beach, CA, June 1995.

Sato, K. (1995b) 'Northridge and disaster-response telework centers: the need for crisis management and decentralization', *International Flexwork Forum* 5, 17: 12–14.

Sato, K. (1995c) 'The policy, social and cultural contexts of ITS: A case study of telecommuting in Japan and the United States', The Second World Congress on Intelligent Transport Systems '95 Yokohama Proceedings, V: 2397–2405.

Sato, K. (1996) 'The development of telework centers and related public policy issues', *The Review of Economics and Commerce* [Kanagawa University] 31, 2. (In Japanese.)

Sato, K. and Spinks, W.A. (1996) 'Survey Results on Changes in Commute and Work Environments after the Great Hanshin Earthquake', STB Research Institute. (In Japanese.)

Spinks, W.A. (1991) 'Satellite and resort offices in Japan', *Transportation* 18, 4: 343–63.

—— (1995) 'Telework Crisis Management: Work-At-Home Keeps Business Functioning', *Nihon Keizai Shimbun*, April.

15

INTEGRATING THE TELEWORKING PERSPECTIVE INTO ORGANISATIONAL ANALYSIS AND LEARNING

Paul J. Jackson

Introduction

Work concepts such as telework provide us with a way of looking at the world. By highlighting certain characteristics of work phenomena, they allow us to interpret things in a meaningful and communicable way. In cases of teleworking, certain attributes of working modes – the use of IT, operating at a distance, the home as a place of work – become the identifying features by which we place phenomena into conceptual categories and thus make them amenable to examination and analysis. On this basis, we can enquire why the working modes in question came about, develop knowledge about the way they operate in practice and make generalisations that can be applied in other cases. There are shortcomings in this approach, though.

Where such approaches introduce a priori derived issues and concepts into the situation under study, ideas may be abstracted out of the interpretative contexts in which the actors normally make sense of and contend with the phenomena concerned. This is particularly so where we wish to explore telework-related issues in companies that do not consider themselves 'teleworking organisations'. We can overcome these problems by getting inside such organisations and conceptualising and analysing telework within the milieu of organisational change, in which decisions are made about a whole range of operational and strategic matters. By doing this we are likely to identify concepts and rationales most meaningful and useful to the context involved. To illustrate this approach, we will turn to research undertaken by the author during the early 1990s in the UK retail banking sector.

Aims and approach of the study

By looking at the subject in a 'non-teleworking' organisation, the intention was to explore teleworking ideas in a more *systemic* way than was often the case in the available literature. In other words, rather than simply studying *instances of* telework, teleworking ideas were used as a *perspective* from which to understand the possibilities for the spatial reorganisation of work, particularly those supported by new technologies. To do this in an in-depth way, a case study approach was adopted. The case in question was one of the main UK retail banks. This was chosen for three main reasons. First, as it was a large, research friendly organisation, it provided the opportunities to gain access to a range of people and functions such that rich data could be collected. Second, given the 'information-based' nature of the work involved, it was thought that teleworking issues would be highly appropriate for banking. Third, and following on from the second point, was the fact that banks were making substantial use of information technologies, in part for facilitating dispersed operations.

The case study was approached in an 'action-research' mode. This involves a 'consultative type' of research, in which organisational actors are helped to examine and address matters of concern to them (see Gummesson 1991). This was done using Checkland's 'soft systems methodology' (SSM) (Checkland and Scholes 1990). In using this, the researcher's key role is to facilitate a *process of learning*. Here, different perceptions of the problem situation are drawn out and examined. Insights are developed and explored with a range of actors such that they can *learn their way* to improvement in the problem situation. In the study, 'improvement' was seen as obtaining a better understanding of the role teleworking ideas might play in the bank's operations and policies.

The use of Checkland's SSM suggested three key stages to the research. Stage 1 involved developing an understanding of the research context. This concentrated on the key pressures that the bank was seeking to deal with, such as technological change and heightened competition resulting from deregulation. In Stage 2, a process of learning was orchestrated, involving personnel from a wide range of areas in the bank. As part of this, the possibilities for, and benefits of, forms of spatial reorganisation were identified. This helped to draw out the meanings and relevance of teleworking ideas to many different actors. These were captured in a four-fold typology which was used to help frame discussions with other members of the bank. Stage 3 focused on the decision-making rationales for telework. It was also thought essential that if the roles of teleworking forms were to be identified, then their merits and demerits *vis-à-vis* alternative solutions and approaches had to be established.

Before we look at the content of the study, we will first examine the wider context of retail banking, in which telework issues had to be understood.

Changes in UK retail banking

To appreciate the relevance of teleworking within banking, an examination of the main areas of organisational change was essential. There were four key areas of change: technological change; deregulation of the financial services industry; branch network reorganisation; and the movement towards a sales and marketing culture in banking.

Until the 1980s, financial services in the UK comprised three well-defined industries: banking, building societies and insurance (Scarbrough 1992a). With the Financial Services Act (1986) and the Building Societies Act (1987), combined with developments such as the 'big bang' in the City and legislation that aided the mobility of pensions, a revolution was in store. The result was an erosion of the demarcation lines between industries, a heightening of competition and a pressure on margins (see *Banking World*, January 1994: 21–2). In response, retail banks looked for more aggressive sales strategies by which to push their products, and sought, through automation and branch closure, to reduce costs (see Mauriello 1996).

Quite apart from the pressures that resulted from deregulation, financial services has traditionally been one of the most information-intensive industries in the service sector, involving massive investments in information technology (Scarbrough 1992a, 1992b; Procter 1992). By the 1990s, banks had even begun to rethink the very nature of their business, placing more emphasis on managing *information* as opposed simply to *money* (*The Banker*, January 1990: 12). Following the introduction of centralised mainframes in the 1960s and 1970s, technology was introduced into the 'back offices' of branches to handle the massive growth in routine processing of items such as cheques (Procter 1992). More recent developments have involved the introduction of terminals into the 'front offices' of branches. This allowed for transactions to be processed automatically and account details integrated to aid customer service and help the cross-selling of products. This wave of new technology also involved the introduction of automated teller machines (ATMs). Benefits from this included the ability to relieve pressure on front office counters and extend service provision to twenty-four hours a day, seven days a week. Additionally, it opened the possibility of siting ATMs away from branches and closer to places, such as shopping centres, which are more convenient for customers (Fincham *et al.* 1994). These latter developments, when combined with the extension of EFTPoS facilities (electronic funds transfer at point-of-sale), bypassed branches entirely but also automated the tasks in question (Child and Loveridge 1990; Scarbrough 1992b; Cressey and Scott 1992). Further automation has been possible thanks to the introduction of bulk processing equipment. This has accompanied the growth of centralised processing centres in banking, used to deal with routine, low added-value work.

Integration of the bank's databases, and use of client-server architectures (which allowed for the remote retrieval and manipulation of data), also opened the possibility of more accurate marketing of products, cross-selling, and the provision of new remote services such as telephone banking. It would be wrong to attribute such developments simply to technological advances and customer preferences, though. With the entry of (technologically advanced) non-banking organisations into retail markets, banks were forced to focus more carefully on the people aspects of their customer base (*The Banker*, February 1994: 29–30). Understanding and catering for customer lifestyle needs therefore became essential. This focused attention on the *human skills* of bank staff and highlighted the need to devote more time to customer service rather than administration (*The Banker*, February 1993: 22–4). In addition, more branch space needed to be released for interactions with customers. Developing a sales culture, and creating a better retail/sales environment, was therefore seen as the key to making effective use of branch staff and space – resources which management increasingly viewed as central for producing high added-value in customer service.

Understanding the bank from the telework perspective

Contextualising teleworking in the bank

One key programme that was taking place in the bank was the reorganisation of the extensive branch network. This was very much a legacy of the 1960s and 1970s, and created a much heavier cost base than that of the building societies. At the time of the study a substantial rationalisation process was in train. This involved moving towards a 'hub-satellite' structure, and was accompanied by the closure of hundreds of branches. Under this new structure, many remaining branches reduced their range of products and were clustered around a head branch (in a town centre) that carried a full complement of staff and services. This presented management with an overstaffing problem and a subsequent redundancies programme in which thousands of positions were eliminated.

Despite redundancies, pressures still existed within the bank for flexible work packages. This was largely due to the 'caring duties' of bank staff – particularly women returning after maternity leave. The bank was especially keen to retain such staff, given their increasing representation in managerial grades. Not only were women returning to work in greater numbers after maternity leave, they were increasingly doing so on a *full-time*, rather than part-time, basis.

During the study then, matters such as technological change, the development of a better retail/sales culture, branch network rationalisation, and responding to greater financial services competition, were the central business problems with which management was grappling. But apart from appreciating the broader business issues, in understanding telework in a banking context, we also need to consider several further factors.

Given that retail banks already exhibit a dispersed structure, in which head offices, processing centres, call-centres, branches and customers may interact remotely with one other, often with IT support, we can already identify certain organisational structures that correspond to teleworking forms. While these matters were not articulated under the teleworking ambit, they were easily translated into issues traditionally discussed in the teleworking literature: for example, saving space and cutting overheads, providing remote services, and so on. Where teleworking issues and concepts could be framed within this context, they were clearly more meaningful to the people involved in the bank and had greater practical relevance.

Undertaking the research

As noted above, the study was undertaken not simply to ascertain the feasibility of introducing teleworking in the bank, but to create a better understanding of the practical relevance for the bank of teleworking issues and concepts. In other words, teleworking provided a *perspective* that offered particular diagnoses of business problems and illuminated certain opportunities for change.

Undertaking the research involved *working with* bank personnel to assist them in framing the matters at hand from a teleworking point of view. As such, a response that involved spatial reorganisation was used to help construct what the problems were. This was done through interviews and meetings conducted over eighteen months. Some eighty people were involved in this, and represented a range of functional and operational areas, as well as management levels. For example, interviews took place with: staff from personnel, marketing, information systems design, network planning; management at central headquarters, regional directors and branch management; and personnel at the 'coal-face' working in branches and other areas.

The three stages of the research

Stage 1

At stage 1 of the research interviews took place with regional directors and staff from personnel, network planning, and information systems design This enabled the breadth of business issues to be drawn out and discussed. Attention was also directed to the teleworking *concept*. We took this to have a broad meaning, relating to the IT-facilitated spatial reorganisation of work. The ideas this generated largely reflected the matters that respondents were concerned with in their particular work area. (For example, personnel saw telework linked to flexible work arrangements.) Secondary material was also collected concerning the reorganisation plans for the bank, statistics on branch network rationalisation, policies on flexible working and details of information systems plans.

Stage 2

Several areas of work were examined in Stage 2 of the research. There were three aspects here. First, gaining a general understanding of communications methods and technologies employed in different task areas, including those parts of bank work thought to demand face-to-face interaction (something especially true in the branch outlets). Second, some relatively novel (telework-like) developments were also visited during the research. These included a remote central typing unit, which used high-speed dictation transmissions, a telephone loan unit, and a central mortgage charging unit. Third, some specific tasks considered as options for remote execution were also examined, including clearing work, telesales, mortgage changing, risk assessment and customer balance sheet monitoring.

Stage 2 of the research therefore concentrated on the sort of practices, problems and issues commonly discussed in telework, so far as they appeared in retail banking. A 'grounded' typology was developed that described four forms of telework-related innovation. These were seen as the (organisational) *means* by which a range of *ends* (the reasons for adopting such changes, e.g. for remote service provision, cutting overheads, etc.) could be achieved. As such, this also reflected the context of the study, as to specific business pressures and change programmes, as well as the spatial dynamics of retail banking.

The typology was explored with research participants to illuminate and evaluate the potential for such innovations in different areas of the bank. The typology also included forms of change (such as centralisation) that we would not call 'telework'. However, given the commonality issues had with conventional programmes of restructuring and rationalisation that also involved spatial dislocation of work activity, it was considered essential to conceptualise and discuss telework in the same context.

Stage 3

Developing a framework for understanding teleworking as part of a wider process of organisational change made it possible to illuminate related decision-making processes and rationales and lay them alongside those posited for possible telework innovations. To ascertain which changes were preferred, the *principal ends* for change options also had to be identified and weighed up against the *associated* costs and benefits involved in each type of change.

The typology of telework-related change in retail banking

The four parts to the typology were:

Homework: which described instances where employees worked at home, either full time or part time, the main incentive being increased flexibility or productivity.

Telecentres Where work was done at a distance to free-up office space and staff time (especially in branches) and to tap into alternative labour markets and use low cost accommodation.

Centralisation Which subsumed changes in which restructuring and rationalisation involved the relocation of work tasks and their concentration in one place. Incentives for this included the opportunity to use bulk-processing equipment and gain economies of scale. Recent developments here included processing centres (or 'factories') which handled the masses of cheques and vouchers.

Specialised units Described the development of business units that provided specific services to remote customers. These included call-centres and telephone loan units.

Ends and means

The study therefore identified four related forms of change that involved a redistribution of work across space. Each of these was linked to *principal ends* (as identified in stages 1 and 2 of the research) towards which the changes would contribute. This also recognised the fact that those programmes and policies within the bank that were subsumed by parts of the typology (such as the setting up of call-centres) were congruent with the ends served by potential, telework-like initiatives (such as telecentres that operated on a regional basis). However, the *means* involved clearly differed. This was not so much so in terms of *spatial* change, but because such innovations were also accompanied by different *organisational structures* – demarcations, lines of responsibility and authority, and so on. For example, specialised units, such as call-centres, were very much autonomous businesses, and contrasted with homeworking, which involved no wider changes in relationships.

There was a need therefore to understand the benefits and costs associated with different means. For example, homeworking, while it provided work flexibility, had the associated cost of a perceived loss of control. Additionally though, each form was associated with a series of associated benefits (for example, the opportunity to develop a particular culture and ethos in the case of the specialised units). The principal ends, and associated costs and benefits, are detailed in Table 13.1.

Exploring the typology

Homework and telecentres

The research into possible forms of reorganisation highlighted a range of problems and issues, and the key criteria by which decisions were made about them. Homeworking was seen as a tool for flexible working, to be judged alongside arrangements such as job-sharing, flexitime and part-time work. However, it was

Table 15.1 Ends, benefits and costs of spatial reorganisation

	Principal ends	*Associated benefits*	*Associated costs*
Homework	Individual work flexibility; avoidance of office distractions	Reduced stress; less commuting	Additional investments in technology; problems of security and confidentiality
Telecentres	Use of cheap accommodation; access to new labour markets; free-up staff time and branch space for high added-value customer contact	Maintenance of security and confidentiality; physical surveillance and control; shared use of office resources	Additional co-ordination activities; additional accommodation costs
Centralisation	Economies of scale; allow for bank-wide rationalisation; lower overheads; use of bulk-processing equipment; use of cheap, 'factory' accommodation	Uniform quality control; access to new labour markets; development of specific competencies	Creation of routine, low-skill jobs; additional co-ordination activities
Specialised units	Provides for new products and ways of serving customers	Customer service culture and ethos can develop; development of specific competencies	May displace customer relationship-building in local branch

thought that formal instances of homework, where they existed for a sustained period, would most likely occur in exceptional cases, where existing alternatives could not satisfy the needs involved. It was therefore thought likely that home-working would be used as means of providing *ad hoc* flexibility, allowing for certain *tasks* (rather than entire jobs) to be conducted away from office distractions. A good example was 'report writing', and, in the case of risk assessment work, building mathematical models. As such, it was something that addressed the concerns of line managers encountering demands for work flexibility and work environments more conducive to concentration.

The scope for homeworking did not depend on elaborate technologies. Indeed, it was thought that the more simple and low-tech the arrangement, the more chance it had of developing. (For example, telesales and customer follow-up activities, which bank staff occasionally undertook in the evenings, could be done with only paper files and the telephone.) The main issue here was *security*. As such, homework that relied on the remote access to banking files, while technically feasible, was cautioned against. Additionally, where such cases needed investment in equipment to support homework (especially where this only occurred occasionally, with staff also needing office facilities) the likely costs involved were thought to outweigh the advantages. This was hardly surprising, of course, given that the principal rationales for homeworking in the first instance were issues of productivity and flexibility, not savings in fixed resources.

Homeworking also shared some issues with telecentres, although the latter also carried the secondary benefits of *on-site* working. These included: the availability of existing resources such as computers, photocopiers, faxes and furniture – much of which could be shared, especially between different shifts. In addition, central workplaces provided for the maintenance of confidentiality and security. The fact that they also allowed for the enclosure and surveillance of workers also meant that managers were comfortable about control aspects of this arrangement.

Specialised units and centralisation

Although many advantages could be (and had been) achieved through home-working and forms we might characterise as telecentres, *centralisation* and the creation of *specialised business units* were seen as the preferred and most likely types of change. Indeed, it was expected that those central units for telephone loan services and central mortgage charging which developed *regionally* (in the tele-centre type of initiative) would be displaced by more encompassing *bank-wide* initiatives in due course. This was because, where it was possible to rationalise activities right across the bank, rather than allowing local, half-way initiatives, economies of scale would be greater, quality standards higher and more easily guaranteed, and specific skills and expertises able to develop. For example, cen-tralised processing factories in cheap, out-of-town locations were seen as ideal for the performance of low added-value work. (Of course, such issues are particu-larly relevant to organisations which have over 2,000 outlets undertaking very similar activities.)

Specialised business units had much in common with centralisation. However, whereas the former were *outward*-focusing and directly served the *ultimate customer*, the latter was *inward*-focusing, service-oriented and involved internal processes. Specialised business units therefore fall into the category of organisation that Holti and Stern (1986) call 'distance working enterprises'. Such developments reflected growing customer expectations for easier forms of access to banking services, something which competition from building societies and niche pro-viders has helped create. The associated benefits of these developments included the relative autonomy created, and the opportunity this offered for developing skills and culture more attuned to sales and marketing activities.

Having discussed possibilities for telework-related innovations within the bank, we can now turn to examine the decision-making context involved in deciding which, if any, form of reorganisation was the preferred way of addressing the bank's problems and opportunities.

Deciding on telework in a business context

The *systemic* approach illustrated above differed considerably from those typically adopted in the study of telework. By understanding and conceptualising phenomena in context, and discussing rationales for change in the milieu of related decision-making, it was possible to evaluate the relative merits and demerits of teleworking in organisational change. In the bank a series of programmes was already in place, including restructuring, relocation, rationalisation, new product development and the provision of flexible working. In many respects, these contributed to the same *ends* which forms of telework could also have addressed. Therefore, considering whether the bank in question was or was not practising teleworking was not really the main research issue. The study illustrated that many contemporary (and often conventional) forms of reorganisation and decision-making reflect matters that can be easily translated in teleworking terms. For example, cutting overheads by saving space and moving to lower-cost areas was already taking place, but this was done through rationalisation of the branch network, and the relocation of branch and head office functions to more peripheral regions. The few opportunities found for homeworking, by contrast, provided little chance of savings in overheads.

The key rationale cited for homeworking – work flexibility – was already high on the personnel agenda in the bank. However, staff involved in this department considered that the bank's existing tools for flexible working largely met the ends sought by workers. Moreover, they did so without the associated costs involved with homework. The centralisation programmes in the bank had also brought about telework-related benefits, such as access to abundant labour markets and cheap premises. So long as the bank deemed such programmes to be the most efficient way of reorganising, therefore, other, more novel, changes were unlikely. However, innovations in telephone loan services and call-centres did show that distance working enterprises were emerging in the bank. And in keeping with the more high-tech vision of telework, these were facilitated by integrated databases that allowed for the remote retrieval and manipulation of information. They also used cheaper, out-of-town accommodation. However, such developments are so commonplace now as to be rarely thought of as 'telework'.

Discussion

There are two typical approaches to understanding telework. In the first, the phenomena under study are commonly recognised as cases undertaking telework, and are studied to gain a more in-depth understanding about their nature and background (for example, Kinsman 1987). In the second, research projects take place in which the central aim is to collect 'objective' survey data about, for example, teleworking forms and penetration, and to test or generate theoretical hypotheses. Both are valid ways of addressing teleworking, of course, if they are commensurate with the overall purpose of the studies involved. This was not so in the organisation mentioned above. Here, while it wanted to gain a greater understanding of how teleworking ideas were relevant to it, the bank did not consider itself to be the embodiment of teleworking. An alternative approach was therefore required in which the researcher *worked with* personnel in the organisation to facilitate a process of learning about telework. In so doing, ideas from the teleworking literature were drawn upon but were translated in terms meaningful to the people involved.

Here, teleworking ideas served as a means of helping the bank to diagnose problems, identify solutions and highlight business opportunities, all from a perspective that involved spatial reorganisation, possibly supported by IT. As such, teleworking ideas represented a 'generic tool' for organisational learning – one that was particularly important as it questioned old assumptions about work location and design, and was based on the possibilities offered by new technologies.

A number of lessons resulted from this. The first was a need to distinguish between the problems and issues considered *relevant to* telework (as commonly identified in the literature) – spatial reorganisation, work flexibility, remote service provision etc. – and the *concept of* telework. This is because the issues pertinent to telework are frequently implicated in organisational change programmes and discourses without the term itself being employed.

There was also a need to understand teleworking within the context of the organisational and spatial dynamics in question. For a UK retail bank, with some 70,000 employees dispersed over 2,000 locations – many with similar business processes and using the same basic databases – the issues connected with spatial reorganisation differ markedly from many other companies. Even within this company, though, telework was far from a homogeneous concept. In parts of the bank involved in the development of IT-supported services, teleworking had most resonance in terms of possibilities for remote service delivery systems. Personnel, on the other hand, being concerned with issues such as an increase in maternity return rates, especially on a full-time basis, saw it as a tool for flexible working.

Some tendencies also emerged that went against certain teleworking orthodoxies. For example, the desire to achieve economies of scale and use capital equipment to automate routine functions illustrated a desire for *centralising* activities or *displacing* them by technology, rather than simply allowing for them to be performed remotely. As such, IT was employed in ways that *foreclosed* teleworking options rather than supported them. In addition, in the branch network, where IT developments were accompanied by greater analytical facilities (or applied in an 'informating' mode, as Zuboff 1988, would put it), this was used to *enhance face-to-face interaction* with customers, and so improve quality of service and opportunities for cross-selling. Indeed, in contrast to centralisation, where routine processes were often involved, sales encounters were recognised as high added-value activities. As such, effective use of staff time and expensive retail space were the main issues, as opposed to lowering operating costs. This contrasts, of course, with the telework logic that suggests a lowering in overheads by avoiding the use of such office space.

Conclusions

While the banking context hardly provides the opportunity to generalise on all organisations, we can make some concluding points. Companies operate in very different industries, vary considerably in size and structure, and have different products and delivery channels. An appreciation of the *spatial dynamics* involved should therefore be the starting point for understanding both teleworking opportunities, but also the very *meaning(s)* of the concept itself. By taking this approach in the banking sector, recognising the importance of the branch network as a key means of service delivery, and the fact that similar processes are replicated in thousands of different locations, is essential.

In contrast to simple, one-dimensional views of IT found in some discussions of telework (e.g. that it can be used to transcend space and thus cut down on commuting), we were forced to consider telework in a way that recognised the other readings and applications of the technology. Even where the choice may exist to undertake work at a distance, the preference for automation, or to use the technology to enhance face-to-face interactions, may foreclose the teleworking option. While telework orthodoxies suggest that technologies can be used to reduce operating costs and gain access to other labour markets, this may be eclipsed by restructuring programmes that involve a rationalisation of staff and premises, and relocation to more peripheral areas. Finally, while the term itself may not be employed, developments such as call-centres represent the creation of new business units, based on technology-supported remote service, that can be easily interpreted in classic teleworking terms. In these instances, the wealth of knowledge created in the study of telework stands by to inform and facilitate developments. But also, such initiatives represent new phenomena from which researchers into telework, keen to codify developments, must learn.

References

Checkland, P.B. and Scholes, J. (1990) *Soft Systems Methodology in Action*, Chichester: Wiley.

Child, J. and Loveridge, R. (1990) *Information Technology in European Services*, Oxford: Blackwell.

Cressey, P. and Scott, P. (1992) 'Employment, Technology and Industrial Relations in UK Clearing Banks: Is the Honeymoon Over?', *New Technology, Work and Employment* 7, 2: 83–96.

Fincham, R., Fleck, J., Proctor, R., Scarbrough, H., Tierney, M. and Williams R. (1994) *Expertise and Innovation: Information Technology Strategies in the Financial Services Sector*, Oxford: Clarendon.

Gummesson, E. (1991) *Qualitative Methods in Management Research*, London: Sage.

Holti, R. and Stern, E. (1986) *Distance Working: Origins, Diffusion, Prospects*, Paris: Futuribles.

Kinsman, F. (1987) *The Telecommuters*, Chichester: Wiley.

Mauriello, M. (1996) 'Economics of Retail Banking: What is Really Happening Here Anyway', *Bankers Magazine* 179, 6: 47–51.

Procter, R. (1992) 'Information Technology in the Financial Services Sector', in Scarbrough, H. (ed.) *The IT Challenge: IT and Strategy in Financial Services*, London: Prentice-Hall.

Scarbrough, H. (1992a) 'The UK Financial Services Marketplace', in Scarbrough, H. (ed.) *The IT Challenge: IT and Strategy in Financial Services*, London: Prentice-Hall.

—— (1992b) 'IT, Products and Infrastructures in Financial Services', in Scarbrough, H. (ed.) *The IT Challenge: IT and Strategy in Financial Services*, London: Prentice-Hall.

Zuboff, S. (1988) *In the Age of the Smart Machine*, Oxford: Heinemann.

Part 4

ACTORS, NETWORKS AND EXPERIENCES
International cases of telework

In Part 4 we take a closer look at particular strategies and experiences of different teleworking actors and networks from around the world. This includes cases from Canada, USA, Austria, Italy, Sweden and Finland. The forms in question range from individual teleworkers and networks of dispersed workers, to telecentres and even 'tele-villages'. These cases not only highlight different forms and aspects of telework, they also show the differing aims and interests of the actors involved.

Chapter 16, by Dima Dimitrova and Janet Salaff, concerns two groups of office-based administrative workers, each of which interacts with their clients (both in-house and external) at a distance. The authors examine the relationship between different types of technology, task characteristics and organisational processes. They identify a range of factors under dispersed arrangements that influence the way technology is employed. These include, for instance, the predictability of work, the network relations (including customers and co-workers) needed to get work done, and the interdependence of the tasks undertaken.

In Chapter 17 by Steven Fireman, attention is focused on the individual teleworker, and the reasons he or she may choose to refrain from or reduce their amount of teleworking. He develops a model for explaining the reasons for 'withdrawal' from telework. There are three parts to this: 'community', which describes an employee's desire for interaction in an office environment; 'compulsion', which highlights those factors outside of work that influence an employee's reasons for teleworking; and 'comfort', which refers to the overall support employees receive from management. The model helps us to understand how individuals, across a range of cultures, adapt to teleworking in specific organisational contexts. It can therefore be used to predict a likely fit between the individual and the work arrangements involved.

In Chapter 18 by Georg Aichholzer, the viability of centre-based teleworking is examined. The author describes several projects in which telecentres were

259

established in the form of neighbourhood offices, satellite offices and resort offices. He examines the reasons for the success or failure of these arrangements, and suggests how these experiences can inform future centre-based practices.

In Chapter 19, the main actors of interest are the telecom companies. Patrizio Di Nicola and Ruggero Parrotto describe how these companies, whilst keen to promote telework as a business product, have also been engaged in using it themselves. One obvious reason for this has been their ownership of a substantial infrastructure which can support telework. The authors suggest a number of lessons that can be learned from these experiences, particularly the need to share knowledge and cultural values in order for such innovations to develop and stabilise.

In Chapter 20 Lennart Sturesson highlights the vendor's perspective on teleworking. In this case, the role of IT and telecom companies as active promoters of telework forms the central matter of interest. He argues, though, that in promoting telework as a new form of work, symbolic values are often marketed rather than those of utility. Sturesson shows the array of actors that have taken an interest in teleworking, and the attempts made to place teleworking ideas at the centre of the design of new tele-villages.

In the final chapter, Reima Suomi, Ari Luukinen, Juhani Pekkola and Marya Zamindar point to the critical role played by management capabilities and opinions in the introduction of telework. They provide an overview of changes in Finnish working life and the role telework adoption has played in this. The authors argue that the spread of telework will depend on an adequate technological and communication infrastructure, appropriate technological skills and the reorganisation of corporate structures and cultures.

16

TELEWORK AS SOCIAL INNOVATION

How remote employees work together

Dima Dimitrova and Janet W. Salaff

Introduction

Our study on teleworkers helps us understand how people in decentralised organisations work remotely. How remote employees get work done, control and co-ordinate work and maintain social relations from afar starts with their communication. We study corporate teleworkers in a large telecommunications firm, which we call the company. Although they work in their home offices, all have partners and clients inside and outside the company at some distance from them. Technology can bridge space, and many expect teleworkers will use mediated technology to communicate. Communications technologies are their lifelines. But what technology most helps them work together from afar?

The company we study equips its middle-level managers, professionals and salespeople with advanced computer-based technologies. Yet, just having computers and modems does not mean these remote workers use them fully. Some start up their modems to share data, whereas others prefer to talk on the phone, or even start up their cars to meet their co-workers. In this Chapter, we compare two groups of employees at roughly the same organisational level in the same firm. We learn why one group depends on mediated technologies to bridge remote locales while the other chooses to meet face to face. They telework differently, and we try to locate the key sources of difference. In this Chapter we focus on the communication patterns which are a central part of how they telework.

Our study has broader implications for the spread of this novel work form. If most employees can use new mediated communications to work at a distance, telework is more likely to spread. If, however, many cannot adapt remote technologies to their tasks, telework will be limited to small circles of corporate workers with just the right kinds of tasks.

How people use different communication techniques to work remotely

Literature review

Organisational research that analyses the work employees do helps us understand the ease with which they telework. Olson's (1982, 1983) early research found that professionals who teleworked most easily were those who had independent, long-term and structured projects and exchanged few resources with others. This finding raises important issues, starting with communication.

Central to remote work is how people communicate at a distance. Matching work tasks with media, 'rational choice' theorists tell us that managers with ambiguous communication tasks prefer rich media. Those that have routine and clearer communications can make do with leaner channels (Daft *et al.* 1987; Trevino *et al.* 1990; Lowry 1996). Applied to teleworkers, we expect that those who can transmit clear messages and use the vast array of computer-mediated communications media can easily work at a distance. At the other extreme, however, this finding limits the extent of successful telework to the set of employees that can convey clear messages.

Next is the degree of structure in their arrangement of tasks. Here we follow Perrow's (1970) emphasis on repetition in structured organisational work. Olson's (1982) study suggested that the employees' work processes are central to how they telework. In another paper, we described managers and professionals with routine work who work at a distance as readily as in the company office while those with novel, negotiated jobs needed considerable support to work remotely (Salaff and Dimitrova 1996). If this is the case, can improved technology more widely extend this novel work form to those with varied work processes?

Finally, is Olson's finding that those who have limited exchanges with their work partners are the most successful teleworkers. Can only the independent worker who exchanges little with co-workers work at a distance? Since corporate employees rarely have independent work and usually work in relation with others, the nature of interdependence needs further study. Organisational theorists distinguish pooled, sequential and reciprocal flows between work partners that exchange the resources they need for their product (Scott 1992: 230). Those that pool their work do not exchange resources; each employee contributes to the final product. Those that work sequentially rely on the input of their partners before them, and in turn provide input for follow-up work. People that are reciprocally interdependent have to take each other's inputs into account to produce their product. While few studies of teleworkers' communication assess modes of employees' interdependence, some are aware of its importance for teleworking (Fritz *et al.*1994; Li 1996). But only by linking modes of interdependence to the work process can we understand how this innovative form of work can be adapted to widely divergent work relationships. Sociologists stress that the work-group shapes how people communicate. Fulk *et al.*'s studies (1990) found that the workgroup provides norms, cues and attitudes about members' communication. Social network theorists study how the structure of social networks shapes distinct uses of communications media (Garton and Wellman 1995; Haythornthwaite and Wellman 1996; Haythornthwaite et al. 1995; Wellman 1995). On the other hand, actor-network theory posits that people use communications technology to relate to their networks. Individuals will be more likely to adapt that new technology which develops the connections they have to others (Latour 1987, 1991; Lea et al. 1995; Axelsson and Easton 1992). Extending these ideas to teleworking as a new set of work techniques, can we expect that more employees will telework if assured that they and their work networks can communicate with ease?

To understand how remote workers work together, we study the media they use and the supports they need. Do they, depending on the ambiguity of their messages, choose media of different degrees of richness? How does the arrangement of their tasks, the degree of routine or novelty of project tasks, shape media choice? And how do their relationships with the work partners with whom they exchange resources affect how they telework? We focus here on the mediated technologies that bridge space. We contrast leaner mainframe, LAN-based computer exchanges, and somewhat richer telephone-mediated forms of communication, with the richest, face-to-face personal interaction. We propose that remote workers with structured projects and stable network structures will choose cool media. In contrast, those with structured projects but complex and unstable work relationships will prefer unmediated and the richest forms of mediated communication.

Our study site

Our study uses the qualitative method of 'paired comparisons'. For this chapter, we focus on two administrative groups of remote workers who work in fairly structured ways but exchange resources differently. We chose them from our larger sample of managers, professionals and salesworkers in the middle ranks of the company who perform complex jobs. The sample as a whole includes 94 employees from 21 administrative groups with a variety of jobs in the firm. Some work in company cubicles, others at home, and still others are mobile workers from 'hotelling' sites. This chapter describes two groups of those that gave up the downtown spot and set up an office in their own home.

Those in this study volunteered to telework. Some were 'guerrilla' teleworkers, working remotely with the agreement of their supervisor, before the company adopted the teleworking policy. All were teleworking before we met them and saw the innovative work form as suitable to their work.

We talked with these employees in several sessions of semi-structured interviews that lasted an hour or more. We discussed how they work, their supervision, setting up the home office, and as home based-workers changes in their home reproductive tasks. We gathered data from individuals on how they work with others. While these are not group-level data, their descriptions capture their work with others.

We taped and transcribed these sessions, and analysed them with the qualitative text package, NUD*IST. We searched the database for themes suggested by the material and by literature on the topic.

Two forms of work

To show how work processes, communication tasks and network characteristics shape use of technology, we compare managers 'provisioning' telecommunication switches for long-distance phone lines with sales consultants to call-centre operations. Both groups are in the management tier but in different divisions of the company. Their projects have a routine structure, while their networks vary. Where there are other differences that affect our comparison, they will be discussed below.

Provisioners: predictable tasks, stable networks

Job function

Provisioners do the paperwork for the installation of new machines in the company switching centres to support long-distance services. As teleworkers, they work from home. Theirs is unheralded, behind-the-scenes, detailed and highly routine project oriented administrative work. In a typical project, provisioners suggest an appropriate switching centre, draw up a budget and write the specs. They order the equipment from a supplier, schedule the installation and pay the bills. Their work is complex, but they and others in their work network impose a routine. Stable work networks facilitate this routine, as seen in three stages of their projects.

Getting the project

Provisioners install new technologies that follow the logic of product development. They are relatively isolated from market pressures, although competition has quickened new installations. Previously programmed two years in advance, now projects may come 'out of the blue'. However, daily operations have changed little.

The routine work of provisioning that lends itself to computer-based communication modes begins with getting the project. Vice Presidents decide whether to go ahead with installations, and determine the budget. They delegate the primary responsibility (project 'ownership') to planners, who set time frames and pull together a project team, and assign the provisioner that we study here. Each provisioner supports the installation of a particular type of machine in her district and the project team composition depends on the machines and the district where they will be installed. Planners contact the appropriate provisioner by e-mail and detail the project further in an electronic file. Provisioners thus follow directives from above, and make few independent decisions of their own.

Provisioners start initial paperwork, and include the work in the plans of their company and that of the equipment manufacturer. Although team members routinely use e-mail, projects have formal paperwork that is physically copied in binders. Binders move from department to department as the project progresses.

Provisioners first confirm the planner's choice of location for the new equipment or recommend another by e-mail. The job is formally introduced in a face-to-face meeting. A dozen involved parties attend, from the manufacturing departments of the supplier, the purchasing department of their company, technical experts and the manager of the provisioners' administrative group. The type of machines, finances, deadlines, and turn-round times of the project are predetermined and the meeting is a one-way exchange: 'OK, this is what we are going to do and this is how we are going to do it and these are the dates we want it . . . the intervals are cut'. They hold the meeting because of the complexities of the projects. A face-to-face meeting allows visuals and questions, and the particularities are discussed. However, this meeting is one of the few they will hold.

Project scheduling 'is all done electronically'. Working backwards from the final deadline set by the planner, provisioners come up with a time frame for each operation. Through e-mail, programmers from the company and the supplier issue a set of job numbers that detail equipment and deadlines. Both company and supplier can access the needed databases electronically. Programmers 'schedule' or 'programme' the job; they file it under a special number and assign the requested time slots on the mainframe databases of incoming jobs. The job numbers, the keystones of all official records, now identify the project work assignments. The assigned codes allow information to be stored electronically, accessed by different departments on the mainframe and communicated among co-workers. The mainframe databases become a tool for co-ordination and control. When the total amount of funding is approved, provisioners start to work on the project.

Doing the work

Provisioners do much of their work electronically, by e-mail messages or entering data on the information system of the supplier (PAQS database) with their passwords. Remote technology helps provisioners confirm the scheduling with the supplier and request records on the machinery previously installed in the designated project switching centre. Ordering the equipment, they work with those who attended the kick-off meeting and add contacts from groups responsible for the installation, maintenance and management of the new equipment. To make a list of the software to go with the new equipment, provisioners exchange spreadsheets over e-mail with the company's software group: 'I give them the job number and what I am putting in, and electronically send it across to them'.

The complex job of working out the specifications and budget, however, requires more face-to-face discussion. Provisioners input the bulk of the equipment; the manufacturing engineers from the allied supplier add the 'nitty-gritty technical details' (like cables). Every change is scrutinised and approved by both sides. Project participants from five to seven groups discuss the specifications in two consecutive meetings. Once agreed upon, the formal approval of the specs, the price quote of the supplier and the actual ordering of the equipment from the manufacturing department of the supplier are done electronically by accessing the databases across the two companies. To finalise the order, the supplier faxes an official order form to the provisioner to sign. This mix of face-to-face, electronic and other contacts in ordering the equipment enables detailed discussion as well as quick remote administrative action. Setting a budget is another iterative process which follows the specifications changes and final prices. Revisions and the finalised budget are entered on the budgeting database of the company. But the approval of financial documents follows a traditional administrative procedure centred on a hard copy document moving along the line of report. The higher executives personally sign a binder copy of the budget: 'How high it goes up depends on how much this estimate is valued at. I can myself approve up to $40,000, my boss can approve $80,000, his boss can approve $200,000.' A mix of technologies allows what is not done electronically to be done remotely. The provisioner faxes a copy of her estimate to a clerk in the office. The clerk may pass the budget estimate to the provisioner's manager and then the provisioner phones her boss to notify him. If 'it is no rush' then the provisioner waits until she gets to the central office and personally hands over the binder. After the final budget draft is revised, it is entered in the mainframe master file and becomes the responsibility of the budgeting group to monitor the charging of labour and money against it.

Handing over the completed project

The provisioner hands over the completed project to the installation co-ordinator at the set time. After the equipment is installed, the provisioners monitor the payment of bills. Different pieces of equipment are processed, verified and billed separately. They send the paperwork to budgeting to fill out the appropriate invoices, sign and fax back the forms, log them, and notify electronically the Accounts Payable department to issue the cheques. When the bills are paid, the provisioner notifies another group in writing to close the project and sends the hard copies of all documents for electronic archiving. The project is officially completed.

Analysis

Predictability

Provisioning is structured and predictable work. While provisioners do diverse tasks within a project, their range and the overall organisation of work remain the same for each new site. The specific 'product' of provisioners, the smooth, without 'hitches', installing of new machines, is unambiguous. Well-developed procedures, rules, agreements and machine codes guide performance. Committee and department rules determine the allocation of work between provisioners and their partners for each operation, fix turn-round times of operations and structure the workflow around them: 'You would probably say it's more a series of steps and we follow them although there are always exceptions to the rule I suppose'. A project takes from six to nine months and provisioners manage up to 12 projects at once. These do not vary. Emergencies are rare. The key is meeting deadlines. If a co-worker delays her input and jeopardises the provisioner's own deadline, this can be problematic. They solve this by 'escalating', which includes higher-level managers by copying them e-mail exchanges. Provisioners do not take major decisions. They follow a set routine. Their tasks, the sequence, turn-round times, the resources they need and how they work, the machines to install, funding, and organisation of work are all set by others. The work has an accepted way of doing things and a temporal structure. While complex, provisioners' work entails little negotiation or politicking. Within this predetermined framework, provisioners can work out their own short-term timetable and organise their work on a small scale. Structured work is predictable, making it easy for provisioners to plan.

Network and relationships

The workflow of installation provisioning links groups in a known fashion. A project passes from one person (or group) to another, each completing a particular operation. In organisational terms, their work is sequential with their work project teams and pooled with the administrative group: 'We all have our little pieces to do and I have to get input from a lot of them for me to be able to complete my tasks, and they also have to get input from me for them to be able to complete their tasks. But nobody does what I do and I don't do what anybody else does.'

ADMINISTRATIVE GROUP

Provisioners belong to an administrative group of eight to ten people, which supports the installation of machinery and its software. They do not work together as a group on projects.

SUPERVISOR

The provisioners' supervisor is kept informed but rarely gets involved in the day-to-day work. As a formal authority, the supervisor has to approve budgets. But he neither provides concrete resources for the provisioners' projects, nor needs their input in his work. Once higher executives launch a project, the type of equipment to be installed and the location determines who is responsible. Because of the existence of rules and deadlines, work is readily tracked and measured. Clear and uncomplicated responsibilities on both sides demand few elaborate supervisory procedures. Provisioners handle their structured tasks without consulting their supervisor: 'Why should we burden him with a lot of little things?' If several new projects start together and threaten overload, provisioners may notify their supervisor who negotiates with higher executives on their behalf. The rare escalation involves him in the loop, but it is the threat to take action that matters more than intervention.

Two 'peers' share the same function for different districts. Peers help out each other in emergencies and take over each other's projects during longer absences. They keep each other informed. The rest of the administrative group provisions different machines or software and does not work with provisioners. A few other co-workers from the administrative group of the provisioners are contacted in the course of their work. Provisioners need *clerical* help to type hand-written budget estimates not on the mainframe. But they try to reduce that by learning new software when work slows down: 'I should be able to do that . . . It is my project for the winter. I haven't got around to it yet'.

WORK FLOW NETWORK

The project work team is drawn from administrative groups in many locations. Provisioners contact the same groups and the same people for each project. They work with designated contact persons. They may work with about 30 co-workers and partners from a number of workgroups in diverse company departments. They exchange resources with two external companies, but these do not vary and are closely allied to them. They have a single supplier.

During a project lasting several months, provisioners switch from group to group as required. But since they handle a number of projects at a time and their work relationships in them are the same, in practice they contact their network members at fixed but long intervals.

Planners, software provisioners or maintenance form the core project team responsible for a distinct set of project tasks. They get involved most frequently in the project. Remaining network members are designated contacts who, while not responsible for the project, have well-defined roles: they supply old equipment, give information on the software for the new equipment, or schedule a task. They get involved at a certain stage of work, finish their tasks within a fixed time, and end involvement. In these ways, workflow relationships are structured; the resources exchanged are fixed.

CLIENT

The client for each project is the co-ordinator responsible for the installation of the provisioned machine. Provisioners inform the co-ordinator on the project status, but the co-ordinator does not provide input, and does not play much of a role in the work.

COMMUNICATION

Provisioners communicate in the context of structured work, stable relationships and networks anchored in a limited circle of co-workers and partners. They communicate at set times and the text is clear. Negotiation, if it occurs, is over technical issues not their political nature. Provisioners contact their supervisor, their peer and the clerk supporting their administrative group frequently, even daily. They do so in a routine manner and over a wide range of three or four forms of media. They use a narrower range of media with other projects' participants.

Provisioners use mediated technology to communicate with their core group of co-workers and partners. By far the highest percentage of mediated technology is e-mail. A sizeable amount of their communication with project members is indirect, mediated by the mainframe. On the mainframe, the information is open for other project team members to review and use without directly contacting provisioners. They exchange data with their work partners through the mainframe, inputting or pulling budget estimates, equipment information and other data from mainframe databases.

The telephone follows e-mail in frequency. Live calls outrank voice-mail. Lest it be thought that the live calls are responses to emergencies, or negotiation, even here this is not the case. Phone calls include team or group voice-conferencing; sometimes up to 70 people can 'participate', ordered by a strict agenda. Further, they are prompted to use multiple contacts to make up for the deficiencies of mediation. For example, they use e-mail or fax to transfer bulky numerical information but back-up such transfers by phone calls to clarify their requests or indicate urgency. They arrange face-to-face meetings electronically. They also try to add face-to-face contacts where the normal course of projects' workflow require only mediated communication. Whenever they are in town, provisioners will 'pop in and say Hi' to their contact persons in the budgeting group, informal ways to support their mail and fax contacts. Using several media for the same contact combines the strength of each, but also raises the incidence of non-mediated contact.

Faxed and written exchanges are next frequent. There are few real time meetings. Overall communication, thus, is not only mediated, but also dominated by leaner media.

Formal and informal contacts are distinct. Formal face-to-face interaction supports a limited number of work operations (like specification discussion), while informal face-to-face interaction maintains smooth relationships. Although such informal contacts ease their duties, work relationships typically do not evolve into social ties. Provisioners keep their workflow and friendship networks separate.

Predictability of work and stable relationships drive other communication patterns. Provisioners work in an established group with regular contacts. They have known most of their co-workers and partners for years. Provisioners know the time frames of their tasks. There are no emergencies, and they do not need to be available outside regular office hours: 'Nobody ever calls at weekends'. Their meetings, either voice-conference calls or face-to-face meetings, are scheduled. Hence, they know when communication with co-workers and partners is likely and when contacts may involve urgent issues. They can choose the right time for contacts and delay communication if needed: 'In my particular job, it's not like real time. It's not like the phone has to be answered this second.' They plan and initiate their contacts, gaining control over communications, which routine and predictability make possible. Stable networks further reinforce provisioners' control over communication.

In the interplay of predictable work and established relationships, communication emerges as mediated, delayed, structured by the flow of tasks. Provisioners none the less control the workflow.

Team call-centre sales consultants: varied networks

The company's permanent consultants to the 1–800 call-centres in corporate industry are organised as a 40-member team call-centre. The sales consultants advise Canada's largest national financial and manufacturing industries on call-centre operations. We describe here an 11-member industry vertical administrative group within team call-centre. They are called consultants because they do not charge the customer for their advice. Their mandate is to increase long-distance usage, which both increases the client's customers and the telecommunications company's revenue. While the range of project tasks vary with the client, internal procedures and products are similar, with predictable stages.

Job function

Team call-centre consultants are the cream of the company sales force, and they have to provide quality service to their important accounts. They deliver a range of 'value-added services' to powerful companies, whose national and international customers contact them through their 1–800 numbers.

Call-centre consultants analyse clients' call-centres needs, recommend a call centre where needed, specify the number of lines and staffing based on the customer's calling patterns, and help hire and train call-centre operators: 'Our role is to consult with our clients on developing new call-centres, on improving the performance of existing call centres'. They discuss with and make presentations to clients, for which they pull together information from a variety of sources and do independent analytical work. But the central part of their work is 'politicking', persuasion and negotiation, a source of task and network diversity.

Their large national accounts generate millions of revenue for the company. They have often been the dedicated representative to these accounts for years. The consultant to one of Canada's national banks spends most of her time on projects for her one-million dollar account. This anchor account jostles with a dozen other substantial, yet smaller-scale, national accounts, such as a chain real-estate agent: 'The Bank has a lot of needs from a telecommunications point of view. I mean they get service to the 'nines'; these are big customers of ours . . . The Bank, generates, it's like maybe $12 million worth of long-distance revenue and I'm working with maybe $5 million of that.'

Getting the project

With 'ownership' of their accounts, consultants generate their own projects and make the major project decisions. A project can start in a number of ways, from visits to the customer to referrals from previous projects. The consultant has a mandate to visit two customers a day for 15 days of the month to generate new projects. Often potential clients themselves seek out the consultant either because they know she is their special representative or because their colleagues with similar needs referred her: 'Sometimes they call in here. A lot of companies know team call-centre services, so they will call our switchboard and they will say, "We're looking for some training." ' They may also contact her assistant who is working 'in front of the customer all the time'. While relations with the client company are ongoing, consultants work with different groups within it. Within each account, consultants provide advice and recommendations for different departments and sites, each of which is a project. Clearly, consultants have to be proactive to secure their own job; negotiation and communication are central to a good consulting strategy.

Doing the work

After the client employs the consultant's services, the work itself becomes tech-nical and routine, and less political. While the range of their tasks vary, all have guidelines and turn-round times. Most of their work is based on modules.

At the first stage, the consultant clarifies the client's objectives and expect-ations. The consultant, her supervisor and often her support person meet with clients to discuss the project: 'I sit in meetings and strategise how the programme is going to go . . . Then we decide on a course of action depending on what they need and you have to prepare a report outlining what it is we're going to do for them, so I do that.'

The content of subsequent work rests on the needs of the client. In a full-range project, the consultant performs a 'needs analysis' to find out if a call-centre is needed. But even where the call-centre is already installed, she must analyse the phone representatives' work. She collects data from diverse sources for this analysis. Discussions with the client provide some information: 'We would sit in a room and talk to the managers and find out what their problems are and what their hot buttons are and what they want to do . . . They have certain needs, they don't feel that their people have got enough etiquette on the phone, or don't know how to sell, or they don't know how to be courteous or end a call – they could've given a million reasons.'

Assistants do the more routine part of collecting the data. A designated support 'would go and actually monitor their calls and see where their weaknesses are'. Meanwhile, the clerk gathers long-distance phone call data from the mainframe. She 'brings off reports that tell me how busy they are, how busy they're not, in a given time'. The consultant analyses the collected data on the computer, outlines a plan for her services, then discusses the proposal with the client: 'My job is to go in there and say, "Mr Customer, by the way, look at this report. You're missing a lot of calls. People are hanging, people are waiting on the phone ten minutes before they get through." "Oh, really, what am I to do?" "This is what we recommend. This is what we offer." '

After her needs analysis, she takes two days to write the account plan. She also e-mails or faxes the proposal to her manager to file as her activity report. After having sold the client on the proposal, the consultant starts implementation.

Her assistant takes over, and orders the services that the consultant recommends. She does the recommended training, using standard training modules. Although the assistant may adjust the formal training modules to the client's need, the work is repetitive. For example, a traders' manager asked her to give the training course in eight one-hour time slots instead of two four-hour sessions. To do so, she revised the course by changing the order and adding information from old courses.

After the initial start-up, the consultant supervises her assistant, helps her with problems and keeps ongoing communication with the customer to follow up. Depending on the project, the consultant may bring in other co-workers from the sales team or a technician from the mechanisation group to install equipment and work up a quotation. She does post-sales service but others in the sales department do the actual technical back-up. Other groups install lines, equipment and applications.

Handing over the completed project

The active involvement of the consultant in a project ends with the completion of training. She sees the Vice Presidents in the client company to ensure they are happy with the results. But the consultant remains the contact person for her company and personnel from her client firm may call later with queries and requests. In that sense, the project is open-ended.

Analysis

Predictability

The uncertainty in consulting is rooted in customer satisfaction. Developing and maintaining relationships with the client firm is an ongoing and highly political task. Apart from relationship building, the actual consulting work is structured.

Call-centres operate in a similar way. The 'product' of consultants – an efficient call-centre – entails a limited number of technical and administration problems. Their solutions are clear and consultants do not have to invent them. There is a ratio of operators to lines and calls. There are rules and turn-round times to guide work. Most projects are within the same client firm. This single industry framework does not allow a wide variation in the technical and administrative solutions. It also introduces a common business strategy and objective in most sites.

However, projects are client driven and consultants choose equipment and training modules to suit a particular site or department. These may or may not already have a call-centre, they may plan the expansion in a slightly different way and they may have some site-specific problems. Hence, while consultants apply known solutions each time, their tasks across projects vary. Such work demands independent decisions in selecting the right mix of software and training courses.

Project durations are also varied. Helping a supervisor customise a software package takes a week, training the sales team takes two to three months. Installing a new call-centre takes much longer. At any one time the consultant works with about three active projects at different stages of completion, with more in the pre-proposal pipeline.

The work a consultant does is conceptual and analytic and there are relatively few emergencies. Most crises are client generated: a client advertises a telephone number without providing enough telephone lines and operators for an inevitable peak: 'And experience tells me, when the customers [of the client's firm] see the [advertised] number, they're going to call, so your peaks are going to go like this' and the system will crash. Consultants anticipate such crises and can prevent them, but are often called in after the event to help sort it out: 'Now if a system crashed . . . they would call the . . . technical person rather than me but anuu I can't fix it. I might be responsible for it if I set it up badly or something but I can't fix. They fix it.'

However, crises may be of a political nature, the product of a company's hurt ego, and the consultant is called to put out the fire. But these are not common. She has few weekend calls, and few customers know her home phone number.

Networks and relationships

The workflow of consultants links groups that have diverse roles, and therefore their interdependence is complex. They have reciprocal interdependence with clients, sequential work with workflow members, and they pool input from their peers.

That consultants most depend for their work on their external clients is foremost in shaping network relationships. The client-driven nature of consulting work that requires them to suit projects to client needs is at the centre of their interdependent work relations. There is constant input to projects from both the client and the consultant.

As the link between their client and a number of workgroups in the company, consultants serve as contact persons who funnel down solutions from various company experts to their client. Their work also demands an input of unstructured, political, strategic information. To get such expertise, they cultivate numerous and diverse relationships in and outside the company. These work networks are large and diverse and not stable. Because they need a wide range of information, their workflow members vary across projects depending on the need of the clients, and they switch between contacts. Some are formally involved in the work. Others provide consultants with specialised knowledge 'on demand'. After consultants receive the necessary information, they may not need formal contact for a while. Nevertheless, they maintain contact with many colleagues, anticipating this need for diverse information.

ADMINISTRATIVE GROUP

They normally work with a core of four co-workers, and add others depending on the project. They cultivate a broader base of network members as advisors for support and services, especially to get information.

Supervisor The supervisor has an important role to play in their projects. Consultants bring her to the first meeting with the client when strategic decisions are made. The supervisor is a back-up and support because 'she has got more experience with banks than I do'. Her authority also adds credibility to the consultant; she also comes 'for clout'. Because of the political nature of their work, consultants get more involved in negotiations and power struggles and have to be aware of power imbalances. Client meetings with the supervisor offer opportunities for coaching; they end with an immediate review of personal performance and advice for the future. At the same time, the consultant and the supervisor work out a plan for handling the project. These are so important that the company has mandated two joint visits to clients per month.

Involved in the projects, the supervisor is well aware of her team's work. However, this is not enough to track a consultant's progress. Performance is measured as the amount of new long-distance revenue an account generates. This amount is not known immediately and there is no visible link between the consultants' performance and the long-distance revenue. Clients are unpredictable, can change their minds, and the relationships with the client can be volatile. The supervisor needs constant updates and soft, unstructured information on consultant–client relations.

Explicit control and reporting procedures take the form of an electronic log to the database of client visits, with names and telephone numbers of contacts, the service rendered and other details of the project. In addition, once a month section meetings filter down information on company policy, restructuring, or changes in account measurement.

Supports Consultants work closely with an assistant when the project entails training. While three consultants share one assistant, assistants are personally responsible for the projects they work on. After the contract is signed, the supports do the routine work of observing, collecting, recording, counting. They spend long hours at the call-centre, collecting information on existing problems and delivering training courses. In the process, they develop relationships with these contacts and become a conduit for messages from the client, feed-back and a source of new projects. The clerk helps with needs analysis. She compiles data from the mainframe databases on long-distance calling. She may type documents. The receptionist, in turn, is a 'buffer' between consultants and their contacts: she tracks down consultants when clients need them urgently.

Other consultants Consultants work independently, each immersed in her own accounts. But all consultants in the group keep in touch and exchange tips and information about their work. The organisation of work, the group objective set for the whole team, as well as their need for unstructured, subtle, political information makes such contacts a part of the job.

WORKFLOW NETWORK MEMBERS

Account team Consultants do not have the same formal team for each project: their formal working relationships are account based. They work closely with sales people who handle the same client. Depending on the client's needs and the project, partners from three to four other groups from the company may come in to install the call-centre equipment or other services. There are about ten technical experts comprising the wider work team.

Peers As the dedicated representative to her client, she has national counterparts that perform similar services for the same client company in different provinces: 'Of course the Bank is almost [as big as] our company. I mean it's massive, it's across the country. Now I'm not responsible for that, I'm only responsible for the immediate area here but they have divisions everywhere.' These national counterparts do not co-ordinate on a project, and instead give advice. Even though their peers across the country work for different telephone companies, they are brought together in an alliance. Consultants co-ordinate their work with them to achieve uniformity and share information about the client. Peers have regular meetings or may contact each other on an individual basis: 'I can't be in Vancouver and I can't be in Montreal because we have territory assigned but we are working with the same customer so I would call my counterpart in B.C., in Montreal, all over the country. We exchange information and say, "this is what we are doing in Toronto, what are you doing in Vancouver?"'

The consultant's overall work network extends beyond these formal categories. Besides those who get directly involved and co-ordinate their work with the consultant, she has numerous contacts across the company and outside it. She consults often with other peers who deal with her client in capacities other than call-centres. Company experts have information about their new products and services, business tips, and technical details. There are product managers, co-workers who handle software services for call-centres, videoconferencing, smaller business office products, and others. This array of different sales people, consultants and experts help her provide a wide range of services for the client.

Clients Consultants work with constant accounts but most projects are on different sites and involve new people from the client company. Consultants develop an extensive client network: some are one-shot contacts while others are stable relationships which evolve into social ties or even friendships. These ties provide the 'soft' information and referrals crucial for getting projects. In addition, clients are the most important source of project-specific knowledge like department objectives, problems, preferences and interpretations of the situation. In every project, their input determines the choice of equipment, software, or training modules. Clients, hence, affect to a large extent how consultants go about their work.

COMMUNICATION

The political nature of their work and the centrality of the clients in their network give rise to the consultants' communication patterns. Contacts with clients and experts dominate their communication. Negotiation is critical and the timing of the contacts cannot be easily planned. Such negotiated, political communication demands rich media. At the same time, network members are dispersed and the use of communication media inevitable. Consultants' communication is a compromise between these two contradictory demands.

Consultants contact their assistant and supervisor most frequently, both of whom have specific responsibilities in their projects. To communicate with them, consultants use a range of technologies.

In sheer numbers, there are more mediated than face-to-face contacts. Phone messages and phone calls outnumber the rest. They are more than routine communications and contain vital negotiated information. E-mail, regular mail and fax follow in frequency.

While face-to-face communications are less numerous than mediated communications, they are lengthy, take much of the consultant's time, and support the most significant steps in the workflow. Consultants spend two to three days a week in face-to-face meetings. As they spend much of their time on client sites and many of their experts and peers are remote, other contacts are by necessity mediated. When unable to meet face to face, consultants use richer and real time media to communicate with clients. Out of these demands comes a strong preference for the phone and voice-mail. Consultants call the telephone their 'lifeline', and make sure they have all services and equipment: individual voice-mail, group voice-mail for broadcasting, calling cards and a cellular phone. One consultant proudly displayed her new tilted handset that let her talk and dial without taxing her wrist. This preference for real time contacts is reflected in the sales culture which portrays itself as resting on verbal communication: 'we are talkers'. They 'find the voice-mail very effective' and check it hourly throughout the day. The bulk of personal contacts is with representatives of the client. While the consultant comes to the downtown office once a week or once every two weeks, she meets clients several times a week for lengthy discussions and presentations. These numerous meetings with the client are necessary and time consuming. Unstructured complex discussions with co-workers add demands on consultants' time although they have less priority in the workflow. To handle the volume of face-to-face contacts and at the same time meet the needs of complex discussions with co-workers, consultants combine meetings. Their joint meetings with the client are attended by their supervisor, various sales representatives or their assistant.

The political and less structured nature of contacts blur work and social relationships. To get referrals and projects, consultants keep on good terms with clients and peers. At the same time, relationships are not totally structured by workflow. For necessary pieces of information, the consultant has to know and select the best source and cultivate the relationship in advance. She has to cultivate relationships with experts and clients in case they are needed in the future. As a result, work contacts evolve into friendships.

This is seen in the multiplexity of relationships. The consultant socialises with many in her work network. Her administrative group meets informally once a month, after the formal group meeting. She lunches with co-workers who are important sources of information. The consultant considers some of the representatives of her client company friends. Her company encourages socialising with clients and organises yearly informal meetings. Golf tournaments and lunches combine work and social gatherings. 'It is wonderful to meet people at a social level ... you get a chance to meet all kinds of people that you wouldn't[usually]'.

Comparisons

We wondered why the use of advanced computer-mediated technologies to communicate with co-workers varied so greatly for teleworkers in one company. Provisioners consistently used advanced computer-mediated communications, while the phone was the consultants' lifeline. We began our comparison by exploring their work processes. These, while complex, have routines. Both workgroups put together a product or service for which they gather and pass on information. Projects have clear-cut stages and final deadlines. They repeat many of the sequences for the same product each time.

Despite the predictability of the projects of provisioners and consultants, consultants have more complex interdependence with their work networks than provisioners. The differences are reflected in the varied role of client, administrative group and workflow members. Provisioners do not depend on the client for work, but consultants do. Assigning projects for provisioners is automatic; consultants have to be proactive to secure their own job. Distinct workflow network relations follow. Provisioners get input from a limited group where relations are formally regulated. Consultants need experts 'on demand' and have to build relationships with others inside and outside the company. Finally, provisioners do not communicate with their administrative group. In contrast, consultants exchange tips and information with their group. Whereas provisioners consider their work independent, consultants see themselves as part of a team.

With the role of clients and experts come different degrees of politicking, negotiation and ambiguity of communication. Provisioners deal with clear unambiguous facts, often technical information. Consultants need 'soft' political, unstructured information. Media use is consistent. Provisioners are on-line with their workflow networks, even those in other firms. They use other media for back-up mostly. Consultants rely on face-to-face meetings and prefer real time rich media. Telephone is the acceptable avenue.

We found that information-rich technologies help with relationship building and negotiation. Provisioners who do not negotiate with their work partners can use information-sparse technologies. Since provisioners do not need to negotiate, much of their work-related communications can be done on-line. The consultants' need to negotiate with work partners turns them towards socially richer media. It should be noted that the phone is a complex computer-based phone system. But it is one that permits richer exchange than on-line e-mail messaging. Even though e-mail is versatile and can support a variety of relationships, these two groups use this electronic technology for different ends. We find that the media which supports the most important workflow relationships spills over to the rest of the network and dominates communication patterns.

Conclusion

Successful teleworking depends on the job, which should be put in context. By placing the work process and work relations at the centre of our analysis, we reconstruct the work environment of the teleworker and the process through which it is reproduced. In this study of employees working together at a distance, we focus on their choice of technologies that aid them to collaborate at a distance.

Our work confirms previous research that routineness, predictability, as well as low interdependence are important teleworking determinants. Those with routine tasks and limited dependence on their work partners can telework most easily. They do not require complex elaborate control and co-ordination procedures. However, unlike early studies, our study shows that interdependent jobs can be performed remotely, but require different supports. The particular supports depend on the analysis of interdependence.

By adding work networks and the flow of resources we expand our understanding of the context. The major finding of this study is that work relationships determine how people telework and are a central part of how they communicate remotely. Our study makes its contribution in this realm. Understanding the relationship between the group and the choice of media is an important goal, but one that needs more precision. Communications theorists assert that the group's influence on choice of media lies in group attitudes and values.

We depart from this path and instead look at typical networks that people construct for their jobs. Some are given to them, others are fashioned for the job. They all vary in composition, complexity and stability. To understand how those in a position to choose their media decide, we have to locate the major network players and analyse their specific relationships to the teleworker. Since each set of players is supported by different communication media and styles, the resulting work networks will have distinct communication patterns. Patterns like these must be understood.

Thus, teleworking firms need to analyse the work process and work networks of their employees if they want to determine what we call the teleworking potential of the job (Salaff *et al.* 1996). They need to develop predictive tools rooted in the real work context to anticipate strengths and weaknesses of the job as it becomes a teleworking job and to support productive and efficient teleworking experiences.

Acknowledgements

The theme of telework as social innovation draws on our wider project on corporate telework and virtual organisation. Although we cannot name the firm that we researched, we are most grateful to those employees that shared their time and experiences with us. We wish to thank the funding organisations, ITRC through the Ontario Telepresence project, SSIIRCC (Canada) and Bell Ontario Research Grant to Ontario Universities. For their collegial help in this chapter, we wish especially to thank Barry Wellman for exchanges of ideas and bibliography, Milena Gulia for her conceptual input, and Suzanne Brandreth for organisational back-up.

References

Axelsson, B. and Easton, G. (eds) (1992) *Industrial Networks. A New View of Reality*, London: Routledge.

Daft, R., Lengel, R. and Trevino, L.(1987) 'Message Equivocality, Media Selection and

Manager Performance: Implications for Information Systems', *MIS Quarterly*, September: 355–66.

Fritz, M.E., Watson, K.H. and Sridhar N. (1994) 'Telework: Exploring the Borderless Office', in J.F. Nunamaker and R.H. Sprague, jun. (eds) *Proceedings of the 27th Annual Hawaii International Conference on System Sciences* IV, Washington, DC: IEEE Press: 149–59.

Fulk, J., Schmitz, J. and Steinfield, C. (1990), 'A Social Influence Model of Technology Use,' in J. Fulk, and C. Steinfield (eds) *Organizations and Communication Technology*, California: Sage Publications: 117–40.

Garton, L. and Wellman, B. (1995) 'Social Impacts of Electronic Mail in Organizations: A review of the Research Literature', *Communication Yearbook* 18: 434–53.

Haythornthwaite, C. and Wellman, B. (1996) 'What Kinds of Network Members Communicate by Email or Face-to-Face for What Kinds of Work?', Presented at the 'Annual Meeting, American Sociological Association', New York, August.

Haythornthwaite, C., Wellman, B. and Mantei, M. (1995) 'Work Relationships and Media Use: A Social Network Analysis', *Group Decision and Negotiation* 4: 193–211.

Latour, B. (1987) *Science in Action*, Cambridge, Mass.: Harvard University Press.

——(1991) 'Technology is Society Made Durable', in J. Law (ed.) *Sociology of Monsters*, London: Routledge, 103–31.

Lea, M., O'Shea, T. and Fung, P. (1995) 'Constructing the Networked Organisation: Content and Context in the Development of Electronic Communication', *Organisation Science* 6: 462–78.

Li, Feng (1996) 'Team-Telework as an Organisational Innovation: A Theoretical Perspective', in P.J. Jackson and J. van der Wielen (eds) Proceedings of the Workshop *New International Perspectives on Telework: From Telecommuting to the Virtual Organisation*, London, 31 July–2 August, Tilburg, The Netherlands: Tilburg University Press: 231–45.

Lowry, T. (1996) *Alternative Work Arrangements: The Effects of Distance and Media Use on the Supervisor–Subordinate Relationship (Telecommuting)*, unpublished Ph.D. dissertation.

Olson, M. (1982) 'Information technology and Organisational Culture', *MIS Quarterly*, Special Issue: 71–92.

——(1983) 'Remote Office Work: Changing Work Patterns in Space and Time', *Communications of the ACM*, 26,3 March: 182–7.

Perrow, C. (1970). *Organizational Analysis: A Sociological View*, Belmont, Ca.: Wadsworth.

Salaff, J. and Dimitrova, D. (1996) 'Telework as Work: Negotiating Uncertainty in Distance Work', in P.J. Jackson and J. van der Wielen (eds) Proceedings of the Workshop *New International Perspectives on Telework: From Telecommuting to the Virtual Organisation*, London, 31 July–2 August, Tilburg, The Netherlands: Tilburg University Press: 417–34.

Salaff, J., Dimitrova, D. and Hardwick, D. (1996) 'Bureaucratic Telework: Hot and Cool Jobs,' in *Notiziario del Lavoro* XIV, 81, November, Telecom Italia: 46–51.

Salaff, J.W., Dimitrova, D., Hardwick, D., Hoski, K., Mar, H. and Wellman, B. (1996) *Teleworking Potential: Evaluating Corporate Jobs*, Centre for Urban and Community Studies, University of Toronto Teleworking Project, December.

Scott, R.W. (1992) *Organizations. Rational, Natural and Open Systems*, 3rd edn, Englewood Cliffs, NJ: Prentice-Hall.

Trevino, L., Daft, R. and Lengel, R. (1990) 'Understanding Managers' Media Choices: A Symbolic Interactionist Perspective', in J. Fulk and C. Steinfield (eds) *Organizations and Communication Technology*, Newbury Park: Sage Publications: 71–94.

Wellman, B. (1997) 'An Electronic Group is Virtually a Social Network', in S. Kiesler (ed.) *Culture of the Internet*, Hillsdale, NJ: Lawrence Erlbaum.

17

EVOLUTION OF THE TELECOMMUTING WITHDRAWAL MODEL

A US perspective

Steven Fireman

Introduction

In this chapter telecommuting is defined as the phenomenon of core organisational employees regularly working off-site for at least part of their normal work hours. Withdrawal is the voluntary stopping or cutting back of the time committed to telecommuting. The Telecommuting Withdrawal Model (TWM), (Fireman 1996) is the result of a search for key variables that influence the individual to suspend telecommuting in an organisational context.

Withdrawal is a critical issue because telecommuting in the US is promoted as a management practice which can reduce cost and increase output. Annual net benefits of $8,000 per telecommuter have been realised by large employers after covering sizable investments in start-up, training and evaluation (Nilles 1994: 145). Therefore, employees withdrawing from telecommuting before recurring gains can be realised or investments recovered are lost opportunities for the organisation.

The enduring goal of TWM is to better understand and predict why employees choose to stop or cut back their telecommuting. Accordingly, the TWM is the result of a process to isolate and develop a parsimonious model that would be applicable across countries. However, one would expect the model to play out differently within varying political, social and cultural milieus. In this chapter I will briefly review the current TWM, how my personal experiences and involvement with the Puget Sound Telecommuting Demonstration (PSTD), (Ulberg, *et al.* 1992) influenced the development of the TWM, current trends in management policy and strategy, a proposed target for testing and potential international applications. In addition, throughout this chapter a recurring focus will be the conditions under which the independent variables of TWM may come into play.

The latest TWM

The original TWM (Fireman 1996) has been streamlined to three independent variables influencing the dependent variable of Withdrawal (see Figure 17.1). The first independent variable, Community, is concerned with affect for office social interactions (Christensen 1988, 1989; Connelly 1995; Ramsower 1985). An employee's desire for the social interactions in the office environment need not centre around friendship ties. Liking co-workers may make the office appealing to some, while others may derive part of their identity from the position they have in the office, and so on. Community can be related to a variety of social facilitation cues (presence or actions of others in a particular context influencing the target person's behaviour) that may be missed over time (Daft and Lengel 1984; Ferris and Mitchell 1987). For example, one might miss a general sense of importance from just being in proximity to others or one might miss the stimulation of direct or vicarious involvement in office rivalries.

Compulsion is the second independent variable and is the employee's belief that personal reasons outside of work make telecommuting a necessity. For instance, this belief may stem from having to take care of children or other dependents. Unusually long or arduous commute trips may also make an employee consider telecommuting a necessity.

Finally, the third independent variable, Comfort, is the individual's overall perception of the support for telecommuting by management. How does the boss and other important organisation players really feel about employees being away from the office? Is the organisation's or relevant sub-group's climate friendly to out-of-sight workers? Criticality, a sub-dimension of Comfort, looks at how telecommuting may create or aggravate role conflicts based on the role(s) played by the telecommuter in the office. For example, the supervisor and co-workers may depend on the telecommuter for certain knowledge/expertise or the telecommuter's problem-solving ability is relied upon for repeated problems or major crises. Comfort's other sub-dimension is concerned with support for telecommuting at several levels of management as well as organisational control norms concerned with being visible and accessible. For example, do the telecommuter's absences from the office raise the supervisor's nervousness quotient – causing distress in the supervisor?

As defined, Community will encourage Withdrawal from telecommuting; high Compulsion and high Comfort will discourage Withdrawal. Community, the

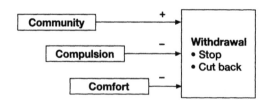

Figure 17.1 The Telecommuting Withdrawal Model

intensity of the desire for office social interactions, is most distinct from the others and can only be reliably evoked after experience with telecommuting. The likely explanation, using the concept of strain being caused by poor person-environment fit, is that strain builds up when telecommuting reduces the supply of opportunity for Community. This reduced opportunity for Community can no longer meet the telecommuter's present demand for Community, and strain results. Compulsion is concerned with constraints stemming from *personal* non-work sources, whereas Comfort assesses the *organisational* environment's support or lack of support for telecommuting.

Experiences of an early adopter

In the mid-1970s, as a fresh MBA, many of my technology-literate associates and I found ourselves highly sought after by computer timesharing companies to help them develop strong relationships with higher-level management decision-makers in major corporations and public organisations. At the time, the role of consultant/account executive required consultative sales skills as well as a solid understanding of specific business problems and how the creative use of existing information technology could effectively solve these problems. The company leased computer terminals and paid for a dedicated phone line for all employees in their homes. We were encouraged to work remotely (portable terminals were available for travel) whenever it made sense to us.

Co-operation and mutual learning abounded. The weekly office business meeting occurred in the early morning over breakfast. Compared to typical experiences in other organisations, the trust and respect we felt for each other seemed to create an almost utopian work environment. However, the company may have been encouraged to implement these humanistic management practices that created an invigorating ambience because productivity could be precisely monitored. The revenue growth of each existing account and the number of new accounts were omnipresent for management review and mutually determined targets were all that were needed to spur performance.

Clearly my early telework amounted to a perquisite ('perk' in US vernacular) for an elite employee. Even when working remotely at odd hours of the night, one didn't feel like the company was abusive, because the job entailed long hours when necessary. My own positive experiences with self-regulated telecommuting were the result of sufficient opportunity for Community combined with high Comfort and an absence of Compulsion.

Intermittent remote work primarily at the discretion of the employee is probably still the hallmark of telework as a perquisite. However, the interest in telework by US companies today is generally focused on achieving a competitive advantage or meeting current or anticipated legal requirements (e.g. environmental protection – requiring reduced automobile commuter trips). Therefore, *regularly scheduled telework* for a wider variety of employees has been the target of several US studies. Before reviewing the Puget Sound Telecommuting

Demonstration's (PSTD) specific influence on the development of TWM, some American peculiarities are highlighted.

An American bias

Clearly the TWM has been influenced by an admitted North American ethno-centrism. First, my review of 'international' literature on telework has been limited to the English language. Although I have adopted the use of telecommuting and telework as equivalent terms, the etymology of these words do identify elements of distinct national tendencies.

Several European languages do not have a word for 'commuting'. On the other hand, people in the United States are obsessed with traffic congestion, particularly as it makes getting to or from work difficult and unpleasant. In fact much of the impetus and money for studying telecommuting is an offshoot of an American fixation that living in the suburbs or the countryside is better or safer than more urban alternatives. Exploring various means to effectively deal with transportation problems in metropolitan and suburban areas has been the driving force behind the current American experiments in telework.

The Puget Sound Telecommuting Demonstration

The Puget Sound Telecommuting Demonstration (PSTD) (Ulberg *et al.* 1992), was funded primarily to look at potential impacts on traffic patterns and energy usage as a supplement to the State of Washington's Growth Management Act (GMA). GMA was enacted in response to explosive population growth in western Washington State. Up until the time of PSTD, American studies of any significant size were confined to public (governmental) entities. However, to attract private organisations and ensure their participation, PSTD needed to be responsive to these private organisations' concerns. It became evident that productivity was the 'hot button' in the private sector. Interviews with managers of telecommuters revealed that for the most part very few of the companies measured individual productivity (as an economic ratio) for the type of workers allowed to telecommute. There was one instance where a supervisor attributed telecommuting as enabling an employee to achieve more of the goals set as part of the employee's performance appraisal process. However, while believing that telecommuting increased productivity, most supervisors were unable to enumerate concrete indicators of increased productivity.

An analysis of 1,200 random US household interviews, in a non-PSTD survey, revealed that telecommuting growth was strongly associated with occupations involving organisational information work (Miller 1996). This trend coincides with the projections that more and more of the workforce will be characterised as 'knowledge workers', much of whose work product will consist primarily of intangibles (Zuboff 1988). For instance, members of a software design team contribute to the development of a product or service through their abilities which are primarily knowledge based. Their contributions are not easily measured and are therefore labeled 'intangible'. This is consistent with the view that the true assets of post-industrial companies are not the physical ones (e.g. plant and equipment), but the knowledge resources that are tied to the individual workers and work teams.

The PSTD productivity interviews also confirmed that productivity, if measured, was for aggregate units (e.g. group, division, company, department) while individuals were most often evaluated by formal annual performance appraisals (PA). Organisations seemed to change their PA systems every three to five years, sometimes adopting the most current direction in PA effectiveness and sometimes reversing it. The tacit assumption seemed to be that change regardless of direction was thought to rekindle the drive for individual performance in the absence of hard individual measures.

Many authors of 'how to' books and articles (Hamilton 1987; Nilles 1994) suggest that managers of telecommuters may benefit from switching from an observational to an output-oriented evaluation mode (e.g. deliverables, milestones, etc.). For knowledge workers, engaged in problem-solving and other creative duties, this may be easier said than done. Furthermore, many managers may be disinclined to change their own ingrained behaviours. The literature reveals widespread concern about an instinctive (unconscious) or conscious 'out-of-sight, out-of-mind' mentality which may result in negative attributions about an employee's contributions to the workgroup or organisation. For example, a large financial services company found that within a few months of encouraging telecommuting for employees who performed most of their work on the phone or computer, 'almost everyone abandoned telecommuting or cut it back to one day a week . . . People perceived their loss of face-time at work was not helping their careers' (Connelly 1995: 222).

However, the employee's perceived lack of Comfort with telework may not always be credited as the actual reason for Withdrawal. In PSTD, 33 per cent of the teleworkers dropped out over the course of a year, only 46 per cent 'were able to telecommute at least once a week without having to cut back during the year', and 9 per cent of the teleworkers completing the final survey indicated they would be discontinuing telework (Ulberg et al. 1992: 38, 47, 56). Among the PSTD Withdrawers, 'conditions at work' (e.g. rush project, new job responsibilities, understaffing) were most often cited as the cause. Inasmuch as the organisations were officially encouraging telework and the teleworkers were interested volunteers, the attribution of Withdrawal to external forces (job change, special project, etc.) may have been less awkward than admitting that the office climate did not seem to genuinely support remote work (a shortage of Comfort) or that the teleworker missed the office environment permeating the work day (Community).

Furthermore, it should be noted that all of the jobs of the telecommuters in PSTD had sufficient activities that could be accomplished on the days scheduled for telework. This indicates that despite the existence of activities that could potentially benefit from fewer interruptions, and so on, adjusting to telework may be unsettling. This is not surprising when one considers that, on average, office workers spend about 65 per cent of their time in interpersonal communication of which 32 per cent is face to face and the majority of this is with the immediate work group (Bair 1987: 187). Understandably, some employees ill at ease with the voluntary telework trial arrangements they initiated, would be reluctant to admit that they missed the office more than they thought (Community) or that they were afraid that their reduced visibility made them seem less important (reduced Comfort). Thus, indicating that one's telework arrangement failed because of an uncontrollable externality may have been a way to save face in some cases.

In the productivity interviews and focus group discussions that were part of the PSTD (Ulberg *et al.* 1992), the most commonly mentioned reason for terminating or reducing telecommuting among employees insisting that they believed in the value of telecommuting and expressing the desire to telecommute, was a rush project, new job responsibilities or a need to solve problems on-site. However, these work-related exigencies may have also been used as a convenient rationale for telecommuting withdrawal by employees concerned about how their 'absence' was being viewed (whether it was antithetical to perceived organisational cultural norms of achievement or success). The model (TWM) is particularly concerned with the teleworker's perceptions of the extent to which his/her supervisor/managers are comfortable with his/her remote work. Therefore, it would be appropriate to investigate whether some of the control norm tendencies ascribed to managers are in fact commonplace.

Managerial control norms

Managerial uneasiness with telecommuting is closely tied to fear of loss of control, which is most common among top decision-makers when considering telecommuting for clerical jobs (Tomaskovic-Devey and Risman 1993). Control generally does not worry top management when it is an option for professionals who make up a small percentage of the organisation. However, when professionals make up a larger share of the workforce of an organisation, as may be expected as the information/knowledge revolution progresses, top decision-makers are not as comfortable with telecommuting for professionals (Tomaskovic-Devey and Risman 1993). Clearly top management's fear of loss of control may permeate all levels of the organisation. Furthermore, when no indisputable metrics of productivity or simple means of monitoring performance exist at the individual level, employees may be justly concerned that being away from the office may negatively affect outcomes such as rewards and promotions. This is consistent with prevalent management philosophy since the beginning of industrialisation, where the possibility of being observed is the prominent control strategy (Perin 1991).

Mere toleration of telecommuting by managers as opposed to real support may be more prevalent than reported in pilot studies and demonstrations that are being promoted by organisation policy-makers (perhaps in response to the threat of government mandates). Indicative of this possibility is the fact that, on the whole, American surveys show that the majority of managers expressed the need to have direct interaction in the office with employees in order to assure work effectiveness, while only a small number of managers are actually in favour of telecommuting (Huws *et al.* 1990). Furthermore, the US is not alone in that traditional management style, organisational culture and institutional inertia continue to be major social forces that represent barriers to the utilisation of telework in both the US and Europe (Qvortrup 1992).

This view of telecommuting as a possible threat to management control was exhibited in the recruitment of organisations for the PSTD.

> At the extreme, some candidate organisations (more private than public) were so concerned about the implications of this change in the nature of work and supervision that they opted not to participate in the study. Thus, for some organisations, telecommuting via this project became the first attempt to experiment with long-standing supervisory styles.
>
> (Ulberg *et al.* 1992: 19)

Comfort utilises the social information processing model as its footing (Salancik and Pfeffer 1978; Zalesny and Ford 1990). Employees are likely to adopt attitudes and behaviours in response to social cues. Social cues from superiors are more likely to influence the perceptions of core employees who believe that continued success in the organisation depends on meeting superiors' expectations of commitment and persistence. Thus, being busy in the office when the boss happens by is an important social cue that the ambitious employee may want to provide for the boss.

The strength of this entrenched managerial perspective is part of the reason that the second independent variable of TWM is given the forceful label of Compulsion. While Compulsion stems from personal situations that necessitate telecommuting, psychologically telecommuters may feel that they have to be especially grateful to the people allowing them to telecommute and may even feel that they have to accept less favourable treatment because of the special consideration they are receiving. Rodgers (1992) found that there is a great demand for flexibility in the workforce among white-collar and service employees of large corporations. However, the employees' consistent message was '[that their] company does not acknowledge – in the way [they] are managed or evaluated – that anything exists for [them] but work. [They] need flexibility to be successful' (Rodgers 1992: 183). Thus, for some, the privilege of telecommuting will generate a strong sense of obligation to the enabling parties. This sense of obligation may account for some telecommuters working more hours at home than the 'missed' hours at the office as an implicit element of the exchange relationship.

Personal situation as weakness

The variable Compulsion pertains to the employee's *belief* in the power (ability to dominate) that the supervisor or organisation holds over him or her, because of a need to telecommute. To the extent that the employee regards telecommuting as essential to continue working (often for strong personal reasons external to the office) and that finding another job with telecommuting would be difficult or impossible, the employee's belief in being somewhat of a captive employee will discourage Withdrawal.

Leidner's (1988) characterisation of two extremes of employer-run homework programmes is helpful in focusing on the discriminating ingredients that relate to the underlying power dimension of the Compulsion variable. Those who epitomise lack of Compulsion are employees with bargaining power and reasonable alternatives who possess valued skills and proven loyalty. Moreover, the employer views homework as a voluntary career option for work that is primarily professional/technical or managerial in nature. In contrast, those who epitomise Compulsion are employees without bargaining power, few or no alternative work opportunities, who have primary child-care responsibility or are (illegal) immigrants. For these workers the employer's rationale is to cut costs for work that is largely clerical in nature.

Given the perception of no options, the supervisor may be credited as having more power because in power relationships, power is often seen as being possessed by the dominant party (Emerson 1964): 'Bargaining strength [or] power in social exchange relationships may be broadly defined as the inverse of dependence' (Bazerman *et al.* 1990: 27). Shellenbarger (1992) points out that many companies try to project an image of being family friendly, without substantive policies. Among the few who have adopted substantively new work–family policies and programmes, most have 'primarily benefited skilled professionals or a few categories of hourly workers whose skills are in short supply such as nurses' (Shellenbarger 1992: 157).

Initial target population

Given the organisational focus of TWM and the upward trend of employees engaging in knowledge work, initial testing of the model (TWM) will focus on knowledge work occupations that have historically been well suited to their work environments. The Theory of Work Adjustment (TWA), (Dawis and Lofquist 1984), concerned with long tenure in occupations, focuses on the *habitual interaction of the individual and a work environment.* TWA's basic tenet is that each must meet a minimum level of the other's requirements. The individual's satisfaction will be affected by the customary stock of work environment conditions that tend to reinforce the individual's chief values. Based on an individual interests instrument, Occupational Reinforcer Patterns (ORPs) have been established for 90 occupations.

Programmers (business, engineering and science) and technical publication writers have the highest correspondence index (degree of fit) with their predominant ORP (Dawis and Lofquist 1984: 221). Their ORP consists of high achievement (ACH), high status (STA) and moderate comfort (COM) which conveniently stresses a self, a social and an environmental reinforcer, respectively. Fortunately, these are the very type of jobs that are often identified as being most compatible with telework. Therefore the Telecommuting Withdrawal Model (TWM) will be tested on organisations that have significant numbers of information workers that are programmers, technical writers or in similarly related occupations (e.g. systems analysts, technical designers, and so on). Limiting the occupations to ones with the highest satisfaction with the ORP dominant for that occupation, may also allow the elimination of some of the control variables that would be necessary with a more diverse cross-section of telecommutable occupations as in PSTD.

The primary control variables would be the extent to which the employee is evaluated on specific output measures and the level of potential monitoring available to the supervisor. The TWM model should also be tested in other countries, in which case, country would be the fourth major control variable.

International implications

In the PSTD, we 'found that the differences among workgroups within the same organisation are often as important as the differences between organisations' (Ulberg et al. 1992: 18). Therefore, the TWM's focus on the individual in the workgroup may be most appropriate for understanding adaptation to telecommuting in specific organisational contexts that may transcend national and cultural differences.

However, national cultural norms supporting flexibility in the workplace do vary considerably. Nations also vary in the degree to which labour laws protect workers and support families. Does evolving telework need supportive social norms and/or legal protection of the workers? If the work itself is not inherently rewarding, one could imagine the situation where mandatory telecommuting accompanied by electronic monitoring or output requirements would have a particularly dire Orwellian tone.

How telework flourishes amid differing levels of support may eventually be moot, if the pressures of the increasingly global economy result in the dismantling of governmental safety nets and worker protection (labour regulations) in many Western countries and thwart the development of these policies in developing countries. However, enlightened management would be well advised to understand how environment- and people-friendly policies such as telework have the potential to truly benefit the organisation, the workers and society.

References

Bair, J. H. (1987) 'User needs for office system solutions', in R.E. Kraut (ed.) *Technology and the Transformation of White-Collar Work*, Hillsdale, NJ: Erlbaum: 177–94.

Bazerman, M.H., Mannix, E., Sondak, H. and Thompson, L. (1990) 'Negotiator behavior and decision processes in dyads, groups, and markets', in J.S. Carroll (ed.) *Applied Social Psychology and Organizational Setting*, Hillsdale, NJ: Erlbaum: 13–44.

Christensen, K. (1988) *Women and Home-based Work*, New York: Holt.

—— (1989) 'Home-based clerical work: No simple truth, no single reality', in E. Boris and C.R. Daniels (eds) *Homework: Historical and Contemporary Perspectives on Paid Labor at Home*, Urbana, IL: University of Illinois Press: 183–197.

Connelly, J. (1995) 'Let's hear it for the office', *Fortune* 131: 221–2.

Daft, R.L. and Lengel, R.H. (1984) 'Information richness: A new approach to managerial behavior and organizational design', in B. Staw and L. L. Cummings (eds) *Research in Oganizational Behavior* 6, Greenwich, CT: JAI Press: 191–233.

Dawis, R.V. and Lofquist, L.H. (1984) *A Psychological Theory of Work Adjustment: An Individual-Differences Model and Its Applications*, Minneapolis, MN: University of Minnesota Press.

Emerson, R.M. (1964) 'Power-dependence relations: Two experiments', *Sociometry* 27: 282–98.

Ferris, G.R. and Mitchell, T.R. (1987) 'The components of social influence and their importance for human resources research', in K.M. Rowland and G.R. Ferris (eds) *Research in Personnel and Human Resources Management*, 5: Greenwich, CT: JAI Press: 103–28.

Fireman, S.M. (1996) 'A proposed model for telecommuting withdrawal', in P.J. Jackson and J.M.M. van der Wielen (eds) Proceedings of the Workshop *New International Perspectives on Telework: From Telecommuting to the Virtual Organisation*, WORC (Work and Organisation Research Center) Tilburg, NL: 136–152.

Hamilton, C.A. (1987) 'Telecommuting', *Personnel Journal* 66: 91–101.

Huws, U., Korte, W.B. and Robinson, S. (1990) *Telework: Toward the Elusive Office*, Chichester, UK: Wiley and Sons.

Leidner, R. (1988) 'Home work: A study in the interaction of work and family organization', in *Research in the Sociology of Work*, 4: 69–94. Greenwich, CT: JAI Press.

Miller, T.E. (1996) '1995 Telecommuting fact sheet', *FIND/SVP's Telecommuting Data*, 21 March 1996. Available: http://etrg.findsvp.com/telework/teleindx.html

Nilles, J.M. (1994) *Making Telecommuting Happen*, New York: Van Nostrand Reinhold.

Perin, C. (1991) 'The moral fabric of the office: Panopticon discourse and schedule flexibilities', in *Research in the Sociology of Organizations* 8: 241–68, Greenwich, CT: JAI Press.

Qvortrup, L. (1992) 'Telework: Visions, definitions, realities, barriers', in *Cities and New Technologies*: 77–108. Paris: OECD (Organisation for Economic Co-operation and Development).

Ramsower, R.M. (1985) *Telecommuting: The Organizational and Behavioral Effects of Working at Home*, Ann Arbor, MI: UMI Research Press.

Rodgers, C.S. (1992) 'The flexible workplace: What have we learned?', *Human Resource Management* 31, 3: 183–99.

Salancik, G.R. and Pfeffer, J. (1978) 'A social information processing approach to job attitudes and task design', *Administrative Science Quarterly* 23: 224–53.

Shellenbarger, S. (1992), 'Lessons from the workplace: How corporate policies and attitudes lag behind workers' changing needs', *Human Resource Management* 31, 3: 157–69.

Tomaskovic-Devey, D. and Risman, B.J. (1993) 'Telecommuting innovation and organization: A contingency theory of labor process change', *Social Science Quarterly* 74: 367–
85.

Ulberg, C., Gordon, A., Spain, D., Fortenbery, L., Whitaker, B. and Fireman, S. (1992)
Evaluation of the Puget Sound Telecommuting Demonstration, Seattle, WA: TRAC (Washington
State Transportation Center).

Zalesny, M.D. and Ford, K.J. (1990) 'Extending the social information processing perspective: New links to attitudes, behaviors, and perceptions', *Organizational Behavior and
Human Decision Processes* 47: 205–46.

Zuboff, S. (1988) *In the Age of the Smart Machine*, New York: Basic Books.

18

A SOCIAL INNOVATION IN ITS INFANCY

Experiences with telework centres

Georg Aichholzer

Centre-based teleworking as a social innovation

There is a strange division between assessments of teleworking as a new phenomenon in the world of work: some people regard working at a distance, supported by telecommunications and computer equipment as nothing different from using these means of work within a traditional office or see it as just one element of continuous change without major significance; others, however, stressing mainly the newness of locational independence, call it an innovation with far-reaching implications for the historical evolution of work. Obviously remote working builds on the results of *technological* innovation in information and communication technology. But does teleworking itself represent a genuine innovation and, if so, does this hold true for all forms?

A look into the literature on innovations leads us to William F. Ogburn's distinction between 'material and *social* inventions'. He lists 50 exemplary social inventions containing such diverse items as an auto-tourist camp, a correspondence school, group insurance, the Ku-Klux-Klan, and the 'visiting teacher' (Ogburn 1983: 162). While he sees mechanical inventions as causal factors and the role of social inventions as being able to reduce the 'cultural lag', there is no such hierarchical conception of innovations in Schumpeter's innovation theory (1939). New products as well as new production processes, and new market organisations as well as new marketing procedures are all conceived as innovations under one dominant goal dimension, which is economic profit. A systematic account of the present approaches to an understanding of social innovations is provided by Zapf (1989: 174). He distinguishes the following seven conceptions of *social innovations*:

- organisational changes in enterprises
- new services (e.g. in planning, design, training, therapy, etc.)

- social technologies (e.g. participation)
- self-generated social inventions (e.g. in development projects)
- political innovations (e.g. non-proliferation treaty)
- new patterns of needs satisfaction (e.g. self-service)
- new life-styles (e.g. new consumer behaviour).

A partially overlapping classification offered by Brooks (1982) differentiates between 'technical', 'sociotechnical' (combinations) and 'social innovations' as the main types. 'Market innovations' (e.g. leasing), 'management innovations' and 'institutional innovations' are all regarded as variants of 'social innovations'.

Against this background teleworking can be qualified as a social (sociotechnical) innovation on several grounds, representing:

1   a form of *organisational change*, eventually including a particular process innovation (from work organised in traditional offices established/provided by the employer to an organisation including work from remote locations);
2   a *new pattern of needs satisfaction* (teleworking reflects needs/preferences concerning work location, choice of social contacts to co-workers, clients, family members, friends and other non-work contacts); and
3   a *new lifestyle* (teleworking may offer opportunities for autonomous and flexible co-ordination of work and private life as well as use of time, with associated status gains).

Basically, these characteristics apply to all forms of teleworking in one way or another. However, one of the generic categories adds a particular innovation aspect: a variety of new institutions have been created which are comprised under a common term, so-called *telework centres*. They provide facilities and telematics equipment which are shared by clients to enable teleworking. What is unique with centre-based teleworking, as will be illustrated later, is that it is built on *institutional innovations* (not just on traditional institutions like market, firm or household).

One could ask what makes these innovations significant enough to deserve to be called 'social innovations'. The following conclusion drawn by Zapf adds a decisive element which can serve as a reference and yardstick for this purpose:

> Social innovations are new ways to achieve goals, in particular new forms of organisation, new regulations, new life styles which shape the direction of social change, solve problems better than previous practices and which therefore are worth being imitated and institutionalised.
>
> (Zapf 1989: 177, in German)

The decisive criterion which allows us to speak of (centre-based) teleworking as a social innovation then, is the aspect of institutionalisation and imitation. In other words, the question is to what extent have such models of new work arrangements and practices been implemented and diffused? Some evidence on this will be presented in the following.

The role of telework centres in the evolution of new spatial arrangements of work

Three generic forms of *teleworking* can be distinguished: *home-based*, *centre-based* and *mobile*. They have become the core of a widely shared classification (cf. ILO 1990: 3–4; Gray *et al.* 1993: 9–25; Gillespie *et al.* 1995; Birchall and Lyons 1995: 108). Within each of them a number of sub-types have emerged (see Table 18.1). Alternating telework (partial home-based working) is the dominant form both in Europe and the US and also has the largest future potential according to European survey results (Korte and Wynne 1996: 38). Centres which are dedicated to house teleworkers still play a much less important role in quantitative terms. Nevertheless the category of centre-based teleworking represents an umbrella for a variety of collective organisational forms and has been seen as an alternative to 'electronic homeworking' since the early days of the telework discussion, at least in Europe.

Telework centres are generally expected to offer specific advantages which teleworking in the form of individual homeworking does not, or does to a lesser degree. For the teleworker it is mainly the opportunity to have social and vocational contacts together with professional support at the workplace, to separate work and the private sphere and to enjoy higher workplace quality in technical terms. Seen from the employer's perspective, above all higher resource efficiency, support efficiency, management and supervision, support and advantages concerning customer reception are the pros. For the local and regional society a centre offers better chances to profit from the diffusion of new technology, innovative working methods and business strategies. Furthermore the visibility of a business unit is more likely to attract additional service businesses. On the other hand there are also real or perceived costs and certain disadvantages as compared to individual teleworking arrangements, such as the remaining work travel, the need to co-ordinate resource sharing, greater demands concerning data security and less privacy.

The present discussion is complicated by a multitude of concepts used in a non-uniform way. Already centre-based telework as a generic term is addressed under different names, such as 'telecommuting centre' (Eldib and Minoli 1995: 107; Nilles 1988), 'remote work facility', 'telebusiness centre', 'shared-facility centre' or, in abridged form, 'telecentre' (Bagley *et al.* 1994: 2–7; Gray *et al.* 1993: 11). This terminology is mainly used in the US whereas in Europe the term 'telecentre' or 'telecottage' describes a specific variant which typically has allowed for additional regional development or community-related functions rather than just housing teleworkers (it is also known under names like 'community- or multi-service telecentre', 'electronic cottage' and, in an urban milieu, 'electronic village hall'). Therefore the term 'telework centre' as a common umbrella for centre-based teleworking is less ambiguous. Table 18.1 gives an overview of teleworking options and puts the various forms of telework centres in a wider context.

Centre-based models of teleworking can be *single- or multi-employer units*. The 'satellite office' is usually characterised as being set up and run by a parent company, as a rule in the form of a proprietary unit, housing only its own tele-commuting staff. A number of companies in Europe as well as in the US have established and successfully operated satellite offices, such as Groupe PBS Telergos in France, and Crédit Suisse in Switzerland (ILO 1990; Duerrenberger *et al.* 1994; Bagley *et al.* 1994). A special variant of this model is the '*offshore* satellite office' such as the Travelers software centre in Ireland which is wholly owned by its parent company in Hartford, US (Brain and Page 1991: 74). Similar facilities have been established by overseas companies in other low-wage regions, espe-cially in the Caribbean area, India and the Philippines, sometimes promoted by a deliberate government policy – as in Barbados – in order to attract work from higher-wage economies (Birchall and Lyons 1995: 104). India especially has become a major place for outsourcing software engineering and back-office work, for instance, for airlines like SWISSAIR and Austrian Airlines, via telework.

The 'neighbourhood office', on the other hand, is the dominant model of a multi-employer teleworking facility, run by a third party. It offers office space and advanced communication facilities to be shared by teleworkers from different employers, allowing them to work in or near residential areas. Size and proximity to the teleworkers' homes vary from small local units to larger regional centres (more about this model in the next section). Most other variants of telework centres also tend to be organised as multi-employer facilities but differ from the neighbourhood office model in other respects. The rural 'telecentre' or 'telecot-tage', for instance, as well as its more recent urban twin are oriented towards offering teleworking opportunities as a major function within a set of regional development goals based on the use of telematics. Nine years after the first tele-cottages had been established in Sweden and Denmark in 1985, a world-wide

Table 18.1 Variants of centre-based teleworking in the context of other telework categories

Home based	Centre-based	Mobile / multiple sites
Tele-homework	Neighbourhood office	Working on travel
Alternating telework	Satellite office	Office train
	Offshore facility	Non-territorial office
	Telecottage	Temporary (floating,
	Electronic village hall	unassigned) office
	Business exchange	Shared office space
	Executive office suite	Hot-desking
	Resort office	Hoteling
	Creative office	Virtual office
	Call-centre	

survey on 'community teleservice centres' already counted 237 workers (Qvortrup 1995). The UK especially shows a high growth rate: according to the British Telecottage Association there are already more than one hundred tele-cottages in the UK and Ireland alone (Bertin and Denbigh 1996).

'Executive office suites' are upscale 'cousins' of neighbourhood offices accord-ing to Bagley *et al.* (1994: section 3, 30) and tend to be located on prime com-mercial estate. A hybrid variant is trademarked under the name 'Comm centre' in the US. The 'resort office', first introduced in Japan, has now also found followers in Europe, with facilities on Crete and Majorca. Located in a resort area, the function is mainly in use for short periods or occasionally during holi-days in cases when a continuous contact with the primary office, supported by special facilities is required (cf. Holloway 1994: 5–7, 26–28; Spinks 1991: 350). 'Call centres' are a special variant dedicated to a variety of teleservices like tele-marketing. Because of their work characteristics and larger size (around 100 teleworkers) they resemble 'customer service factories' (Richardson 1996).

All these variants are constituted by factors like special type of career, type of users, functional profile and location and most of them represent new insti-tutional models. It is worth taking account of the conceptual evolution of tele-working and to mention also the 'virtual office' concept as an expression of 'networked teleworking'. It stands for new work arrangements and forms of co-operation based on telematics which do not presuppose fixed locations, central premises and stable organisational structures but which tend to be project bound. The notion of the 'elusive office' as coined in a prominent book title (Huws *et al.* 1990) accentuates this aspect of teleworking. It also includes forms of networked co-operation enabled by telematics called *teleco-operation* as well as group or team telework (Gillespie *et al.* 1995: 15; Commission of the European Communities 1994: 9).

The spread of neighbourhood offices in Europe and world-wide

One of the earliest institutional work arrangements which was invented to enable working for a distant employer from one's residential area is the neighbourhood office. However, while quantitative information on the spread of home-based teleworking is increasingly available, there is no exact evidence available on the number of existing neighbourhood offices. What is clear is that the majority of telematics-oriented projects established have been telecottages rather than neigh-bourhood offices in the more narrow sense. Nevertheless, recent studies under-taken by Bagley *et al.* (1994) and Becker *et al.* (1993), together with a number of other sources (Murphy 1996; Pekkola 1993; ILO 1990) including personal communication with project managers, provide a lot of empirical examples.

The history of neighbourhood offices started with the opening of pioneering projects in Maine-la-Vale, France (1981) and Nykvarn, Sweden (1982), followed by similar centres in Benglen, Switzerland (1985) and a second Swedish facility.

The first known neighbourhood office outside Europe was established consider-ably later by the State of Hawaii in the US (1989). From the beginning of the 1990s, an increasing upswing of projects can be observed, especially in the US but also in Europe. In some countries such as Switzerland, Denmark and Fin-land, neighbourhood offices or its variants have been stimulated by national ini-tiatives (cf. Rotach and Keller 1993; Storgaard 1995). At least a dozen new neighbourhood office projects (in the more narrow sense) have been implemented in Europe during the nineties to date, while the number of telecentres and tele-cottages is much higher (cf. Gordexola database, MONIREG database): a num-ber of promising start-ups of neighbourhood offices most recently in the UK, especially in Wales, as well as in Scotland (Antur Teifi, Grampian region or Scottish Highlands and Islands Enterprise), Ireland (Kinawley, Cork), The Neth-erlands (Friesland, Lochem), Denmark (Veile), Finland (Archipelago of South-West Finland), Sweden (Nynaeshamn), Germany (Unterfranken, Fraenkische Schweiz), and Austria (Waldviertel). An Austrian 'televillage' project with inte-grated neighbourhood office facilities near Vienna has been in planning since 1994. A most ambitious project is reported in the MONIREG database (MONI-toring for information society initiatives and policies in REGions) for France: by 1996 one hundred neighbourhood offices (*bureaux de voisinage*) were planned to be created in the Ile de France region around Paris.

On the other hand, there are also projects which have meanwhile stopped their operation, such as the Nykvarn neighbourhood office – one of the most promin-ent experimental cases, or the 'telebureau' in Goms, a very remote Swiss moun-tain village. In a Dutch case, Purmerend Telewerkkantoor, the starting stage has been extremely long and progress has been much below initial expectations. Where the project was not deliberately designed to be an experiment of limited duration, a number of problem areas have come to the fore (cf. Bagley *et al.* 1994): underestimation of required marketing efforts; insufficient resources for centre management; low inclination of client organisations in conurbation areas to use neighbourhood offices in remote rural regions; lack of ability to provide anticipated social contacts because of small size and infrequent presence of tele-workers. This gives a rather mixed picture with indications of serious hurdles on the one hand but quite promising aspects, including an overall positive evaluation of the pioneering Nykvarn project, on the whole.

The development of neighbourhood offices outside Europe is still more in flux, especially in North America. A major initiative is the Residential Area-Based Offices (RABO) project, also known as the Neighbourhood Telecentres Project (Mokhtarian *et al.* 1996). This three-year programme financed by the Federal Highway Administration and the California Department of Transportation has established a total of 15 neighbourhood offices in or near residential areas, accompanied by a research programme at the Institute of Transportation Stud-ies, University of California, Davis. Bagley *et al.* (1994: section 3, 32–49) describe similar plans for Colorado, Kansas, Kentucky, Minnesota, North Dakota and Washington State together with further projects underway. According to

Mokhtarian (1995: 97) this amounts to at least 30 telework centres in the operation or serious planning stages in the US alone. The Australian government also approved funding for up to 30 telecentres over four years in 1992, of which at least some will be neighbourhood office-like. Japan also has a number of projects, although not all of them are neighbourhood offices in the full sense (Spinks 1991: 343). Interestingly, there is a strong presence of state and other public sector agencies behind almost all of these initiatives, especially in the US.

Evaluation results

Major findings of available evaluation studies from the US (Bagley et al. 1994; Mokhtarian et al. 1996; Becker et al. 1993) included the following:

- While there was certainly some variation in goals and objectives among centres, improving transportation, stimulating local business, and serving as a basis for research were overarching concerns.
- Implementation time span from six weeks to three years. (The mean for US telecentres was about six months (less time should have been spent on facility development and more time on critical marketing tasks for the sake of a higher utilisation rate).
- Training of telecommuters is important for a successful use of the neighbourhood office.

Factors which are of key importance for success:

- An intensive and comprehensive marketing approach is important. Bagley et al. (1994) suggest putting the strongest emphasis on sound and systematic marketing which has to include all components from product development and design to positioning, pricing and promotion. As guidelines for this task ('a formidable challenge for some time to come') the authors suggest: 'be serious about marketing; hire professional consulting if in-house expertise is not available; market early in the planning process and continue throughout the project; and use every available tool to promote the telecentre – mass media, phone, speeches, direct mailing, newspaper articles, flyers, e-mail, electronic bulletin board, and so on' (Bagley et al. 1994: Summary, 11 12).
- Presentation of telework centres as a new form of work which has the potential to increase efficiency (instead of viewing them primarily as solutions to traffic congestion and as demonstrations of new technologies (Becker et al. 1993)).
- Careful site selection with consideration of local availability of restaurants, shopping opportunities, post office, etc.
- High-quality facilities and management (full-time site administrator).

Major implementation barriers were identified in the study by Bagley et al. (1994) in the following four circumstances:

- Costs to tenant employers: one of the most important hurdles has been found to be a disinclination on the part of the tenants to pay market-level rents or, indeed, any rent at all: 'As long as telecommuters retain a desk at their conventional office and telecommute on average only one day a week, this barrier may be extremely difficult to overcome. Claiming hard-to-quantify benefits, such as increased productivity, to offset the added cost is not yet convincing the prospective tenant employers' (Bagley *et al.* 1994: Summary, 20). This problem has been reemphasised by the earlier than anticipated closure of two telecommuting centre projects in the California Bay Area Telecommuting Development Program (BATDP). The two neighbourhood offices in Concord and San Jose had to face a significant under-utilisation because employers were not willing to pay rents for alternative workplaces in addition to the traditional office (*Telecommuting Review* 1994).
- Discomfort with remote supervision (uneasiness and problems for managers to supervise remote workers).
- Security concerns (security of proprietary information; some employers were declining to use neighbourhood offices which did not have private offices and were not satisfied with lockers, passwords, security codes, etc., as substitutes).
- The differential distribution of costs and benefits over teleworkers, employers and regional public (direct costs such as office rents, reorganising use of office space and work-groups, training managers, etc. have to be carried by the employers of teleworkers).

In a comparative assessment of multi-employer centres and others, in particular of satellite offices and telecottages, the study concluded that multi-employer centres in general had found it more difficult to achieve sustained commercial viability. This parallels to some extent the mixed picture found for European projects of this type. However, there are also encouraging signs of higher utilisation among more recent projects which have started with significantly improved implementation and marketing strategies.

A European case study of networked neighbourhood offices

An EC-supported project (OFFNET Project Team 1995) investigated the neighbourhood office model of teleworking in combination with gathering experience in establishing and running pilot neighbourhood offices within multi-service telecentres in three countries (UK, Germany and Austria). During the 18-month project (ending August 1995), efforts were made to establish neighbourhood offices at the following six sites: WREN Telecottage, Warwickshire (UK); Anglesey Business Centre, and Antur Teifi Telematics Centre (Wales); Apenburg Community, Sachsen-Anhalt (Germany); Telehaus Freiwald, and Telehaus Waldviertel Management (Austria). The telecottages not only strived to implement neighbourhood offices but also undertook efforts to develop networked services among them (first steps concerned translation services in the form of small-scale practical tests based on the delivery of texts via e-mail).

Four neighbourhood offices were established as pilots during the 18-month period. The teleworking tasks comprised a variety of professions and qualifications: social workers in field service, architectural planning and inspection, data entry for an agricultural database, marketing and administrative tasks for a small business, production of course materials for distance education. Although the most successful of these pilots (Antur Teifi) closely matched the original definition and comprised more than a dozen teleworkers, practical experience showed that the market generally demanded a more flexible interpretation of a neighbourhood office than envisaged by the project. One telecentre (Freiwald) ended its operation before the project finished but triggered a teleworking trial with its former client, a province government administration. Practically all except the Welsh telecottages were faced with difficulties in acquiring clients for the neighbourhood offices. The resources required to market the neighbourhood office were greatly underestimated. A combination of the low level of awareness amongst medium to large organisations of the neighbourhood office model and the fact that this model involved some sort of agreement between user organisations and a third party (the multi-service telecentre) increased utilisation barriers. Lead-in times for the establishment of pilot schemes are far longer in such cases than with home-based teleworking schemes which often develop from individual homeworking arrangements.

Critical factors and future prospects of centre-based teleworking

Insights from innovation research can contribute to explain the difficulties with which telework centres are confronted. Among the critical barriers are challenges such as: the need to convince potential clients of the economic advantage of using a neighbourhood office (visibility, observability, triability of the innovation are important here); appropriate institutional frameworks to take risks and to limit uncertainty (clear regulations, devices to guarantee information security); social attractiveness to prospective teleworkers (site location, services); acceptance of changes in working arrangements by managers (adaptation of management styles); awareness, communication and marketing of comparative advantages.

The future prospects for telework centres will very much be shaped by a continuing conflict between economic and social demands: adaptation to intensified competition (cost-effectiveness, home-based teleworking) on one side and social goals like reducing regional disparities, providing social contacts at the work place, etc. on the other. Demand and economic viability will remain crucial questions in the medium and long term. Multi-functional telecottages can be suitable carriers of neighbourhood offices, but the development and improvement of appropriate business strategies is an absolute pre-condition. Strategic options include: diversification, seeking contracts from public sector institutions, subsidised premises, etc. Among key requirements to achieve attractiveness and viability are the following:

- comparative advantages of neighbourhood offices versus other forms of teleworking need to be pointed out and demonstrated
- clear strategic decisions and professional management
- market analysis and intensive marketing strategies
- low-cost rent conditions
- attraction of anchor clients
- balancing of social and economic functions.

Without significant steps forward on these dimensions the diffusion of multi-employer telework centres cannot be expected to take off. They will remain institutional models irrespective of how innovative they may be.

References

Bagley, M.N., Mannering, J.S. and Mokhtarian, P.L. (1994) *Telecommuting Centres and Related Concepts: A Review of Practice*, University of California, Institute of Transportation Studies, Davis.

Becker, F., Rappaport, A.J., Quinn, K.L. and Sims, W.R. (1993) *Telework Centres. An Evaluation of the North American and Japanese Experience*, International Workplace Studies Program, Cornell University, Ithaca, NY.

Bertin, I. and Denbigh, A. (1996) *The Teleworking Handbook. New Ways of Working in the Information Society*, Kenilworth: Telework, Telecottage and Telecentre Association (TCA).

Birchall, D. and Lyons, L. (1995) *Creating Tomorrow's Organization. Unlocking the Benefits of Future Work*, London: Pitman Publishing.

Brain, D.J. and Page, A.C. (1991) 'Review of Current Experiences and Prospects for Teleworking, ORA–Teleworking 1992', Commission of the European Communities (DG XIII).

Brooks, H. (1982) 'Social and Technical Innovation', in S.B. Lundstedt and E.W. Colglazier (eds) *Managing Innovation*, New York: Pergamon Press.

Commission of the European Communities (1994) 'Actions for the stimulation of transborder telework and research cooperation in Europe', Brussels.

Duerrenberger, G., Jaeger, C., Bierri, L. and Dahinden, U. (1994) 'Telework and vocational contact', unpublished manuscript, Zurich.

Eldib, O. and Minoh, D. (1995) *Telecommuting*, Boston and London: Artech House.

Gillespie, A., Richardson, R. and Cornford, J. (1995) *Review of Telework in Britain: Implications for Public Policy*, Centre for Urban and Regional Development Studies, University of Newcastle upon Tyne.

Gordexola database: http://www.telecentro.net/english/europa.html

Gray, M., Hodson, N. and Gordon, G. (1993) *Teleworking Explained*, Chichester and New York: John Wiley and Sons.

Holloway, L. (1994) 'Telecottages, teleworking and telelearning', Teldok Report.

Huws, U., Korte, W.B. and Robinson, S. (1990) *Telework. Towards the Elusive Office*, Chichester and New York: John Wiley and Sons.

International Labour Office (ILO) (1990) 'Telework', *Conditions of Work Digest* 9, 1.

Korte, W.B. and Wynne, R. (1996) *Telework: Penetration, Potential and Practice in Europe*, Amsterdam: IOS Press Ohmsha.

Mokhtarian, P.L. (1995) 'Country report – USA', in F. van Reisen and M. Tacken (eds) *A future of telework. Towards a new urban planning concept?* Netherlands Geographical Studies 189, Utrecht/Delft.

Mokhtarian, P.L., Balepur, N., Derr, M., Ho, Ch.-I., Stanek, D. and Varma, K. (1996) 'Residential Area-Based Offices Project: Interim Findings Report on the Evaluation of Impacts', University of California, Institute of Transportation Studies, Davis.

MONIREG database, http://www.idate.fr/actu/monireg/Fiches/FR028.html

Murphy, E. (1996) *Flexible Work*, Hemel Hempstead: Director Books.

Nilles, J. (1988) 'Traffic reduction by telecommuting: a status review and selected bibliography', *Transportation Research* A, 22A, 4: 301–17.

OFFNET Project Team (1995) 'Networked European Neighbourhood Offices: An Evaluation of the Neighbourhood Office Model of Teleworking', research report, Austrian Academy of Sciences/ITA, Vienna.

Ogburn, W.F. (1983) *Recent Social Trends in the United States*, New York: McGraw Hill.

Pekkola, J. (ed.) (1993) '*Telework – a new touch. Flexiwork perspectives in the European and Nordic labour markets*', Ministry of Labour, Working Environment Division, Helsinki.

Qvortrup, L. (1995) 'Community teleservice centres', unpublished research report, University of Odense.

Richardson, R. (1996) 'Teleservices and the relocation of employment: evidence from Western Europe', unpublished paper, Centre for Urban and Regional Development Studies, University of Newcastle upon Tyne.

Rotach M.C. and Keller, P. (1993) *Telematik und qualitatives Wachstum* (Telematics and Quantitative Growth), Zurich: Fachverlag.

Schumpeter, J.A. (1939) *Business Cycles*, London: McGraw Hill.

Spinks, W.A. (1991) 'Satellite and resort offices in Japan', *Transportation* 18, 4: 343–63.

Storgaard, K. (1995) 'Telework – Danish experiences', in F. van Reisen and M. Tacken (eds) *A Future of Telework. Towards a New Urban Planning Concept?* Netherlands Geographical Studies 189, Utrecht/Delft: 77–84.

Telecommuting Review (1994) 'The Gordon Report. Telecommuting Applications', March, 11, 3.

Zapf, W. (1989) 'Über soziale Innovationen' ('On social innovations'), *Soziale Welt* 40, 1/2: 170–83.

19

ORGANISATIONAL FITTING AND DIFFUSION OF NEW CULTURE

Internal telework at telecoms

Patrizio Di Nicola and Ruggero Parrotto

Introduction

This chapter has two main aims. First, proving foremost that teleworking involves cultural and organisational matters before technical issues; second, demonstrating that traditional theoretical models about management styles, leadership models and power-recognition mechanisms can be applied in order to analyse the impact of new technology on labour relations. To this end, we will analyse internal telework in telecommunications 'carriers', where there is full availability of the newest technologies. In fact:

1   The telecoms are companies of giant size, with tens of thousands of employees. Their presence is truly capillary, with personnel, offices and structures in practically every corner of the country they serve. Their product – the processing and transfer of information – is non-material, obtained by means of advanced technologies and, almost by definition, readily teleworkable. De-localisation of activities would render their production process more flexible, as well as their relations with users and the supply of their services. Lastly, telework represents a low-cost innovation for the telecoms because ownership of the networks and the communication technologies is vested in them. Often exclusively so.
2   Experimenting, producing and 'selling' integrated solutions for telework could constitute an important line of business for the telecoms. There is the possibility of stimulating new markets for hard- and software dedicated to a wide variety of specific sectors, from SOHO (Small Office Home Office) right through to the great company networks, tackling aspects like data security, productivity instruments for dispersed workgroups, multimedia, and the ergonomics of integrated telework stations. Lastly, of course, telework has an immediate impact on the basic products of the telecoms: networks, high-speed links and data traffic.

It is evident, therefore, that research regarding the spread or, rather, the non-spread of telework must draw from the experiences of the telecommunication companies. Some of these companies, as we shall see, have used telework internally, more or less in laboratory conditions, and in a strategic manner, generating – at the time more by accident than design – a cultural management fertilisation process. The solutions they offer the market are 'global': though they take due account of the technological problems, they embrace also the psycho-sociology of work, the repositioning of the productive organisation, contractual problems and trade union relations, the problems associated with data security, intellectual property and other legal aspects. As we shall see in the eight cases analysed in the present study (plus Telecom Italia, our national carrier), these telecoms have contributed – each according to their own company traditions – to the growth both within and without their own structures of an extensive culture that sees telework as a modern instrument, though certainly not the only one, for promoting organisational flexibility.

Internal telework experience: an overview

The following cases involve telecommunication managers with extensive telework experience. Some of these cases, though not ones we consider 'excellent', are particularly interesting on account of the fact that they develop formal and, even more often, informal approaches to telework that readily lend themselves to being repeated outside the immediate company environment.

Table 19.1 Teleworking cases A–H

Case	Typology of teleworking	Typology of work	Year starting	Implementation
Company A	Satellite office	Technical writers	1995	Formal
Company B	Mobile and Hoteling	Field sellers	1994–6	Formal
Company C	Home	Professionals	1992	Formal
	Mobile	Technical assistance	1994	Formal
	Virtual office	Account executives	1995	Informal
Company D	Home and mobile	Medium-high-rank employees	1970s	Informal
Company D	Home and mobile	Medium-high-rank employees	1980s	Informal
	Home	Low-rank employees	1991	Formal
Company F	Home	Dial-assistance operators	1991	Formal
	Home	Managers	1992	Mix
Company G	Home	Employees	1970s	Informal
	Home	Employees	1994	Formal
Company H	Home	Researchers	1995	Mix

Case A

Company A is realising a telework experiment for their own employees, although it has not received a great deal of publicity. About twenty technicians forming part of the 'New Projects' Division have been moved from the central office to a satellite office, obtained by restructuring an old building in a small centre situated about 30 km from the capital. Contact with the central office is maintained by means of ISDN links and interaction between the various subjects is supported by software dedicated to the management of remote groupwork (groupware). The declared purpose of the experiment is to study the technical and feasibility requirements of telework and, more particularly, telework performed at telecentres.

Case B

The telework strategy of Company B is centered on the personnel in charge of sales and the technicians who provide customer assistance. This company commenced the automation of about 5,000 employees, supplied with computers, software and network technologies. The investment involved was of the order of $50 million. The second phase of the experiment consisted of the setting up of a 'rally centre', a meeting-place for the company's sales personnel who normally telework. In the centre there is a very extensive rotation of people, this being made possible by a computerised space booking system. According to his/her particular needs, each salesperson books a desk (or a meeting table) on a certain day and at a certain time. The booking system gives the telephone number assigned for the length of the stay at the centre, and provides the names of the colleagues who will be there on that occasion.

Case C

Company C is running three telework experiments: telework from home for a wide range of professional figures, mobile telework for technicians engaged in assistance work, each of whom can access the central office database via a portable computer, and a 'virtual office' for the account executives. The first of these experiments is the oldest and the most important of the three. In May 1992, the company launched a telework experiment for 31 employees, who could work at home for two or three days each week. By September of the first year only 22 people were still continuing the experiment, thus demonstrating that, notwithstanding the very best intentions that had led the original group to volunteer for the experiment, the problems deriving from the need to reconfigure one's family and social life constituted, at least in the short term, a very real and a constant obstacle.

Case D

Company D, unlike the others, has made very little ado about their internal telework experiments, because they consider them to constitute a normal practice in support of work flexibility. Ever since the 1970s, in fact, many employees, especially those of a medium to high level, have engaged in occasional work from home, generally for some days each week or some hours each day. Contact with the office evolved in the course of time and was maintained in various ways: access to internal electronic mail, dispatch by telefax, telephone communications, etc. These initiatives, however, were not co-ordinated at the central level and were generally taken on the basis of informal agreements reached between the worker and his/her direct superior. In this case the decisive stimulus for the further development of telework came in 1990 with the passing of a law on environmental protection. In this context, Company D faced a great demand for services, equipment and consultancies to transform office jobs into telework activities.

Case E

The genesis of telework in the case of Company E was not substantially different from what we have already seen in the case of Company D. The first telework experiments came into being in a wholly informal manner at the beginning of the 1980s, when it was made possible for some of the company's employees to access the internal data networks from their homes. As from 1991 onwards, however, the experiments were formalised by the drafting of an internal telework regulation, which established access parameters and rules to ensure data security and protect the health of employees. This was accompanied by the preparation and approval of a teleworking agreement, which to this day has been applied to about 20,000 employees (10 per cent of the total), most of whom (about 12,500) work in the conditions of a virtual or mobile office or a satellite office. Telework has also been given a great deal of publicity.

The excellent cases

Case F

The first experiment

The first telework experiment lasted for a year, starting in June 1992. It involved 11 telephone operators of the dial-assistance service. The declared purpose of the experiment was as follows:

- to demonstrate that telephone operators of the assistance centres could do their work from home;

- to explore the extent to which normal office equipment could be transferred to an employee's home without having to undergo far-reaching modifications;
- to understand how telework problems, be they technical or otherwise, could be successfully solved;
- to investigate the manner in which technology can support the work of operators and supervisors;
- to see whether the benefits expected from telework really represent concrete advantages for the parties involved;
- to determine the requirements that are indispensable for applying telework on a large scale at the dial-assistance centres.

The results obtained from this experiment were in line with expectations, but also furnished a stream of additional information that proved particularly useful. Indeed, over and above confirming both the advantages (reduction of stress, greater work flexibility, greater leisure time) and the drawbacks (maintenance problems in the event of equipment failure, fewer external relations of the employees concerned), the experiment also provided numerous other indications:

- the importance of the audio-visual means (videotelephone) as instruments that substantially facilitate communication and interaction;
- the support that the supervisor gave to the teleworkers tended to drop after the initial phases of the experiment;
- the sense of isolation had not really constituted a problem;
- working at home does not change the hourly productivity of the workers and does not even exert any effects on the absence rates due to illness.

The second experiment

Notwithstanding the experience acquired as a result of the first experiment, Company F did not introduce the practice of telework to any appreciable extent among their employees working at the dial-assistance centres. Two years were to pass from the end of this experiment before a telesales centre implemented a pilot project that caused 12 of their 25 telephone operators to be transferred to a workstation at home. Participation was wholly on a voluntary basis and subject to a selection test. Following extensive negotiations with the trade unions, the candidates, who originally were full-time employees, were told that they could participate in the telework experiment if they accepted a part-time job for 25 hours per week, a figure that was subsequently raised to 30 hours when the company came face to face with the difficulty of recruiting volunteers who were prepared to accept such a sharp downturn in their working hours and income. This experiment is still in progress.

Telework among executives

Company F implemented a form of telework that is particularly innovative. In 1992, in fact, the company and the trade union representing the higher and executive grades signed an agreement that made it possible for these higher-grade employees to work at home on an individual and voluntary basis. In its general approach, this agreement prefigured a 'quasi-definitive removal' from the office environment. What happened in actual practice, however, is very different from expectations. Even though no official figures illustrating the magnitude of the phenomenon are available, outside observers affirm that the greater part of the managers who requested the facility of engaging in telework continued to come to the office with a certain regularity, limiting their work at home to the tasks that best lent themselves to being undertaken in a quieter and more peaceful environment (for example, reading or writing important documents) or the occasions when particular circumstances made their presence at home desirable.

Case G

Implicit telework

Telework within Company G commenced in a rather subdued manner: from the beginning of the 1970s onwards, a number of local managers allowed some of their employees to access the company networks from home, mainly with a view to enabling them to carry out urgent work outside office hours or to avoid loss of working time on the occasions when adverse weather conditions prevented them from reaching the office. There thus came into being the first telework programmes, which became known as *Alternative Work Arrangement*, a name that did not even make express use of such words as telework or telecommuting. This process of 'implicit telework' tended to expand with the further development of the informatics and telematics technologies, which not only made it possible for the employees to perform an ever larger number of even complex tasks from their own homes, but also provided the companies with the necessary means for 'opening' the company networks to external connections at a low cost, while yet maintaining reasonable levels of data security. According to a recent survey, almost 70 per cent of the employees of Company G are now authorised to access the company information system from their own homes.

Explicit telework

Company G officialised their internal telework in March 1995. Administration of the new programme, now known as *Teleworking Option*, was entrusted to a newly set up inter-company committee. A practical teleworking guide was prepared at the beginning of 1996. It consists of a basic document and six appendices, each of which is intended to solve some specific operational aspect bound up with telework. The publication also includes a teleworking contract agreed with the unions.

Case H

Company H is a major telecommunications operator and sells a wide range of technical solutions capable of being applied to teleworking. Circulation of information about teleworking is considered as a strategic operation for promoting its further expansion. Internal telework is widely used in this company, but it is not equally well-documented and, as elsewhere in this particular country, springs more from an empirical practice than a rigorous contractual approach. In this rather informal context, therefore, considerable importance attaches to an experiment, designed for a duration of 12 months, that set out to study 11 tele-workers within the company and a control group of identical size made up of people who have become indirectly involved in teleworking problematics: colleagues, husbands or wives of teleworkers, personnel responsible for computer maintenance, middle-grade employees who have teleworkers among the staff they control, executives and administrators of the services affected by teleworking. The first results of this study highlighted no less than the following four paradoxes:

The rigidity/flexibility paradox

Even before they were selected for the experiment, all the teleworkers involved enjoyed a great deal of freedom in planning their day. Being generally inserted in some team or workgroup, all the co-ordination activities within the group were performed, generally in a rather informal manner, during their stay at the office, often in the form of a one-to-one interaction. There were only rare occasions when the group had to call meetings that required the presence of all the team members. The first effect of the decentralisation of some of the team members is therefore that the resource of informal co-ordination is no longer available at the office. This immediately gives rise to the need for a codified exchange of information, which obliges all the members of the group to reorganise their activities in such a way as to leave room for frequent meetings. This becomes an element of greater rigidity not only for the teleworker, who is obliged to go to the office at pre-established times, but also for his colleagues, who now have to arrange their work schedules around meeting cycles at set times.

The leisure time paradox

The greater part of the time gained by having to do less travelling is dedicated to the work itself. But the interviews arranged at intervals of six months bring out very substantial modifications in the organisation of family life: more time can be dedicated to any children and some of the teleworkers have started cooking their own meals. The periods of extra work would therefore seem to be bound up more with the progress of the project in which the teleworker is involved than with an intrinsic propension for hyperactivity induced by telework itself.

The creativity paradox

Creativity can be categorised as the *analytic generation of new ideas*. According to the researchers responsible for the experiment, working from home tends to increase analytical creativity, because the working environment in one's own home, being free from disturbance, makes possible greater concentration and therefore better problem-solving activities. But there is a downturn in the capacity of creating new concepts, because the separation from one's colleagues reduces the creative stimuli and the occasions for checking one's ideas against those of the others.

The isolation / communication paradox

There are times when the office is the least suitable place for carrying out certain activities that, above all, call for isolation. But the experiment brought out the fact that, side by side with the need for remaining isolated if certain activities are to be properly performed, the workers voiced an almost obsessive demand for having at their disposal the greatest possible number of technological devices that facilitate communication with others. These devices can be divided into two great families: the *interactive* technologies, like the telephone and the videoconference, which in real time recreate the interaction that exists at the office; and the *asynchronous* technologies, which include telefax, the voice-box systems and electronic mail and make it possible to be reached without being accessible.

Telecom Italia: between organisational flexibility and workforce rebalancing

The implementation of telework at the Italian carrier was a very special process: it was reached with the agreement of the unions through an extensive process of bargaining, discussion and mutual education. The collective agreement signed in 1996 by the Italian telecommunications companies and the trade unions is the first agreement concluded above individual company level that envisages generalised recourse to telework in all the signatory companies.

But it is also the first time that a collective agreement draws its inspiration not from a simple employment defence logic in the face of a crisis or company restructuring (the so-called defensive telework), but rather from the goal of promoting telework as such, recognising it as possessing a valency that goes well beyond the traditional approach, which saw it as a mere instrument for limiting surplus labour.

The agreement is underlain by a widely drawn notion of telework subdivided into three categories: *at home* (but envisaging periodic returns of the teleworker to the office), *working out* (in this case the returns to the office are to be agreed with the direct superior and the daily duration of the telework (without in any way altering the contractual working hours), its precise location of work during the day and the performance assessment criteria may be characterised by innovative features), and *remote* (in which case the working activity is performed at a distance, generally from centres far removed from the company's office that is responsible for the activity in both hierarchical and substantial terms).

The legal connotation of the labour relationship remains the one traditionally associated with subordinate work. For the purposes of the implementation experiments, subsequent and more specific agreements will define the activities and professional figures to be included, the modalities of the experiments and the professional and social guarantees for the employees involved. The ordinary hierarchical functions may be carried out via telematics and/or by means of target assessments. The teleworkers are to adopt every possible precaution to ensure absolute secrecy of the company information made available to enable them to carry out their tasks.

Over and above the novelties already set out, it seems interesting to note that this is also the first time that a company–union agreement contemplates mobile telework (called *working out* in the agreement), which during late 1997 and early 1998 will find a first application among the salesmen of Telecom Italia.

An explicit provision of the agreement recognises that in the case of teleworkers, performance and hierarchical control may henceforth follow new paradigms that are more in keeping with the effective working situation: even though it did not prove possible to avoid the sacred reference to the contractual working hours, which remain valid also for the teleworkers, the agreement yet represents an undeniable step forward as compared with the contractual experience hitherto matured in Italy.

Each company that signed the collective agreement could apply it according to company needs. Telecom Italia initiated a telework project as part of two company-level agreements signed together with the trade unions in the wide area of management of personnel redundancy and mobility processes. All the three kinds of teleworking have been implemented.

Remote teleworking affected the existing operator-assistance work centres. This choice aims, above all, at balancing the workforce geographically by remote-siting part of the operator services (i.e. directory enquiries) and by assigning them to a business unit which physically operates outside its area of jurisdiction. In practice, workloads of other geographic sites will be transferred to distant work centres. This project will involve about 400 workers, but it is likely to be extended to all the workforce employed in directory enquiries.

Home teleworking is currently going to involve 50 employees of the operator services. Telecom Italia will bear the costs associated with the performance of the job at the employee's home, namely those related to occupancy of the required space and consumption of electricity. This project is going to be extended to a maximum of 5 per cent of the workforce employed in directory enquiries (that is to say 250 employees).

'*Working out*' is the name of the project involving 725 salespersons in Telecom Italia. They will always be in touch with the company, through a little suitcase containing a computer, a printer and connection with all the company information systems. In this way, the sellers may always (and from wherever they are) manage their electronic agenda, enter the databank of the company, have all the information they need in order to manage the commercial relation with the customer, monitor all the selling activities and the connected incentives.

Conclusions

General

The telecoms constitute a reliable sample, because – for wholly legitimate reasons closely bound up with their business – they are both beneficiaries and providers of telework services. And it is equally beyond doubt that coming to the potential customer with actual firsthand experience of successful applications can ensure greater credibility and authority, and not only at the commercial level, but also at the institutional level.

The analysis performed shows very clearly that the telecoms who have already matured significant experiences of telework in their own midst also have a very pronounced capacity for spreading the culture of telework among the public at large. And, in an appropriate ranking list in order of importance, this takes precedence over 'ability' in 'selling the telework product', although they are undoubtedly also well provided with this latter capacity. More particularly, all the 'excellent' cases analysed by us show that the problems that had to be overcome were not by any means solely of a technical nature, but also involved human resource management, here understood as agreement, motivation and valuation. This made it possible for the managers to become fully conscious of the extra-technological problematic associated with telework. This consciousness also derives from the fact that in all these excellent experiments the managers were themselves involved in telework activities and therefore have firsthand experience of it. This is the second aim of the paper, but we shall leave this aspect for discussion at a later stage.

Side by side with internal telework, the telecoms have also developed their range of services intended to solve organisational, trade union, psychological, training and attitudinal problems. It does not seem a mere matter of chance, for example, that quite a few companies not only place the accent on the need to undertake a careful in-depth evaluation of the persons to be authorised to engage in telework, but also stress the desirability of *developing individualised teleworking models*, approaches that we might define as attempts to formulate micro-sociological indicators of an individual teleworking capacity. Others, working in environments that are potentially favourable and well suited to the introduction of telework, are trying to gain greater insight into the multi-dimensional relationship that exists between the factors that speak in favour of telework and those that counsel against it.

The organisation for telework

'Selling telework' is not only a market operation of the telecoms, but also a cultural and knowledge-spreading process that gathers momentum from within and thus constitutes a virtuous spiral. In fact, the experiments so far carried out and reported in the relevant literature highlight the fact that the development of telework in the industrialised societies invariably involves a number of well-defined and fundamental elements:

- the demand for flexibility expressed by the workers (and to a lesser extent also by the companies), was almost always bound up with the existence of unfavourable geographic or climatic conditions, and was intended to facilitate and optimise the manner in which individuals distribute their time between life and work. This, for example, is the variable that contributes to explaining the rapid growth of telework in such vast, cold and sparsely populated regions as Canada and Sweden;
- the support of the public authorities, who by means of appropriate laws and regulations, often with the ultimate aim of reducing environmental pollution and traffic, grant fiscal facilitation to companies who adopt teleworking. This is the case, for example, of the state of California and of the US in general;
- the birth of a telework culture production sponsored by the managers of the telecommunication networks.

We are here concerned with an obligatory process that can not be given up: telework breaks up and puts an end to many of the schemes and patterns underlying the pre-existing culture of the industrial societies that, starting with Adam Smith and right through to Taylorism and Fordism, gave rise not only to a particular production mode, *but also* to a cultural model that is today being called into question by these new forms of work. It is precisely for these reasons that many of the authors today tend to underline the fact that the chains that have so far prevented telework from really getting off the ground are inherent to our old and timeworn management paradigms.

Telework twixt codification and informality

Yet another important characteristic that can be found in all the cases of internal telework so far implemented by the telecoms is the existence of *two levels* at which the relevant experimental work was carried out.

At the first level, which one might call the *formal* or *codified* level, the work was advanced by involving personnel of homogeneous qualifications for whom the technicians had designed a specific workstation, while an appropriate teleworking agreement was reached with the unions that represented them and acted on their behalf. All said and done, these experiments tended to create traditional work-places in the worker's home and the desk used there had to become as far as possible a mere appendage of the office. Though often not admitted, the ultimate scope of these experiments was to transform into telework a number of activities characterised by a low variance, and therefore distinguished by the substantial repetitiveness of the individual tasks and few unforeseeable factors, this with a view to producing work 'mechanisms' that could be sold and adopted outside the company without in any way interfering with the buyer's pre-existing organisa-tion. We are here concerned with an approach that, being rigid on the labour side, seeks to have a minimal impact on business or company culture. The design idea underlying these experiments accepted all the principal Taylorist paradigms: the division between those who design the work and those who carry it out, the rigid determination of the tasks obtained by means of a scientific study of what has to be done, the ambition of creating a single 'best way', in this case of a purely technological nature, conceiving domestic workstations dedicated to a sin-gle type of work (for example: answering the telephone, searching for specified information in an appropriate database and then communicating the findings to the caller). These attempts, which sought to introduce telework without modify-ing the pre-existing organisation, in the end proved to be useful means of collect-ing data and information about behaviour patterns, but did little or nothing as regards the repeatability or expansion of the proposed solution.

The second and more profitable line along which the telework experiments of the telecoms have hitherto been pushed forward is the *informal* one. In these cases, peripheral management, subject to complying with a set of rules or principles (generally in the form of recommendations), were given the possibility of agree-ing specific teleworking modalities with interested employees, and the arrange-ments therefore had to be convenient and advantageous for both parties. The central office in these cases offered consultancy services on telework and instru-ments to support the decision, but the responsibility for codifying the work rela-tionship, at times in a somewhat slack manner, was left with the periphery, together with an ample margin of discretion. In support of this practice there always existed some kind of framework agreement with the unions, often setting out mere principles, that established the minimum criteria that had to be observed. The subjects of these telework relationships were almost invariably high-grade officials, often the managers themselves, whose activities, or at least some part of them, lent themselves to being more efficiently performed at home.

Strictly speaking, therefore, we are here concerned with part-time forms of telework, this in the sense that the teleworkers' work was done partly at home and partly in the office. These attempts substantially reduced not only the fear of isolation and exclusion, but also the risk of weakening the teleworker's identifica-tion with the company, and they were truly innovative because they were always

implemented as part of work scenarios characterised by a maximum of performance flexibility.

Authorising the higher-grade employees to do their work from home – always,
of course, in accordance with their specificities – also has the enormous advantage of facilitating the expansion of the experience and therefore makes it easier
to pass from a managerial culture of 'controlling the work' to the new approach
of 'controlling the result'.

As is readily shown by the cases studied by us and the whole of the relevant
scientific literature, the true obstacle to overcome in the endeavour of expanding
telework consists of the passage from the paradigm of the *office in the first place*, that
is to say, the office seen as the place where all the activities can be and are best
performed, to a paradigm of the *work in the first place*. This implies that one has to
see the work environment with the eyes of a layman: the office remains the place
where ideas are born and verified and where creativity and project promotion
find stimuli, drive and collective verification, but not necessarily the ideal place
for coming to grips with every type of work. There will inevitably be cases where
the optimal working environment is the drawing room of one's own home.

A mixture of formal and informal experience and a constant interchange
between the two types of experience therefore seems to have constituted the most
fruitful road for the growth and development of telework.

Informal experiments often come into being as pioneer operations and at times
spring from the entrepreneurial genius (Schumpeter 1932) of a number of managers who feel the need to render more flexible both their own work relationships
and those of their subordinates (though they must, of course, dispose of the
operational autonomy necessary to do so). The typical effect obtained in such
situations is that of combining new work modalities with the diffusion of a telework culture understood as a practice of flexibility and informality.

The mixture of formality and informality: adapting before adopting

At this point one cannot but wonder, seeing that such a linear procedure is quite
sufficient to produce a telework culture within a company organisation, why there
are still so few cases in which this actually happened, as is also borne out by our
own study. The informal approach requires one essential condition to be satisfied:
there should exist a hierarchical structure that will make it possible. All said and
done, therefore, an organisation must in some way envisage the possibility of
innovating its own paradigms, its own reference standards: innovation must be a
value to be pursued as a source of benefit.

Although the scope of the present study does not extend to analysing the
managerial cultures of present-day company organisations, it nevertheless seems
unavoidable at least to attempt a problem-setting operation with a view to
pin-pointing the principal variables that have to be taken into account and, if
possible, also the interrelations between them.

Telework is a rather more complex and articulated phenomenon than is generally believed. This is borne out, above all, by witnesses from countries that are more advanced in this field. To say that the Information Society is an irreversible scenario does not automatically permit one to say that this scenario will be simpler and more positive. Though it is reasonable to think that the Information Society will upset the social, organisational, juridical and technological equilibrium that underlies the consolidation of industrial society, it seems equally foreseeable that, notwithstanding protective intervention by the institutions, there will eventually be winning companies, businesses and individuals, but also losing companies, businesses and individuals.

Acknowledgement

While carrying out the present study, the authors enjoyed the benefit of the counsel, help and courtesy of numerous people, many of whom are known only via electronic mail. The authors are in debt especially to Francesca Sacchi and Mario Iannaccone: they were an invaluable help to this study.

References

Adr – Empirica – Tavistock (1986), *Le Travail à distance en Milieux Urbains et Ruraux Européens*, Fast-Fop Report No. 117, Brussels.

Adr – Empirica – Tavistock (1986) *Distance Working Project in the Federal Republic of Germany, France and United Kingdom*, Fast-Fop Report No. 79, Brussels.

Bianco, M.L. (1990) 'Sentieri di innovazione organizzativa: come è stato progettato un esperimento di telelavoro', in *Rassegna Italiana di Sociologia*, No. 1.

—— (1991) 'Tra necessità e scelta: atteggiamenti nei confronti del telelavoro', in *Industria e Sindacato*, No. 23/24.

Bibby, A. (1995) *Teleworking. Thirteen Journeys to the Future of Work*, Calouste Gulbenkian Foundation, London.

—— (1996) 'Teleworking: how the Trade Unions are responding', in *Flexible Working*, No. 2, February.

Bonazzi, G., (1994) *Storia del pensiero organizzativo*, F. Angeli, Milan.

Borgna, P., Ceri, P. and Failla, A. (1996) *Telelavoro in movimento*, Etaslibri, Milan.

Bracchi, G. and Campodall'Orto, S., (1997), *Progettare il telelavoro*, F. Angeli, Milan.

Brain, D.J. and Page, A.C. (1991) *Review of Current Experience and Prospects for Teleworking*, European Commission, Brussels.

Bruun, N. and Johnson, M. (1995) *Legal and Contractual Situation of Teleworkers*, Swedish report, mimeograph prepared for the 'Telework Study Project' of the European Foundation – EU (DG V).

BT Research Laboratories (1990) (J. Withnell), *An Overview of Teleworking*, Ipswich, 28 June.

—— (1991) (L. Haddon), *Disability and Telework*, Ipswich, 5 April.

—— (1991) *Clerical Teleworking. How it affects Family Life*, Ipswich.

—— (1992) (A. McGrath), *A Study of Homeworking Environments*, Ipswich, 24 April.

Ceiil–O'Group (1989) *Telelavoro: i miti e le prospettive concrete per l'Italia*, F. Angeli, Milan.

Cepollaro, C. (1986) 'Il turno in vestaglia. La prospettiva del telelavoro tra mito, problemi e realtà', in *Sociologia del lavoro*, No. 28.

Chiesa, E. (1995) 'Il telelavoro. Aspetti organizzativi e psicologici', Ceiil–European Informatics and Labour Information Centre, mimeograph.

Ciborra, C. and Maggiolini, P. (1985) 'Il telelavoro: organizzazione e implicazioni sindacali', in *Quaderni di Rassegna Sindacale*, No. 113.

Craipeau, S. (1984) *Telework: Impact on Living and Working Conditions*, European Foundation, Dublin.

Di Martino, V. and Wirth, L. (1990) 'Le teletravail: un nouveau mode de travail et de vie', in *Revue Internationale de Travail*, No. 5: 129.

—— (1990), *Condition of Work Digest*, International Labour Office, Geneva: 9.

Empirica (1987) *Tendances et perspectives dans le travail a domicile par ordinateur. Resultats d'une enquête dans quatre pays européens*, European Union, Fast Report No. 20.

Ettighoffer, D. (1993) *L'impresa virtuale*, Muzzio, Padua.

European Commission Green Paper(1996) *Living and Working in the Information Society: People First*, COM(96) 389, Draft 22 July 1996.

Forester, T. (1988) 'The Myth of the Electronic Cottage', *Futures* 3, June: 227–40.

Formez, (1991) 'Il telelavoro: una opportunità per lo sviluppo sociale e organizzativo, Proceedings of the European Meeting held in Rome on 23 April 1991 and organized by Formez in collaboration with the 'La Sapienza' University of Rome, F. Angeli, Milan.

Gaeta, L. (1993) *Lavoro a distanza e subordinazione*, Esi, Naples.

Gaeta, L., Manacorda, P. and Rizzo, R. (1995) *Telelavoro. L'ufficio a distanza*, Ediesse, Rome.

Gallino, L. (1993) *Dizionario di sociologia*, TEA, Turin.

—— (1996) 'Mutamenti in corso nell'organizzazione del lavoro', in CNEL *Nuove forme di lavoro tra subordinazione, coordinamento, autonomia*, Materials of the Study Meeting held in Rome on 27 May 1996.

Goldman, M. and Richter, G., (1986) *Telehomework by Women*, results of an Empirical Study in Germany, Fast-Fop Report No. 120, Brussels.

Gouldner, A.W. (1970) *Modelli di burocrazia aziendale*, Etas Kompass, Milan.

Grasso, B. (ed.) (1986) *Il telelavoro: lavoreremo tutti a casa?*, Edizioni Sud, Bari.

Gray, M., Hodson, N. and Gordon G. (1993) *Telework Explained*, John Wiley and Sons, Chichester.

Huws, U. (1984) *The New Homeworkers, New Technology and the Changing Location of White-Collar Work*, Low Pay Unit, London.

—— (1984), 'Le nuove tecnologie e il lavoro a domicilio', in *Economia del Lavoro*, No. 3/4, July December. (Original edition, 'New Technology Home Workers', in *Employment Gazette*, January 1984).

Huws, U. *et al.* (1990) *Telework: Toward the Elusive Office*, John Wiley and Sons, Chichester.

Jouet, J. (1988) 'Les usages professionnels de la micro-informatique', in *Sociologie du Travail*, No. 1.

Korte, W.B. and Wynne, R. (1995) *Telework. Penetration, Potential and Practice in Europe*, TELDET Project, Final Report, mimeograph, Bonn.

Marrow, A., Bowers, D. and Seashore, S. (1967) *Management by Participation*, Harper and Row, New York.

Martin, J. and Norman, A.R. (1970) *The Computerized Society: An Appraisal of the Impact of Computers on Society in the Next Fifteen Years*, Englewood Cliffs, Prentice-Hall.

Mitchell, W.J. (1995) *City of Bits: Space, Place, and the Infobahn*, MIT Press, Cambridge, Mass.

Nilles, J.M., Carlson, F.R., Gray, P. and Hannemann, G.J. (1976) *The Telecommunications-Transportation Tradeoff: Options for Tomorrow*, New York, John Wiley and Sons.

Perrow, C. (1977) *Le organizzazioni complesse*, F. Angeli, Milan.

Reid, A. (1994) *Teleworking: A Guide to Good Practice*, New York, Blackwell.

Robins, K. and Hetworth, M. (1988) 'Electronic Spaces: New Technologies and the Future of Cities', in *Futures* No. 2, April: 155–76.

Rognes, J., Rogberg, M., Forslund, K. and Virtanen M.T. (1996) 'Paradoxes and Some Unexpected Consequences in Telecommuting', Paper read to the 'Telecommuting 96' conference, Jacksonville, Florida, 25–26 April.

Romagnoli, U. (1986) 'Noi e loro: diritto del lavoro e nuove tecnologie', in *Rivista trimestrale di diritto e procedura civile*.

Scarpitti, G. and Zingarelli, D. (1993) *Il telelavoro. Teorie e applicazioni*, F. Angeli, Milan.

Schumpeter, J.A. (1932) *La teoria dello sviluppo economico*, Utet, Turin.

Sgrosso, U. (1992) 'Telelavoro: ieri e oggi', *Sistemi e reti*, No. 8.

Soete, L., *et al.* (1996), *Building the European Information Society for Us All*, EC–DG V, Brussels.

Tasca, A. (1995) 'Un nuovo modo di lavorare', *Media Duemila*, No. 1, 13 February: 62–5.

Teldok, (1995) *20 Seconds to Work*, Report 101E, Stockholm.

Telecom Italia (1994) *Potenzialità e fattori critici del telelavoro in Italia*, December.

—— (1996) *Osservatorio sul telelavoro. Prospettive di integrazione delle telecomunicazioni nei processi produttivi in venti aziende leader italiane*, mimeograph, June.

Telecom Italia, Industrial Relations Research Office (1995) *Notiziario del Lavoro*, No. 75, Special Issue: Teleworking.

—— (1996) *Notiziario del Lavoro*, No. 81: Special Issue: Teleworking.

Times Mirror Center for the People and the Press (1994) *The Role of Technology in American Life*, New York, mimeograph.

Toffler, A. (1989) *La terza ondata*, Sperling and Kupfer, Milan. (Original edition 1980.)

Vendramin, P. and Valenduc, G. (1989) *Le teletravail: quels enjeux pour les relations sociales?*, in *Cahiers de la Fondation Travail-Université, No. 5*.

Webber, M.M. (1968) *The Post-City Age*, in *Daedalus, 97: 1091–110*.

20

THE MIS-MATCH BETWEEN SUPPLIERS AND USERS IN TELEWORK

Lennart Sturesson

Introduction

Since the 1970s there have been many over-optimistic predictions on the growth of teleworking. For instance, in 1971 AT&T was anticipating that all Americans would be working from home by 1990. More recent predictions, though, have been modified, with teleworking now viewed as an evolutionary rather than revolutionary development. Despite this, Gray, Hodson and Gordon – three telework promoters – write: 'with the increasing availability, and decreasing cost, of the enabling technology, the end of the [world] recession could signal the start of the teleworking boom' (1993: 22).

Surveys based on Swedish Statistics in 1986 and 1995, analysed by the research institute Nordplan in Stockholm, indicate that the amount of employed people working at home for at least six hours per week has increased from 240,000 to 350,000 during the period 1986 to 1995, which is respectively six and ten per cent of the workforce (Engström *et al.* 1990, and personal information from unpublished survey results). This cannot be interpreted as a large success for telework, although it is perhaps still too early to evaluate the efforts of different actors to promote telework.

In waiting for a possible boom, it is worth looking at explanations other than the recession for the slow evolution of telework. In doing this, it is necessary to look at both promoters and users of telework, and the technology which is supposed to support it. It is also time to go beyond the question of why people *are* teleworking to ask the question why they do *not* telework. As such, it is important to search for the mis-matches between what promoters of telework can offer and what teleworkers want and need. In this chapter I will identify actors that promote telework in Sweden, drawn largely from two cases of municipal telework promotion, and will relate the actors' ambitions to teleworkers' experiences.

Definition of telework

Given my empirical study, I will concentrate on telework performed in the tele-worker's home or neighbourhood, and consider employees as well as self-employed teleworkers. I have defined people as teleworkers if they are working at least 5–8 hours (one day) per week at a distance from their employer or customer. I have not excluded people working without the use of telecommunication or computers – for me it is an empirical question as to how dependent telework is of information and communication technology (ICT) use.

Identifying the actors

In the literature on teleworking developments, promoters of telework are com-monly identified among three types of actors, namely the *employers*, the *teleworkers* and their families, and *public actors* (authorities). Telework is described primarily as an affair between employers and employees, sometimes also involving public act-ors who promote telework for the sake of employment or the environment. How-ever, in the 1990s in Sweden, the strongest promoters of telework are the *suppliers* of telecommunication and ICT equipment.

Concepts and theory

The difficulty in implementing telework on a large scale raises the issue of new technology – for instance, in this case, whether ICTs are important to the introduction of telework. There is a common belief that such technologies are the key to working at home or in a neighbourhood office. It is therefore necessary to see if the homeworkers use and need telecommunications, or if they behave just like they used to: reading information, writing a text on a home computer, or making some phone calls – things that white-collar employees have done for decades.

To be able to analyse a possible mis-match between promoters and tele-workers, it is appropriate to look at telework from an actor perspective: who are the promoters, why do they promote telework, which are their strategies and arguments, and how do they act to introduce telework? But it is also important to look at the teleworkers' motives and needs, and not only the need for technology and technical artifacts, but also their needs to organise their lives, to win time, to minimise conflicts, etc.

A central question will be: What are suppliers selling? Is it 'telework', or is it computers and other equipment, telecommunication, or a lifestyle? Are the 'commodities' which they propose to users the same as what they deliver? And are the commodities the same as the teleworkers need and ask for?

Conservative technology

Faced with new technologies or social innovations, it is common for people to behave in their normal way – doing what they would have done before such changes. In an article on automobiles, Hård and Jamison (1996) write that alternative technology seldom succeeds if it poses an alternative on all of three levels that they identify. These levels involve the three kinds of reinforcing structures that define stabilised technologies (Hård and Jamison 1996: 5–6).

The *symbolic* level refers to the values that are associated with technologies – the visions, expectations and desires – on both the individual and collective level.

The *organisational* level refers to the social systems that support the dominant technologies and from where attacks on alternatives are often launched. Success, according to Hård and Jamison, is often based on a promoter's ability to break through established institutional frameworks and devise social innovations for technical development.

The *behavioural* level includes the habits and routines that are found in everyday life. Technologies have little chance unless they adapt themselves to standard routines of behaviour, and to personal expectations that users have of their technical artifacts.

Hård and Jamison suggest that a too ambitious alternative is less likely to succeed than a conservative one, conservative meaning that the technology is not a radical innovation but is related to an established set of ideas.

Symbolic values

Hård and Jamison note that certain symbols are a part of the technology context. It is therefore necessary for people to be connected to the right type of symbols. They take as an example early automobiles, where the electric car came to symbolise femininity, an ideal not favoured in the persisting male car-culture.

There is also another way of looking at symbols. Suppliers of a commodity try to give it a symbolic value to persuade the consumer of its advantages. But in the end, the commodity must have a use value, valuable enough for the users to buy and use the commodity, and to recommend it to their personal networks.

Thus, by *symbolic value* I mean the value accredited to an artefact, not because of its direct usefulness, but because of its perceived potential to give the owner a means to make her/his dreams and visions come true (i.e. it is perceived as increasing the person's social and cultural capital, to speak of Bourdieu). The symbolic value is added to by making the artefact a symbol for something tempting. The meaning of *use value* in this sense is the immediate technical or practical function of the artefact as perceived by the owner.

From this I make the presumption that for a social innovation like ICT-based telework, a main actor has to build a network which enrols strong promoters as well as a broad population of potential teleworkers. And for teleworkers to join the party the social innovation offered has to be conservative, meaning that it is

321

not radical on all the three levels of symbols, organisation, and behaviour. In this concept, successful symbols must be accepted by the users either as a value as such on the symbolic level, or give users values that have or can be transformed into use values on the behavioural level.

Telework in Sweden

Nykvarn

The idea of telecommuting was discussed intensely in Sweden in the first-half of the 1980s. In 1982–84 there was an experiment centred around a neighbourhood office in Nykvarn, about 60 km south west of Stockholm, where seven employers agreed to rent an office for a total of ten employees. These people shared their working hours between the Nykvarn office and their main workplace in Stockholm or Södertälje, 15 km away.

The actors promoting the experiment were: a Nordic research institute, Nordplan; several suppliers of telecommunication, IT and office equipment; and Södertälje municipality and its housing company. After the experimental period, the neighbourhood office existed for another year, after which it was closed down. The employers no longer wished to foot the costs of the extra workplace. Scepticism from white-collar unions is also considered to have contributed to the failure (Ranhagen *et al.* 1986). Reports from the UK that telework can be a trap for women amplified this scepticism.

Sweden in the early 1990s

After the Nykvarn office was closed, there was little discussion about telework in Sweden, although some telecottages were established (local centres which supply ICT equipment to local people). The telecottage teams formed an association which became a strong voice for the telecottage idea in Sweden – as well as for distributing work in general, independent of distance.

This was supported by Swedish authorities like NUTEK (Swedish National Board for Industrial and Technological Development) and Glesbygdsmyndigheten (National Rural Area Development Agency). Swedish municipalities, especially in regions far from big cities, have been very eager to attract small firms and convince larger companies to outsource some departments to their region, supported by ICT.

Another organisation interested in telework is ECTF, the European Community Telework/Telematics Forum, aimed at promoting teleworking, launched under the auspices of DG XIII in 1992, and having a co-ordinator in Sweden co-operating with NUTEK.

In this period discussion on telework was mainly concentrated on telecottages and on employers having some of their business decentralised into smaller places and rural areas or the archipelago.

Nyköping

At the start of the 1990s the municipality of Nyköping, with about 45,000 inhabitants, planned a vast new construction project, Nya Nyköping (New Nyköping). The new site was described like this on the front page of a prospectus:

The intelligent society is soon here!
In a charming small-town environment.
Now we start building!

According to the prospectus, the meaning of 'the intelligent society' is the possibility of replacing commuting by working at home or at a telework centre or telecottage in the neighbourhood. By using new technologies (such as AXE, fibre optics and ISDN [Integrated Services Digital Network]) it was suggested that you can work at home but still feel as if you are sitting in your office. As such, it would be possible for commuters to work some days at home instead of travelling 100 km to Stockholm.

This project was operated by the municipality in a separate company, Nya Nyköping HB. Initiated by municipality politicians and HSB (which is a Swedish co-operative housing society in which the local tenants own their apartments, and their local co-operative society owns the buildings), the project company became the main actor for introducing telework. The project manager employed an information officer who made contact with the telecom operator Telia (formerly Swedish Telecom), which became involved by installing ISDN in Nyköping and the new district. The manager also looked for teleworkers, admittedly with the purpose of achieving early success stories of telework.

In the municipality there were different opinions on the Nya Nyköping project. Started by the Social Democratic Party, the non-socialist parties were reluctant to make the project company as independent as suggested. And the local daily newspaper *Södermanlands Nyheter* was critical of the way in which the project was operated, and presented it almost entirely as a housing project, not as one for telework or new lifestyles.

After the first 120 apartments were built on the new site of Brandholmen, 3 km away from the city centre of Nyköping, there was a deep recession in the Swedish economy, and the rest of the planned 1,000 apartments were postponed for years to come. Thereby the goal of the project to make Nya Nyköping an 'information village' became impossible to achieve. Some teleworkers moved into the new houses, but the proportion was not extraordinary when compared with amounts in other places.

Nynäshamn

In Nynäshamn, a town with 25,000 inhabitants situated on a Baltic peninsula 60 km south of Stockholm, the starting basis was different from that of Nyköping.

The main actors consisted of a little group of enthusiasts who were themselves practising both commuting and teleworking, with one of them becoming project manager. Their network included municipality politicians and officials. One of the initiators worked with a Telia subsidiary, Telia Promoter, which was searching for a municipality for a pilot experiment with telework. With Nyköping hesitating about it, they instead chose Nynäshamn. Telia was then one of the sponsors in building the information office for telework in Nynäshamn.

Information was given to as many as possible of the 4,000 commuters living in the municipality but working elsewhere (most of them in Stockholm, which meant about one hour's journey in each direction). During the project period, 1994–96, contact was established with 321 commuters showing interest in telework. One year later the work resulted in a neighbourhood office which, among other telecom-related services, offered an office for teleworkers on a regular or *ad hoc* basis.

Before the telework project started, at the beginning of the 1990s, HSB in Nynäshamn built two housing areas, with about 50 apartments and about 60 co-operative terrace houses. These were designed for ISDN installation, which was also a marketing argument. Neither in Nynäshamn then, was the housing project a mark of success in the teleworking story.

The late 1990s

At about the same time that Nya Nyköping was built, companies such as Telia, Canon, Compaq and others, began large advertising campaigns promoting telework. Additionally, in the 1990s some employers have also started to show interest in home- or telecentre-based telework. When researchers are trying to find objects to study, however, it seems that the number is quite limited: Ericsson, Telia Research, Siemens-Nixdorf, Intel, DIAL Försäkring (insurance), and a few others, are the companies always referred to.

At this time a telework discourse also became manifest. Almost everybody was talking about telework – newspapers, magazines and other media reported about projects or single teleworkers. A new magazine devoted to teleworking, *Distans* [Distance] was even started.

Telework, at least for some period, has been a distinct part of the 'IT hype', which is also connected to other concepts like the 'Information Society', the Internet, the World Wide Web, and so on. As such, telework functions as one of the symbols of the Information Society.

The empirical material

The two projects of Nyköping and Nynäshamn constitute my empirical material. Questionnaires were directed to people moving into the housing sites, and to people identified through the telework project in Nynäshamn – having responded to the various information and advertising activities. They were either working at home for some of the time, or were interested in doing so.

In Nya Nyköping, 143 adults out of the population of about 200 (73 per cent) answered a questionnaire (sent out in December 1994) on the living area, work, work travel and homework. In Nynäshamn, a corresponding questionnaire was sent out in March 1995 to 162 adults in the HSB blocks; 100 of them replied (62 per cent). Another questionnaire to the group 'interested in telework' was sent to 128 persons; 89 of whom replied (70 per cent). From these 332 respondents I have identified 52 teleworkers, qualifying according to my definition. I have also undertaken interviews with teleworkers in Nyköping. The interviews have been focused on the history of the person's telework experience and their use of ICT, so far as it relates to the expectations of the Nya Nyköping project.

My investigation indicates that the teleworkers consist mainly of two groups: the self-employed and employees well advanced in their careers. Professionals and qualified employees are markedly over-represented, while women in general are under-represented.

The teleworkers have long working hours – a great part of the homework is in fact unpaid overtime. For four of the ten teleworkers in Nyköping, the homework is a spare-time job. This leaves three persons working for their employer at home for at least 5–8 hours per week.

The interviews indicate that teleworkers make conscious and well-considered choices. Two of the teleworkers, both self-employed, are engaged in starting a neighbourhood office, which could not be realised first time round. They are convinced of the usefulness of ICT for remote work, but frustrated by promises of the Nya Nyköping marketing which were not fulfilled. Some teleworkers in Nynäshamn also indicate the same mis-match.

Teleworkers use information and communication technology more frequently than others – most obviously in the use of fax machines and modems. Most of them use their own equipment, although they consider it to be not good enough for the job. This is in line with the results of another Swedish study which interviewed teleworkers in four companies. Here, information technology was important and was necessary for communication with the workplace. Nevertheless, although workers were reasonably well-equipped with ICT, they still asked for more technical equipment. However, this does not mean that ICT alone is enough for teleworking to function well (Larsen 1996).

Teleworkers, therefore, seem to have a very practical attitude towards information technologies. They are aware that they have to evaluate the marketing message against their own demands, and decide whether the benefit is worth the price of the product.

Interpreting the story

None of the described projects has resulted in a take-off for telework. In Nykvarn, the employers withdrew, citing the costs involved in the office, and the clerical unions did not give their support. In Nyköping, the municipality ceased to be an actor for telework after the apartments were built and no new construction projects were in sight. In Nynäshamn, the teleworking project has left some traces, not so much as a telework boom but rather in IT programmes for schools and in a neighbourhood office (although this acts as more of a service centre for small companies than for teleworkers). But this still functions as a base for promoting telework in Nynäshamn, as well as other places where affiliated offices are established – one of them in Brandholmen, Nyköping!

Does this mean that teleworking is too radical an innovation to be accepted by a considerable amount of workers? Let us look at the three levels suggested by Hård and Jamison.

Suppliers and symbolic level

ISDN and 'intelligent society' was used by the actors of Nya Nyköping as symbols of telework. As such, they were active in forming and reproducing the 'telework discourse', or the image of teleworking. Contributing to this discourse were, above all, suppliers of ICT equipment and services, but also other central public authorities (e.g. European Union and the Swedish government's IT commission in speaking about the Information Society – where telework is seen as a prominent ingredient), mass media, consultants and even researchers.

Thus telework is constructed as a symbol of *modernity* – urging you to take part in the 'Information Society'. Modern in this context is not the same as urban: on the contrary, *nature* is very close to the teleworker, the archetype of the little red Swedish cottage being a standard image.

The symbol of *flexibility* is also a key element, not meaning freedom from work, but freedom to work where and when you want, or to put it another way: freedom to be in control of your life.

Taken together one can find telework symbolising a lifestyle with a large amount of freedom, where it is possible to combine work and family without conflicts, to live and work close to nature, and to be modern in the Information Society. It is a Swedish middle-class dream of being able to combine a work career with family life, which normally means a lot of planning and switching between different duties in life.

Such symbols ought to appeal to many Swedes, so they should not be hindrances to teleworking. But some questionnaire answers indicate that teleworkers do not believe in these pictures: telework in practice is not so unproblematic as the adverts suggest, and communication technology is not so easy to handle as suppliers want employees to believe.

Employers and organisational level

Employers are quite invisible in the local projects I have studied. Answers from teleworkers indicate that employers' support is not satisfactory. This is also a main explanation for the slow rate of expansion in many other telework studies. Consequently, the teleworkers in my studies are persons with the will and capacity to telework on their own premises, whether they be salaried employees or self employed.

This can be interpreted in two quite different ways. One is that the social systems consisting of work relations do not support the social innovation of telework. The other interpretation is that the large amount of overtime indicates that employees adjust themselves to heavy working conditions by means of teleworking.

However, there are some reports of companies in Sweden having programmes for teleworking. They show that telework is possible to establish on a company basis, but to succeed, management has to be an active supporter of the idea. From a study in Sweden, Constance Perin highlights the great differences between the work system, believed to be rationally organised, and the household system, believed to be effectively ordered and relatively unpredictable. Co-ordinating these two systems obviously needs some efforts (Perin 1996; Baumann 1995; Larsen 1996).

One of the messages from telework promoters is that work will be organised in rather different ways when ICT makes us more flexible and mobile, and when companies want just-in-time workers and consultants instead of life time employees – working at home and mobile work being solutions for this.

Teleworkers and behaviour level

According to the responses to my questionnaires, the teleworkers' arguments *for* teleworking are advantages such as: 'more effective work', 'undisturbed working conditions', 'reducing work journeys', 'independence in work design' and 'possibility to combine work and spare time' (which does *not* include taking care of children while working). They indicate that teleworkers are interested in performing a job well, at the same time as having the 'flexibility' that is suggested.

But there are disadvantages, most of them connected to work: 'poorer contacts with colleagues', 'more difficult to relax from work', 'fewer or bad technical utilities'. These are more frequently noted than 'missing work material', 'disturbance from family' and 'intrusion in dwelling'. The conclusion must be that even if many people want to work at home, this is not always comfortable.

Technology

As indicated above, teleworkers use information and communication technology more frequently than other respondents, but most of them are not satisfied with their equipment. Most of them use their own equipment, which they consider to be not good enough. To be able to work more at home one-third remark that they need better technical equipment. This means that although promoters of telework argue that 'technology is not a problem', teleworkers do consider it to be a problem.

327

The answer to the question of whether ICT matters, thus, is that it does, but that few teleworkers have been equipped with adequate technology, which is another indication of a mis-match between promoters' visions and users' needs.

Conclusion

Telework, for many employees, seems to mean radical change – in organising work and its social system, in the 'organisational level' (according to Hård and Jamison 1996), as well as in the 'behavioural level' in everyday life. In my studies on telework in Sweden I have found that teleworkers have unmet demands concerning work conditions that would help combine work with family life, as well as concerning ICT equipment. Thus, there are mis-matches on the organisational as well as on the behavioural level.

This can be interpreted as a failure by promoters to ensure that the symbolic and use values offered are high enough to sell telework as a social innovation. As symbolic values have been dominating until now, it may be, therefore, that there is a need for messages with higher use values.

References

Baumann, F. (1995) *Teleworking from an organisational point of view: critical success factors and limits*, London: City University Business School.

Engström, M., Eriksson, G. and Johanson, R. (1990) *To be flexible in time and space. Structures and tendencies of distance work*, Stockholm Byggforskningsrådet, Report T8. (In Swedish: *Att flexa i tid och rum. Distansarbetets struktur och tendenser.*)

Gray, M., Hodson, N. and Gordon, G. (1993) *Teleworking explained*, Chichester: John Wiley and Sons.

Hård, M. and Jamison, A. (1996) *Successful and Failing Challengers: Diesel and Steam as Alternatives to the Gasoline Automotive Engine*, Stockholm: KFB-meddelande: 14.

Larsen, K. (1996) *Prerequisites and limitations for remote work – experiences from four Swedish companies*, Linköping University. (In Swedish: *Förutsättningar och begränsningar för arbete på distans – erfarenheter från fyra svenska företag.*)

Perin, C. (1996) 'Project Management Models as Social, Cultural, and Cognitive Systems: Relating Paid and Unpaid Work Schedules', in P.J. Jackson and J. van der Wielen (eds) Proceedings of the Workshop *New International Perspectives on Telework: From Telecommuting to the Virtual Organisation*, London, 31 July–2 August 1996, 2, Tilburg, The Netherlands: Tilburg University Press.

Ranhagen, U., Jägbeck A.H., Berg, H. and Stjernberg, T. (1986) *Workplaces near home with new technology. The neighbourhood central in Nykvarn, and other visions*, Stockholm: Arbetarskyddsfonden: Abstract 899. (In Swedish: *Bostadsnära arbetsplatser med ny teknik. Grannskapscentralen i Nykvarn och andra visioner.*)

21

TELEWORK – THE CRITICAL MANAGEMENT DIMENSION

Reima Suomi, Ari Luukinen, Juhani Pekkola and Marya Zamindar

Introduction

In our chapter, we adopt a management point of view on telework. This is based on the following assumptions we have about the current situation of telework:

1 in most cases, the feasibility of telework is easy to see from the point of view of macroeconomics, participating organisations, as well as from participating individuals;
2 though technical problems can be severe in individual cases, they can usually be overcome; telework is not primarily a technical problem;
3 in spite of its feasibility and technical soundness, telework has not invaded classical hierarchical organisations as fast as could be expected. Something must therefore inhibit the invasion of telework;
4 the reason for the slow adoption of telework especially in larger organisations can be found in management communication styles and practices.

A profile of telework: the nature, extent and potential of telework in Finland

Statistical findings: flexibility in Finnish working life according to the Finnish 1995 Working Life Barometer

In Finland, the Working Life Barometer (Ylöstalo *et al.* 1996) is used by the Ministry of Labour each year to collect data of contemporary interest. The Barometer is a sensitive instrument which can be used to examine many aspects of the transformation of Finnish working life. The data are collected by the Central Statistical Office by means of telephone interviews of approximately 1,000 wage earners (between the age of 18–64 years). An analysis of the collected data from the years 1992 to 1995 shows the changes in the quality of Finnish working life, including data on wage earners, expectations regarding the future.

Using these data, we now highlight some results that support our hypotheses above.

Working in groups

In order to meet sophisticated customer demands, 'group work' is necessary because services for customers can only be produced through complicated value chains, involving many employees. In 1995, 28 per cent of employees reported that they were working in some kind of organised group. Approximately the same number of employees reported that they did not work in any kind of group. The remainder of the sample (43 per cent) worked only occasionally in groups. The differences between the sectors are considerable. Groupwork was most popular in the state sector and most unpopular in the service sector. On the whole, one can say that working in groups is popular in Finland. Groupwork can cause difficulties in implementing telework practices, because the cohesion and integrity of a group requires delicate management practices that can be difficult to implement in a telework context.

Development programmes

The implementation of several kinds of official development programmes is a strong signal from management that organisations must change. In 1995, the question of whether or not organisations had adopted development programmes was included in the Barometer for the first time. According to the response, development programmes were surprisingly common in Finnish workplaces. An astonishing two out of three workplaces have some kind of programme. Due to the nature of the question, it was not possible to clarify the content of the programmes. This result can be interpreted as a general willingness on the part of management to adopt new practices and, in such an environment, even telework programmes are easier to implement.

Recruitment practices and the amount of permanent positions

According to the Barometer, work arrangements have become more diversified in Finland. In 1995, 23 per cent of all companies recruited personnel. The majority of the recruited individuals did not receive permanent positions and permanent employment relations have been breaking down very rapidly. Only 29 per cent of the 23 per cent of companies that had experienced a growth were able to offer permanent positions, and two-thirds of the new working relationships were atypical. Trends indicate a diminishing core of permanent employees within companies. This shows, in our opinion, that employers are preparing for flexibility through the manipulation of the amount of core and flexible workers. Flexibility, in the form of efficiency and working time adjustments of the contemporary workforce (for example, in the form of telework) is not supported by this trend.

Nevertheless, we should bear in mind that most telework arrangements in Finland are a result of non-systematic and informal developments. In general, telework arrangements are not regarded as part of the organisational strategies aimed at improving the flexibility of companies.

Factors behind the adoption of telework as discovered through statistical analysis of employer opinions

Current context of telework in Finland

The proportion of teleworkers in Finland is a little more than 8 per cent of all wage earners (Zamindar 1995). In all, the figure amounts to 150,000 Finns. In the Finnish Working Life Barometer study, 'teleworkers' were referred to as employees who work outside the employer's facilities at least some hours per month by using modern information technology. About 3 per cent of Finnish wage earners, or about 50,000 Finns, are teleworking quite frequently, that is to say at least one day per week on average. Proportionally, the extent of telework in Finland is at the same level as it is in Sweden and Norway (Pekkola *et al.* 1996).

Teleworkers are mainly employees in higher-income groups who have a strong educational background. They are usually independent professionals who work under pressure, but are satisfied with their position in the firm and with their firm's working conditions. Typically, relationships with superiors and colleagues are strong, and employees who became teleworkers report that their output is worthwhile and influential.

Three out of four Finnish teleworkers are male. About 40 per cent of the persons who telework are upper-level executives. Telework is used particularly in technical planning areas. Every fifth teleworker belongs to a small work organisation of 20 to 50 employees. Relatively more teleworkers work in small- to mid-size organisations comprising about 100 to 200 employees.

Understanding organisational change in the workplace is essential to appreciate telework. Telework is part of an ongoing industrial transformation of organisations to post-industrial systems whereby products are becoming more tailored and customer-oriented, while at the same time the mass-production and standardisation of products decreases. Nowadays, to be able to produce more sophisticated products and supply specific market niches, production methods must be more flexible and decentralised as compared to the mass-production era. Information and information technology are also becoming more important as companies need to be increasingly sensitive to market changes in order to capitalise on emerging market niches. A greater need for geographically dispersed specialists, for example, makes telework arrangements more attractive for businesses.

331

Thus, in one sense, telework is dependent on post-industrialism and a feature in the process toward labour evolution and modern production methods.

To summarise, telework is not merely a technological innovation, it is also a sociological innovation. The reasons behind telework take-up include social-organisational factors like moving away from a lack of flexibility in old, industrial-production structures.

Statistical analysis using a survey-built database from the FET project in co-operation with the Finnish Information Processing Association (Tietotekniikan Liitto) reveals three factors determining whether or not an organisation will adopt telework. The greatest predictor for the implementation of telework is the existence of an appropriate information technology infrastructure. These results show that technical infrastructure provides a conducive atmosphere for telework.

Second, organisational size proves to be important in predicting whether or not a firm will implement telework. The parameter value for this variable is large and *negative*, indicating that the larger the size of the organisation, the less likely it is they will have telework arrangements.

The last significant variable in the model shows that teamwork is positively related to the practice of telework. This significant, positive relationship shows that teamwork acts as a catalyst for telework. Teamwork structures may allow employees to overcome fears about social isolation that might result from teleworking.

The correlation between high-wage employees and telework practice was measured by analysing the relationship between motivation to recruit and retain key personnel (high-skill, high-wage employees) and the use of telework. The correlation between the desire to *recruit* skilled staff and the use of telework is so low that it precludes inclusion into a regression model. Similarly, the correlation between the desire to *retain* skilled personnel and telework use is also too low to include it in the model. These results, however, must be read with some caution. The correlations reflect the *opinions* of managers regarding the amount of tele-work that already exists (or should exist) in their organisation. These variables do not measure the objective existence of a category of skilled workers against the actual use of telework. Although such measurement would be ideal, in practice this is not always a feasible method for measurement.

The perceived impact of labour unions on telework also proves to be insignificant. It is possible that Nordic managers do not regard the influence of labour unions as anything out of the ordinary, even though labour unions have more of a role in the Nordic countries, if such managers have no experience with which to compare their own situation.

Finally, analysis showed that none of the negative influences described in the literature is hampering the spread of telework – neither the cost of setting up a teleworker, nor the expected career problems caused by a lack of social inter-action, nor supervisory difficulties for managers. Furthermore, the perceived positive productivity advantages correlate significantly with the actual practice of telework. Regression modelling shows that belief in productivity gain is relatively important, but still not as influential as use of teamwork, handling of simple information technology problems, or firm size.

Through such analysis, it can be inferred that the statistically ideal company for adopting telework in Finland is a small, teamwork-oriented firm which already possesses an adequate information technology infrastructure. Regression modelling shows that it is this type of firm which is most likely to introduce telework. Policy implications derived from these results indicate that policy-makers should, for example, concentrate on promoting telework especially within small firms which are most likely to respond favourably to telework initiatives. Policy-makers can also make their policies more effective by promoting techno-logical innovation and network-based information technology. Advanced technological infrastructure proves to be an important condition behind telework adoption. The lack of statistical significance of labour union opposition and fear of social isolation, together with the statistical significance of data regarding the receptivity to telework, strengthens the conclusion that well-constructed telework promotion policies can be successful in Finland.

Practical telework management in Finnish enterprises

Based on the results of the 'Telework for Change' project and our earlier case studies among some Finnish companies, we believe that there are several ways in which the introduction of telework can take its course and materialise in organisational settings. Furthermore, we suggest that these changes occur mostly in a concealed way and that they are closely related to the evolving new working culture which manifests itself in the management of resources and communication.

As described above, at least two developmental trends can be distinguished regarding the adoption of telework in the Finnish business environment. The first trend is associated with the development of flexible and distributed work patterns in small enterprises. The second deals with telework applications in larger organ-isations. To avoid extreme simplifications, we would like to stress also that there are important differences within these categories in respect to the way telework is perceived.

Telework in small Finnish enterprises

In Finland, there is a growing number of small enterprises which have adopted flexible modes of production and new ways of working as a basis of their busi-ness operations. Flexible work arrangements are introduced to create competitive advantage when establishing the organisation.

Many of the small firms that are utilising telework are characterised by the effective use of telecommunications in relation to internal communication, net-working with subcontractors and other organisations, and in delivering products to clients. Moreover, they can be characterised as innovative, especially with respect to the way in which they manage resources and organise business operations. We can conclude that such developments reflect a newly emerging work culture.

Innovative small businesses can be regarded as forerunners of the growing information society, or as agents of change in the working environment, because they are showing other businesses how market needs can be met in a flexible, efficient and also profitable way. Most important of all, they are the 'carriers of change', influencing organisational and management culture. In this context, telework and other distributed work patterns, like dispersed groupwork arrangements or business networking, can be seen as natural consequences of flexible modes of operation and an emerging new culture. Likewise, telework arrangements appear to be unofficial and hidden by nature. Systematic and official telework schemes seldom exist in these circumstances.

Telework in large Finnish enterprises

Large Finnish corporations have developed telework arrangements mostly along with their other pursuits for organisational development. Basically, most of the motives to introduce telework are related to rationalisation of the use of labour, or changes to make work processes more effective and productive. Nowadays, telework arrangements are in many cases the result of extensive investments in information and telecommunication technology. However, other motives, arguments and reasons also exist.

There are also enterprises which have looked for the possibilities offered by telework arrangements to utilise opportunities to motivate, recruit or retain their key personnel. Although these kind of arrangements (which derive from managerial pursuits to develop an active human resource management policy) are especially uncommon in Finland, they do exist. In some cases, the companies mentioned above also have some explicit elements of proactive personnel policies built into their telework arrangements.

Telework in virtual organisations

It can be suggested that the most prominent base for the future spread of innovative telework schemes is related to the emerging 'virtual organisation'. As noticed above, virtual organisations can originate in small enterprises under favourable circumstances. Likewise, such structures and modes of operation can be developed in existing large companies. ICL Data can be regarded as one of the leading companies in Finland in this respect.

We expect that the fundamental factor behind the development of virtual organisations and telework arrangements is related to what people really want to do and how they would like to do it, not where or in which organisational surroundings this is going to happen. As Peter Johnson puts it: 'work is what you do, not where you go'.

Without much disagreement, we can assume that virtual work arrangements that comprise telework are by definition based not only on the innovative organisation of work and new perception of management culture but also on effective use of human intellect.

Conclusions

One of the reasons why we conclude that telework arrangements have not spread as fast as could be expected is the lack of market pressure on many organisations. Changes in organisational structures and processes are usually painful, and organisations postpone these changes until they are unavoidable.

With regard to telework promotion, it is important to pay attention (in a client-oriented fashion) to the way in which businesses are organised and control their resources. A 'need-driven' approach to telework is demanded. Specifically, it is essential to recognise three conditions which are necessary for businesses to initiate telework. An adequate technological and communication infrastructure, sufficient technological skills, and a reorganisation of corporate structures and cultures is needed to provide for successful and lasting telework arrangements. Telework should not only be seen as a new way of working, but in the most extreme case as a virtual way of organising that supports organisational adaptation to environmental changes.

To summarise, our theoretical discussion and our empirical findings both point out that there are no major obstacles to the successful adoption of telework in Finland. The technical facilities are available together with the willingness of workers to engage in telework arrangements.

Current governance structures indicate that large organisations outsource work and make use of smaller organisations as buffers against fluctuations in demand. As a result, small organisations have been the first to learn how to create flexible organisational structures. As small organisations are very dependent on knowledge owned by the workers, they are not usually willing to hire and fire employees all the time, but look for other means to add flexibility. This is where telework comes in. Small organisations have management techniques that support and allow for telework. With regard to this we have to realise that telework arrangements, in the way researchers define them, are not always understood by small organisations as such. For them, telework is just a normal way of doing business.

We can conclude that management capabilities and opinions seem to be the critical factor for the introduction of telework. Small organisations seem to have an advantage over larger corporations. Larger organisational units should therefore try to learn from smaller ones.

References

Pekkola, J., Heikkilä, A. and Zamindar, M. (1996) 'Directions of Telework in Finland', in Luukinen, A. (ed.) *Report by the Finnish Experience with Telework Project*, Ministry of Labour, Publication of the Labour Administration, 143, Helsinki.

Ylöstalo, P., Kauppinen, T. and Heikkilä, A. (1996) *Työolobarometri marraskuu 1995*, Ministry of Labour, Työpoliittinen tutkimus 145, Helsinki.

Zamindar, M. (1995) *Telework in Finland. Factors behind Telework Use as Seen From an Employer Perspective*, Ministry of Labour, Publication of the Labour Administration, 116, Helsinki.

CONCLUSION

New networks and agendas

Paul J. Jackson and Jos M. van der Wielen

The contributions to this book can be read in two ways: first, as a range of insights into different issues bound up with teleworking and virtual organisation; second, as a demonstration of the different standpoints, interests and agendas concerned with these. As such, it provides an overview of recent developments (both practical and theoretical) on the state of teleworking and offers new perspectives and lines of analysis to help move things forward. We would therefore like to use this conclusion to discuss some of the consequences these two readings have for future research and practice. To begin, we will draw together the main ideas discussed in the book's four parts.

Drawing the parts of the book together

Part 1 of this book showed that teleworking is a complex subject, about which many standpoints can be brought to bear. If we look at the history of teleworking ideas, starting with the initial discussion of telecommuting back in the 1970s, we find that perspectives on telework have continued to change over time. The meaning and significance of the concept has thus varied depending on the contexts in which it has been used.

At one level, it is looked upon in concrete, practical terms – as an effective approach to a range of organisational and social problems, such as traffic growth and demands for flexible working. At another, more abstract, level – particularly when it forms part of the debate about the Information Society – telework is seen as embodying a new set of ideas and principles. In short, it is looked upon as part of a new paradigm that challenges old assumptions about the design of organisations and the way work and private life have traditionally been compartmentalised.

There can be little doubt that while developments such as telework do indeed embrace new sets of temporal and spatial relations, supported by advanced information technologies, they cannot be looked upon as an inevitable consequence of such technologies, nor as a cornerstone of a new (post-)industrial era. We instead need to establish more thoughtful, integrative approaches that provide robust linkages between teleworking, the technologies that support it, new organisational forms, and wider developments in societal and industrial structures.

In Part 2 we saw the way in which the compartmentalisation of industrial and social structures into distinct, geographically separated sets of social relations and practices has been subject to change – leading to new ways of integrating work, family and leisure. However, we have also seen that such developments raise their own issues and problems – such as the management of role conflict. This heightens the demands placed on those concerned – workers, family members, employers, etc. – in managing the boundaries between work and family relations.

Teleworking developments also highlighted the cultural significance of temporal and spatial structures in work and family life. We have seen how the meanings and descriptions of 'work' have traditionally been bound up with activities and experiences undertaken at particular places – buildings, offices – and at particular times (typically, 9 a.m. to 5 p.m.). The ideas and practices involved in this have become deeply rooted in the habits, norms and values of industrial culture. The consequence of this is that certain times (hours of the day, days of the week), as well as particulars places (the boardroom, the office, the living room) carry with them strong symbolic connotations. These stand by to inform and reproduce different sets of meaning and experiences (concerning work, leisure, and so on) and cannot therefore be looked upon as socially *neutral*. This helps to explain, for instance, why those productive activities that take place outside of workplaces and work times are often looked upon as 'non-work' and are devalued economically and culturally as a result.

Part 3 illustrates the web of interrelated issues and agendas involved in temporal and spatial work innovations. For organisations looking to reap the benefits of dispersed working, this raises questions about a range of matters – from business strategy, technology policy and organisational learning, to team building and collaborative working, and management and control. In the broader context of the city, we have seen that matters of 'public good' (such as economic renewal) are not necessarily high on the agenda of individuals and organisations planning teleworking.

Clearly, these are not matters that can be treated as narrow, 'technical' problems. They are inherently complex, as well as being innately social and political. To deal with them, two sets of tools and abilities are in demand. First, we need *methodologies* that help to relate and integrate issues from a wide range of areas, disciplines and viewpoints. For instance, in the organisational context, a teleworking perspective requires interweaving perspective from business strategy, facilities management and human resource management. Second, given the different actors involved, it is imperative to find ways of *managing the different interests and expertises* of the actors. Rather than eliminating different viewpoints then, we must embrace the richness and diversity these provide. At the same time, those involved must recognise the existence and interdependence of other stakeholders involved in developments.

Many of these stakeholders were discussed in Part 4 of the book. Here, we examined the interests, experiences and strategies of a number of actors, and the networks they were engaged in or sought to create. When it comes to teleworking, no actor is an island. The success and stability of teleworking networks depends on a range of people adapting to their required role in the teleworking network over time. Ensuring an appropriate alignment of business strategies on the part of client organisations, telework centres, even televillages, etc. is essential for the durability of initiatives. Teleworking networks are often fragile because of the amount of (often institutionalised) forces acting against them. For example, the conservative attitudes of managers and workers alike may act as a brake on innovation. They strongly embedded in industrial culture and are often slow to change. The examples from Part 4 illustrate that we need to create a more encompassing realignment of work-related values and business models for tele-working to develop.

Future networks and agendas

The above has raised a number of questions and directions for future telework-ing developments. First, there is the need for new management tools which can aid the task of integrating teleworking issues and perspectives into planning and business strategy. Second, skills are required to manage the new boundary relations, particularly those created by homeworking and virtual teams. Third, there is a need to create new networks for both research and practice, which respectively should be based on multi-disciplinary and multi-party collaboration.

A number of key issues are now firmly placed on the teleworking agenda. For example, understanding the symbolism of time and space and the shifting mean-ings of work and non-work, are matters at the heart of teleworking. We need to raise the general consciousness about these factors in order to redefine underlying assumptions about the nature of work, how it is organised and the institutions that support it (such as government bodies, training establishments, trade unions, and so on). Attitudes and values – often deeply culturally embedded – may need revising as part of a wider rethink on the way we live and work.

In creating and managing new ways of working – for instance, in managing dispersed workforces, temporary teams and inter-organisational alliances – new modes of co-ordination, co-operation and control are required. If such innov-ations are to succeed and mature, organisations must ensure a shared understand-ing between constituent parts, create identity, loyalty, commitment and trust among members, as well as maintaining learning and knowledge development in the organisation as a whole.

As far as individuals are concerned, there is a requirement to develop a set of skills, with self-management and entrepreneurship abilities becoming increasingly important. For those working alone, the formation of coping strategies is essential for dealing with new sources of stress.

Where teleworking and virtual working arrangements are built, based on the solutions offered by a single prominent and powerful actor (such as an IT or telecom company), there is a danger of over-simplifying the needs and interests of the other actors in the network. As we have seen, virtual teams need to engender a sense of shared enterprise, individuals need to find ways of managing revised social boundaries. These cannot be solved simply by new technologies. This points to the need for *social* innovation – new attitudes and forms of behaviour – as well as *technical* innovation – if new forms of working are to succeed. As such, a wider understanding of issues and work dynamics is required.

There is a clear requirement, therefore, to integrate teleworking ideas and issues into both broader *social agendas* (such as urban planning, transport management, etc.) as well as *corporate strategies* (for example, in creating inter-organisational alliances or new forms of service delivery). Because these challenge many established institutions and practices – the central workplace, the work–family divide, the functional divides within organisations – new modes of thinking and planning are required.

This points to the need to draw on the expertise of parties and experts who can provide a broader diagnosis of the problems at hand, as well as offering a more encompassing view of what the strategic aims of such innovations might be. This also recognises the different rationales for such developments – economic growth, social inclusion, environmental protection, corporate restructuring, traffic management, work flexibility, and so forth. Such an approach to teleworking could help to ensure more encompassing methods of problem solving, but more importantly could help to create a shared vision of the desired future.

INDEX

Note: page numbers in italics denote figures or tables.